ELEVENTH HEAVEN

Ed O'Bannon and the 1995 national basketball champion
UCLA Bruins

ROB MIECH

BRIAN !
I HOPE YOU
ENJOY !

R. M

MARCH 2015

For Sally

Chapter One

AT NINETY-FOUR feet long, fifty feet wide, it is the final resting place for buckets of sweat, sprinkles of tears, globules of oil, and beads of blood—the claret droplets are unmistakable—from Alcindor, Allen, Bibby, Johnson, Walton, Wicks, Wilkes, et al, some of the game's luminaries. The center is occupied by a big powder blue donut. Four gold block letters curl around both halves of the circle. A thick band of powder blue outlines the four thousand seven hundred square feet of maple wood that gets resurfaced, with a fresh coat of gooey lacquer and intense polish, every September. It is the most acclaimed timber in college basketball history.

It is the UCLA basketball court on whose southern sideline every Bruin aligns himself soon after the first official practice of the season begins on October 15, 1994. Seventeens. The drill those players most loathe. Someone has screwed up, missed a cut, clanked a jumper when a bank shot had been in order, flubbed a bounce pass, or botched a basic assignment that the plebes will come to perfect in their sleep. The shrill from the shiny silver whistle coach Jim Harrick angrily blurts between his clenched teeth echoes off Pauley Pavilion's twenty-nine-year-old concrete walls. He points to the sideline, at the floor. Many of his charges know what's coming without him even saying the word. Four freshmen are confused. Seventeens.

They must haul ass to the other sideline, back to this one, down to that one, then back ... they must touch seventeen sidelines within sixty seconds; almost three football fields. Covering a hundred yards in twenty seconds, three times in a row, might not sound like an Olympian feat for an elite Division-I athlete. Chop it all up, however, into seventeen pieces, and toss it into a hoops practice at any given moment, and watch some of the nation's most fit young men grimace, grind, growl, and grunt. Harrick might have devised the diabolical drill himself, but he also believes he could have lifted it from one of former Los Angeles Lakers coach Pat Riley's practices ten years ago, when Harrick coached Pepperdine University and visited Riley's runs often, for pointers, at the Fabulous Forum.

The Bruins don't make it. If one doesn't, none do. They will run it, over and over, until all of them complete it within sixty seconds. They fray. Some vector off and bellow at the ten blue national championship banners that hang from Pauley's rafters. Some of the young bucks bend, hands on hips, eyes closed ... *Why ... did I ... come ... here?* Cameron Dollar, the sophomore point guard from Atlanta whose facial features, deadpan expressions, and contagious laughter resemble the archcomedian Chris Rock, would deplore seventeens so much he would murmur, just loud enough for Harrick to hear, *Just like plantation days; Run, nigger. Run!* Kevin Dempsey, a bit player, just acts as if he's touching that far line. He crouches and reaches, fingertips purposefully falling six or eight inches shy, for an edge. He heads the other way, but Harrick's vigilant lieutenants always catch him. They have to do it again. They need nearly half an hour to execute this arduous exercise. Harrick strolls, as if he's on holiday in the South of France. To punish was rarely the point, Harrick says. It's about conditioning, being in peak shape, for each other, for the program, to leave opponents gasping in UCLA's wake.

Tony Luftman scurries to mop the area below veteran forward Ed O'Bannon. Wiping the star's perspiration from the court is one of Luftman's many responsibilities as one of five student managers, or glorified gofers. Such moisture could have been the culprit in the John R. Wooden Center that fateful October day in 1990, when O'Bannon ripped his left knee apart upon his re-entry from a powerful dunk in a pick-up game. The anterior cruciate ligament (ACL) snapped in half. Residual damage complicated significantly an unusual operation in which an Achilles tendon from a cadaver was used to replace O'Bannon's ACL. The allograft procedure is still considered controversial and radical today.

The injury dramatically alters O'Bannon's goals, his objectives, indeed the course of his life. Adding to college basketball's dynasty, whose crowns are dusty, becomes his obsession. His self-centered dreams of NBA fame and fortune get shelved. He learns about allegiance, dedication, and resolve. His new mission would consume O'Bannon. Since the devastating injury Harrick always ensures that someone—this season it's Luftman—shadows O'Bannon to sop up his sweat, a sagacious stratagem to protect the bellwether of the Bruins.

Luftman, short and thin among fellow eighteen-year-olds, has a dark crop of hair and bushy Groucho Marxian eyebrows. It's eerie how he looks like Harrick at the same age. Luftman crab-scampers, with some extra zip; he's an earnest greenhorn who has only been on the UCLA campus a few weeks. Luftman knows his way around, though, for he had been a Bruins ballboy, huddling with other kids behind each basket and scampering out to mop up moisture at a referee's wave during games. Moreover, Harrick utilized a special admission allowance, usually reserved for athletes, to ensure Luftman's entrance to UCLA. In his managerial interview, for which Cameron Dollar was present in Harrick's office, Luftman predicted that the Bruins would win several titles in the coming years. Harrick turned to Dollar and said, "You hear that Dollar? We're gonna win *mulllll-ti-pullll champ-yunnnnn-chips.*"

Harrick refers to the very center of the mid-court circle as the *egg yolk*. He showed Luftman how oil sometimes drips from the center scoreboard near the egg yolk—it does not fall directly on the yolk because the scoreboard does not hover over the exact centerline of the court, one of the pantheon's quirks. That oil had to be minded. For Harrick, Luftman would take out the trash and do the windows. Luftman would soon regard Ed O'Bannon with the same regal disposition.

Something catches Luftman's attention in the lull after that first seventeen. Above him, a few feet away, the former national prep player of the year has morphed into a southpaw combination of Muhammad Ali and Mike Tyson. Luftman gawks at assistant coach Lorenzo Romar. A man of deep faith and scant words, Romar returns a half-grin to Luftman. Romar slightly nods with his eyes closed. Down the line, to the west end of the arena, players gape at O'Bannon. Mark Gottfried and Steve Lavin, Harrick's other assistants, stare at O'Bannon.

Nobody wants to run another seventeen. O'Bannon never hesitates. He barely pauses before toeing back to the line. Harrick's next *Go!* will ignite another torturous series of fifty-foot sprints, back and forth, back and forth. There will be hundreds more before O'Bannon can truly sleep at the end of his fifth-year senior season, his final shot at an NCAA championship that has so dominated his desires and tormented his soul, and eluded him.

He will rage. He will rejoice after only one victory. The burden will be heavy. He shows his fellow teammates that he is ready for anything Harrick will throw at him. Are they? O'Bannon bobs and weaves. He floats. Punches sting thin air. He shuffles his Reeboks. He has tunnel vision, sort of; he catches blurred glimpses of astonished players and coaches. Every potential foe that could possibly confront him over the next six months firmly presents itself in his crosshairs. Left jab. Right jab. Right hook. Left uppercut. The six-foot-eight, twenty-three-year-old bald man

with the Whoppers complexion, narrow face, and high cheekbones, and blue nylon wrap around his left knee—wearing a white UCLA practice jersey and long white shorts—appears ready for the heavyweight match of his life.

Ed O'Bannon shadowboxes.

Luftman widens his eyes. O'Bannon's teammates keep stealing glances at him. They straighten themselves. They shake off their weariness. Moans fade. They toe the line, too. The returnees realize he meant it back in March in Oklahoma City, when he exploded at them during halftime of yet another debacle of an NCAA Tournament showing. His mien is mean.

Jim Harrick had supplied one of O'Bannon's triggers. During Harrick's first few weeks of practice as UCLA's coach, in the fall of 1988, he had repeatedly blown a fuse at point guard Jerome "Pooh" Richardson, who carried the requisite edge of a Philadelphia native. Biggest hot dog Harrick had ever witnessed. Pooh then broke curfew in Moscow, Idaho, after a one-point victory over Washington State. Harrick made him run a solo seventeen at the next practice. Pooh barked, That all you got? Harrick made him run another one. *That all you got?* And another. *That ALL you GOT!* And another. Ran 'em like they were candy, Harrick says, "He was a *stuuuuud.*" Pooh rattled off Jumping Jacks in front of everybody, begging for more. Pooh wanted that to be the best-conditioned team in America. All of Harrick's players have heard that story early in their UCLA careers.

Harrick also finally told Pooh, "Shut your fuckin' mouth! Don't say another word!" Pooh acquiesced. He would play nine solid seasons in the National Basketball Association.

Another scene also empowered O'Bannon. Former UCLA teammates Don MacLean and Mitchell Butler had played the 1993-94 NBA season for the Washington Bullets (now Wizards).

Butler was a rookie. For MacLean, it would be his second professional campaign and, by far, the most productive of his nine pro seasons. In the summer of 1994, Butler had told O'Bannon how MacLean had been so energetic at that preseason camp in the fall of 1993, out-running everybody, never tired, always the first player ready for the next drill. MacLean topped it off by shadowboxing between drills. O'Bannon directly related how MacLean had prepared for and attacked that camp to his subsequent productivity.

"One person is completely ready, so ready he can't wait to get to the next drill," O'Bannon says many years later. "And he's shadowboxing! He's ready. I was like, Hell, yeah! I just thought that was the coolest thing. So when that opportunity came for me … I wanted to get to that point, to be in such good shape that I could do it. I finished that [first] seventeen. I wasn't breathing hard at all; I was in the best shape of my life. Everything was coming together at that point. I was fired up."

It was a fuck-you-this-doesn't-affect-me type of gesture toward Harrick, says one player. Seeing something like that from your leader, says another, is fuel. You feed off it. "There were some intense practice battles. [O'Bannon] was really driven to win. He wanted to prove we could do it," says Toby Bailey today. "Following a guy like that, you have to suck it up and get back on that line. No excuses."

Long after those pugilistic flashes, O'Bannon pauses. He is not given to hype or hyperbole, flowery lingo or self-promotion, highs or lows in actions or words. His steadiness is his backbone. He says he did not know how much that scene, after that first seventeen, would affect every other Bruin on that court, that … he catches himself. He did know. It had been premeditated. "I knew it had been done before and knew the impact it had had on the people who were watching. I wanted that."

As the dynamic components of that 1995 championship squad began to ponder how to celebrate the twentieth anniversary of that scintillating season, it seemed probable that those festivities would also likely coincide, in the spring of 2015, with a startling forty-year stretch in which college basketball's most distinguished program has added only one banner—theirs—to Pauley's crossbeams. That it is the lone basketball championship trophy among the eleven in the glass case in Westwood that does not bear the signature of John Wooden further enhances the achievement. It might be the most remarkable of the lot; at least one qualified observer is certain it shines the most.

Many coaches and players regard that first seventeen, at that first practice, as the switch that propelled this version of the Bruins onto an entirely new plane of dedication and seriousness. This court had served as the platform for so much friction and toil—"ups and downs and fights and love, literally tears and blood and teeth knocked out," says Ed O'Bannon—and would continue to do so in the days and practices and weeks and games and months to come. In fact, O'Bannon, in a fit of outrage, would quit the team on this maple wood.

Harrick certainly saw O'Bannon take command of the Bruins at halftime of that shoddy performance against Tulsa the previous March in the NCAAs. The shadowboxing showed another level of purpose for the man who had been one of the most reposeful Bruins. Introverted country boy J.R. Henderson might have been the quietest player Jim Harrick has ever mentored, but Henderson had some sullenness in there, too. Point guard Tyus Edney also bore an unobtrusive manner, which totally belied the forceful way he played. But Harrick witnessed years of turmoil manifest and funnel into O'Bannon at the end of that first seventeen. Tulsa proved he would no longer speak only when spoken to. His ownership was complete. This was fiat. "A coming out for Ed," Harrick says. "He wanted everybody to know,

'I'm the leader! Give us all you got. We want to be in good shape. Nothing you can do will peter our enthusiasm.' "

Luftman tingles when he recalls O'Bannon duckin' and jukin' and jabbin' and shufflin'. Mark Gottfried thought, *The warrior.* Lorenzo Romar interpreted O'Bannon's hooking and upper-cutting of all those ghosts from UCLA's glorious days of yore as not-so-subtle messages to his teammates; *Get on my back ... we're about to go on a ride ... I'm about to show you the way.* Romar had played in the NBA, and he had coached three collegiate programs for nearly twenty years through 2014. He slowly licks an orange Creamsicle in the late hours of a steamy Las Vegas summer evening in the glitzy foyer of the Wynn. He smiles. He again shuts his eyes. He sees Ed O'Bannon shadowboxing that October afternoon in 1994. Romar has never witnessed a floor motivator of O'Bannon's magnitude. "He wasn't gonna let anyone get in the way of how he was gonna lead that team."

O'Bannon points to the strenuous off-season conditioning program he had devised and adhered to as the physical catalyst to his sweet science display. He truly wanted to get himself into peak physical condition so, if the situation materialized, he could actually step into a ring, between the ropes and onto canvas, and fight someone. Anyone.

In November 2012, Pauley Pavilion opens after a resplendent $136-million renovation, more than twenty-seven times the cost of the original concrete, bricks, and mortar. In a fitting tribute, John Wooden's great grandson Tyler Trapani—who would play a total of fourteen minutes in his UCLA career—scored the last basket on the original hallowed grounds on February 26, 2011. Once again, as they did in the 1950s and '60s, the Bruins played home games on the road, at the Sports Arena and Honda Center in Anaheim, during the refurbishment.

Some consider a modern UCLA in script scrawled across the middle of the new wood to be a far less venerable, even sacrilegious, nod to the tradition of the place. A replica of that sublime center-court powder blue circle, with the block letters, now serves as the bottom of the huge scoreboard that hangs from the middle of the ceiling, over the exact center of the new court. Sticklers are further incensed that the seat that commemorates John Wooden is on the *opposite side* of the arena from where he actually sat as a fan. Hallowed? In the arena in which the Bruins were 149-2 when their monumental coaching figure exited the profession, these commemorative attempts ring hollow.

Someone who has bled powder blue for decades sends me a photo of Mickey Mouse ears, when I ask about the script lettering and the Wooden seat, and says, "Absolutely ridiculous. If UCLA [officials] were in charge of renovating the Lincoln Memorial, they would change it to Daniel Day Lewis. I just don't get it." The John Wooden statue outside the north doors, though, is dignified—and looks nothing like Lincoln or Lewis.

Half of the center circle from the original floor is encased in glass out on Wooden Way, in an inviting new main entrance. In his final act as a UCLA player in this building, when Jim Harrick pulled him from his last game on that maple wood, after all of those daunting and dreadful seventeens, O'Bannon knelt down and smooched the very center of that egg yolk.

Years later, O'Bannon attends the grand re-opening festivities. Jim Harrick is here, too, but several haughty inhabitants of UCLA's ivory tower, and maybe a few others, shudder at his presence. *Persona non grata*, says someone who thought he had an idea of what the UCLA hierarchy thought about Harrick, whose exit from Westwood was as tarnished as Wooden's was celebrated.

At halftime, O'Bannon and Harrick knot in a bottleneck at the side of the floor, just about where Ed finished that first seventeen in October 1994. Fans high-five O'Bannon as they inch by him. They pat him on his back. *Thanks, Ed!* They want to touch his eminence. That O'Bannon three years earlier became the face of an epic lawsuit against the NCAA should surprise none of them, but they can't possibly fathom the toll that has taken on him or his family. *Thanks, Ed!* O'Bannon and Harrick can't move.

The cheers and hurrahs arrive in waves. The former coach plucks at his former player's left elbow, yanks at his shirt. Ed leans over so his left ear hovers around Harrick's mouth. In his syrupy West Virginia drawl, Harrick whispers, "They have no idea."

Chapter 2

JOHN WOODEN OVERHAULED his entire system in late August 1960. He had just experienced the worst of his twelve seasons as UCLA's basketball coach, and it had not even been a losing campaign; the Bruins had won fourteen games and lost twelve in 1959-60. But Wooden sensed something was amiss. UCLA was oh-for-three in the NCAAs. Wooden did not attempt anything to be mediocre. Just getting to the tournament was not the point, either. To win in a big way, to dominate, he believed his program required a major rebuild, not just a tune-up. He examined recruiting methods and strategy, the practice regimen, even socks with a critical eye. In the process Wooden would raise the game's ceiling of excellence into the stratosphere. He called it a *total analysis of everything.*

Socks? "Believe it or not, there's an art to doing it right," Wooden wrote in *They Call Me Coach*. He deplored blisters, which can be caused by a wrinkle in a sock and sideline a player. He wanted the feet of his pupils to withstand a season's worth of relentless pounding and punishment.

Jim Milhorn doesn't remember the sock lessons. Then again, at that time he was antsy to play for Wooden and was much more interested in soaking up lessons about the high-post offense and breaking down other teams, making them wince for even thinking they could hang with the Bruins. He would be just as uncompromising on a racquetball court. Milhorn had been a scrappy guard at Long Beach Jordan High School and spent his freshman collegiate year at Long Beach City College.

Pete Dalis, a student manager for Bruins football coach Red Sanders in the 1950s, was a year into master's-degree studies. He was also working in an entry-level athletic department capacity at UCLA, the only employer Dalis would ever know. J.D. Morgan, an associate business manager at the university, had just coached the UCLA men's tennis team to its sixth NCAA championship, and he would win another in 1961. In Redlands, out near San Bernardino, Jerry Tarkanian was earning a master's degree at Redlands University and prepping for his second season as hoops coach at Redlands High School. In West Virginia, Jim Harrick had just married Sally Marple. A teacher-placement agency had landed Harrick a job in California near the Oregon border. The newlyweds packed their few possessions in a U-Haul trailer behind a new Chevy Bel-Air. They bolted west out of Charleston.

Jim Harrick set himself on a collision course with John Wooden, J.D. Morgan, Jim Milhorn, Pete Dalis, Jerry Tarkanian, and Ed O'Bannon.

Major Harrick ran several businesses, but none adequately supported a wife, daughter, and son in Charleston. He hustled. He boasted of having once played billiards against the legendary Willie Mosconi. Jim and his sister, Dee, did not grow up in a house, but the apartment was clean and warm. Helen Harrick was the rock of the family. Her odd jobs ensured that her two children would always have food and clothes. They would mirror her drive and personality, although some of Major's hucksterism would rub off on his only son.

Jim met Sally at a mutual friend's birthday party when he was a freshman at Stonewall Jackson High School. She was a grade younger. They became inseparable. He often held his own on the court, in summer pick-up runs and during the season, against East Bank High School ace Jerry West—who would eclipse his peers in the second half of his senior campaign. Harrick earned degrees in speech and physical education from Morris Harvey College (now the University of Charleston), becoming only the second member of his extended family to graduate from college. A few months later, after the wedding, the newlyweds barely glanced at Charleston in the rear-view mirrors of the Bel-Air.

After a year in Northern California the Harricks relocated to Southern California, near relatives in El Segundo. Coaching had not yet captivated Jim Harrick. He obtained a master's degree and teacher's credential. He worked in plants assembling automatic water rifles and spraying primer on airplane parts. The Lakers' propitious 1960 move from Minneapolis to Los Angeles enabled Harrick to follow Jerry West at the elite level. On April 10, 1962, a Tuesday, Harrick joined a record Los Angeles Sports Arena crowd of 15,180 that watched West steal a pass from Sam Jones, with three seconds left in a tie game against Boston, and dash thirty feet for a layup to beat the Celtics in Game 3 of the NBA Finals. The play cemented itself in Harrick's memory. Elgin Baylor scored thirty-nine points and West tallied thirty-six in the dramatic victory, but the Lakers would lose the title to their nemeses in seven games.

Harrick began observing John Wooden direct UCLA at Venice High School, the Pan-Pacific Auditorium, Long Beach City College, Santa Monica City College, the Long Beach Arena, and the Sports Arena. Harrick marveled how Wooden, without the stability of a bona fide home, had guided the Bruins to their first Final Four just a few weeks before Jerry West's mad dash. Coaching youth sports on the side became the first seed of a career, and two years later Harrick was hired as junior varsity baseball and basketball coach at Morningside High School in Inglewood. He also taught driver's training. At the corner of Manchester and Prairie, where the Forum would open in late 1967, a student slammed the brakes to jolt the dumpy vehicle to a stop at a red light. Jerry West rolled to a halt, beside the jalopy, in a luxurious Lincoln Continental. An embarrassed Harrick shrank in the passenger seat of the clown car.

When he took over as Morningside's varsity head coach, Harrick applied what he had learned in many John Wooden clinics. Harrick adopted the high-post offense into his plans. He developed a relationship with Wooden by working his summer camps. Harrick and others hustled to occupy a seat by Wooden at lunch and dinner breaks, and Wooden answered every query patiently.

Harrick detailed Wooden's practice regimen on three-by-five index cards, which Harrick's assistants would copy decades later. Harrick would mimic Wooden's sayings, like *Goodness gracious sakes alive!* Like Wooden, Harrick coached with a rolled-up program in his right grip. In his *Embracing the Legend*, published in November 1995, Harrick elaborated how honesty became a cornerstone of his philosophy. *Be fair and up-front with [people] … all the time.* He frequently mentioned fate. Harrick would eventually assemble a seventy-one-page Guidebook, which largely reflected the Wooden way, that he would deign on any interested party; *organization, discipline, patience, self-control,* and *poise* would all describe Harrick's version of the successful coach. All would clash with his legacy.

Wooden did transform his program. UCLA started rolling. He altered his practices by rotating players more frequently to ensure that they would all have a feel for each other's strengths and weaknesses, nuances and tendencies, which—he hoped— would also strengthen the team's overall late-season stamina. He became flexible, agreeable to change strategy posthaste. The two-two-one basic zone press became a staple. University of Southern

California coach Forrest "Toogie" Twogood compared trying to break down UCLA's pressure defense to being locked in a casket for six days. Wooden would acquire talent that made the Bruins' man-to-man defense peerless, season after season. But he wouldn't hesitate to switch to a one-two-one-one version or a diamond-and-one zone, to further confuse the enemy.

The stout, gruff, and pontificating J.D. Morgan took over as athletic director—for Wilbur Johns, who had hired Wooden after Johns coached only two basketball winners over nine seasons—in July 1963 and placed a WINNING SOLVES ALL PROBLEMS placard on his desk. A versatile high school athlete in Oklahoma, Morgan had been a four-year UCLA tennis letterman. He seized hoops-scheduling duties and paid Wooden's assistants as full-time employees, which allowed them to intensify their recruiting efforts. Fewer distractions enabled Wooden to further refine tactics. Many of the assistants Wooden hired, namely Jerry Norman and Denny Crum, were not yes-men; he did not seek lieutenants who would say what they thought he wanted to hear.

Morgan also increased Wooden's salary before he had won his first national title. "What we wanted to do was remove everything from his way so he could coach to the maximum," Morgan said in *The Wizard of Westwood*. "We wanted him to do just one thing: Win!" Arthur Ashe, who played tennis for Morgan, wrote about his "forceful, high-voltage" coach's contagious will to win in his *Advantage Ashe* autobiography. Sitting beside Wooden on the bench during games, Morgan chastised officials at his wont. Infuriated league coaches finally passed a proclamation to remove administrators (primarily UCLA's) from the sideline. As an example of his persuasiveness, Morgan once coerced a TWA pilot into executing an unscheduled landing in St. Louis, rather than Pittsburgh, to best facilitate a train trek to snowbound Chicago.

Finally, a major issue was resolved when University of California chancellor Edwin Pauley staked a million dollars, to be matched by fellow donors, for the construction of a long-sought arena on the UCLA campus. It would be called Pauley Pavilion, cost five million dollars, and open in June 1965. The project received significant early publicity boosts from UCLA alums John Ehrlichman and H.R. Haldeman. Pauley was an oilman who advised presidents, and he once had a stake in the Los Angeles Rams of the National Football League. Welton Becket, whose dozens of civic and corporate landmarks—which include the Capitol Records building and the spider-legged Theme Building at Los Angeles International Airport (LAX)—would mark the L.A. skyline for decades, would design the arena.

Wooden would have his own palace, and someone else would sweep the place before and after practices for a change. Perhaps that would help the Bruins finally beat the Trojans. The University of Southern California had made the first roundball noise in the region when coach Sam Barry guided it to the Final Four of the NCAAs in 1940, when only one victory advanced a team to the national semifinals. USC had won fifty-six of the first seventy games against UCLA, which included forty-two victories in a row from the 1932-33 season through 1942. They often played four times a campaign in that era. The Trojans returned to the NCAAs in 1954, '60, and '61.

The pendulum started swinging the other way in the few weeks before Harrick watched Jerry West's sprint against the Celtics, when the Bruins beat Utah State and Oregon State in Provo, Utah, to earn the program's first Final Four berth. Beginning that season, UCLA won seventeen of its ensuing eighteen conference championships, vital since that provided passage to the NCAAs. It claimed its first national championship, over Duke in Kansas City, Missouri, in 1964. The Bruins successfully defended that title in '65 against Michigan, in Portland, Oregon. The home-court comforts of Pauley, starting in

1967, launched the Bruins to seven consecutive national titles and drew comparisons to the Green Bay Packers, Boston Celtics, and Montreal Canadiens, other dynasties of the era.

Before the 1970s were half over, Wooden had evened the slate with his adversary on the other side of the tracks. The Trojans were relegated to the city's cellar. Wooden wrote about his pavilion, "It seemed to give us a little more incentive." He confided in the splendor of having his own complex just dozens of steps from his office. He admitted not having worked with the same "deep-seated purpose that is inspired by playing in your own facility." Triumph by triumph, however, the imperious reign of J.D. Morgan demanded more winning, a gluttonous condition that could conclude only one way.

All of that success pleased Bill and Helen Gillette, who celebrated their sixty-second anniversary on August 1, 2014. They had met in an Art Specialty class at UCLA in 1951, bought season tickets for the new arena in 1965, and held them for twenty-one years. Both would forge long careers in education, and Helen would nearly hyperventilate discussing UCLA sports, particularly basketball. Eternally positive, she could only listen so long to demanding, critical fans that called the post-game radio show—about the margin of victory not being enough, or strategy of which they had no grasp—on the drive home. Yappers sat all around the Gillettes in Pauley. Wrote renowned *Los Angeles Times* sports columnist Jim Murray; *The crowd there was … contemptuous, derisive, abusive … insulting, impatient, intolerant of mistakes. Smug in the knowledge it was the citadel of all basketball … insufferable in victory … mocking of opponents. They came to watch a slaughter, not a game … they wanted the head of the enemy on a platter. They usually got it.*

Helen cringed at snide remarks aimed at opposing fans and teams that were constant. She would not wish the enemy well or luck, not against her Bruins, but Gillette would genuinely welcome them to Pauley Pavilion. Well, she was told by one out-of-towner, "that's the nicest thing I've heard today!"

Morningside High was also winning big, at roughly a ninety-percent clip, under Jim Harrick. One team was 28-0, but Harrick became flustered when he discovered that three players had smoked marijuana before a playoff defeat. Harrick was devoting more and more time to the game, and developing fine players like Billy Ingram and Jackie Robinson (no relation to the former UCLA star and great Brooklyn Dodger). The latter would entangle Harrick in a major fracas with Jerry Tarkanian in the spring of 1973.

Harrick was about to accept an assistant's post at Utah State; the Yoda-like, damp-towel-chompin' Tarkanian had established Long Beach State as a burgeoning regional power and was about to take over at Nevada-Las Vegas. In 1970, '71, and '72, Long Beach State lost to the Bruins in the NCAAs, the last two times for spots in the Final Four. UCLA won national championships all three seasons. During that era J.D. Morgan, with nothing to gain and everything to lose, would not schedule Long Beach State. "I really wanted to beat UCLA," Tarkanian wrote in his *Runnin' Rebel* autobiography. "They were the kings of college basketball and obviously the Goliath to our David."

Jerry Tarkanian and John Wooden supposedly got along well. Wooden once promoted Tarkanian for an opening at Indiana University. The NCAA snooped into Long Beach State, though, in 1973. Tarkanian became incensed that his program would be so scrutinized yet those investigators, in Tarkanian's view, allowed UCLA—and notorious booster Sam Gilbert—to seemingly operate so freely. In *Runnin' Rebel*, Tarkanian said Gilbert had the Bruins "so far over the salary cap it was ridiculous." Tarkanian became friendly with Gilbert and even called him a good guy.

Tarkanian had no qualms with Wooden or Gilbert, he said, but there would be friction with J.D. Morgan, the NCAA, and Jim Harrick.

"There was an implication that we weren't on the up and up, all the while Sam Gilbert was hovering around the Bruins," wrote Tarkanian, in *Tark* in 1988.

> I ... found out in court proceedings that ... J.D. Morgan had turned us in to the NCAA. He wanted to hurt our program because we were getting close to knocking UCLA off. To my face, J.D. had always been nice. He used to come up to me and say in this slow voice, "Jerry, what a marvelous job you do," and all this bullshit. J.D. was a powerful guy, though, and if he wanted the NCAA investigating us, then the NCAA was going to investigate us. They got us on some ridiculous things, nothing like what was happening up in Westwood, and I let the NCAA know about it. And they let me know about it, which started our longtime feud. But I don't regret it. They can say what they want, but the NCAA will not investigate or punish the big schools like they investigate the small schools. They won't. They never have, and they never will. And I have been right about that from Day One.

Tarkanian became especially enraged at Jim Harrick. Jackie Robinson had wanted to follow Tarkanian, a longtime friend to the Robinson family, to UNLV. Harrick, however, hoped to take Robinson with him to Utah State in Logan, Utah. Harrick informed the NCAA about a potential UNLV rules violation when Robinson's ill mother, Lois, flew to Las Vegas to be with her son during a recruiting weekend. An NCAA investigator interviewed Jackie and Lois Robinson about the source of those expenses, but nothing came from the allegation. The publication of a transcript of Harrick's telephone conversation with an NCAA investigator— *... she stayed at the Dunes ... was taken to the Bill Cosby Show ...*— cast Harrick in a dubious light.

Jackie Robinson played for Tarkanian at UNLV. "[Harrick] tried to be a friend. I'd say hello, but I didn't respect him at all," Tarkanian told me in 2008. "The stuff he said was all B.S." Harrick becomes increasingly agitated when pressed about Tarkanian and the Jackie Robinson affair. "[Tarkanian] hates John Wooden. How can you *hate* John Wooden?" *In Runnin' Rebel*, Tarkanian praised Wooden as if he were a relative, calling the UCLA legend one of the *classiest* and *greatest* men to ever coach basketball. Tarkanian and his wife, Lois, seemed to have a bottomless reservoir of compliments for John Wooden.

Harrick steams ahead, saying, "[Tarkanian has] always been a sick, demented ... he thought people were squealing on him. He hates me to this day." About the transcripts of that chat with NCAA officials that were released to the public, Harrick says, "Anybody would have done what I did. Jackie told me, for three years, he'd never go to Vegas. Never. Tark comes in and pays all the bills. I get the Utah State [assistant's] job. I try to recruit him. Yeah, [Tarkanian] hadn't signed him yet. Tark got mad. The last thing I'd do is tell the fucking NCAA anything, [the] asshole."

For new Utah State coach Dutch Belnap, Jim Harrick recruited Southern California, scouted opponents, and coordinated the Aggies' defense. In 1975, Utah State had just finished a 21-6 season when Harrick felt the tremors from Southern California; John Wooden retired after the Bruins beat Kentucky in the NCAA finale in San Diego. Wooden had told his players about his imminent departure before the finale. They gave him an appropriate going-away gift, the capstone—the tenth and final championship building block—to his Pyramid of Success.

A year earlier UCLA had lost a national semifinal after leading North Carolina State by seven points in overtime. In San Diego a fan told Wooden, "Well, you let us down last season, but we got 'em back this time." What, Wooden told *Sports Illustrated*, do you say to that? "Ten championships in twelve seasons wasn't [sic] enough. It's laughable. But the UCLA coaching job has never been difficult." A host of successors could have argued with Wooden about the veracity of that statement. Internal and external forces whirred in Westwood, spitting out coaches with the best of intentions and soundest of ideas. Harrick looked on from afar as Gene Bartow quit after two seasons; someone had threatened to kill his beagle. Next up, Gary Cunningham called Harrick in Logan for help. After a brief interview in which J.D. Morgan vetted Harrick, he accepted Cunningham's offer to become a UCLA assistant coach. Harrick talked hoops and played competitive racquetball with Jim Milhorn, who had eased into athletic administration at UCLA.

Having learned how to sell himself and his institution at Utah State, Harrick was now visiting the homes of Ralph Sampson, Sam Bowie, and other top national recruits while representing UCLA. The Bruins beat Pepperdine in the 1979 NCAA Tournament; the Waves went to two NCAAs in the 1970s, winning a game before losing to UCLA in both. Before the Bruins played again in '79, Pepperdine athletic director Wayne Wright gave Harrick a tour of the school's gorgeous Malibu campus to lure him into coaching the Waves.

On cue, as if in a sappy television soap opera, Gary Cunningham informed Harrick that he was quitting UCLA. Harrick met with John Wooden, to gauge his chances of taking over for Cunningham. Wooden shook his head. Harrick went to J.D. Morgan anyway; Morgan also shrugged. For such a hot seat,

Morgan would need someone with top-flight experience as a head coach and a solid track record. Harrick understood. Morgan tapped the quirky, insecure Larry Brown, who had spent his previous eight seasons coaching in the professional ranks and would last only two seasons in Westwood. That started a vagabond run in which Brown would hold eleven different head coaching jobs by the time he took over at Southern Methodist University in 2012.

Morgan was bold, which he showed in 1976 when he hired thirty-one-year-old Terry Donahue to coach the UCLA football team. He could not take such a risk with the supervision of the nation's premier basketball program. Morgan retired in the summer of 1980 and died, from a heart ailment at age sixty-one, in December 1980. After Bob Fischer served as caretaker AD for three years, UCLA chancellor Charles Young made his own bold move by replacing Fischer with Pete Dalis, the school's cultural and recreational affairs director.

Many would bristle at the caustic, critical, and cynical nature of Dalis. Even after a major basketball victory—not something of the middling variety but a big one, against the University of Arizona in Tucson—his greeting to assistant coaches would be negative. Big deal. The corners of Dalis's mouth rarely turned upward, a distinguishing feature noted by many of his underlings. By contrast, they enjoyed rare visits by Gus Dalis, Pete's affable older brother.

Pete and Gus were sons of Greek immigrants. Their father, Tom, was twelve when he came to the States in 1910. He became an ardent baseball fan, especially of the minor-league Los Angeles Angels that played in Wrigley Field a couple of miles east of the Los Angeles Memorial Coliseum. Tom Dalis was in the Rose Bowl the first day of 1929, when University of California center Roy "Wrong Way" Riegels picked up a fumble and ran sixty-nine yards the other way, to Georgia Tech's benefit, in one of college football's more infamous plays. Tom Dalis also favored the Rams.

When his mother died in 1952 and Gus went to fight in Korea, Pete became tighter with his father, adopting his enjoyment of sports and his quiet, no-nonsense, business-like demeanor. Tom Dalis was part owner of a market at Olympic and Crenshaw, from which he sold and delivered produce after World War II. Pete was seventeen when he entered UCLA in 1955. Tom Dalis died before his youngest son ascended the UCLA athletics structure.

Pete Dalis recognizes that he wasn't as gregarious as Gus, but Gus Dalis was not charged with running a world-class athletic department whose budget would become sketchier by the year and force some difficult fiscal decisions. Gus need not worry about friendliness being misconstrued as a sign of weakness or a threat to his superiority. To Pete Dalis, sycophants or cronies of certain cliques, like coaches sticking up for one another, were bootlickers. He talked of his time overseeing UCLA athletics as his watch, as if he were the guardian of Faberge eggs or his post atop the fortress kept the barbarians outside the gate.

His personality might have been challenging, but Pete Dalis was a savvy businessman. He spearheaded the construction of the Wooden Center, a 95,000 square-foot facility just north of the Morgan Center that opened in May 1985. That would be the site of a low point in Ed O'Bannon's life. Wooden's only stipulation to Dalis, for putting the vaunted surname on the edifice, was that the entire student body had to have access to its many amenities, a given to Dalis, anyway.

Wooden, Dalis, and a regular group of about a dozen UCLA administrators, coaches, and a professor or two often lunched together in the student union in the late 1960s. As women's sports began growing and attracting attention—Title IX, the landmark gender-equity legislation, would be instituted in

1972—Wooden foresaw conflicts and tension in facility usage. As Dalis observed a women's hoops practice, he noticed a figure hunched in a dark corner way atop Pauley. It was Wooden, who told Dalis the following day, "Pete, I'm changing my mind. They play the game the right way, the way it's supposed to be played."

Highlighting his business acuity, Dalis arranged a lifetime six-figure annuity for Terry Donahue if the football coach remained at UCLA for twenty years—he did. When Donahue left the profession, some doubted his departure was under his own volition. But years later it appeared that both sides were at peace when a wing of Rose Bowl suites was named after Donahue. An area of luxury seats in Pauley Pavilion, by contrast, would never bear the name of Jim Harrick.

Peter T. Dalis would become a central figure in the sensational highs and lows of UCLA basketball.

Pepperdine groomed Jim Harrick. He would have his son, Jim Jr., play for him, and Senior would aptly call his offspring Headache for his wildness on the court, stubbornness, and academic woes that would require Junior to attend a junior college. Harrick hired Tom Asbury, who stayed at Pepperdine for all of Harrick's nine seasons and would succeed Harrick in fine fashion. Harrick coined a term in Malibu that became a mantra—*Everything's fiiiine at the Diiiine.* Jim Milhorn navigated the short, magnificent jaunt up the coast to continue his racquetball domination of Harrick.

In 1983, a defeat fell upon Harrick that will haunt him until his final breath. The Waves held a six-point advantage on North Carolina State and possessed the ball with twenty seconds left in the first round of the NCAAs in Corvallis, Oregon ... and lost, in double overtime. Wolfpack coach Jim Valvano won four more times, two by a point, to reach the championship. North Carolina

State then stymied powerful Houston in one of the tournament's all-time championship upsets. Harrick landed one of the best leapers in L.A. prep hoops history when Dwayne Polee, out of Manual Arts High School, transferred out of Tarkanian's lair in Las Vegas to play for the Waves.

Harrick admitted to being a bit loose in Malibu. Once or twice a season, he'd do or say something to embarrass himself and the school. He almost fought an opposing coach. A thousand-yard stare would glaze over his dark beady pupils. Assistant coaches could not restrain him. But he believed he was maturing and becoming a commodity, as Arizona State, Ohio State, USC, Nebraska, Wichita State, Colorado, and Houston all rang to gauge his interest in jobs or potential openings.

Genuine interest, on either side, varied. He checked into one hotel as Gertrude; an athletic director wanted to keep their meeting hush. Still, it made headlines in Phoenix. Harrick knew where he stood with USC when athletic director Mike McGee arranged an interview in a room at the Hilton by LAX. They ordered room service, McGee emptied five beers out of a six-pack, and he pelted Harrick with questions about this shady character called Sam Gilbert. McGee left, sticking Harrick with the check, and hired George Raveling.

Harrick believed he would be at Pepperdine for the rest of his coaching days, hardly a wretched prospect. From his office, he could watch the sun set over a fairway-size swath of lush bluegrass that seemed to slip right into the Pacific Ocean. Gazing the other way he witnessed the country's elite basketball program sink "into the muck of mediocrity," Harrick wrote in *Embracing*. "The great tradition that Coach Wooden established was slowly eroding, fading into memory." There were fewer top national rankings and coast-to-coast appearances on television, and the best West Coast schoolboys were not even considering UCLA.

Unreasonable expectations in the wake of John Wooden's preposterous achievements had spelled the demise of Gene Bartow, Gary Cunningham, Larry Brown, Larry Farmer, and Walt Hazzard. A toxic brand of venom—stirred by alums, fans, and media—took its toll on every coach. Wooden claimed Bartow was too sensitive to the "kook letters and the radio talk shows. Gracious sakes alive, I had lots of awful letters written about me, too. You just show weakness if you let them get to you." Wooden even shared Bartow's office, ostensibly to aid in the transition. Bartow heard Wooden answer his phone, *Hello, Coach Bartow's office* ... after a few months Wooden realized the discomfort his presence caused Bartow and truly stepped aside.

In 1987, UCLA lost to Wyoming and Fennis Dembo, who had poured in forty-one points, in the second round of the NCAAs. A victory would have pit the Bruins against UNLV. That was Reggie Miller's final collegiate season. His lone positive NCAA Tournament experience had been a victory over Central Michigan before that nineteen-point disaster against the Cowboys. As a junior and senior, he had jacked 948 shots. In a long NBA career, Miller would ring up more than twenty-five thousand points. But he embodied the post-Wooden era, in which future professional success hardly meant anything prestigious had occurred in the college ranks.

A season later the Bruins went 16-14, and UCLA generals Charles Young and Pete Dalis fired Hazzard. He was the first of Wooden's successors not to leave Westwood on his own accord, which sparked a tidal shift in how UCLA would run its basketball business. Spend even a brief time within the unique setting and circumstances of the place and the past becomes clear and unavoidable.

"Larry Brown was so temperamental; they said he wanted the office walls painted and he was upset when his office wasn't cleaned nightly," says Steve Lavin, who would eventually be called upon to pull the strings in Westwood.

> Bartow had issues with the outside pressure, and he was from the south so he could never acclimate. Cunningham was a worrywart; nerves got to him, and he lost hair. Hazzard was too militant. Farmer was too young; [players] called him "Farms" … it all gets back to, there's a certain pathology with places like the Yankees. There are certain sports entities, or institutions, like UCLA … what it's achieved is unparalleled in the history of sports, not just basketball … [detractors] want to have some cause and effect, some rationale, some reasoning. They say, "He only gets hot in the N-C-double-A Tournament … he's a country bumpkin … a duck outta water … he can't recruit … he can recruit, but he can't coach." It's endless. At the end, there's only one John Wooden.

Jim Valvano was etched in ink atop Pete Dalis's wish list. Valvano and his wife, Pam, flew to Los Angeles to meet Dalis, tour the campus, and house hunt. Sticker shock, in Bel Air and Beverly Hills, made the Valvanos sprint to LAX for the next plane back home to Raleigh, North Carolina. At that point, Jim Harrick rang Dalis to inform him of his interest only to be told, *Jim, we want a high-profile coach.*

Dalis contacted Mike Krzyzewski at Duke, but the chat was as brief as it was uncouth; the Blue Devils' season hadn't ended. Krzyzewski declined an interview offer after the season. Dalis discovered that Arizona boss Lute Olson had a clause in his contract that forbade him to coach in the Pacific-10 Conference within five years if he ever left Tucson. Longtime Villanova coach Rollie Massimino, who had won an NCAA title in 1985, was somewhere on the list. Larry Brown, fresh off coaching Kansas to a national championship over Oklahoma, flew to L.A. He accepted the same post he had left seven years earlier. But he insisted Dalis and Young remain mum because he wanted to announce it on his own terms the following day, a Friday, at Kansas. At that press conference, Brown revealed he would stay with the Jayhawks. Two months later he became the head coach of the NBA's San Antonio Spurs.

Before the sun set that Friday, Dalis called Harrick to arrange an interview the morning of Saturday, April 9, 1988. Charles E. Young got delayed trying to leave University Residence, the eleven thousand square-foot Florentine-style two-story brick home—decorated with Oriental rugs, a Picasso, a Warhol, and an Utrillo, and a rich wood-paneled library, built on seven lush acres in 1930—in which he had resided for nearly twenty years. He had earned a political science doctorate at UCLA in 1960. Eight years later, at thirty-six, he became the youngest chancellor in the history of the University of California system.

At fifty-six, Young could almost have body-doubled for actor Charlton Heston in his later years. Small birds seemed to nest in those thick gray eyebrows. He'd stalk the Rose Bowl sideline during UCLA football games, just a few paces behind Terry Donahue, and the agony of losing or ecstasy of winning would be etched all over Young's mug. When the brash six-foot-three chancellor finally showed that Saturday, he was full of bombast. He erupted. He slammed a fist on a table and complained about being treated so shabbily by Larry Brown. Dalis had to settle Young. Harrick thought, *What am I getting into?* He now had a prime seat inside the big top.

Still, he wanted the responsibility. UCLA represented Jim Harrick's dream job, but it required three evenings of fret and worry and waiting. In his Newbury Park home, Harrick received the phone call of his life at 7 A.M. on Tuesday, April 12. Pete Dalis said, "Jim, are you ready to take the toughest basketball coaching job in America?"

Three months shy of his fiftieth birthday, Harrick didn't hesitate. He told Dalis he'd been waiting twenty-eight years for the opportunity. Harrick accepted the offer and said he would not let Dalis down. Harrick's most staunch supporter during the thirteen-day lull that UCLA had not had a basketball coach had been John Wooden, who believed Harrick was uniquely qualified for the job. To top it all off, Wooden said, Harrick didn't have to be coaxed, like those other guys. He *wanted* the job.

Dalis had settled, in the eyes and typewriters of many pundits and outsiders. Harrick had been fifth or sixth on Dalis's candidate list. Acrimony developed between the two men, in Harrick's view, before he had even inked the deal. An hour after that phone call, before an 11 A.M. press conference to introduce him as the next UCLA basketball coach, Harrick drove to Westwood to discuss benefits and sign contracts with Dalis.

They were, Harrick says, a few steps inside the ground floor of the Morgan Center. On a brick-walled open staircase, they scaled metallic treads that switched back 180 degrees halfway up. According to Harrick many years later, they reached that halfway landing and Dalis said, *We don't give country-club memberships here at UCLA, either!* Harrick says Dalis screamed at him. "It was my mistake in, right then, not saying, 'Hey, wait a minute. Don't ever yell at me again,' " Harrick says. "I should have said, 'Please don't ever yell at me again.' I didn't do that. Right then and there I know what's coming. I *know* what's coming. And we hadn't coached a game yet."

However, Dalis denies that he made any sort of country-club comment to Harrick or raised his voice. "No, I would have never said that," says Dalis, who was somewhat amused that Harrick would write nothing but accolades about Dalis in *Embracing* if, in fact, such animus existed between them. "There's always been a lot of stuff between me and him. Jim's a complex person, very complex, but a helluva good coach."

Harrick says slights continued. He claims that at a formal dinner among UCLA brass, a vice chancellor's wife sitting next to Sally Harrick told her, in a hushed tone, "Don't sell your home." (The Harricks had bought a high-end condo on Wilshire Boulevard, for its proximity to Westwood, but would keep their Newbury Park home, too.) Jim Harrick says he has a hundred more examples. "I knew [Dalis] was throwing me under the bus for all eight seasons I was there. I knew it was coming, I just didn't know when. I'm disappointed I didn't do a better job of diffusing anything."

Chapter 3

SIX-MONTH-OLD Marques Johnson sits, in diapers, spine straight on a rust-blotched metal chair on the porch of the family home in Natchitoches, Louisiana. "The Natch," he says. His parents ordained his future by writing UCLA BOUND at the bottom of the black-and-white photograph that bears the characteristic sepia tinges of a snapshot from 1956. Jeff and Baasha Johnson were determined to move to Los Angeles, so their four children could matriculate into the University of California system.

Friends and kin believed the Johnsons were crazy, that they were not being practical when, five years later, they uprooted their young family and left secure teaching positions to go to Los Angeles on a lark. "But it was not a lark," says Marques. Relatives awaited them in Southern California, and UCLA had represented a beacon of racial equality and opportunity to the Johnsons due to Dr. Ralph J. Bunche and Jackie Robinson. Bunche had played basketball and football at UCLA. He became the first black person to earn a Ph.D. in political science from an American university, at Howard. He was the first person of color to earn the Nobel Peace Prize, an honor bestowed upon Bunche in 1950 for his role in Palestine peace talks. He debated with Israeli leader Moshe Dayan over a billiards table. Robinson was a four-sport star at UCLA and broke Major League Baseball's color barrier, in 1947, with the Brooklyn Dodgers.

Marques and his sisters, of which a fourth would arrive in Southern California, would all graduate from either UCLA or UC-

Santa Barbara. As a sophomore in 1975, Marques would help John Wooden win his final NCAA championship. During the 1994-95 season, Marques provided insight and analysis on UCLA radio broadcasts, next to play-by-play veteran Chris Roberts. Johnson's eldest son Kristaan was a freshman on the team; another son, Josiah, served as a ballboy.

Tyus Edney, the senior floor general, would be revealed as a cousin to Marques at a family reunion. (Edney also had distant blood ties to Ed O'Bannon.) As the most direct living, breathing link to the UCLA glory days, Marques Johnson experienced the program's national resurgence with elan. He would steadily learn what made Ed O'Bannon tick.

Marques Johnson steers his black Mercedes SUV into a primo parking spot outside Earvin "Magic" Johnson's Friday's restaurant at La Cienega and La Tijera. At six-feet-seven, Marques has a smooth gait and easy smile, framed by a neatly trimmed grayish goatee, for the many friends and familiar bystanders who greet him. He is fifty-seven and carries just a few more pounds than the 220 he lugged during eleven NBA seasons. However, four months earlier, a bum ankle made him sidestep a birthday dunk that had become a YouTube ritual. The marine layer dissipates and Ben E. King serenades the energetic patio area with "Spanish Harlem." Three men and a woman argue, sometimes vehemently, about the NBA playoffs. Dominoes click on another table.

Marques recalls National Guardsmen splayed atop Manchester Elementary School, rifles pointed on upside-down V bases, during the Watts riots of August 1965. Uncle Junior, his mother's younger brother, lived with the family and sometimes had to inform police officers, who stopped his car after curfew, of his overnight shift at North American Aviation.

Jeff Johnson had named his only son after Marques Haynes, a bewitching ball-handler for the Harlem Globetrotters. Marques polished his street game in the Run, Shoot and Dunk League, first at Denker Park (now Denker Recreation Center)—less than a mile west of the USC campus—and then at L.A. Trade Tech College. One official carried a .22 pistol, just in case. Nearby gunfire sometimes interrupted the action. Charles Bloodworth, Donald Strong, Walter Ned, Jerry "Money" Chambers, David "Airplane" Payne, Jimmy "Helicopter" Payne, James "Arkansas Red" Allen, and the outstanding Raymond Lewis all fashioned their roundball credibility in the Run, Shoot and Dunk, and on other asphalt proving grounds in Los Angeles.

At Sportsman's (now Jesse Owens) Park on Manchester and Western, Marques drooled over the agility and keen shooting of Alfonso Brigham, Johnson's first idol. A strong consensus, though, insists Raymond Lewis was the greatest player Los Angeles has ever produced. When Lorenzo Romar became an assistant coach at UCLA, he always regaled wide-eyed Bruins with stories about Lewis's cunning and exploits.

Lewis had met John Wooden via a meeting arranged by George McQuarn, his coach at the all-boys parochial Verbum Dei High School in battle-scarred Watts. But neither UCLA nor Wooden impressed Lewis. A red Corvette, offered to him if he went to Cal State Los Angeles, did turn his head; Lewis drove the sports car around town—often circling blocks, just to show off— while he was a senior in high school. He averaged thirty-nine points as a CSLA freshman, thirty-three as a sophomore. A dalliance with the NBA fizzled, and Lewis never left the dark duplex, and its constant temptations of drugs and alcohol, across the railroad tracks from Verbum Dei's track and football field. He was forty-eight and blind when he died, in 2001, during leg-amputation surgery.

Brigham helped CSLA reach its lone NCAA Tournament, an 88-80 defeat to Dayton in 1974—the Flyers were ousted in the next round by UCLA in a three-overtime thriller. Brigham graduated from CSLA and began studying medicine at UC-Irvine just as Peter Schultz, who had defected from Bratislava, Czechoslovakia, was admitted into CSLA. Fifteen years later, Schultz would give a clandestine assist to the UCLA hoops program. Dr. Alfonso L. Brigham specialized in internal medicine, and he conducted annual physicals for prospective Crenshaw High School athletes for years.

Marques Johnson began attending Dorsey High School in the fall of 1969. Twelve miles to the southeast Ed O'Bannon stood with his pals along the lockers to view the parade of girls gallivanting into Compton Dominguez High School on the first day of classes. High-fives and howls greeted the females. Ed favored football but played hoops to stay in shape; basketball teammate Dennis Johnson would wind up in the Naismith Memorial Basketball Hall of Fame. A young DJ stood with O'Bannon and an army of males that day when a six-foot sophomore named Madeline Hamilton made eye contact with the brawny six-five senior who was drawing considerable interest from UCLA football coaches.

Best friend Robin, as usual, strolled next to Madeline when they entered Ed's sweet spot. Madeline angled her head toward Robin and said, Who is that? "That's Ed O'Bannon," Robin said, "the guy we've been telling you about since the eighth grade!" Ed saw Madeline's big, soft Afro and that electric mini-skirt and, well, in his basso profondo that belongs in La Scala, he elbowed his buddies and pointed at them. "OK, fellas, nobody—NOBODY—talks to this one right here. This is the one I'm gonna pursue."

Jeff and Bashaa Johnson, who became a librarian, worked with Willie West at John Muir Junior High at Vermont and King, at the southwest corner of the Coliseum. Jeff Johnson also welded and became a master barber. West left for Crenshaw High, and when he became its basketball coach Jeff plotted to have him take a look at Marques. West invited them to a Tuesday night open run at Crenshaw. Sides were chosen. Willie West, in his early thirties, was five-feet-ten and could dunk. He defended sixteen-year-old Marques Johnson, who was north of six feet and growing. "You ain't gonna get a rebound!" West barked. You ain't gonna do *this*, you ain't gonna do *that*. "I'm gonna get up in you!" Marques had been impressionable. He had just seen Crenshaw dominate in a semifinal and final, in which it defeated Jordan High School, of the city tournament inside Pauley Pavilion. Jordan coach Bobby Brown garnered attention with his up-tempo style, but it looked like a loose brand of street ball to Marques. Crenshaw had under-rated point guard Donnie Aaron, who ran West's disciplined and structured system to perfection.

West always looked proper in crisp suits and stylish ties. Suited and booted, Marques says with a smile. West liked the kid's potential and told Jeff, as they left Crenshaw's gym, that he'd like Marques to play for him. A powerful dunk by Marques might have also swayed West's opinion. "My father asked me about the move, about going to Crenshaw," Marques says. "Coach West was intense, but cool. I had a good feeling when I left there."

The younger Johnson kept tabs on all the standout players in the area, from Jackie Robinson at Morningside to Lewis Brown at Verbum Dei, Greg Lee at Reseda, Greg White at Palisades, and Crenshaw's George Arteberry, a future best friend whose brother, Melvin, played center at Stanford. Johnson gauged the national scene by dog-earing the *Street & Smith's College Basketball* annual that hit the newsstands every fall, bugging his parents for the four quarters to obtain the magazine. His imagination got the best of Marques when he read about Wesley Cox of Louisville and Walter Luckett of Ohio University. "They talked about how muscular Wesley was. I thought, 'I could never compete with that dude.' Luckett was a six-foot-five lefty guard. I'm thinking all these guys were the shit, the greatest ever, that there was no way I could ever measure up to be anywhere near them."

Willie West, however, taught Marques about confidence and self-esteem. Twenty years later, West would run Kristaan Johnson—one of four Marques Johnson sons to play for the illustrious coach—and his Crenshaw teammates through a month of weekday six-hour practices after a stinging loss to Washington High. Crenshaw's next game? Washington. Crenshaw won the rematch handily and added another state title to its trophy case. When West called it quits after thirty-seven years, in 2007, he owned a record eight state titles and would be the fourth coach in California history with at least eight hundred victories.

In two seasons at Crenshaw, Marques kept improving. He and teammate Napoleon Gaither visited Drake University, in Des Moines, Iowa, but Marques was not going to endure Midwest winters. He also visited Washington State, Oregon State, and California. The UCLA dynasty, steered by John Wooden, was in full steam. The Final Four had become The UCLA Invitational, according to Texas Pan-American coach Abe Lemons. Playing for the Bruins had major allure, but what if Wooden wouldn't want Marques? He took his trips—recruits are allowed five—but the most appealing reserve plan turned out to be Long Beach State, where Jerry Tarkanian had been threatening UCLA's regional monopoly.

Marques had an enjoyable lunch, during an unofficial visit, with Jerry and Lois Tarkanian in their Long Beach home. "I fell in love with Tark," Marques says. "They jumped right up there." During Marques's senior season at Crenshaw, Long Beach State had been ranked third in the country. But 49ers assistant coach Paul Landreaux rang Marques to inquire if he would consider going to Las Vegas if Tarkanian took over at UNLV? The player had never visited the desert oasis and barely knew about UNLV. "At that time, Vegas meant nothing to me. When [Landreaux] said that, arrrgh. That took them out of the picture." Crenshaw teammate Robert Smith would go to UNLV and rave, in telephone conversations, about the celebrities and casinos and nightlife—"it's just a *live* situation!"—to Marques.

Tarkanian leaving for Las Vegas increased Marques's interest in UCLA, as did Sidney Wicks, whom Marques once saw tip a jump ball from the nearest circle into a basket when he played for Hamilton High. Fremont High product Curtis Rowe also became a favorite. Marques always watched the Bruins on the eleven o'clock replays on KTLA-Channel 5. (The station did not replay an original live broadcast; it was the actual first airing of a UCLA game, with a young Dick Enberg calling the action.) The first Bruins televised game from Pauley Pavilion, technically unofficial, especially captivated Johnson and the rest of Los Angeles in November 1965 when seven-foot-two center Lew Alcindor (now Kareem Abdul-Jabbar) and UCLA's freshmen, ineligible under NCAA rules at the time, defeated the Bruins' varsity squad, 75-60. Alcindor scored thirty-one points and hauled in twenty-one rebounds. The late-night TV replays gave Johnny Carson stiff competition.

Jim Milhorn, John Wooden's former reserve guard on that first Final Four squad, served as a media liaison. He sat in the front row of the new arena and enjoyed Alcindor's fantastic talents. UCLA had won the two previous NCAA titles. Milhorn thought, *We're going to win a few more.* As a sophomore, in his varsity debut, Alcindor set a school record with fifty-six points in a 105-90 victory over USC. Later that season he'd tally sixty-one points, still the Pauley record. With the big man as UCLA's anchor the Bruins won eighty-eight of ninety games, and three consecutive national championships.

But Marques insists that UCLA's pull was not overwhelming. The early part of its reign created a matter-of-fact, expectant mood, he says. Other teams had contributed to spoiling L.A. sports fans. From the time the Johnsons had moved from Louisiana to when Marques was a senior at Crenshaw, the Lakers had won eight conference championships and an NBA title in 1972, the Dodgers—having bolted from Brooklyn after the 1957 season—had played in consecutive World Series and won one (in 1965), and USC football had gone 100-23-6, with three national championships. UCLA football was mostly average or poor during that stretch, although the Bruins did finish fifth in one of the polls in 1965 and 1966.

Moreover, Marques had to keep his options open. What if John Wooden would not be interested in his services? But playing down the street, at USC, did not appeal to him. Ironically, a star beach boy who had been weaned on the UCLA way would favor the Trojans. The season before Marques entered high school, Paul Westphal averaged thirty-two points as a senior at Aviation High School in Redondo Beach. He had attended John Wooden's basketball camps four consecutive summers. Westphal's father hated USC, too. But Trojans assistant coach Jim Hefner persisted in wooing Paul, and the slick player reached his own conclusions. "It would have been just another championship at UCLA," Westphal told *Sports Illustrated*. "If we win here, it will be unique. It's more of an achievement to beat Coach Wooden than to win for him."

Those were foreboding words. The Trojans with Westphal—and many other top-notch players—could not defeat Wooden. The day Notre Dame upended the top-rated Bruins during the 1970-71 season USC defeated Loyola of Illinois and basked in its first national number-one ranking. The Trojans were 16-0. They just didn't do well against their powerful neighbors, losing both times that season to UCLA and stellar guard Henry Bibby. USC finished 24-2, yet Westphal and his mates watched on television as UCLA obtained its fifth consecutive crown. Jim Hefner believed USC was the second-best team in the nation that season. He had read in *Sports Illustrated* how, had the Trojans been in a different conference than UCLA, the two adversaries very likely would have met in the Final Four in Houston. Westphal had a superb twelve-year NBA career.

In Westwood, one sport ruled, and that team dominated the country. Marques finally, formally, met John Wooden. At a recruiting dinner at the famous Chasen's, on Beverly Boulevard at Doheny Drive, UCLA assistant coach Frank Arnold and Wooden entertained Jeff and Bashaa Johnson, and Marques. Burgundy-leather booths were named after Frank Sinatra, Alfred Hitchcock, and Groucho Marx, and Clark Gable, Howard Hughes, W.C. Fields, Humphrey Bogart, and Spencer Tracy had feasted on the tasty hobo steak and chili of owner Dave Chasen, a one-time Three Stooges fill-in during their prime. Elizabeth Taylor had gallons of the chili shipped to Rome when she was filming *Cleopatra*.

Marques Johnson licks his lips at the memory of something else from the Chasen's menu; the most succulent slice of white coconut cake that he has ever tasted. Frank Arnold called Marques often, always reinforcing a positive impression John Wooden harbored about Marques. But they were also wooing Jackie Robinson, Ricky "Tex" Walker, and Gavin Smith, all of who were talented forwards of similar six-five or six-six frames.

A timely clash in the Watts summer games, before Marques's senior season at Crenshaw, helped gain more of Arnold's attention. Marques went up against Jackie Robinson, whose team was stocked with Morningside players and won, 72-71. But Marques, in cut-off blue sweats and a flamboyant Afro that he parted in the middle and combed down on each side, thoroughly dominated with thirty-five points and twenty rebounds. Dunking wasn't allowed, but Robinson still tried to jam twice on Marques, who swatted both away. Arnold told Marques, "OK, you passed Jackie Robinson [on UCLA's wish list]. So much for Jackie, just keep playing well and everything will work out."

On the television in the family den in early 1973, Marques watched UCLA defeat Memphis State, and Larry Kenon and Larry Finch, in Tennessee. Less than ten minutes later, the telephone rang. Jeff Johnson said, "Uh huh, uh huh, hold on." He passed the receiver to Marques. John Wooden was calling.

"Marques, did you see the game?"

"Yeah, coach."

"Well, we want you to be a part of this next season."

"I'd love to be a part of it, coach. Thank you. Thank you very much. I'd love to be a part of it."

"OK. Well, we'd love to have you. Just wanted to make sure you were watching."

The attention stunned Marques. John Wooden *wanted* him. Still, he had not signed a National Letter-of-Intent, a written agreement binding a prospect to a college. Marques had agreed to join some friends for a weekend excursion in Santa Barbara, but his father quashed the plan. A squabble became a heated argument, as Jeff forbade Marques to leave town. Jeff figured UC-Santa Barbara basketball coaches might have something to do with the get-away, so Jeff finally said, "You say you're going to UCLA, but you haven't signed that Letter-of-Intent yet!" Marques said, "Where's the letter?" He found it. He signed it. "Now are you happy?" Jeff still restricted Marques from visiting Santa Barbara with his friends, which Marques laughs about today. "Knowing me back in those days, as wild as I was ... probably saved me from something. Everything happens for a reason."

Marques led Crenshaw to the Los Angeles City Section championship, capping a senior season in which he averaged 26.4 points and was named the section's player of the year. Fifteen-year-old Lorenzo Romar had watched the Cougars beat Jordan, 71-66, for the title on television at home. It was Romar's freshman year at Verbum Dei; locals dubbed it "the Verb." Romar was about five-feet-six and seeking direction.

Archie Chapman, a prominent football player for the Eagles, went to train at the Verb's track one day when a gang member, leaning on the other side of the fence, told Chapman to scat. The punk held a gun against the chain links. Chapman ran back inside the school. Gang members would saunter brazenly into Verbum Dei classes, stroll up and down aisles, spot shoes they would like to procure, and take them off kids' feet. Teachers were helpless, Romar says. "They better not do anything; [hoodlums] would beat them up." That violence would compel Romar's parents— who, like Johnson's, moved from Louisiana when he was very young—to relocate Lorenzo to Saint Pius X High School, where Morningside coach Jim Harrick first took note of him. That gang mayhem would also cause Madeline and Ed O'Bannon Sr. to move their two sons away from the area in about fifteen years.

But in 1973 Marques Johnson had become a household name in Southern California. That summer, he and Tex Walker formed a powerful tandem for the Denker Bucks in the Run, Shoot and Dunk. In the finale, however, they ran into a star-studded lineup that featured Sidney Wicks, Curtis Rowe, Henry Bibby, Jim Price, and Ricky Hawthorne, all of who either played at UCLA or were already professionals. Marques brushed off the shellacking. With UCLA as his next stop, he planned to win national championships in each of his four seasons as a Bruin.

By the time Marques had autographed that UCLA commitment, he had devoured *They Call Me Coach*, penned by Wooden. Before he played his first game as a freshman, Johnson had also consumed *The Wizard of Westwood*, written by Dwight Chapin and Jeff Prugh. Johnson inherited a voracious reading appetite from his parents, which has served him well in a long broadcasting career in which he chooses his words carefully and often enunciates mellifluous sentences. And he cuts to the chase. When a defender slammed into a particularly strong pick, Johnson said of the poor guy *it shook his family tree.*

In the former tome, Johnson learned how Wooden, among his many athletic exploits, had covered one hundred yards in ten seconds for the track team at Martinsville High School in Indiana; wrote about himself in the third person on occasion; turned down a barnstorming offer from the New York Celtics just before learning that his life savings of $909.05 had evaporated in a bank failure in the Great Depression, and probably had his life spared when an appendix operation kept him from duty on the USS *Franklin* in the South Pacific during World War II. A Purdue fraternity brother had replaced Wooden and was killed, in his gun-turret battle station, by a direct kamikaze hit.

Wooden would have accepted the basketball post at the University of Minnesota in 1948, but a snowstorm downed telephone lines to delay Golden Gophers athletic director Frank McCormick's attempts to reach Wooden. In the meantime, Wooden accepted the UCLA gig from Wilbur Johns. When McCormick finally reached Wooden, he would not retract his commitment to Johns. He was headed to the school that, in 1929, had been called L.A. State Normal when it moved its campus from between downtown and Hollywood to the acreage on the west side that had for so long been fields of beans and barley. Up sprouted UCLA, and the area known as Westwood Village. A stubby man named Sam Gilbert attended UCLA classes in the

1930s. He did not graduate, but he would display his affinity for Bruins basketball in significant ways.

The campus is situated immediately east of Interstate 405. Wilshire Boulevard, on the south fringe, is wide but congested with vehicles and high-rise condominiums—where Jim and Sally Harrick would one day purchase a fifth-floor unit in the sixteen-story Park Wilshire. To the east lies Beverly Hills; Hugh Hefner's Playboy Mansion is within walking distance. To the north, across Sunset Boulevard, Bel Air features luxurious mansions atop its hills and in its canyons, where Marques Johnson would one day reside. To the left is Brentwood, to the right Beverly Hills and the Hollywood Hills.

The narrow Sunset Strip has its own eminence, and a 2012 namesake documentary. Just a few winding miles east, past mansions once owned by actor Charles Bronson, and singers Michael Jackson and Elvis Presley, a sharp left bend past actor Gene Hackman's shack leads to the famous Beverly Hills Hotel and its Polo Lounge. A few minutes later, the Rainbow Bar and Grill (formerly the Villa Nova, where Judy Garland first met director Vincente Minneli, and baseball star Joe DiMaggio was introduced to movie star Marilyn Monroe), the Whisky A-Go-Go (whose stage has been graced by the Doors, Jimi Hendrix, the Who, and Led Zeppelin), and The Comedy Store—which featured Redd Foxx, Johnny Carson, Robin Williams, John Belushi, and many others in its long run—provide a haven of entertainment options.

For new and veteran Bruins alike, the Strip has always been an intoxicating seduction. I once spotted a UCLA reserve quarterback from Texas cruisin' it slowly in a white T-shirt as he drove an old, battered white Ford truck, windows down, country music blarin', him grinnin'. Looked like *Midnight Cowboy*. In a mile or two, he'd brush by his doppelganger passing under the seventy-foot Marlboro Man billboard, an iconic landmark to some that had been erected in 1982 (and would be torn down in 1999). When Jim Harrick was gearing up for the 1994-95 season, the House of Blues, Viper Room, and the Roxy—which was shunning under-age UCLA basketball players—were hot. Bruins could get the latest CDs nearby at the famous Tower Records store. Down past Hollywood High School, Roscoe's House of Chicken N Waffles would tug at the taste buds of many Bruins, especially Kris Johnson.

That UCLA is tucked into the most affluent, and glitzy, real estate of any college in the country is a vast understatement. It would be just as silly to say driving, and parking, in the area can be challenging. It was brutal in the mid-1990s. When Ed O'Bannon returned to the reincarnation of Pauley Pavilion, a massive, years-long construction project on the 405 created the automotive ninth circle. Then UCLA chiefs opted to tear down a parking structure, maybe fifty steps southeast of Pauley, in favor of a hotel. Those benign waves of barley and bean fields were most definitely long gone.

In 1948, when John Wooden arrived, The Garden of Allah Hotel, a sprawling twenty-three-bungalow den of debauchery whose frequent guests included Erroll Flynn, Sir Laurence Olivier, Ernest Hemingway, Orson Welles, and the Marx Brothers still existed down at the other end of Sunset. Across the way the seven stories of the Chateau Marmont, where dissipation tales ran rampant, towered over the area. Ciro's was about to play host to Sammy Davis Jr., Frank Sinatra, Dean Martin, Ava Gardner, Humphrey Bogart, Lauren Bacall, Sidney Poitier, and many other celebrities in a golden era of Sunset revelry.

By contrast, the other end of the strip, at UCLA, was staid. Not that Wooden sought amusement or distractions, but something close to contemporary amenities might have been nice.

Minnesota's facilities had impressed Wooden. At UCLA, its bandbox of a men's gym on the second floor of an ancient block of a recreation building, aptly called The B.O. Barn, wouldn't even accommodate twenty-five hundred fans on its fold-out bleachers. It received its derisive nickname from *Los Angeles Times* sportswriter Jack Geyer. "The place was hotter than hell," Geyer said in *The Wizard of Westwood.* "There was just one little window open in the whole place … they'd come out roaring in that old gym like it was the hundred-meter finals in the Olympics."

That barn would become the unofficial summer meeting point for scores of top-flight players, to prepare for professional preseason camps or collegiate practices, for decades. Blue-chip prospects like Baron Davis would test themselves against Earvin "Magic" Johnson, James Worthy, Kevin Garnett, and many other pros inside its dusty confines. Ed O'Bannon would not; he found adequate competition around Lakewood. On a glorious Tuesday in early October 1990, Marques Johnson mistakenly believed that the B.O. Barn was where O'Bannon was headed when Johnson saw him strolling across campus. Johnson daydreamed of seeing the nation's high school player of the year in a UCLA uniform.

For Wooden, the accommodations were so stale he thought about bolting not long after he had arrived in Westwood. Halfway through Wooden's book, Johnson read how Wooden wanted out after his second season. Purdue, his alma mater, had called. But Wilbur Johns and associated students graduate manager Bill Ackerman were flabbergasted that Wooden would even consider leaving with a year left on his contract, a three-year deal upon which Wooden had insisted. Wooden was peeved, but he honored the deal. In fact, his growing family enjoyed Southern California so much there would be few further words about relocating, even though the chatter among the UCLA hierarchy about building an on-campus arena for Wooden amounted to many rounds of bluster. By 1955, the hot air inside the barn had attracted fire officials, who declared the room unsafe with more than a thousand spectators. That ignited UCLA's travel odyssey in its own basin.

Wooden would parlay that ignominy into an updated barn of his own, but that would take a while. He had learned about angles, touch, and timing on the green felt of a pool hall in Martinsville. Marques Johnson read about Wooden's proficiency on a billiards table but was still curious, until one afternoon Wooden strolled by Johnson playing nine-ball on a table in the UCLA student union. Johnson froze. Wooden, wearing a powder blue, button-down sweater, with a toothpick between his lips, didn't say a word. He coolly took Johnson's cue, sank six or seven balls in a row, handed the stick back to a stunned Johnson, and slipped away. Lucius Allen, Mike Warren, and Kareem Abdul-Jabbar all had similar tales of Wooden silently showing off his billiards prowess.

Johnson discovered that Wooden began planting the seeds of what would become his famous Pyramid of Success in the mid-1930s; he toyed with building blocks, foundations of strength and mental fortitude. "If you lose self-control everything will fall," Wooden wrote. Reliability, integrity, honesty, and sincerity were the mortar of the pyramid, which he did not copyright. He would answer a request with a signed copy. He kept stacks of the pyramid, by the hundreds, in his office.

The pyramid did not include grift as a building block. Johnson read that, during the first title season, the Bruins received extra benefits based on performance; five dollars per rebound, up to ten, and ten bucks for every rebound beyond ten. Jack Hirsch noted a "helluva great feeling" when he collected an envelope stuffed with one hundred dollars. Athletic director J.D. Morgan and Wooden ended the scheme the moment they heard about it. (The NCAA, which prohibits such stimulus, never learned of the payments.) Farther under the radar, UCLA players learned how they could obtain free burgers, fries, and Cokes—provided they come in the back way and eat on orange crates in the storage room—at Hollis Johnson's Fountain and Grill in the village. That first title turned the Bruins into celebrities.

Johnson knew all about the famed full-court two-two-one zone press, its genesis and philosophy, before he first slipped on a Bruins jersey. He knew Dr. Ralph Bunche, who died in 1971, had tried to help Wooden recruit Lew Alcindor out of Power Memorial Academy in New York City. In a letter to Alcindor, Bunche stressed that the tutelage he would receive in the classroom would equal the education he'd receive on the court in Westwood. Johnson degusted every word about Alcindor, Henry Bibby, Keith Wilkes, Curtis Rowe, and Sidney Wicks, and about the 1971-72 Bill Walton-led squad that went 30-0 and established an NCAA season record for margin of victory, at 30.3 points, that still stands today.

The more Johnson read, the more he wanted to know every detail of the dynasty. *The Wizard of Westwood* explored the legend of Wooden, comparing the myth to the man. UCLA had won nine of the previous ten national championships, a span in which it went 281-15 over ten seasons—eight of those defeats coming in one season, 1965-66—and included a run of thirty-eight consecutive NCAA Tournament victories. All while being guided by a little man with a *saintly, professorial countenance, who looks like an English teacher ... and talks like a church deacon.* Duke coach Mike Krzyzewski is succinct in his admiration of Wooden; "You can have a pretty good argument about who is the second-greatest college coach of all time. There's absolutely no argument about who is the greatest."

Wooden spoke with a Hoosier sonant, wore bifocals and a tight haircut, always had that rolled-up program in his right fist, and he shunned tobacco, strong drink, and profanity. UCLA students came to liken their hoops games to religious experiences. The *Daily Bruin* sports editor believed Bob Boyd, coach of hated rival USC, drew the most ire because his slowdown tactics were "a direct affront to 'Saint John.' [UCLA fans] feel they have to protect their religion, their saint, the sacred traditions—the NCAA titles." Monty's Steakhouse, a restaurant atop the twenty-two-story Westwood Center building on Glendon Avenue in Westwood, became a popular nightspot for a bite to eat or a drink after games when it opened in 1969. For a future UCLA coach, that loft would be the site of a hard fall.

Word was spreading about Wooden's high-post offense. In the strategy, a center or forward would slink just beyond the free-throw line. The ball would be passed to him, and manifold options kick-started from that action. The "high post" would become synonymous with the UCLA offense, from AYSO contests to college programs to NBA arenas. Within a few days in early 2013, I heard coaches holler *U-C-L-A!* in a Japanese Basketball League team practice in Kariya, Japan, and in a youth-league game in Garden Grove, California. At all levels of hoops, and in all corners of the world, those four letters ignited the high-post set and represented a quest for perfection.

Johnson, in *Wizard*, also read how Wooden had pulled his first Indiana State team from a postseason tournament in 1947 because those officials would not allow Clarence Walker, a black player for the Sycamores, to participate. (It was not by coincidence that Indiana State was the guest for the debut of the renovated Pauley Pavilion in November 2012.) When a whites-only hotel in Lexington, Kentucky, refused to house the Bruins, during the 1951-52 season, Wooden took his team three hours away to accommodations in Cincinnati, Ohio. UCLA lost by thirty-one points. As the Bruins' contingent left Lexington on a bus, Wooden turned to a friend and said, "Someday, somehow, somewhere, a few superstars would emerge from California's high schools."

Curtis Rowe, Sidney Wicks, Henry Bibby, Bill Walton, Marques Johnson, and Ed O'Bannon would make that forecast golden. Wooden lost two more times, by slim margins, to Kentucky coach Adolph Rupp, but the Wizard would trump the Baron prodigiously in national championships. Along the way, Wooden would be challenged in many ways. At a 1972 speaking engagement in Pullman, Washington, someone asked him about the upstart American Basketball Association's raiding of undergraduate collegiate players. "Greed devours itself," he said. "It's bad for everyone ... I cannot say that the rare individual player does not profit." Those were portentous words, in relation to Marques Johnson. The ABA, Sam Gilbert, and greed nearly pried the splendid player away from UCLA early.

Marques Johnson had met Sam Gilbert, a multimillionaire contractor who handed out apples and oranges to UCLA basketball players in the early 1960s, not long after landing in Westwood. Gilbert wore a Bavarian fedora with a pheasant-feather band as he sat near the home bench. He often traveled with the team, too. He allegedly paid for players' girlfriends' abortions and helped athletes get discounts on stereos, airline tickets, and cars.

Gilbert dispensed advice when Bruins stopped by his twelfth-story penthouse office in Encino or his stylish Pacific Palisades home on Seabreeze Drive. The license plate on the Mercedes to the left read PAPA G. The one on the right, for Gilbert's wife, Rose, read MAMA G. Marques recalls many weekends with teammates at the retreat. They'd swim in the pool, feast on sumptuous barbecues, bet on who could spend the most seconds on a skateboard zipping down Surfwood Road or Blue Sail Drive, and play paddle ball on a neighbor's court. They'd hike into the hills of Topanga State Park, up at the end of Surfview Drive, to indulge in marijuana. "We'd go up into the mountains and smoke a joint, and just trip on the Palisades and ocean," Johnson says. "It was just a great hangout, mostly on Sunday afternoons."

When Bruins needed coats, Gilbert sent them to a store whose owner would offer sweet deals. Johnson once acquired a lambskin coat, a leather jacket, and another garment, "and I probably got fifty percent off. Instead of paying a hundred bucks, I paid fifty, or whatever it was in those days." Gilbert befriended the Bruins to look like a bigwig, Johnson believes. Gilbert would invite a few of them to dinners at the Ram's Horn—a restaurant popular among pro athletes and celebrities, run by former UCLA linebacker and Rams enforcer Don "The Turk" Paul—on Ventura Boulevard in Encino, or B'nai B'rith lodges and functions. "He would 'floss' us, as they say nowadays ... he'd walk in with us, [and say] 'My guys, these are my boys.' "

Former UCLA All-America Willie Naulls, who met Gilbert in 1967, first took disgruntled sophomores Lew Alcindor and Lucius Allen—who pondered transferring to Michigan and Kansas, respectively—to seek counsel from this fiery figure. They would remain at UCLA. They brought other teammates to the Palisades. Gilbert wore one of Larry Farmer's NCAA championship rings. He negotiated professional contracts for Alcindor, Allen, Sidney Wicks, Henry Bibby, and Swen Nater, and probably would have for Johnson had they not feuded.

A balding, barrel-chested five-foot-seven dynamo, Gilbert referred to himself as a "fat little matzo ball." A product of Lithuanian immigrants, Gilbert claimed to be fluent in French, Russian, and German. He served in the OSS, the precursor to the CIA, in World War II. He professed to be just a middling middleweight boxer in his youth. He invented metal frame studs and a door lock, which made him wealthy.

"Enemies refer to him contemptuously as 'Kareem Abdul' Gilbert," wrote Jim Murray. Gilbert once threatened to have a reporter tossed out of his office window. "I'm warning you to stop harassing me," he told two writers on another occasion. "If you know my history, you'll stay out of my hair. You don't understand ... there are some things I'd be willing to go to jail for." In *Wizard*, J.D. Morgan praised Gilbert, calling him a humanitarian and a volunteer advisor, someone in a unique position to help "the kids" after college. Pete Dalis even tapped Gilbert for advice during his watch.

Marques Johnson figures he and teammate Richard Washington were enlightened, about life and business, by Gilbert. Johnson says some Bruins would get better deals in their housing arrangements via Gilbert, "but nothing was free with Sam. No free shit. That's the biggest misconception, I think, people have. Sam was smart. Sam was a businessman, a frugal businessman. I think the perception people have is that he was buying cars [for players]. Sam never bought me a car."

Marques's parents bought a used Volvo for him. They had been saving money for his college education, just in case he did not win a basketball scholarship. Since he did, they purchased the Volvo, which they used more frequently than Marques. Jeff Johnson refurbished a green 1961 Volkswagen Beetle and painted it glossy black for Marques. But when Marques wheeled into Crenshaw in the Volvo, his friends oohed and aahed at him. "They thought it was a Mercedes," he says, laughing. "They were saying, 'UCLA got Marques a Mercedes!'"

Gilbert and Johnson went their separate ways when Gilbert tried arranging a professional contract for Marques after his junior season in 1976. Gilbert had bought airline tickets for him and Marques to attend the ABA Finals in Denver that May. The high-flying dunks by Julius Erving of the New York Nets and David Thompson of the Nuggets produced highlights that Johnson can still envision. Denver general manager Carl Scheer worked out a deal with Gilbert in which if Marques would declare hardship to leave UCLA early, the Nuggets, coached by budding peregrinator Larry Brown, would sign him to a million-dollar deal, or fifty grand a year for twenty years. "After five years, I'd still have fifty grand a year coming to me for fifteen years," Johnson says. "OK, sounds good to me."

The NBA's Detroit Pistons, coached by Larry Brown's brother Herb, had the fourth pick in that league's draft on June 8 and wanted Johnson. NBA owners were scheduled to vote on absorbing four ABA teams—which included Denver—into its league on June 17. Pistons general manager Oscar "Ozzie" Feldman had told Gilbert, when the Nuggets were in Johnson's picture, that Detroit would give Johnson a four-year deal worth $100,000 the first season, then increase it to $125,000, $150,000, and finally $200,000.

The day Johnson was scheduled to sign the Nuggets contract, Carl Scheer informed Gilbert that NBA officials had told him that the pending merger would be jeopardized if the Nuggets ink Johnson. "Denver couldn't just sign a player out of college without going through the draft, before the merger, and get away with it," Johnson says. Days later, with the Nuggets out of the picture, Feldman rang Gilbert's office to tell Sam, with Marques in the room, that the Pistons could offer only a three-year deal, for $90,000, $95,000 and then $100,000. "My heart sunk," says Johnson, who knew he'd return to UCLA for his senior season.

On Thursday, June 17, NBA owners voted to absorb the Nuggets, Indiana Pacers, San Antonio Spurs, and New York Nets into their exclusive basketball fraternity, creating a sixteen-team NBA. Johnson has heard that Larry Brown didn't speak to his brother Herb for nearly twenty years at least partly because of whatever role Detroit might have played in the bungling of Marques's potential deal with the Nuggets.

Later that summer Johnson met with Beverly Hills attorney Jerry Roth, who believed Marques could still get into the NBA via a special supplemental draft. Johnson arrived in Roth's office but didn't feel comfortable there unless he notified Gilbert. Roth nodded to his telephone. Johnson rang Gilbert and told him he was sitting in Roth's office, exploring a possible avenue to the NBA.

"Sam starts cussing me," Johnson says. " 'You son of a bitch!' Blah, blah, blah. 'How dare you!' Blah, blah, blah. 'Fuck you, Marques Johnson!' And he hangs up the phone. I'm sitting there ... wow, what happened?" Two minutes later, the phone rings. TV sportscaster Stu Nahan speaks with Roth, who hands the phone to Marques. Stu tells Marques he just heard from a reliable source (no doubt Gilbert) that Marques had signed a contract to become a professional player and, if so, that would mean he's no longer eligible to play college basketball. Marques told Nahan he hadn't signed anything. Nahan said, "Okay, okay, I hope not, for your sake. Just double-checking." Johnson laughs. "Imagine ... I thought, 'what the fuck is going on?' "

He and Gilbert never exchanged another word. Johnson scratched a check for two thousand dollars and sent it to Gilbert, who had presented Johnson with a bill for all the discounted merchandise he had received over the years. Johnson thought it would be best to completely sever ties with the man. Gilbert's association with Marques Johnson would have surely violated NCAA amateurism rules on agent activities and improper benefits.

"You got me talkin'," says Johnson, who hesitates; he's mulling writing his own book. I press him, asking if Gilbert's relationship with UCLA basketball players should affect, to any degree or in any way, the Bruins' dynasty that is attributed to John Wooden. "Uh, no, not at all. For one, you [didn't] go to UCLA because of Sam Gilbert; you [went] to UCLA because of John Wooden. Sam ...

it's a weird dynamic to describe. But it wasn't like you went to Sam with your hand out. He was a grandfatherly millionaire business guy. And you're not getting paid, you're not getting payouts."

Johnson never received a hundred-dollar handshake, for a game well played, from Gilbert. He did, however, get several from a certain doctor. "Around tournament time, yeah. I ain't gonna lie. It didn't happen all the time; if it happened three times in four years that was a lot. One doctor in particular, [I would] always try to find him. Sam wasn't the hundred-dollar-handshake guy. He wasn't giving anything. He kept records of everything. Coach Wooden would caution the team, without going over the line. He'd say, 'If he's giving you stuff, don't take it.' "

The black paint on the Mercedes that Johnson steered into Friday's is shiny, spotless. The grille gleams. The rims appear to have just rolled off a showroom floor. Gilbert, a clean freak, had more of an impact on UCLA players than just enlightening them with business acumen. He always told the Bruins, *If you take care of things, they'll take care of you.* During his fifth season as a professional, Johnson, in a multiple-story expose on Gilbert in the *Los Angeles Times*, recited that line. Washing and waxing their vehicles became part of the Sunday ritual at the Gilbert compound. Sam would even have the soap, bucket, and rags ready to do the job himself if the players were too lazy or disappeared for hours up in those hills. Johnson told the *Times*, "Even now, I'll be driving and notice that my car is dirty [and clean it], and I think Sam wouldn't have liked that."

In early 1982, Gilbert appeared on a Los Angeles television program to deny paying for, or arranging, abortions for UCLA players' friends, and refuted other *Los Angeles Times* assertions. Two months earlier, UCLA was placed on probation for violations that included Gilbert co-signing a promissory note for a player to buy a car, arranging the sale of complimentary tickets, and helping a player obtain an apartment at a reduced rate, but none of those charges involved players from Wooden's era. Because of those penalties, UCLA was ordered to vacate the run it made, under Larry Brown, to the 1980 title game—which it lost to Louisville and coach Denny Crum in Indianapolis. Even the Bruins' single chapter of success after Wooden and before Harrick was soiled and sullied.

Federal prosecutors from Miami indicted Gilbert in November 1987 for racketeering and money laundering, and sought the return of more than eleven million dollars in illegal drug profits that had allegedly been used to build the Bicycle Club gambling joint in Bell Gardens in 1984. They had hoped to arrest him when they visited Seabreeze Drive on a Tuesday night. They discovered that the seventy-four-year-old Gilbert had died, after a two-year battle with cancer and heart disease, the previous Saturday.

Rose Gilbert, whom Sam had married in 1950, taught high school English for sixty-three years before retiring, at age ninety-four, from Palisades Charter High School in February 2013. Upon her passing, in December 2013, Toby Bailey wrote *A UCLA legend. You will be missed* on his Twitter page as a tribute to Mama G. She had graduated from UCLA in 1940 and earned a Ph.D. from the institution in 1987. All-America forward David Greenwood claimed Mama G just about taught him to write, which kept him out of remedial writing classes. "If that's a violation, then to hell with the NCAA," Greenwood said. A feature about her retirement noted her avid support of the UCLA men's and women's basketball teams.

Wooden said he hardly knew Gilbert and thought he was a person who was trying to be helpful, but ... "I sometimes feel that in his interest to be helpful it's in direct contrast with what I would like to have him do to be helpful." In *The New York Times,* Wooden admitted knowing that Gilbert lurked, that his players went to Gilbert's home and were close to him. "But you can't pick someone's friends," Wooden said.

> I talked to the players and tried to make them aware of what was good and bad, but I didn't try to run their lives. I can't object to anyone being a friend of the players. And I certainly see nothing wrong having players at your house for dinner or, as a friend, helping them. I suspect if you're going to buy a new car or furniture, don't you shop a little and get someone to help you? I do. I see nothing wrong with a person trying to get a good deal. I'm not talking about something that's out of line where it becomes wrong if the help is unusual.

Wooden was not embarrassed by renewed allegations against Gilbert because Wooden knew he himself hadn't done anything "to be ashamed of." Wooden called "ridiculous" assertions that the NCAA declined to investigate the Bruins during his tenure because of the program's stature, a frequent Jerry Tarkanian charge. Wooden said UCLA was probably checked more frequently because when outstanding players went to Westwood, others wanted to know why. "You know when they're checking you," Wooden said of NCAA gumshoes. "They don't do it without your knowing it. They don't do it unless they were checking what somebody wanted them to look into."

Just before Marques Johnson landed on the UCLA campus, his next coach received another honor to set him apart from his peers. John Wooden was inducted into the Naismith Hall of Fame as a coach, the first person to receive that accolade twice; he had earned a spot in the hall as a player in 1960. Through 2014, only two others had been so dually honored.

The windfall from which Johnson benefited was the abolishment of the freshman-eligibility rule, which the NCAA had instituted in 1954. But Johnson still had a rocky beginning, whether he would be able to play as a freshman or not. He struggled the moment he donned a Bruins practice jersey. Keith Wilkes seemed to shove every shot attempt by Marques back at his nose. The ones Wilkes didn't deflect, Dave Myers or Bill Walton clouted into Pauley's nether regions. Weeping, Marques called his father. "I can't play here! These guys are too good. I should have gone to Santa Barbara. See, Daddy, I told you! I should have gone to UC-Santa Barbara."

"Well, who's giving you the most trouble?"

"Keith Wilkes. Every day!"

"Keith Wilkes is one of the best forwards in the country. Dave Myers might be the second best. You'll be okay. You're playing against two great defensive forwards. You'll be okay."

Johnson grins and says, "And I was. Eventually, I started to figure things out. All that was overwhelming." The 1973-74 season ended as salty as it had begun for Johnson, though, in that heartbreaking double-overtime defeat to North Carolina State in the Final Four. Right away, his hopes for four national championships vaporized. That season, however, Milwaukee Bucks general manager Wayne Embry visited a Pauley practice to scout Walton. But the guy named after Marques Haynes demanded Embry's attention with his strength and style. Embry told a colleague, "We're scouting the wrong kid."

One day Marques saw his friend Robin pushing a stroller across campus. He investigated. Inside was an infant Edward Charles O'Bannon Jr. Robin knew in junior high that her best friend Madeline should be with Ed O'Bannon, now Senior. Robin rejoiced when Madeline allowed her to babysit the tyke. "Who do we have here?" Marques said with a big smile as he reached into the stroller. Marques had known Ed Sr., a UCLA football player, and he pinched the left cheek of Ed Jr. Marques elevated Junior high into the air with both hands. Junior widened his eyes and supposedly enjoyed the view.

Ed Sr. had been on scholarship, but freshmen weren't eligible when he went to UCLA, and he needed to tend to his flailing academics as a sophomore. When Ed Jr. came along, on August 14, 1972, Senior quit football to concentrate on his studies and begin working to support his family. Eleven weeks later, ground was broken in Seattle to build the Kingdome.

Robin called Madeline and said, "Guess who held Ed Jr. today?" About forty years later, Madeline sits at her kitchen table in Cerritos, California, and slowly raises her right index finger. "When you think about it, one John Wooden Award winner holding another." Marques Johnson and Ed O'Bannon Jr., and Sidney Wicks and Walt Hazzard, would all have their UCLA jerseys and numbers retired at Pauley on February 1, 1996.

As a sophomore, Johnson learned what it took to become a champion, with an extra incentive. Three of UCLA's first four NCAA games were tight victories, and two came in overtime. After beating Louisville and Denny Crum, 75-74, in overtime of a national semifinal at the Sports Arena in San Diego, Wooden announced his plan to retire after the finale against Kentucky. I'm bowing out, he told his players.

At least, that's the widely believed timeline of events. It should not have been a surprise because in six months Wooden would turn sixty-five, the mandatory retirement age in the University of California system. However, Pete Dalis, the former football student manager who would rise to become UCLA's athletic director, contends that the mandatory retirement age mostly pertained to the upper levels of the ivory towers across the UC system. Still, the real-time events have been challenged. In his *Wooden: A Coach's Life*, author Seth Davis wrote that Wooden approached J.D. Morgan in the autumn of 1974 to tell him he would leave the following spring. Morgan allegedly interviewed Gene Bartow in February 1975.

Johnson was one of only six players Wooden used to beat Kentucky, 92-85, for his final national championship. Four Bruins logged forty minutes. Marques played twenty-four, making three of nine shots, grabbing seven rebounds, giving out an assist, and turning the ball over twice. It was Wooden's lone victory over Adolph Rupp. Stamina was no issue at UCLA. Wooden's pyramid was complete. Bartow took over, and Johnson says not a day of his life passes that he does not regret playing all four seasons for Wooden. "A bit of a loss," Marques says. "I was so used to doing things one way."

Wooden had rarely been concerned with the other guys. If UCLA played properly and followed his directions, there would be no need to worry about a foe. He never talked about victories or losses. Conversely, Bartow was concerned about the opposition; he would unveil elaborate opponent scouting reports. He was also a genuinely nice person whose interest in others was unimpeachable. Ask him, in passing, how he's doing, and Bartow might say, *Well the tummy is actin' up a bit ... might be too much sodium from the Chinese food I ate last night ... yeah, it's actin' up. Need some Bromo ... how are you?*

Street & Smith's experts had been watching Johnson, and he and Notre Dame's Adrian Dantley donned the cover of the basketball annual that hit the newsstands in the fall of 1975. The nation's impressionable young basketball players would daydream about one day playing like Marques Johnson, or have nightmares trying to stop him. He made the all-NCAA-

Tournament team that junior season, but Indiana—which would record college basketball's last undefeated season, through 2014—belted UCLA in a national semifinal.

Johnson endured those ABA and NBA dalliances, after a disagreeable season of playing for someone not named Wooden, and he returned to Westwood for his senior season with a renewed vigor to show pro scouts he belonged in the NBA. Craig Impelman, a grandson of Wooden's whom Gene Bartow had hired as an assistant, saw Johnson's drive and spirit one day in the fall of 1976. That morning Impelman saw Marques Johnson and Malek Abdul-Mansour—a UCLA student formerly known as Fred Warren who had befriended Lew Alcindor, and who would play a critical role in the development of seven-foot center George Zidek almost twenty years later—running laps and negotiating the stairs at Drake Stadium.

Later that morning, Impelman cruised by Pauley Pavilion to find Johnson, Kiki Vandeweghe, Reggie Theus, and others executing shooting drills. Vandweghe, about to begin his UCLA career, much preferred his short monicker to his given name of Ernest Maurice. Theus, nineteen years old and on his way to becoming a star at UNLV, hailed from Inglewood. He determined that UCLA, after Wooden retired, "sort of lost its magic." He said he also got "bad vibes" in a meeting with J.D. Morgan.

Early that afternoon, Impelman heard more commotion inside Pauley. Johnson and some mates were playing pick-up ball. Around six that night Impelman found Johnson shooting alone inside the arena. "The kicker, and I remember this vividly, is that at about nine o'clock Craig was in the Palms area, where I had an apartment." Johnson smiles. "On a court at a park across the street, he saw a shadowy figure shooting jumpers. He was like, 'Noooooooo, noooooooo!' I was workin' on my shot ... obsessive."

Johnson earned the first John R. Wooden Award, as the nation's top collegiate basketball player, after averaging 21.4 points and 11.1 rebounds as a senior. He shot nearly sixty percent from the field. He was polished. On breaks, Johnson owned the right wing. His play demanded more time, and powerful dunks—outlawed by the NCAA from 1967 through 1976—became standard his final season as a Bruin. He had a feathery touch on his jump shot, but he became known as someone defenders had to constantly monitor after he released the ball because he was so adept under the offensive glass.

Lorenzo Romar was a freshman at Cerritos College, a two-year institution, and he and his teammates made Channel 5's 11 P.M. tape-delayed games mandatory viewing that season, he says, "to watch Marques. We'd talk to each other, 'You see what Marques did? See that dunk he did this time!' He had an unbelievable senior year. He just dominated college basketball. That's when I really knew who Marques Johnson was."

Johnson played seventy-nine out of a combined eighty possible minutes in an NCAA victory over Louisville and a 76-75 defeat to Idaho State. He had scored a total of thirty-eight points and snatched twenty-seven rebounds in the two games. For years, Kristaan Johnson irritated his father with, How could the Bruins lose to *Idaho State*? Marques explained that the Bengals had three future NBA players on their roster. But he evened the score with his eldest son when UCLA was ousted by Princeton, in Indianapolis, in the first round of the 1996 tournament.

Kristaan, how could you lose to *Princeton*?

The pressure of following Wooden, however, was too much for Bartow, even though he was 52-9. He developed stomach issues and lost weight. He went to Alabama to start his own basketball program in Birmingham. For his accomplishments and exploits at UCLA, Marques Johnson earned a spot in the

Collegiate Basketball Hall of Fame, in Kansas City, Missouri, in November 2013. Johnson inserted an old photo of him and Wooden, Johnson in a leather jacket and Wooden in a suit and skinny tie in a garage, as the avatar on his Twitter page.

Milwaukee had the top pick in the 1977 NBA draft, after finishing the previous season at a woeful 30-52. Wayne Embry wanted Kent Benson, a center from Indiana. But he also wanted Johnson, so Embry traded seven-foot center Swen Nater to Buffalo for the third pick in the draft, which he used to select Johnson. Milwaukee had only one losing campaign during Johnson's seven seasons, but the Bucks lost in the Eastern Conference finals in the last two playoffs that Johnson wore the team's forest green uniform.

Contending with Larry Bird and the Boston Celtics, and Julius Erving and the Philadelphia 76ers in the East were tough chores. But Marques and Dr. J became tight. When the Bucks played in Philadelphia, Doc would pick up Marques and take him directly to the Old Original Bookbinder's delicatessen for lunch. "And we'd have to play that night," Marques says. "He'd say, 'C'mon, Marques, eat that cheesecake!' He'd try to fatten me up like a Christmas turkey. Took me a couple of years to catch on." As a member of the Bucks, Johnson won only five of twenty-four games in Philadelphia.

Of the eighty UCLA Bruins who had played in the NBA through 2014, only Kareem Abdul-Jabbar, Marques Johnson, and Russell Westbrook averaged at least twenty points during their professional careers. Westbrook joined that dynamic duo in an injury-shortened but productive 2013-14 season for Oklahoma City, but it remains to be seen if he can retain his membership. Johnson admitted that it was no accident that he thrived among the world's best players.

Dr. Michael R. Shapiro would rave how Ed O'Bannon played such a corollary to *A Sense Of Where You Are*, John McPhee's fine 1978 book about Princeton basketball star Bill Bradley. The title is a take-off of a shot Bradley—whom Marques Johnson idolized—attempted with his back to the basket, a blind flick over a shoulder that routinely fluttered through the net. "You develop a sense of where you are," Bradley told McPhee. It's how Shapiro, a former Princeton tennis player who befriended McPhee, would view Ed O'Bannon.

And it's how Marques Johnson explained his preternatural senses during his fourth season in the NBA. "I always know where I am and where I must get to," Johnson told *Sports Illustrated*. In Houston, he once fielded a lob that was short and low. With his back to the basket, Johnson bent down, scooped the ball into his hands, and blindly dunked it backward. He was asked how he knew where he was. "I *always* know where I am." Erring by even a centimeter would have been comical. "Not," he said, "if you know *precisely* where you are."

Marques Johnson had some personal issues—a stint in a drug rehabilitation clinic in Minnesota, an arrest on a felony spousal battery charge—at the end of his career, with the Los Angeles Clippers. A 1987 comeback attempt with the Golden State Warriors was brief.

By then Johnson had been living in his seemingly secure pad up among the chateaus and mansions in Bel Air for two years. A gate protected Stradella Court, and another guarded the short driveway at 10725, a modest one-story ranch compared to some of its ostentatious neighbors. It featured four bedrooms and three bathrooms on its 3,263 square feet, with a view to the south, of his college and beyond, past a kidney-shaped pool that would play a tragic role in the lives of Marques and Kristaan Johnson. Singer Tom Jones and actor Henry Fonda all once owned homes nearby, as did actress Maureen O'Hara, who risked her life but saved her home when she climbed upon the wooden roof and hosed it down during a 1961 fire that swept through Bel Air and Brentwood. *Life* magazine dubbed the disaster, "A Tragedy Trimmed in Mink."

That he resided amid such opulence and Hollywood royalty was not so far-fetched for someone who always fancied acting stardom. At Audubon Junior High, the tall and quiet Johnson took drama as an elective on a whim. Much-adored theater instructor Mario Lomeli arranged elaborate plays, with orchestral accompaniment, background choirs, and wardrobe shipped in from New York. Eric Laneuville preceded Johnson by a few years at Audobon, which launched him to acting (*Room 222, Sanford and Son*, and *St. Elsewhere*) and directing notoriety. Johnson had a bit role in *Damn Yankees*, and he played lead characters Li'l Abner Yokum in *Li'l Abner* and Conrad Birdie in *Bye Bye Birdie* for Lomeli, who died, at sixty-five, in 1997.

Johnson studied Theater Arts at UCLA, and he has acted in *White Men Can't Jump, Blue Chips, Forget Paris*, and *Sunset Strip*. He's had television gigs in *Boston Legal, Baywatch*, and *L.A. Law*. Of his twenty-two acting credits, one stands out. In 1994, Johnson spoke at the John R. Wooden Award presentation at the Los Angeles Athletic Club and asked Grant Hill of Duke, Glenn Robinson of Purdue, Donyell Marshall of Connecticut, and Jason Kidd of California what they knew about his playing career. He saw sheets of blank stares. They had no clue that he had won a national title as a Bruin or that he had a JOHNSON'S LAW poster—he sails at you for a two-handed jam with his white Adidas sneakers dangling above the unimpressive skyline of Milwaukee—which Michael Jordan had affixed to his North Carolina dorm wall.

But when Johnson rattled off his famous line as pick-up hoops ringer Raymond in *White Men Can't Jump*—"I'm gonna go get my *other* gun!"—Hill, Robinson, Marshall, and Kidd, and the rest of the crowd clapped in familiar appreciation. Johnson was just finishing *The Senator*, a short film in which he played the title role, when I met with him in the summer of 2013.

Long ago, Johnson had said *Pyramid, Schmyramid* in response to an inquiry about playing for John Wooden at UCLA. He says that was youthful hubris. Johnson showed his appreciation for Wooden when his Point Forward production company oversaw the creation of *The Wooden Effect*, a twenty-three-minute documentary that was partly directed and written by son Josiah, who played at UCLA in the early 2000s. Another Johnson son, Moriah, earned some renown for three seasons as a member of the Black Entertainment Television reality series *Baldwin Hills*, and he played basketball at Tuskegee University in Alabama.

In the documentary Wooden talks about race relations over the span of his life, and Kareem Abdul-Jabbar, Bill Walton, Keith Wilkes, former UCLA coach Ben Howland, and others impart their admiration for the coaching legend. Marques Johnson was particularly impressed when Wooden mentioned playing semi-pro baseball in his youth and learning how to properly turn a double play from Negro Leagues star Josh Gibson. The documentary was unveiled in June 2011, on the first anniversary of John Wooden's death at the age of ninety-nine. It has raised more than two hundred thousand dollars, which was earmarked for UCLA scholarships.

Johnson is working on his third marriage. He and his wife have a toddler daughter, his seventh child. He sold his Bel Air home in 1997, for $750,000, and now lives near this little plaza at La Tijera and La Cienega, where his roots surround him. Marques explains how much of an honor and privilege it was to play for the man who molded the little school with the barn of a gym, whose walls were saturated with body odor, in the former bean and barley field into a basketball powerhouse, who made those four letters synonymous with hoops utopia. "He was a deity, all the way," Johnson says.

> He was God. I mean, yeah, at that time, he had won nine championships in ten years. Crazy. But it was the way he carried himself, first. I had read his book. I knew all the anecdotes. Bill Walton was coming back for my first season, and Jamaal [Keith] Wilkes and Dave Myers ... all that was in the pot for me. To be plugged into that as a seventeen-year-old, for me ... talk about overwhelming. I wanted four [titles]. I wound up with one. There was initial frustration, some disappointment. But even though it's trite to say decades later, it's just something I'll always have, to be a champion and to be a part of the Wooden legacy, to have been a major contributor on his last championship team.

Johnson was giddy watching another major contributor to UCLA basketball glory, but victories were no time for Ed O'Bannon to rejoice. There was always another game, another conquest, one more block to scale en route to the top of his own pyramid. Marques always saw the heavy burden Ed carried, which told Marques all he needed to know about the kid's determination, will and spine. Those traits again surfaced when O'Bannon became the face of unprecedented legal action—"the sports trial of the century," according to one publication—against the NCAA in 2009. "For him to be the spearhead of this whole lawsuit ... that's the guy you want," Johnson says. "Certain guys, like Jackie Robinson or Jason Collins [who had declared his homosexuality in a *Sports Illustrated* cover a few weeks before I met with Johnson] ... it takes a special type of person to spearhead something like that, something of that magnitude. He's the one guy who has what it takes, inside and out, in terms of being a warrior and being comfortable with himself."

Johnson is certain that Ed O'Bannon would have thrived playing for Wooden, and coaching O'Bannon would have gratified Wooden. Johnson smiles when, in his mind, he replays the highlights, and ruminates over the subplots and struggles, of the one UCLA championship season that arrived after John Wooden. "He knew what it took to be a champion," Johnson says of O'Bannon. "Watching him that season was one of the special moments of my life. Whenever I see Ed, I light up inside. I just light up."

Chapter 4

ED O'BANNON JR. did not grow up pining to play hoops on Pauley's powder blue-framed maple wood. That sport would eventually consume him. But his first athletic dreams involved diamonds, specifically the pitcher's mound at Dodger Stadium. Dr. Michael R. Shapiro would use apposite lingo one day when talking about fixing O'Bannon to get him *back to the ballpark*.

O'Bannon swooned for the elegant canopies and lines of Chavez Ravine the moment he first sat in those bleachers beside his father to watch the Dodgers play the Houston Astros. Los Angeles outfielder Ken Landreaux had attended Dominguez High in Compton with Senior. Landreaux had also played Little League ball with Lorenzo Romar, future Major Leaguer Hubie Brooks, and John O'Bannon, the younger brother of Ed Sr. whom everyone called Sonny and whose right arm was a cannon. Landreaux made the final out of the 1981 World Series by catching a fly ball off Bob Watson's bat to seal a championship over the New York Yankees, whom nine-year-old Ed Jr. despised. So when Landreaux dropped by the Victoria Park Little League fields in Carson for an instructional session Junior received his first taste of celebrity; Landreaux picked him out of the large group. "Ed, how ya doin'?" Junior's heartbeat raced. His school popularity skyrocketed.

Ed wore number twelve on his jersey in tribute to Dusty Baker, his favorite Dodger. At ten, Ed threw a fastball and a curve. Even then, his left arm was formidable. Years later, that wind-up

68

would unleash a midnight blue eighteen-pound bowling ball in the lanes of UCLA's student recreation center that would obliterate a pin ... well, the top chipped off at an acute angle, wowing his teammates and even O'Bannon. "But I had a heckuva curve," he says of his repertoire. He threw a six-inning perfect game in the district playoffs. His approach to every hitter was fastball, fastball, curve. In the middle of the perfecto, he had an oh-two count on a batter whose coach hollered from the dugout, "Hey! Look out for the curve! Here comes the curve!" O'Bannon's coach yelled back, "Yeah, here it comes! See if you can hit it!" Ed threw the wicked pitch. The hitter missed wildly.

When selections were made for a district all-star squad that would attempt to qualify for the Little League World Series, in Williamsport, Pennsylvania, Ed was left on the other side of the fence because he was too young. The team failed to reach Williamsport. O'Bannon's three kids grew up hearing their father explain, judiciously and methodically, how that team surely would have advanced to Williamsport with him on it.

Baseball fell by the wayside after the eighth grade, as basketball wooed Junior into its web. Without telling his eldest son, Senior had periodically raised the rim in the backyard. When youngest son Charles Edward O'Bannon took to basketball, Junior routinely swatted his shots into Mr. McGrew's fenced-in yard next door. Big bro called little bro Beagle-Beagle and coerced Charles, a chubby kid whose cheeks Ed enjoyed pinching, to finish Ed's chores. The threat of Senior's wide leather belt kept both sons in check. Junior would continue his merciless badgering of Charles into adulthood.

Ed Jr. played on a summer club basketball team, the Stars, that represented Victoria Park. O'Bannon and most of those teammates went to Verbum Dei High, where Raymond Lewis and Lewis Brown had flourished. On the last Sunday of November 1986, Ed Sr. and Junior drove to Pauley Pavilion to watch the

University of North Carolina practice for its game the next day against UCLA. Someone on the Stars knew someone on Tar Heels coach Dean Smith's staff and arranged the exclusive meeting. The O'Bannons arrived early. Senior knew to pull the far left of six metal doors—the only one not locked—at the bottom of a flight of concrete stairs in the northeast corner of the arena.

Junior ogled the place in slow, complete turns. "Fell in love with Pauley Pavilion," he says. The building is austere. Its pavement-level doors lead patrons to a high-level concourse, maybe two dozen rows of seats rise above that level once inside. Much of the seating is below ground level. The luster of the arena hangs from its rafters. The floor, O'Bannon would learn, would produce the pain. He became a fan of J.R. Reid, a powerful freshman forward for the Heels, at that practice. The Bruins beat North Carolina, 89-84, one of only four losses by the Tar Heels that season; Syracuse and Derrick Coleman would defeat them for a spot in the Final Four. Later, Ed Jr. met Mark Raveling when both participated in a tournament inside Pauley. Mark stood next to Ed and pointed to two big guys sitting next to each other in the stands. Mark told Ed that the guy on the left is his father, George, the USC coach.

"He's asking about you," Mark told Ed.

"Cool. Who's the guy on the right?"

"He coaches at UCLA," Mark said of Walt Hazzard.

Ed paused. "How come *he* ain't askin' about me?"

When Ed O'Bannon's freshman hoops season ended at the Verb, his teammates opted to run track rather than play baseball—at track meets, they conspired, they'd surely meet girls from other schools. O'Bannon competed in the long jump and high jump, but he was clumsy. He owes that to feet that grew from size eights when he was eight, to nines when he was nine,

70

tens when he was ten ... all the way to seventeens (where they settled) when he was seventeen. After their freshmen years, O'Bannon and those friends all went their separate ways.

Gang violence kept metastasizing throughout South-Central Los Angeles. Crenshaw High was referred to as Fort Crenshaw due to the violence in the neighborhood. Ed had ridden a bike to and from the Verb, always passing rough neighborhoods and seeing Brickheads, a faction of Crips that buzzed around the high school. Ed would glide around the far end of the school, entering through a backdoor, to avoid the Brickheads.

Madeline O'Bannon feared for Ed on a daily basis. She'd peek around the curtains and nearly cry when he walked through the front door. When Charles came home from Perry Junior High and announced that he would be forced to join a gang or wage daily survival battles, Ed Sr. had heard enough. A deliveryman for United Parcel Service, he moved his family several miles west to a home in a safer area at Rosecrans and San Pedro. They also took an apartment in Lakewood, so the two boys could attend Artesia High School and be coached by Wayne Merino. Ed Sr. would sell the house when the family spent most of its time in the apartment.

Senior's UPS route regularly took him by the home of Lorenzo Romar, so Romar received periodic updates about Junior's hoops progress. (Ed Sr. now works for a title company, and Madeline O'Bannon is a notary public.) Ed Jr. thrived at Artesia as he concentrated on basketball, to capitalize on his growing physical stature—he stood about six-feet-six at the start of his sophomore year. But quitting baseball still rankles him. As soon as he arrived in Artesia's halls, he was reminded of his prowess on a baseball diamond. A catcher on the Pioneers' baseball team had played Little League ball against O'Bannon. "You gotta come out for baseball," the kid begged Ed. "You gotta play baseball!" New schoolmates looked up to Ed and said, "Ohhhh, you've *got* to be a basketball player!" Ed angrily responded, "No, I play baseball." He had difficulty shaking those Dodger Stadium daydreams. "They'd go, 'What, you play *baseball?*' " O'Bannon says.

> So after a while I started thinking maybe I should just stick with basketball. That's how it happened. There was that voice telling me, "You are tall and you're good at basketball, pursue that. That's the sport you should play." I wish I hadn't listened to that, to be honest with you. If I could do it over again, I would play both. I would not *not* play basketball; I'd definitely play both.

Ed Sr. continued jaunts southeast, lugging his two boys to Orange County to continue training with Marv Marinovich in Mission Viejo. His most infamous experiment was his own son, Todd, the former USC Robo Quarterback whose hamstrings Marv stretched when Todd was an infant. Marv had Todd teethe on frozen kidney, and the kid took carrot sticks and carob muffins—to avoid cake—to birthday parties. He was on a steady diet of sit-ups and pull-ups by his third birthday. Big Macs and Cokes were outlawed by pop, although Todd's mother, Trudi, secretly whisked him to McDonald's. By 2010, Todd Marinovich had been arrested nine times, charged with five felonies, and served a year in jail, all as a result of hard-core drug addictions.

Marv Marinovich knew tyranny was in his blood. His Croatian grandfather had amputated his own arm in a battlefield when he was a general in the Russian army. Marv played on both lines of USC's 1962 national championship football team, but he got booted from that season's Rose Bowl for fighting with a Wisconsin player. His athletic career plunged due to his vigor; he'd chain hundred-pound dumbbells on the ends of fully loaded weight bars to squat more than half a ton. He discovered too late that speed and flexibility trumped tonnage. His body broke down. His high-tech gym featured core programs and swimming-pool activities to increase swiftness and agility. Ed Sr. always insisted that his boys ride bikes to school, believing miles of roadwork strengthened their ankles, calves, knee joints, and lungs. And he swears by Marinovich's tactics. "That helped. He used to work out a lot of kids, and Ed and Charles were two of them. They worked on muscles, did drills we never thought they'd see. These kids were jumping out of the gym once Marv got through with them."

Madeline O'Bannon proudly reveals a yellowed Los Angeles *Daily News* clip from 1952 that shows a drawing of Alton Hamilton, her father, in his Jordan High track outfit above a host of times and distances and events, approximating *Ripley's Believe It or Not!* Hamilton finished second in the high jump in the 1951 state meet in Berkeley. Madeline smiles at the newspaper clipping but her eyes are sad, for Alton is battling stage-four renal disease. "My hero. It's heart breaking. He's where the kids get all their talent from." Ed Sr. diplomatically doesn't say a peep. The six-five former football player is formidable, tipping the scales at about 275 pounds. He fills the doorframe when he greets visitors. He resembles Mike Singleterry, the tough former Chicago Bears linebacker who deciphered opponents' plans with laser-like glares. Turhon O'Bannon, a son of Senior's from a previous relationship, was a wide receiver at the University of New Mexico and played two seasons for Winnipeg in the Canadian Football League.

Madeline touched athletic royalty in her youth. She tagged along with her mother to visit a best friend on Pepper Street in Pasadena. The families were so close, everyone seemed to be an uncle this or aunt that ... Madeline learned that Uncle Jack was Jackie Robinson, the legendary Bruin and Dodger. Uncle Mack was Mack Robinson, who finished second to Jesse Owens in the two-hundred-meter dash at the Summer Olympics in Berlin in

1936. The few degrees of separation between Ed O'Bannon Jr., Madeline O'Bannon, Marques Johnson, and Jackie Robinson were precious.

At Artesia High, Ed O'Bannon Jr. adopted a habit that Kareem Abdul-Jabbar had perfected when he was Lew Alcindor at UCLA. In his *Giant Steps* autobiography, Abdul-Jabbar documented how he'd stroll halls with his eyes straight ahead, the less eye contact the seven-foot-two center made with his peers—and potential enemies, that he believed were many—the better. O'Bannon related to looking over a sea of heads, "and not being bothered, as opposed to looking down and having to say hello to everybody or certain people, or look into the eyes of rude people," he says.

> Rather than acknowledge the world, [Abdul-Jabbar] would keep his eyes straight ahead. The rest of the world didn't exist to him. I thought, *Man, it's gotta be tough to be him.* You get to a point where you have a lot of friends, a lot of people who recognize you. You don't want to be bothered, but you have to go somewhere. What you do is, you look straight ahead. You're not trying to be mean or aloof ... but I guess you are.

O'Bannon's short roster of idols includes Mark Hendrickson, the former Washington State forward whom Ed played against in college. A six-foot-nine lefty who was a class behind Ed, Hendrickson also pitched for the Cougars' baseball team and earned All-Pac-10 Conference recognition. He spent four uneventful seasons in the NBA. Ed was shocked when he flipped on his flat screen during the 2006 season to see Hendrickson as the Dodgers' starting pitcher. Hendrickson spent ten pedestrian seasons in the majors. He won only two of his starts wearing the home whites in Chavez Ravine. But the idea of throwing on that famed bump just once makes O'Bannon salivate.

In his vehicle a baseball has always been O'Bannon's best friend. He grips two- or four-seam fastballs with his left hand. He flops the ball up and down in the palm of his right hand. A deep azure size-7½ Dodgers cap is always within reach. One of his few life regrets is discontinuing baseball. "I was good at it. I absolutely loved it." Had he stuck with baseball he believes a major league team would have drafted him.

So he has always coerced his two sons and daughter to play various sports, to get a feel for other fields, other talents. But his children discovered early how dear baseball is to Ed O'Bannon Jr. Edward III, his youngest, was going to quit the game to focus on hoops. But pop objected. Strenuously. He made Edward III play baseball so the lad would never have to regret giving up what the old man considers to be the most beautiful sport in the world.

Ed O'Bannon, however, did discard baseball. Fame and fortune slipped into his hoop dreams. And Sonny Vaccaro would slip into O'Bannon's life, creating a relationship that would eventually cast both in a titanic battle against the NCAA in another court a few decades later.

In an English class at Artesia High, fate—well, the alphabet—placed LeRoy Pedigo behind Ed O'Bannon when they were sophomores. Pedigo was six-foot-five but still sat in O'Bannon's shadow. Pedigo barked at O'Bannon, to scoot over so he could see the chalkboard, that first day of class. O'Bannon coaxed Pedigo to try out for the basketball team, barking back at Pedigo when he lagged behind in sprints on the football field. The two are tight to this day.

O'Bannon would knock on the door of Pedigo's home at first light on weekends. They'd sneak into the Artesia gym. Instead of attending parties, they went to that gym. "Our safe haven," O'Bannon says. They took what Wayne Merino taught them in practice—cuts, free throws, three-point form, weaves, picks—and relentlessly repeated the drills. They'd fetch grub at a McDonald's, then return to the gym. "Nonstop," Pedigo says. "He pushed me, and he wanted to get to where he could do those drills with his eyes closed."

The prep legend of Ed O'Bannon started forming. Toby Bailey recalls O'Bannon completely jumping over a kid, who had settled in to take a charge, en route to an extravagant dunk. Dr. Michael Shapiro relays how O'Bannon once leapt from the free-throw line, turning 360 degrees in flight and finishing with a ferocious reverse jam; never mind that such a full turn would have left O'Bannon facing the rim. O'Bannon frowns and shakes his head about the validity of such tales. He sighs when others talk about what he used to do on a basketball court.

The summer after his sophomore year, O'Bannon first met Vaccaro at Princeton University for the Nike/ABCD camp. He would participate in the Roundball Classic in Pittsburgh and earn MVP honors, and the recruiting letters besieged the apartment in Lakewood. O'Bannon would get thirty to forty a day. At the end of the process, he had eight cardboard filing boxes jammed with letters; by contrast, Beagle-Beagle would wind up with three boxes of correspondence. Ed Jr. averaged almost twenty-five points and ten rebounds as a senior, when Artesia went 29-2 and claimed a state Division-II championship. O'Bannon won a coveted spot on the McDonald's All-America team, a second *Parade* All-America listing, and he was chosen as the *Basketball Times* national high school player of the year.

Opposing coaches and other observers compared O'Bannon to Michael Jordan, Larry Bird, Earvin "Magic" Johnson, and James

Worthy, at similar ages. But his *joie de vivre* was bus rides with cheerleaders and the Artesia varsity girls' team. He was always the serious and shy O'Bannon, reflecting his mom's low-key characteristics; Charles, like Ed Sr., is boisterous and garrulous, the extrovert, the one who'd dance and prance and flex. A punctuation jam did Ed's talking. The thrill was holding the hand of a cheerleader he had hoped to take to the movies. He was too shy to ever kiss a girl on that bus. He sat in the back. "One big social hour," he says with a wide smile.

> Whomever you got a crush on, you're sittin' next to. We're throwin' paper at each other, yellin' out the windows. It was just a blast. Things were easy back then. No responsibilities. My responsibility was puttin' the ball into the hole. My parents didn't even let me have a job. "You're gonna go to school and concentrate on hoopin'. That's your job," they told me. It was an easy life.

That existence yielded to reality when he took his first recruiting trip to Tempe, Arizona, to visit Arizona State. Sun Devils coach Bill Frieder called O'Bannon the best player he ever tried to recruit. O'Bannon met and dined with assistants and players, toured the arena and campus, and was quite impressed with ASU's coeds. No doubt about it, Ed O'Bannon was going to Tempe. He'd be a Sun Devil. "Your first visit is always your best," he says. His parents put up a unified front, though, and told him to chill ... he had four other programs to visit.

O'Bannon went to Syracuse just to see the ballyhooed Carrier Dome, which held thirty-five thousand rabid basketball fans. It was the end of a decade when the Big East Conference had exploded in a wildly successful marriage with ESPN. Ed grew up watching Syracuse, Georgetown, Connecticut, and the rest of the Big East bullies bruise each other on *Big Monday*. O'Bannon hung out with Syracuse forward Billy Owens.

He was also enjoying watching Sean Elliott of Arizona and Danny Manning of Kansas. When O'Bannon started playing at Artesia, as a sophomore, he watched Manning lead Kansas to an NCAA championship on television in 1988—a few days later Jim Harrick got his dream job. O'Bannon watched because he knew Wayne Merino was attending the Final Four festivities in Kansas City. Manning's impressive efforts hooked O'Bannon on the madness that is March. "He made me want to play in the NCAA Tournament," O'Bannon says. "When I saw Manning do what he did ... that's when I fell in love with the tournament. I said, 'I *gotta* play in this tournament. I *gotta* be a part of this! If I could do *that*, put a team on my back ...' "

Elliott, Manning, and Owens were forwards who could play close to the rim and shoot from range. Most important, O'Bannon says, they were *team* guys. But like Marques Johnson, he abhorred freezing temperatures, snow, and perpetual gray, weather O'Bannon would not be able to dodge forever. He crossed 'Cuse off his list. He next gave George Raveling—who had been tight with Sonny Vaccaro—a courtesy call, nothing more, at USC. O'Bannon was much more familiar with UCLA, despite uncomfortable recruiting phone calls from Bruins assistant coach Tony Fuller. Both Fuller and Ed Jr. were guarded, which led to awkward conversation lulls. Madeline and Ed Sr. knew when Junior fidgeted with the long telephone cord and appeared disinterested, and silent stretches were painfully obvious, that Fuller was on the other line.

Conversely, Ed O'Bannon Jr. could not contain his excitement when he visited a Nevada-Las Vegas program poised for national domination. Unlike Marques Johnson, O'Bannon felt a strong desert pull from the gnome-like patron with the droopy eyes known as Tark the Shark. After all, the Artesia Pioneers wore black and red uniforms, like UNLV, with touches of white or gray. At the center of the Artesia court was a rebellious, scruffy, white-mustachioed Yosemite Sam-like character in a wild hat that somehow had to figure in the lineage of UNLV's *Hey Reb!* mascot. Wayne Merino liked to press the issue on both sides of the court, just like Jerry Tarkanian. They didn't light off indoor fireworks during Artesia's pre-game introductions, which greeted the Rebels inside the Thomas & Mack Center, but they did turn the lights off and flash a spotlight all over the gym. "We were modeled after the UNLV Rebels," O'Bannon says. "When I was in high school, I felt like it was my destiny to go to UNLV."

He arrived in Las Vegas on a Saturday, in mid-February 1990, for an official recruiting trip. He met guard H Waldman and center George Ackles. O'Bannon lunched with Greg Anthony and was impressed that the star guard had to leave early for a speaking engagement at a grade school. O'Bannon watched UNLV defeat Arizona, 95-87, inside the Mack, a spiffy six-year-old, nineteen-thousand-seat arena in which high-rollin' fans turned courtside seats into Gucci Row. He hung out with Stacey Augmon and Larry Johnson. Those two and Chris Jeter joined O'Bannon—and younger brother Charles, there on an unofficial recruiting visit—to watch Siegfried & Roy perform that Sunday night in a showroom at The Mirage. They slid into a semi-circular booth in the center of the stage, maybe halfway back.

Buster Douglas, seven days after his stunning upset of Mike Tyson in a heavyweight prizefight in Tokyo, strolled in. *Introduced as if he were the President of the United States*, thought Ed O'Bannon. Flashbulbs popped all around the basketballers. Another buzz circulated. Julius Erving, Marques Johnson's on-court adversary and off-court pal, sauntered up to their booth and shook hands with everyone. He told Johnson and Augmon, "Man, I was watchin' y'all today in the plane flyin' here. Great game!"

Ed was floored. *Dang*, he thought, *these guys got heavyweight champs walkin' up to* them, *not the other way around! And Doctor J! And they just got done playing on national television. How do you* not *come to this school?* Several weeks later in Denver, UNLV defeated Duke, 103-73—still a championship-game record margin—to win an NCAA title and cap a 35-5 season. Tarkanian had the Rebels on a roll. They had appeared in eight consecutive NCAAs, advanced to the Final Four in 1987, and fallen a victory short of that grand stage in 1989. Over the previous eight seasons, UNLV's record of 247-39 had been tops in the country. By contrast, UCLA had won only twice in the NCAAs in the 1980s—remember, its run to the championship game in 1980 was vacated due to NCAA penalties. It did win an NIT title in 1985, but that's only whispered about in Westwood. Charles Young might have employed that banner as a doormat over at University House.

In the 1990 tournament, the Bruins beat Alabama-Birmingham and Kansas before losing to Duke, which UNLV would conquer so thoroughly. Tarkanian had all the West Coast glamour and returnees to defend his championship in 1990-91. Ed O'Bannon yearned to join the high-wire hoop act, help the Rebels defend their crown by winning another one, and then enter the NBA draft after that season or in 1992. He would do the bare minimum academic work required to stay eligible. His life was all basketball. He would make tens of millions of dollars in the NBA and be a perennial All-Star, perhaps even help a professional franchise win a few titles, too.

In May, Ed O'Bannon and Shon Tarver, a six-foot-five swingman from Oxnard Santa Clara High School considered to be one of the top players in California, gave oral commitments to UNLV. Tarkanian did not press the pair for binding written commitments because of a threatening NCAA investigation. If penalties were levied, Tarkanian wanted them to be able to pick new schools without having to sit out a year, the requirement for breaking a signed Letter-of-Intent. "I couldn't believe it," O'Bannon says.

> Everybody else would have said, "Sign the [National] Letter-of-Intent." But [Tarkanian] was like, "Things aren't lookin' all that great. So if [penalties] happen, I don't want you tied into this." I thought it was extremely classy. How could you not want to be there, to play for someone who is as classy as that, despite what the N-C-two-A is sayin'? I think Tark has all the class in the world. He's an iconic figure ... the John Wooden of our era. What I mean by that, you walk into that gym and he's that big. Coach Wooden walked into an arena or gym, or restaurant, and everyone knew who he was. The whole place stops. Everyone pays his respects to Coach Wooden; same thing with Coach Tarkanian. He walks in that door and the ten people in the joint would know who he is. They would stop what they're doing and watch him walk all the way across the room and sit down.

Getting O'Bannon and Tarver had been a watershed event for Tarkanian, who had always finished second to UCLA at Long Beach State and never seemed to get a blue-chip recruit who was also considering the Bruins. Tarkanian told me in 2008 that he and his staff "recruited their butts off" to get Ed O'Bannon. "He was the first time we beat UCLA on a [premier] player." The episode with Jim Harrick and Lois Robinson had not settled with Tarkanian, " ... but we fixed him good when we [got] O'Bannon and Tarver." Harrick, however, believes nobody recruited Ed O'Bannon more vigorously than he and his staff, "from April 12, 1988, until he committed to Vegas," Harrick told *The National* in September 1990. "I saw him twenty-one straight days [that] summer, and I never saw [USC coach] George [Raveling] or Tark around."

Once O'Bannon announced for UNLV, Jim Harrick never deliberated about any sequence of events that might plop O'Bannon and Tarver in Westwood, and he says he never brooded over their loss. Can't get emotionally involved in recruiting, he says, "too tough." He did keep several scholarships open, but that was his standard operating procedure, anyway; Harrick never doled out all thirteen of his full rides in any given season at UCLA. He always left himself some leeway, just in case.

In losing O'Bannon and Tarver, Harrick never had a backup plan. He says he was fine going into the 1990-91 season with a foundation of sophomores Mitchell Butler and Tracy Murray, and juniors Darrick Martin, Don MacLean, and Gerald Madkins. The only hope was that neither O'Bannon nor Tarver had signed with UNLV. "But I don't think you can hope on the come [line]. We were rollin' at the time," Harrick says. "We had MacLean and Murray back. We were really, really good." On offense. Harrick is very kind. At the other end of the court his teams lacked, which would be exposed when it mattered most.

On July 20, 1990, the NCAA Committee on Infractions barred UNLV from postseason play after the 1990-91 regular season as a final penalty from a case that caused Tarkanian to sue the NCAA thirteen years earlier. Tarkanian released O'Bannon and Tarver from their UNLV oral commitments. O'Bannon was on the US team participating in the FIBA Americas Junior World Championship tournament in Montevideo, Uruguay, when he heard about the UNLV penalties from US teammate and UCLA guard Darrick Martin. *Hey, buddy, your school's goin' on probation. Whatcha gonna do? You need to come to UCLA.* O'Bannon slammed the door of his dorm room on Martin.

In the fallout George Raveling might have believed there was a chance, however slim, of Ed O'Bannon becoming a Trojan. On the first Saturday of August 1990, Tarver switched his commitment to UCLA. Two days later O'Bannon signed an application letter for financial aid to play for Harrick and also become a Bruin. Athletic department officials cognizant of academic requirements and UCLA scholastic demands were reluctant to admit O'Bannon; very reluctant, according to sources. Harrick placated those concerns. He would have much more difficulty getting a few others admitted into UCLA. It was the first O'Bannon windfall that would be invaluable to the career of Jim Harrick. O'Bannon told a reporter, "I hope that I can contribute in some small way to the great UCLA basketball tradition."

At 5:30 P.M. on October 9, 1990, six days before the official start of UCLA basketball practice, Ed O'Bannon ripped his left knee apart in a pick-up game at the Wooden Center. The group of Bruins was going to quit. They had played several games. Just one more, someone said.

O'Bannon stole a pass from Mitchell Butler on Court 2, the middle of three courts. He toyed with executing a wild windmill jam or throwing down a monster dunk and touching the top of the backboard with his right hand, buoyed by a gym packed with students, as he closed in on the north rim. He settled for a basic two-handed deal. O'Bannon rose so high he had to duck his head so it wouldn't bang into the iron. Upon descending his left foot landed on a wet spot, probably sweat. The leg twisted and bowed out—a varus bend, as opposed to valgus, or "knock kneed"—snapping the ACL and tearing the lateral collateral ligament from his tibia.

Scores of onlookers fell silent as O'Bannon howled and writhed in pain. Totally disheartening, said Mitchell Butler. Internal damage appeared significant but could not be confirmed until swelling—the knee had ballooned to the size of a basketball—had reduced. The exact nature of O'Bannon's injuries would only be discovered via arthroscopic surgery, and the attendant orthopedic surgeon had best have the experience to mend whatever mangled material he found.

That night O'Bannon, moving haltingly on crutches, pegged inside the front door of his parents' home. You know, Junior told his parents, I haven't even cried ... and he broke down. All three released torrents of tears. But that sorrow quickly vanished when Ed said, I'm gonna be all right. "He lifted us up with his attitude," Madeline O'Bannon says. "It was amazing. We were so devastated." LeRoy Pedigo showed to support O'Bannon and would never see his buddy despondent. O'Bannon never preached, but Pedigo knew he was spiritual. "And he put it to God," Pedigo says. "He wasn't going to let it defeat him."

Only until recently damaged knee ligaments had often ended basketball players' careers. The ACL and posterior cruciate ligament cross each other inside the femur and tibia, preventing the two bones from slipping out of joint, forward or backward. For an elite athlete that requires quick stops and starts, with a reliance on jumping and landing, sound knees are vital. Advances in kinesiology and surgical implements in the middle-1980s were invaluable in lengthening such careers.

Until then, knee reparation was primitive. In 1895, Sir Arthur William Mayo Robson became an orthopedic pioneer when, with tough sutures from animal intestines, he re-stitched two torn ligaments in the right knee of a forty-one-year-old miner at Leeds General Infirmary in England. It was the first known case of knee-ligament reparation. The patient would walk without a limp and never miss a day of work. The illiotibial (IT) band (or fascia lata), the tough flat strip that runs down the outside of the femur and into the tibia, was first used to form a new ACL in England in 1917, and a portion of the patellar tendon was first used to replace an ACL in Memphis in 1935. They were autografts, using material from a patient's own body. An entire patella, with its attached tendons, was used in 1923 as the first documented allograft, or tissue from a cadaver.

Those were hallmark stages of knee reparation. The development of the arthroscope paved the way for quantum advances in orthopedic technique. Still, when Ed O'Bannon underwent his allograft procedure it was considered controversial and radical. Tissue from another body could transfer disease or suffer rejection. Stephen Lombardo, a team doctor for the Los Angeles Lakers whose counsel Madeline and Ed Sr. sought, has always favored autografts. He told *Sports Illustrated*, "The best tissue is your own."

In 1985, Bernard King played for the New York Knicks when he tore his right ACL. Dr. Norman Scott, the Knicks' team physician, repaired the injury with ligaments from King's upper thigh, or hamstring. After nearly two years of rehabilitation, which included another operation after he stumbled on a pothole, King returned to All-Star status. He was inducted into the Naismith Hall of Fame in 2013. Within the previous two years of O'Bannon's injury, Danny Manning and Ron Harper of the Los Angeles Clippers both tore ACLs. Both opted for the patellar tendon autograft procedure, and both returned to the game.

Madeline and Ed Sr. struggled with their son's surgical options because of the apparent severity of his injuries. Dr. Gerald Finerman, the lead physician for UCLA's athletic department, would suggest replacing Ed's ACL with a slice of his own hamstring or patellar tendon, the autograft procedure that is still the most popular knee-ligament replacement technique. But Finerman had been attending a medical conference in Hawaii the day O'Bannon went down and was not scheduled to return to the mainland anytime soon. Short, balding, and bespectacled, Finerman wore his long white laboratory coat even when visiting Spaulding Field, the UCLA football team's practice facility. A fellow writer would cringe upon his appearance and call him Doctor Death, since his visits never seemed to bring good news. Some who regularly came in contact with him considered him cantankerous. Finerman did not return many inquiries, for more than a year, seeking comment.

Michael R. Shapiro says he read a sports feature in a Sunday newspaper, most likely on October 21, and became irate at the delay in fixing O'Bannon's knee. A keen lookalike of comedian Tim Conway, Shapiro is an ardent conspiracy theorist regarding the assassination of President John F. Kennedy. He calls famed orthopedist Dr. James Andrews "Jimmy." Shapiro had served on J. Richard Steadman's US Ski Team Physicians staff in Lake Tahoe, so he had seen, and assisted with, severe knee injuries, including alpine racer Steve Mahre. Shapiro had also worked under Marty Blazina, who had established UCLA's department of sports medicine in 1958. Blazina would become an advocate of the Achilles tendon allograft, a technique that Shapiro had performed several dozen times under Blazina's supervision.

An exhaustive search could not unearth the alleged Sunday newspaper feature to which Shapiro referred, but his frustrations cannot be minimized. "It seemed as though Ed was basically being dismissed, that there was nothing they could do for him," he says. "They had [nearly] two weeks to do something, and nobody was doing anything."

Connections were made between Jim Harrick, the O'Bannons, and Shapiro via Shapiro's father, Albert. A retired physician living in Southern California, the elder Shapiro was a member of the UCLA tennis boosters club called Bruins Racketeers. Michael Shapiro quickly recognized that the O'Bannons were in limbo.

"Ed Sr. was going to make the decision," Shapiro says. "He called me up, and we talked about the possibility of using a donor graft as a reconstruction method." Time, Shapiro conveyed to Ed Sr., was of essence since each passing day increased the possibility of atrophy in and around the damaged joint and prolonged a rehabilitation process that already promised to be difficult.

Ed Sr. sought more information. He spoke with six of Shapiro's former patients that had received an Achilles tendon allograft. Not one dissented. The next day, Senior and Madeline, with Jim Harrick and UCLA assistant coach Brad Holland at their side, visited Shapiro at his nondescript L.A. Knee & Sports Medicine Clinic in Tarzana. As Holland entered the office he whispered to Shapiro, "Well, he's a millionaire if you can put him back together, Doc."

In the medical community, the *orthopod* is known as a cowboy. They strut. They return famous athletes to the court—or grass, or snow—and earn status themselves in the process. To O'Bannon and his parents, Shapiro was supremely sure of himself. He knew fellow doctors viewed him as presumptuous, but he didn't give a damn. His only concern was Ed O'Bannon. Many years later, Shapiro is livid, again, about the delay. "I felt any new technique at least needed to be considered. [The Achilles tendon allograft] was something new that we were having success with, that had also been blessed by a senior surgeon [Blazina] who was the founder of the department of sports medicine at UCLA."

Perched later on the foot of his parents' bed, Junior listened to Senior reason why he favored the allograft. Why further weaken the damaged knee or tamper with the healthy one by taking material from either—same with either hamstring—to form a new ACL? That would only complicate an already extremely intricate ordeal. It was also highly unusual for a UCLA athlete to undergo surgery from someone other than a UCLA physician at a non-UCLA medical facility, then to desire rehabilitation on UCLA property. "There's a code—don't go against 'your' doctor," says Jim Harrick. "At the school [Finerman] was the head of the orthopedics department. I stayed out of that. That was a family matter. I knew Ed Sr. and Madeline had a hold of it. Yeah, there was some drama, certainly inside the department; [the O'Bannons] didn't want [UCLA physicians] to do the operation, but they wanted them to rehab him. Not my call."

Many years later Ed Jr. says of Shapiro, "He had a lot of people not liking him. I wasn't in tune as to who and the amount of venom he took, but I know he took some."

Shapiro repairs the left knee of Ed O'Bannon Jr. on Thursday, October 18, 1990, at Sherman Oaks Hospital. Shapiro sits with O'Bannon's left knee extended over his lap. Ed floats in an anesthetic fog. He is covered, except for an opening around his left knee, in baby blue surgical sheets.

For forty-five minutes, Shapiro uses a contraption to suck pools of blood from the knee. The millisecond of extreme torque indeed inflicted severe injuries, but Shapiro is relieved that the lateral femoral condyle—the outer nub of the femur base that looks like two knuckles of a fist—has not sustained micro-fractures. That had concerned others, who believed such damage would restrict O'Bannon from ever playing again. But Shapiro knew a disparity between an X-ray and a magnetic resonance imaging (MRI) test meant micro-fractures weren't certain. In fact, a portion of the condyle had been skived, as if by intermittent hacks from a razor's edge, but a relieved Shapiro could smooth it.

From all the tangled ligaments and tendons he had seen stretchered off the slopes of Lake Tahoe, Shapiro will not be overwhelmed by any damage he finds. Once he cuts O'Bannon's knee and scopes its insides, nothing could possibly surprise Shapiro. He finds plenty. Blood pours from every crevice. He deftly wields an intra-articular shaver, Osteotome, Takahashi rongeur, and other metallic instruments during the five hours of surgery. The blood just keeps coming.

Loose pink fatty tissue and the long end of the curled-up, eggshell-colored ACL make O'Bannon's knee resemble sashimi in a saucer of watery ketchup. Shapiro nods. "This was a fairly high-impact injury. I mean he ripped the hell outta his knee. But he's six-eight, and he has a long lever arm on the knee because he has a long tibia and a long femur." That translates to serious torque.

I watch perhaps the highest-profile case of Shapiro's career almost twenty-three years after he performed it. He found a VHS tape of the ordeal in the garage of his modest ranch home in exclusive Bell Canyon, near Malibu. We sit on the edge of the bed in his master bedroom to view the lone VCR-linked television in his house. With the Takahashi "grabber," Shapiro removes a chunk of loose white cartilage on the screen. "It's like playing Atari," he says as he watches himself. In the ceiling speakers of the operating room he has foregone Bach and Beethoven, the Rolling Stones and Beatles, which typically soothe him. For O'Bannon, Shapiro wants total quiet for the atypical procedures.

Halfway through, Ed awakens. He groggily glances at the computer-screen-sized monitor to his right. He sees the end of the intra-articular shaver, which Shapiro uses to arch the roof of O'Bannon's intercondylar fossa, or notch, between the nubs of Ed's femur. It should be curved, a small dome, to allow the ACL a degree of movement. However, O'Bannon's is more of an A-frame, which predisposes his ACL to being pinched. It's a congenital defect that means O'Bannon, a ferocious player, will most surely tear, or rip, his ACL playing basketball. His brother and daughter will also suffer ACL injuries.

"What's up?" Shapiro says as he grins at O'Bannon, whose eyes roll around the room trying to gauge his surroundings. "Just so you know, we're still operating." O'Bannon tries to digest those words and feels something in the general area of his left knee. Some tinkering. Something odd. "You're more than welcome to watch the rest of the operation," Shapiro says. O'Bannon glances back at the monitor and the shiny shaver. His dilated eyes finally focus on the dull gray lateral condyle of his femur, sinuous chunks of splayed cartilage, loose bloody fat pads … "aw, hell no!" O'Bannon says. "Put me back out!"

"You sure?"

"Yeah, I'm good." Shapiro's female assistant, the only other person in the room, covers O'Bannon's nose and mouth with a black mask that returns him to Wonderland. Shapiro re-attaches the lateral collateral ligament to the tibia with staples. He shaves a smooth surface on the condyle. He slices a centimeter-wide portion of the IT band from the femur and re-attaches it with a washer to Krackow's point F9 on the femur, which will shadow and stabilize the lateral collateral ligament and ACL—a tenodesis Shapiro learned from J. Richard Steadman.

The *coup de grace* of Shapiro's handiwork—via Marty Blazina—arrives when he gently pulls a thin piece of yellow plastic-like tubing through a meticulously drilled hole in O'Bannon's tibia. Inside that tube is the grayish Achilles tendon allograft, protected by a fine white mesh, from a twenty-seven-year-old male cadaver. The tendon will be anchored inside the tibia by a small chunk of heel bone. Shapiro pulls the tube through a hole in O'Bannon's femur. Shapiro calls the allograft a *stout* tendon, at about ten millimeters in diameter more than twice as thick as a sliver of a patellar or hamstring tendon would have been. It's a solid match, Shapiro says, because O'Bannon's original ACL was also quite stout.

(O'Bannon would joke with UCLA student managers, during his lengthy rehabilitation and slow recovery, that the donor had been Caucasian. For fifteen months, from May 2013, Shapiro tried tapping contacts at the Red Cross tissue bank, which supplied the Achilles tendon, to obtain information about that male donor. Sherman Oaks Hospital had also changed ownership, which spelled disaster for its records. Shapiro had agreed that it might be poignant to inform the man's relatives—if any existed—of how he had contributed to the Bruins' rich basketball history. O'Bannon had signed the requisite forms. Alas, Shapiro's valiant efforts went for nought.)

Shapiro gently pulls off the yellow plastic cover and protective mesh. He taps PAUSE. He nods to my digital camera and says this would make a fine photo; the layers of yellow cover, white mesh, and gray Achilles tendon are all in full view. Snap. Shapiro calibrates the proper tension of the allograft and attaches it to the femur with a screw. Stretch the condensed play-by-play above into more than five hours of delicate, taxing maneuvers, and an accurate idea of Shapiro's duress, and skills, can be formed. He tells Madeline and Ed Sr. that Ed Jr. should be able to play ball for another ten years. For inspiration, Ed O'Bannon will tape a Bernard King basketball card inside the door of his Pauley Pavilion locker and keep it there for the rest of his days as a Bruin.

When he awakes in a nearby hotel room, Ed O'Bannon's recuperation venue for twenty-four hours, vases of azaleas, roses, and tulips surround him. A large get-well card, signed by all the kids at Artesia High, stands in a corner. Paula Abdul, George Michael, and Michael Jackson autographed smaller ones. The bill for the operation is seventy-two thousand dollars. Many years later, Ed Sr. and Madeline exhale that Senior's health-insurance coverage was so dependable.

As Junior began convalescing at home the following day, LeRoy Pedigo visited. Ed's private phone rang in his room, but he was in the living room. LeRoy picked it up. "Hello. Yeah? Uh-huh. Can I tell him who's calling? Kareem who? Uh-huh. Sure." Ed lumbered in, rolled his eyes, and demanded the receiver. "Keep your head up. Danny Manning came back from this and you will, too. Best of luck. The entire UCLA family is behind you," said Kareem Abdul-Jabbar. Ed vowed to re-read *Giant Steps*.

Six weeks later the NCAA lifted UNLV's postseason ban when the Rebels accepted an alternative penalty that would prohibit them from appearing on live television during the following (1991-92) season and competing in postseason play in 1992. The 1990-91 UNLV basketball team could, in fact, defend its national championship. The NCAA had never previously reversed its course on such a major ruling. Still, Jerry Tarkanian referred to it as "that horseshit ruling."

However, O'Bannon recalls nothing about that timeline. Had he stuck with his commitment to Tark, he would have been able to help the Rebels defend that title. He would not have been playing pick-up ball in the Wooden Center in October 1990. It's absurd to continue down this path, let's do so anyway ... one writer fancied that O'Bannon probably would have been worth at least three points in UNLV's eventual 79-77 defeat to Duke in a national semifinal in Indianapolis in 1991. But O'Bannon says he never had any regrets. "Absolutely not. Once I made my decision to go to UCLA, or not to go to UNLV, I never looked back. I never followed what the N-C-two-A was doing with UNLV. I couldn't tell you when they actually went on probation. I had moved on."

O'Bannon's rehabilitation was laborious. Pedigo spent some weekends with O'Bannon on campus and tagged along to rehab sessions that included workouts in a swimming pool, a weight room, and in a trainer's facility with electrical-stimulation devices attached to the knee. "He kept going until he was almost crying," Pedigo says. "You could see on his face how much it hurt, but he was not going to let it beat him."

A few weeks after UCLA was embarrassed by Penn State in the first round of the NCAAs, Shapiro removed three washers and a screw from his previous handiwork. Antsy to get back to the court, O'Bannon pushed himself too hard, too quickly, sometimes even playing pick-up ball twice a day. The knee puffed up. In the fall of 1991, Dr. Gerald Finerman removed damaged tissue lining from O'Bannon's left knee in a two-hour procedure.

At that point, O'Bannon had finally worked up the nerve to ask Rosa Bravo, who sat in front of him next to two male friends in a Hispanic Literature class, out on a date. But he'd have to be nonchalant. Rosa's two pals didn't show that Friday. Mid-term exams were returned. Ed saw over Rosa's shoulder that she had done well; he had bombed the test and used that as an excuse to ask her for help. He says, "She obviously knew what she was doing. Of course, she was pretty as hell." He walked her to her car in Parking Structure 4. She agreed to help him with his studies. They discovered when he attended Verbum Dei that she had lived in the same neighborhood. They grew up going to the same skating rinks and arcades.

Restless that evening, he called her. She was free. He picked her up in his blue-black Honda Civic hatchback, a beat-up rig that Pedigo laughingly calls *a piece of shit*. At a stop light under a bridge, conversation steered toward relationships. O'Bannon repeated a line he had first heard a young Earvin "Magic" Johnson utter in an interview; "I am married to basketball. No kids. No marriage." Bravo thought, *Well, this will be a one-date relationship.*

They went to a Del Amo Mall cinema and helped make Wes Craven's comedy horror movie *The People Under The Stairs* the top box-office draw of the weekend. They shared a large Coke and popcorn. Afterward she showed him Crush, a discount women's clothing store that she managed in Manhattan Beach. They strolled on a wooden pier. They sat on a concrete bench. He kissed her and instantly fell in love. He called her Saturday. They went out again and haven't been apart from each other.

Ed O'Bannon finally played in his first UCLA game, a 99-71 thrashing of Oregon at Pauley Pavilion, on January 16, 1992. He walked onto the court as a Ducks player prepared to shoot free throws. The crowd showered him with applause. Ed looked up to his proud parents in the stands. On the verge of tears, O'Bannon inhaled deeply to regain composure. He played twenty-three games, averaging almost thirteen minutes and four points as a redshirt freshman.

NCAA officials also visited Westwood during the season to chat with O'Bannon about the purchaser of an airline ticket he had used to take an unofficial recruiting visit to UNLV more than two years earlier. Nothing came of it, but those visitors infuriated O'Bannon. He was being grilled about the topic maybe a tenth time. The officials shut the door in a conference room and all but raised a spotlight at him. "Dude, you guys are fishin'," Ed said. "What are you lookin' for? What the hell do you guys want from me?"

To O'Bannon, it was typical of how the NCAA had badgered Tarkanian for many years. In April 1998 Tarkanian accepted a $2.5 million settlement from the NCAA, averting the start of a trial scheduled to begin in Las Vegas six weeks later. Tarkanian and the NCAA had jousted since 1973, when he penned a guest column for the *Long Beach Press-Telegram* and wrote how the governing body for collegiate sports went after minnows—small programs—but not whales. "You want vindication? Tark has had his," O'Bannon says. "He sued the N-C-two-A and got, what, two million dollars? But there's a whole lot of other people they hurt in going after him, just a wave of people they hurt and had lives altered because of their beef with him … what a crooked organization." That antagonism would help fuel O'Bannon's own future litigious actions, in concert with Sonny Vaccaro, against the NCAA.

His redshirt freshman season ended with UCLA getting run out of The Pit, in Albuquerque, by Indiana in a 106-79 evisceration that represented the essence of humiliation, not only because the prize was a spot in the Final Four but the Bruins had defeated the Hoosiers, by fifteen points, in the season opener in Massachusetts. The teams finished in quite diametrical places. Moreover, UCLA had nine players on that roster that would play in the NBA. Had the affair been reduced to forty one-minute contests, the Bruins would have gone oh-for-forty. In my twenty-seven-year career, I can count such lopsided games that I have witnessed on one hand, minus the thumb. At halftime, the Hoosiers sprinted up—past their weary, slogging opponents— the steep ramp that leads to both locker rooms.

Jim Harrick had made a calculated move when he benched starting point guard Darrick Martin, a senior, for the NCAAs, letting the Bruins sink or swim with a true freshman, Tyus Edney, at the controls. Fanatical supporters could rail that yet another title opportunity was lost. In reality, Harrick wanted to galvanize and vulcanize his raw little floor general for the future. This team did not possess championship mettle. The tunnel-vision mentality on offense, by some of its key players, made it easy to manipulate at the other end, exploitable by teams and coaches who were elite, like Duke and Indiana, and a big-time liability against an upstart thirteenth-seeded team like Penn State in 1991.

That Edney directed them to four NCAA games in 1992 was commendable, as was Harrick's audacious call to go with him.

For all his faults, Harrick did not receive enough credit for such maneuvers. Nobody saw him when he told his players that they would need to conquer plenty—opponents, road crowds, officials, provocative media, and *Harrick himself*—to be successful. Few bosses are that ballsy. The college basketball coaching fraternity is rife with control freaks and egomaniacs that would never concede their own faults or have their methods questioned. The ugly endings, though, were what weighed heavy to many UCLA fans that had been staring at only ten banners for a long time.

A few days before the debacle in Albuquerque, I had ventured to Las Cruces, New Mexico, to watch New Mexico State practice in the Pan American Center and chat with Aggies coach Neil McCarthy. The Bruins would play the Aggies in the Sweet Sixteen in Albuquerque; many saw UCLA-Indiana as a foregone conclusion in the next round. McCarthy knew that. He saw me sitting in a floor seat and showboated, gathering his players. He riled them. They all clenched hands above McCarthy as he capped his rousing diatribe with, "They're a bunch of pussies!" (En route back to Albuquerque, a highway patrolman pulled my rental car over. Speeding. Where you comin' from? Where you goin'? What are you up to? When he learned I wrote about UCLA basketball, he put his pad away and regaled me with his fondest memories of Alcindor and Walton. Ten minutes later, he smiled and waved me a good evening.)

The Aggies put up a fight but lost, 85-78. Larry Pierce, a forty-three-year-old UCLA administrative analyst whose muscular dystrophy affliction had confined him to a wheelchair for twenty years, attended the game courtesy of Bruins boosters. A practice regular, his knowledge of UCLA hoops was impressive. McCarthy lamented that UCLA didn't want any of his players, and he couldn't get any of UCLA's players—that would change in less than three years.

Five-foot-eight guard Sam Crawford had sixteen points and seven assists for New Mexico State. Just playing in such a spotlight qualified as a feat for him. At ten his mother had sent him away from crime-laden housing projects in Chicago to live with an aunt in Los Angeles, and by sixteen he was living on the streets, around Westchester High School, when that aunt went into a detoxification center. Jim Harrick lauded Crawford, telling media the Bruins had nobody more talented than the rare guard who was shorter than his own playmaker.

Don MacLean begged to differ. Always quotable, he said the Aggies could take this loss and "go back to Las Cruces. They didn't belong here anyway." Less than forty-eight hours later, Indiana showed that UCLA didn't belong here, either. The defensive accountability at UCLA around this time was minimal, at best. Jim Harrick was dismayed that he had cocky, not confident, charges, and they had nothing to be cocky about. That always worried him. MacLean's comment reinforced that cockiness. As talented as he and Tracy Murray were on the offensive side of the court, they did not exactly provide defensive inspiration. Duke coach Mike Krzyzewski once exposed MacLean by isolating Brian Davis on him on a wing. Davis blew by MacLean on the baseline and scored at the rim, and the Blue Devils pulled away for the victory. Christian Laettner and Davis played with passion and precision at both ends of the court, and Coach K always ruthlessly exploited advantages. Those Blue Devils were supremely confident, on offense and defense. Not so with the Bruins.

Another UCLA season had ended in disaster, but that was trivial compared to actual real-world tragedy. In late April, L.A. became a war zone after four Los Angeles Police Department officers were acquitted of using excessive force in the highly publicized videotaped beating of motorist Rodney King. Ground Zero for the rioting was Florence and Normandie, five blocks south of USC's campus and three miles due east of where I had lunch with Marques Johnson. For many Bruins, the arson and looting and murder that made international headlines were occurring on very familiar turf.

As a third-year sophomore O'Bannon began regaining his form, starting full time and averaging almost seventeen points. Only now—for the first time since his initial operation—did he again start soaring like an eagle, canvassing the planet from among the clouds and dipping down to glide over the peaks of the Alps and between skyscrapers, in his dreams, a metaphor of which he was acutely aware. In losses at Washington and Washington State, O'Bannon experienced the first inkling of what it took to lead a team and the ache of how it felt to disappoint teammates, coaches, himself, his family, an entire city, and an empire of global UCLA basketball fans on whom the sun never set. That would gnaw at him for a couple of seasons, as would more sour experiences in the NCAAs.

In January 1993, UCLA dropped a 104-82 decision to California and coach Lou Campanelli, the Bruins' worst Pauley Pavilion defeat. They had split their first six conference games and were 12-5 overall. Jim Harrick's contract only took him through the end of the next season. Senior captain Mitchell Butler and center Rodney Zimmerman, among others, cited their dismay at constant Harrick criticism and bashing on sports-talk radio shows and by zealous newspaper columnists. Booing from his own fans, in his own home arena, shocked Ed O'Bannon. He said he and his teammates should have worn their away powder blues because those supposedly loyal followers had made it feel like a road game.

Harrick did himself no favors with his superiors when he told a Los Angeles *Daily News* columnist that he had beaten Indiana's Bobby Knight, Arizona's Lute Olson, and Denny Crum of

Louisville, but his compensation was hardly commensurate with those prominent coaches. The conversation had started benignly and meandered to salary, and Harrick was embarrassed to see his comments in ink. But he did not say he had been misquoted or that his words were taken out of context. Dalis said if Harrick could land a more lucrative gig that UCLA would not stand in his way. Some fans were furious with Harrick, but then when weren't they? It would eventually quell.

After an eleven-point defeat to Duke in Durham, North Carolina, Ed O'Bannon slinked toward the UCLA bus when a thin voice rang out in the winter dusk. "Ed. ED!" A feeble Jim Valvano, ravaged by cancer, had called the action for television and was stepping gingerly, with an aid, to a car when he spotted O'Bannon. At first startled, Ed saw that it was Valvano and grinned. Valvano pointed to the bus and yelled, "You guys can't afford to fly back to L.A.?" O'Bannon laughed. He waved at Valvano and hiked up into the coach. Valvano died two months later.

Two weeks later, UCLA athletic director Pete Dalis and chancellor Charles Young extended Harrick's contract. It probably wasn't just happenstance that they had dangled him so very close to lame-duck status, especially after the Knight-Olson-Crum paycheck comparisons, an unheard-of penurious scenario at a program of such supposed distinction.

In the NCAAs, UCLA beat Iowa State and Julius Michalik, the Slovakia native whose slovenly appearance and manner during a UCLA recruiting visit had convinced Harrick to instead take a serious look at George Zidek. Harrick had a day to prepare against Michigan and its ballyhooed Fab Five of Chris Webber, Juwan Howard, Jalen Rose, Jimmy King, and Ray Jackson. The hype surrounding the Wolverines irritated Ed O'Bannon. In studying tape of Michigan, O'Bannon said, in a room with a few coaches, "Did they forget I was number one in the country [as a prep senior], too? This stuff isn't new to me. I'm not intimidated." O'Bannon scored seventeen points in the first half. Lorenzo Romar saw outrage in O'Bannon's eyes. UCLA led by as many as nineteen points and settled for a halftime edge of thirteen.

Marques Johnson, sitting courtside for the UCLA radio broadcast, saw Jalen Rose elbow Shon Tarver's jaw early in the second half near the middle of the court. No foul was called. The entire tempo changed. The Wolverines took control. Steve Lavin had noted that Michigan's best play was an offensive rebound. Michigan pounded the Bruins on the boards and led, 86-84, in the final seconds of overtime. Sophomore point guard Tyus Edney drove to the free-throw line. He could either take a shot or pass, to Ed O'Bannon under the basket; Edney passed ... and Michigan's Jimmy King slashed in to intercept the ball and seal the victory. The mistake would haunt Edney.

With Ed O'Bannon as a junior in 1993-94, UCLA won its first fourteen games to snatch the top ranking in the country. Nearly eleven years had passed since it last occupied the top spot in the AP poll. Long Beach State coach Seth Greenberg highlighted the arrival of Charles O'Bannon as a major addition to the team's moxie and poise, and he said George Zidek gave Harrick *presence*, Tyus Edney exuded *direction*, and Ed O'Bannon provided *heart*.

The Bruins had walloped UNLV, 108-83, at Pauley in the Rebels' season opener, an outcome that might have been reversed had two UCLA players stuck to their original decisions and gone to UNLV, and if the main figure had lured his younger brother ... a terrifying vision for any Bruins fan. In his second collegiate game, Charles O'Bannon put up twenty-three points. An auspicious encounter took place when UNLV junior guard Michael Curtis, a former walk-on who would log thirty-five minutes all season, introduced himself to Ed O'Bannon after the game. The repercussion of that meeting would have a major consequence on the collegiate landscape in sixteen years.

The top ranking proved to be a mirage, though, for the Bruins. That was the zenith of their campaign as they split their final fourteen games. They were slipping away on black ice, a familiar scenario for Jim Harrick. "There was a perception at that time that he was not a good coach," says Marques Johnson, "even though he had quality teams that [always] won twenty games ... there was still this perception that he was not the guy who would be able to get [UCLA] over the hump and win a championship."

Near the end of the regular season life was taking a toll on Ed O'Bannon. His baby boy with Rosa was due in mere weeks. Classmates and interlopers were inquiring about him becoming an unwed father. He had not viewed it as a big deal, but the constant nosiness became a nuisance. He had been excited. When others intruded into his personal business he became increasingly irritable. *You know the responsibilities of having a baby? You know you'll be up all night, right?* He tried hard to prove he could deal with it all. "It's just that, I tried too hard."

There was tension with Rosa. At least, that's what Mark Gottfried and Lorenzo Romar sensed at the end of an early-spring practice when they thought they were the only ones in Pauley. They heard sobs. They shifted to better view the padded anchor behind a basketball hoop. Ed sat in a curl, bawling with his head in his hands. "I didn't want to be a father at that time," O'Bannon says today. "But it happened, and I was going through it. I could feel my life changing every day, when I was faced with being a father and being a leader at the same time, and being in college and hanging out with seventeen- and eighteen-year-olds."

His efforts and sacrifices and determination were washing away. He was averaging 18.2 points and 8.8 rebounds. But he did not care about statistics, rankings, or even geography; when it was announced that UCLA would play Tulsa in the first round of the NCAAs, O'Bannon admitted that he neither knew nor cared about the state in whose boundaries Tulsa existed. The Golden Hurricane had already been afforded a unique postseason luxury by requiring only a simple bus ride to reach its NCAA venue in Oklahoma City; now a twelfth-seeded team received the additional windfall of invaluable bulletin-board material from a seemingly superior fifth-seeded squad which just happened to be the king of all college hoops programs.

A couple of practices before Tulsa, UCLA had been crisp and efficient. The ball whipped around. Guys were confident, shooting at high percentages. Shoes were squeaking so much the maple wood nearly smoked. "I learned a lesson [then], that practice isn't as relevant as we all think," says Mark Gottfried. Before he had even settled into a padded seat next to Harrick, in The Myriad Convention Center (now Cox Center) in Oklahoma City, Gottfried watched Tulsa score eighteen of the first twenty-two points. Tulsa pounded UCLA in the first ten minutes, 46-17. "A barrage. We couldn't do anything. It was over at halftime," says Gottfried. O'Bannon wasn't surprised. The harbingers had been all too familiar. Maybe all those allegations of late-season UCLA fades under Jim Harrick held more truth than any Bruin had cared or dared to admit?

O'Bannon's soul and spirit were taking some hits. He went from the exhilaration of helping UNLV establish its own dynasty—albeit for only a few weeks—to suffering a serious knee injury upon landing at UCLA, knowing he was in this college thing for good. He became something of an actual student, taking interest in astronomy and acting; on a trip to New York for the preseason NIT, O'Bannon and Tyus Edney attended a Broadway performance of *Les Miserables*. O'Bannon would later partake in commercial endeavors, even act in a few sitcoms. Like many UCLA basketball players he would major in history because its classes best fit the rigors of their practice and travel demands.

O'Bannon figured his career, on average, as a Bruin consisted of forty hours a week devoted to hoops and about ten to academics.

"That's when the national championship became a goal ... more than a goal, an expectation for me," he says of the climb back from the knee injury. "It was like, I'm not leaving here without one. If I'm going to be here, I have to make it stand for something. I have to leave my mark. I didn't see any other way to do it."

O'Bannon had recognized he had been serving as an apprentice. It wasn't his place to critique strategy, coaches, or teammates. He respected a hierarchy, authority. Oklahoma City changed all of that. After twenty minutes he had seen enough. For four seasons nothing had worked. He had heard plenty of excuses, so much hot air he could recommend several chaps for careers at the International Balloon Fiesta in Albuquerque. O'Bannon took full control of, and complete responsibility for, UCLA's honor, glory, and reputation. He blasted into The Myriad locker room.

"We're going to do it my way! This is all about respect! It's all about doing what I say, cuz this is MY team." He threw chairs. Seniors occupied the tight space, but everyone was in his crosshairs. Charles was not spared. Ed bellowed, "I raised you better than this!" Ed scanned the room. "If no one else is gonna do this, I'll do it! We're getting our *asses* kicked! We're playing like pussies! Like wimps! Enough is enough. At least let's fight back! Don't just stand there in the corner, put your hands at your waist, and continue to take headshots [punches]! The world doesn't end. We still have to go back to campus, to class, to our neighborhoods. How do you hold your head up after playing like this, on national TV? How do you live with yourself?"

Someone had the gall to utter, *Everything will be okay ... if we just do [this] and [that], everything will be fine.* "No! Fuck that!" Ed blared. "It ain't gonna be fine! Enough! We've been talking this same bullshit all season!" Nearly twenty years later, O'Bannon fairly trembles, as if he had just stomped out of that room to try to take on the Golden Hurricane one-on-five. Jim Harrick stood outside with his three assistants. They heard the commotion, and Harrick canned everything he had planned to say about respect and dignity. Ed would not yield the gavel. "I was embarrassed," he says.

> But I was also hurt, that we came out and had completely laid an egg. Completely! On national television! Everything that everyone had said we were, we were ... we were over-rated, we were soft guys from the beach, we should be surfing instead of playing basketball. We were all Hollywood, all California Cool. We had dug ourselves a gigantic hole we couldn't get out of. I was like, Enough! Enough! I had played with and against the best players in the country. I KNEW what it took to get it done.

He had seen Gerald Madkins roar. Harrick told his players that he believed there were three freshman *stuuuuuuds* in UCLA history; Alcindor, Walton, and Madkins. A scooter accident had put Madkins into UCLA Medical Center with multiple pelvis fractures—half of his pelvis had been rotated almost completely around, which Dr. Gerald Finerman called "a big-time injury." But Madkins had rebuilt himself into a leader. In the 1992 collapse against Indiana, Madkins could not contain himself. A timeout was called. On the bench, he berated Tracy Murray and Don MacLean and Darrick Martin, all players of stature. "Yet, the leader was Gerald Madkins!" O'Bannon says. Madkins fumed at each teammate, *Don't you give up!* O'Bannon sat next to Shon

Tarver on the bench. "Man, look at him!" O'Bannon whispered to Tarver. "He's all over these guys! He ain't scared of nobody!"

All of that rushed into O'Bannon's mind in Oklahoma City. "When the time comes, you have to crack your whip," he says. "I wanted to be in that position, where if I crack my whip they would listen. Didn't want to crack it every day, then it falls on deaf ears. But every now and then ... "

He recorded thirty points and eighteen rebounds, his six assists set a career mark, and he tied a career high by blocking four shots. UCLA scored eighty-five points over the final thirty minutes, and still lost by ten. After the 112-102 defeat Madeline O'Bannon and Sally Harrick repaired to a women's restroom and bawled. The ramifications of yet another disappointing display in the NCAAs were clear to them. Jim Harrick took uneven steps across the court and muttered to his assistants, "These are the kinds of games that get coaches fired."

Athletic director Pete Dalis called Harrick, soon after the loss, and demanded individual meetings first thing Monday with him and each assistant. They all wondered, over the ensuing forty-eight hours, who would get axed. All of them? Would Dalis force Harrick to fire every assistant, or just one as a sacrifice? Would Dalis get rid of Harrick and promote an assistant? If so, which one? They contemplated every possibility over the telephone that weekend.

Jim Milhorn had become an associate athletic director to Pete Dalis and always sat next to Dalis at Pauley. Early on, Harrick and his lieutenants became wise to the fact that soon after they chatted with Milhorn, Dalis would soon parrot those exact lines and descriptions. ("Fundamentals" was also a go-to Dalis line, on how Harrick and his staff needed to improve the team in a subsequent season, after the usual sour ending to a campaign.) Milhorn did not deny those scenarios. He did discount them, saying it would only be natural for those comments to be duplicated because Milhorn and Dalis worked so closely together. Because Milhorn had actually played the sport at UCLA, Harrick—and most of his coaches, players, and managers—respected him far more than Pete Dalis or Charles Young, the invisible chancellor to Harrick. "[Milhorn] was genuinely happy for you," Harrick says. "I don't know that the other guys were happy for you."

Harrick believed Dalis was out to get him from the day he signed that first contract in 1988. But the fact is that when Dalis had every justification to sack Harrick and his staff after that horrible showing in Oklahoma City, yet another dismal ending to another basketball season, Dalis chose to stick with Harrick. Dalis listened to each coach's version of what had gone awry over the last half of that season, digested the input, and decided to keep Harrick.

Regardless of what was being said on the radio airwaves or written in letters to editors of Southern California newspapers, Jim Milhorn recalls no serious in-house debates about Harrick's job status after Oklahoma City. "We had gotten our comeuppance," says Milhorn, whose white hair made him seem older than his forty-nine years. "It wasn't a good feeling ... [but] I don't remember anyone saying that was even in the wind, about getting rid of the coaching staff. I don't remember any big thing of [Harrick] getting fired after the Tulsa game." Dalis says, "I was not prepared to make that kind of change at all."

Ed O'Bannon would return as the centerpiece of a trio of seniors, and a quartet of incoming freshman was being hailed as just the infusion that the Bruins would need for the 1994-95 season. Dalis factored all of that. He let it play out. A few hundred furious fans sent letters to Dalis about his decision not to can Harrick. Normally, Dalis would have dismissed the angry and churlish missives. He would have had his secretary dispose of them. Instead, for some reason that he can't even tab today, he told her to keep them. They were all filed together into a cabinet drawer.

As soon as he returned to Los Angeles the following day, a Saturday, O'Bannon got down to business. He whipped the returning Bruins out to the track and field stadium. It had been named after longtime UCLA trainer Ducky Drake, whose famous saying—A FEW WEEKS TO WORK HARD, A LIFETIME TO REMEMBER—was made into a sign that was posted in the training room. O'Bannon led sprints and distance workouts. The Bruins' low stamina after the opening tap against Tulsa had humiliated O'Bannon. He would not allow that to happen again. The laps around Drake were grueling. They pounded each other in pick-up games at Pauley, the Wooden Center, and the B.O. Barn.

Seventeen days after Tulsa, early on a Monday evening, Ed visited Rosa at Crush. They strolled south on the Strand, a concrete strip with a wide swath of Manhattan Beach sand that dissolves into the Pacific Ocean to their right; apartments, bungalows, contemporary mixes of glass, stone, and brick, and a corner mini-mansion that resembled the stern of a Spanish galleon to their left. The NCAA title game, between Arkansas and Duke, waned and waxed in a roller-coaster run of noise from those residences. Ed stopped in the hazy yellow murk between two lampposts and glanced at Rosa, then at those abodes. "Next year these people will be sitting in these same seats, but they'll be watching me. Mark my words. These people have no idea that the person who will be playing in this game next year is right outside their doors. But I promise you, I'm gonna make that happen."

"Dude, shut the hell ... "

"I'm gonna make that happen. It's gonna happen."

Chapter 5

THE SHADOWBOXING ROUTINE had not been a novelty. In preseason testing, administered by strength and conditioning coach Phil Frye, Ed O'Bannon had hit thirty-four inches on his standing vertical jump. Newcomer Toby Bailey, known for his kangaroo hops, led all Bruins with a thirty-eight-inch vertical. Ed hit personal bests on all weight-lifting disciplines.

The Bruins lined up for running vertical tests. O'Bannon soared. His teammates howled and pushed aside bench presses and leg lifts. He soared higher. Frye had players move other machines to the side. He told Ed to start from around the corner in the cramped space. Ed soared higher. His teammates lined up and didn't say a peep. Ed nearly ran a complete circle, and soared higher. He was the lone Bruin to slap a rod, above the colored slats of the vertical contraption, at an even twelve feet. Ed O'Bannon was in the best shape of his life.

Known as Easy Ed to some teammates, others called him Easers, a derivative they dared not utter in his presence. He earned blanket respect, as much with his biting criticisms as with his ferocious actions on the court. Most of the younger Bruins feared him. Tyus Edney, another senior, was mostly called Tyrus by every Bruin since a Freedom Hall p.a. announcer mispronounced his name before a game at Louisville midway through his freshman year. Don MacLean latched onto the error immediately, never again referring to Edney as Tyus; in fact, MacLean often abridged it to Russ, as did many others. MacLean never paused his sense of humor, which could irritate some. For a media-guide questionnaire, MacLean called playing tennis with Argentine ace Gabriela Sabatini a goal. When trainer Tony Spino received a Rogaine package in the mail, he scratched his smooth scalp and all eyes pointed toward MacLean. In one shoot-around, the laziest of practices that required minimal exertion or cognition, Ed O'Bannon had had enough of MacLean's comedy routine and tackled the six-foot-ten forward. That was out of character, unrelated to any heated reaction that can boil during pick-up runs or full-bore practices, and still embarrasses O'Bannon.

Toby Bailey, omm'A Givens, Kristaan Johnson, and Milton Henderson Jr.—whom the public would come to know as J.R. but would be referred to by teammates as Milt, or Nerf, because of how he easily handled a regulation-size basketball—were the fabulous freshmen. In an Irvine summer showcase event Bailey, Johnson, and Henderson had teamed up in a 125-115 victory over a squad comprised of Ricky Price (bound for Duke), Jason Hart (headed to Syracuse), and Miles Simon (committed to Arizona), an extravaganza that highlighted the richness of that recruiting year.

When that UCLA freshman foursome attended study hall, rookie manager Tony Luftman was always with them. He grinned when tutor Deanna Cherry presented them with FAB FOUR caps that had PLUS ONE scrawled at the bottom. That she included Luftman endeared her to him for life. Cherry was in her mid-twenties, slender with dark shoulder-length hair and faintly freckly skin. The Bruins considered her cute and down to earth; she enjoyed traipsing around the Griffin Commons study hall room in bare feet. *Be there, listen attentively,* and *understand* were her simple instructions.

Some weren't so attentive. Kris Johnson once slinked to the floor, in the back of the study hall, and fell asleep. Cherry curled around a corner and said, "Kristaan. Kristaan!" He instantly opened his eyes, sat up with his all-black Dodgers cap askew on his noggin, acted as if he had been perusing some notes, and said, "Man, this stuff is hard to understand." She said, "It's easier when you're awake!" In another study-hall session, Eric White, a sturdy academic liaison in his mid-forties with a wrestling background, tangled with the gangly, six-foot-ten omm'A Givens, who brooded frequently and challenged others often. So the escalation of a mouthy exchange into a grappling round surprised nobody. White dominated Givens, but White felt so horrible about his indiscretion he called Jim Harrick to explain. Harrick wanted to know only one thing—*Did you win?*

Harrick's deadpans were priceless. When Charles O'Bannon actually shot an air ball in one practice, Harrick ordered Tony Luftman up to the councourse level to find the door that someone had carelessly left open. Nature had to have been involved. Luftman scurried around the arena. He landed back at the floor level winded. He reported that no doors were open. Harrick executed a grand, Vegas showman-type pivot at Charles and said, "You just air balled, *Charrrrrullzzzzzz.* Luftman said there are no doors open up there."

Toby Bailey snuck away from his UCLA hoops brethren to meet with Harrick, to reaffirm exactly what would be required of him to get minutes and maybe, just maybe, start. Bailey shut the office door, but the chat was informal. Bailey was told he had to take, and make, jumpers and three-point shots, and beat out Kevin Dempsey for a spot in the rotation. Bailey was buoyant.

The day before practice began the *Pasadena Star-News* published the first report—mine—of Ed O'Bannon and fatherhood. I thought we had had a solid, professional relationship, but O'Bannon confirmed that when he accepted my offer, via a mutual friend, to discuss the rumors and innuendo of him having become a parent. "I needed to get something off my chest," O'Bannon says today. "I needed to reveal what was going on, why I am who I am, that 'this' is what I was going through. If you empathized, cool. If you don't, cool, too. But you gotta know what I'm going through. I remember having those strong feelings."

What he heard others say did not bother him so much. He was affected by what he saw in the mirror. "I knew what I would be thinking, about someone in my position," he says.

> So I knew someone had to be thinking that when they were looking at me. Therefore, I had to say it, just so they can know where I'm coming from and what I was thinking. It's your prerogative to think what you want. I could not have cared less. But I had to show what I was feeling. I wanted to be the leader of the UCLA team. I just didn't know how to do it. Once I knew I'd become a father, I wanted to be the leader. I wanted my guys to follow me. I just didn't know how to make everyone come with me. I'm not the most vocal guy. I knew how to win. I knew how to put the time and work in. They had to believe in me ... heart and soul.

Almost twenty years later, Ed and Rosa are husband and wife. Fiercely protective of her and her three children's privacy, Rosa O'Bannon declined to participate in this project.

On defensive switches that first week of practice, all 265 pounds of the six-foot-four Kristaan Johnson regularly wound up on George Zidek. Like a St. Bernard puppy wantonly floppin' his paws around, Johnson would constantly bump, bruise, and push Zidek. "The asshole. I'll *fuckeeen* kill him," said Zidek, whose

Eastern European accent (especially when reciting lines from *Ace Ventura* and *The Terminator*) and serious nature always elicited laughter from his teammates.

Johnson was turgid, which further inflamed Zidek, as did free throw "rest breaks" in which Harrick so frequently partnered Johnson with him. Kris didn't know mute. He was about eight inches shorter than Zidek, but they were similar on the scales. On the court Johnson always seemed to have the edge. When Harrick slipped a plastic bubble over the hoop, the Bruins' big men banged and elbowed each other for the surefire rebound. Johnson enjoyed every second of the drill that looked like an octopus fumbling for a pearl. "He just destroyed George," Toby Bailey says. Those tussles would pay off handsomely for Zidek and UCLA.

When the seven-foot center first arrived in Westwood, he needed eight appendages to gorge on the unlimited buffet inside the student cafeteria. Zidek had never encountered the all-you-can-eat concept. Welcome to America. Classmates wondered if he were a professional eater or the new bookend tackle to Jonathan Ogden on the UCLA football team.

The start of practice allowed the basketball players to join their football counterparts in weekly training-table barbecue sessions that lasted until the end of the pigskin season. The Bruins played football against USC, at the Rose Bowl, on November 19, which gave the basketball players five barbecues. Those weren't just treats to Zidek; Ed O'Bannon grins when reminiscing about those delectable early Wednesday evenings by the long black grill with the semi-circular lid out on Bruin Walk, behind the Morgan Center.

None of Zidek's teammates—not even Tyus Edney, with whom Zidek shared a dorm suite—ever showed curiosity about Czechoslovakia. But when he treated all that chicken, steak, and brisket like delicacies, only a few pondered, just for a moment, that his youth might have been a bit different than theirs.

The basketball coaches and players participated in a parade to honor the Northridge City Little League baseball team, which had lost the Little League World Series championship game, 4-3, to a squad from Maracaibo, Venezuela, at the end of the summer in Pennsylvania. Ed O'Bannon gleamed at them and treated them like superstars. If it involved Little League, Ed O'Bannon was in. For his entire life, baseball—especially the Little League World Series—would trump anything else on television. Some Bruins asked a Northridge lad how fantastic that experience must have been. "No. We lost the last game," the kid said gloomily. "It sucks. That's all anyone remembers." Those words would resonate with many Bruins.

The practices dragged on. After one, Tony Luftman sprinted up those three sets of foreboding concrete steps, in the northeast corner of Pauley Pavilion, to fetch something for a coach. A minute later Luftman descended those steps to find six-foot-six forward Kevin Dempsey ascending, two steps at a time. Dempsey plucked a mobile phone from his sweat pants, unfolded it, and tapped at numbers. Dempsey was sandy haired and a burgeoning lady's man, and he had a cell! Luftman was certain he was in the midst of one of the coolest cats on the planet.

Luftman returned to the court to find a rash of Bruins frowning at him. Yet again, he had stirred another sour batch of Gatorade in one of the large orange plastic containers. They would always charge the kid with a lawyer father with having a privileged youth, having chugged only bottled Gatorade when he was a kid. He could never mix a batch to please every Bruin. Fellow student manager Andrew Pruter borrowed those containers for parties in his off-campus apartment, and guests never complained about his gin and Gatorade potions. Those two and Brendan Jacobson dubbed themselves The A-Team, after a popular television show from the 1980s. Greg Buonaccorsi and Richard Klinger were older, more serious managers. They never rattled, all business, and were often behind the scenes, tending to locker-room issues.

The A-Team was out front, doing the dirty work, chasing loose balls, running towels to players and coaches. Pruter was a sophomore, Luftman and Jacobson mere rookies. Jacobson would get so wound up in big games he'd pull a wad of Red Man out of a pouch and chew, spittin' into an empty Gatorade cup. It was as if he were about to endure a crash landing in a plane. "It's just too much," he told his two pals. He smoked Marlboro reds—outside Pauley. Of the three assistant coaches, Mark Gottfried was the rudest to the managers. He never called them by name, just *ball* or *manager*. One day Pruter hit his disrespect limit and, when Gottfried wasn't looking, two-hand-chest-zipped a basketball at the coach. It missed his skull by less than twelve inches. Gottfried never noticed. Pruter and Luftman still exchange text messages about that audacious fling.

Pruter once told the band director how much Ed and Charles O'Bannon enjoyed *The A-Team* show theme, which features a rousing intro of snare drums and bass booms, soon accompanied by splashes of brass that could have been used at Normandy. Luftman sat in the middle of Pruter and Jacobson. At the designated time during the pre-game layup line Pruter smiled at his two befuddled buddies seconds before the band played the O'Bannons' request. Luftman and Jacobson nearly fainted. Neither Ed nor Charles acknowledged the band.

Pruter hatched a skit to mimic Harrick, who could turn into a whirling dervish upon the actions, or non-calls, of an official. Mark Gottfried, Lorenzo Romar, and Steve Lavin would instantly form a floating three-man wall to try to contain a furious Harrick from getting a technical foul. Sometimes, they couldn't box him out; he'd weasel his way between two or pull a deke, faking left and dashing right. At a timeout or after a controversial call, Pruter would straighten and, with hot eyes and teeth bared, act as if he were about to dart at the baseline ref, but Luftman would block him and cool him down. They'd perform it two or three times a game. Eventually, Marques Johnson would tell them he'd never seen anything so funny on a basketball court. They were elated.

Toby Bailey did not laugh when he received Ed O'Bannon's early attention. Bailey's younger brother Ryan, better known as Moose throughout Southern California, ridiculed Toby every morning when, as they waited for the school bus, Toby would alternate each foot, every thirty seconds or so, against the curb. He constantly stretched his Achilles tendons, absolutely knowing that that was the anatomical key to being able to vault to the moon in a single bound. Bailey attended Loyola High School, but he nearly went to Artesia. John Bailey, a UCLA graduate, drove a young Toby to Artesia just for some practice *burn*—the hip hoopster's slang for court time—with Ed and Charles. Bailey knew Kris Johnson and Tyus Edney, too, before they all teamed up in Westwood. "The chemistry was great," Bailey says. "This was our dream."

At the beginning it was a nightmare. Ed O'Bannon ran over Bailey, who had settled in to take a charge, for a dramatic dunk in practice. To top it off, O'Bannon grabbed the ball and tossed it, hard, at Bailey's chest. "And he *knew* me," Bailey says. "I wasn't a stranger." Wiped out on the floor, with a reverse imprint of WILSON JET just about stamped across his chest, Bailey sought a measure of sympathy as he aimed puppy dog eyes up at Harrick, who said, *Hell, son, you better get up! That's Ed O'Bannon!*

Grasping Harrick's schemes, and O'Bannon's defensive demands, took some time. Nothing in the middle, Harrick extolled. O'Bannon followed that line with risqué language and more physics lessons to ensure the younger Bruins knew what was expected of them with their backs to the basket. Bailey sailed up for one dunk, threw it down, then hung onto the rim for cameras or contest judges who weren't present. Worse, O'Bannon saw teammates part like the Red Sea to allow Moses access down the middle. Even worse than that, O'Bannon heard Bailey bitch at the slightest touch of a defender. *Pretty boy*, O'Bannon thought.

"It wasn't registering with him," O'Bannon says. He ensured that Bailey wound up on his ass if he attemped any aerial maneuvers close to the rim when O'Bannon was on patrol. Not on *his* watch. "Not havin' it!" O'Bannon screamed at the prostrate Bailey. "This is how we're gonna play this season! What I'm doin' to you is what I need you to do to everybody else! You are gonna help me protect this paint! Understand this! Get your shit together! And let's go out and win." O'Bannon's commands would become the signature of a team for the ages, one that would stand up mightily to some of the program's finest editions.

An intra-squad scrimmage and two exhibitions felt as if they were a few months away rather than a few weeks. Those events would be the team's unveiling to spoiled, if not downright arrogant, factions of alumni and fans that had become quite accustomed to celebrating national championships. Winning was so ingrained with them it was as if it were their divine right, similar to more than a few supporters of USC football, Kentucky basketball, or half a dozen Southeastern Conference football programs. Success breeds magniloquence.

But those eight-claps had rung hollow for nearly twenty years. Would a coach ever add to John Wooden's incredible success? Some close to the program believed this would be a breakthrough season. One of them was pleasant, low-key, and bespectacled assistant sports information director Bill Bennett, who served as the media liaison between the Bruins' basketball coaches and players, and media figures. Bennett enjoyed road trips to Arizona, especially sharing a convertible on a mostly wide-open jaunt from Phoenix to Tucson, and back. He was an ardent fan of *Lonesome Dove* and the Old West, of simpler times. He had a poster of the 1985 movie *To Live and Die in L.A.* inside his cubicle. Bennett had hatched an astute plan—nothing akin to living and dying in Pauley Pavilion, although that described many who sat in its seats—for the cover of the team's 1994-95 media guide of which Jim Harrick had approved.

In a nod to pillars of the program, Charles O'Bannon, Ed O'Bannon, Tyus Edney, and George Zidek were photographed—from left to right—descending Janss Steps, the original university entry of eighty-seven brick-lined steps between Royce Hall and Powell Library. Each player wore black dress shoes, a dapper suit, white dress shirt, and tie. Charles has his right hand in his pants pocket. Two steps below, Ed's hands are by his side—hooks and jabs at the ready? Edney's left hand is in his left pocket. His right hand dangles. Zidek has his left foot on that level, but his right foot is on the next one and his left hand is in a pocket. They're all smiles. The brilliant late afternoon sun bathes the quartet, framed by the steps, trees, a Powell turret, and a brilliant blue sky. A thick band of Bruins blue surrounds the photo on the media guide. UCLA'S ALL-AMERICAN LINEUP is etched in gold at the bottom.

Bill Bennett had recalled a sharp photo of the main figures of John Wooden's first national championship team in 1964. In its edition of April 16, 1984, *Sports Illustrated* ran a story about former All-America guard Walt Hazzard becoming the fifth coach to succeed Wooden. The magazine published a photo of Gail Goodrich, Keith Erickson, Fred Slaughter, Jack Hirsch, and Hazzard—all looking stylish in dress shoes, suits (each showing pocket-square wisps), white shirts, and skinny dark ties—descending from the top of Janss Steps. The 1964 snapshot was taken from below the players, and to their left; thirty years later, the shot was reprised from below the players, and to their right.

Doug Erickson enjoyed the traditional look upon first reviewing the guide. An administrative assistant to Harrick with a penchant for wearing white athletic socks inside black leather loafers, Erickson was in his late twenties. He had thinning hair but thick biceps, due to regular workouts. He slept on the floor of a small apartment he shared with Steve Lavin, a beneficial arrangement owing to their miniscule salaries. Erickson stood in a narrow aisle—cubicles for assistant basketball coaches to the left, cubicles for sports information staff to the right, the open door of Jim Harrick's conventional office straight ahead—of the cramped ground floor of the Morgan Center when he asked me, "Know why we're going to win it all this season?"

I had not given it much thought. Westwood brought unforeseen surprises, dips, and curves at every bend, with forgettable, crushing endings. To think ahead even a few days was dangerous. I tilted my head at Erickson. He was quick and certain. *Senior leadership.* That meant Ed O'Bannon, Edney, and Zidek, in that order. I couldn't disagree with Erickson, but it would be difficult to be disagreeable with him on any topic. He was as levelheaded and unassuming as Bill Bennett, which enhanced any road trip.

That was also when Erickson took the impressionable Tony Luftman, the kid from the San Fernando Valley who had so yearned to be a UCLA student manager, to John Wooden's tiny condo in Encino. A dazed Luftman finally said, Coach, how did it feel to win your first national championship? Wooden gave a two-minute response that somehow included Mother Teresa. Luftman would chomp gum, pass Wooden, and hear, "How's that gum, Tony?" Wooden detested gum. Luftman would immediately toss it in the nearest trashcan. *Leave a place better than you find it* was another Woodenism that Luftman would forever carry with him.

Erickson would forever keep a voicemail from John Wooden on his phone system. Erickson helped Wooden often, driving him to doctor appointments, or breakfasts or lunches, always assisting him with a hand to steady UCLA's famous coach. Erickson tapped his office phone one day to find that Wooden had left him a heartfelt thank-you poem for everything Erickson did for him, which Wooden prefaced with, "To the Floor Sleeper … " Wooden pursed his lips, however, the night he dined with Erickson and Luftman, and Erickson made a *Wiz* or *Wizard* slip to Wooden, who hated the nickname. "I'm no Wizard." He gently but forcefully explained how that denigrated the development and growth of his players. Erickson had a row of VHS tapes, on a UCLA opponent's past few games, at the ready for coaches. To the right were his cherished *Sanford and Son* tapes—his favorite episode is the surprise party the guys threw for Fred upon his *return* from Las Vegas. Erickson shuddered at the thought of Jim Harrick popping a Stanford tape into the machine but finding Grady ranting about something in the junkyard.

Those Morgan Center "office" cubicles offered no privacy for assistant coaches. Anyone of average height could easily peer over the flimsy barriers, check if any were in, and fire away with questions. Privacy wasn't exactly a premium at the nation's most prestigious basketball program. The facilities were fading as quickly as the luster of those banners. Harrick pressed on. He assembled what would become a commendable staff by seeking key traits in the lieutenants, husbands and fathers with faith— Harrick is a devout Mormon, which he would only reveal in detail decades later. ("I just never wanted to bring it into the public sector," he says. "That's my private life. I didn't hide anything; anybody that asked me I'd tell 'em. [But] I didn't want to use religion as part of it. I wanted a kid to come to UCLA because he wanted to come to UCLA. It's a special place. I hold it in high regard.")

Luck, skill, and gut feelings also played into those staff decisions. The players would rue the rare day when personal or professional business kept Harrick from attending practice. Those few times, the deputies—who always believed Harrick was too soft on his players and hated that he allowed media to watch every minute of every session—ran the proceedings, ran the players relentlessly, and the players got away with nothing.

Mark Gottfried had been a standout prep player in Illinois and owned a solid sports pedigree. His father Joe first gained acclaim in Ohio coaching basketball at Ashland College. Toward the end of a long stretch as athletic director at the University of South Alabama they'd name a street after him. Joe's brother Mike coached four Division-I football programs and settled into a career as an ESPN analyst.

At the University of Alabama, Mark Gottfried played for Wimp Sanderson, a coach known as much for his hoops success as his garish plaid sports jackets. Gottfried helped the Crimson Tide reach the Sweet Sixteen of the NCAA Tournament in 1985, '86, and '87—it was ousted, respectively, by North Carolina State and coach Jim Valvano, Kentucky and coach Eddie Sutton, and Providence coach Rick Pitino and plucky guard Billy Donovan, who would own UCLA much later when he coached Florida. Gottfried appropriated a Southern dialect that has stuck with him and evokes swimmin' holes and crawfish boils. It did not, however, compel Gottfried to dash to Sanderson's side the moment Wimp snapped his fingers.

Detroit had picked Gottfried in the seventh round of the draft, but he never played a minute in the NBA. He kept in shape with the faith-based Athletes In Action, which had sprouted from the

Campus Crusade for Christ organization that Bill Bright had founded at UCLA in 1951. Bruins football stars Donn Moomaw and Bob Davenport were among the first converts, as was track star Rafer Johnson, whom John Wooden regretted misusing on his basketball team. AIA hosts an annual Final Four breakfast at which it honors a player or coach with a Keys to Life award, in recognition of "a high level of moral character, integrity and faith"—according to its Web site—and modeled after Wooden.

Sanderson had an opening on his staff and wanted Gottfried, but Gottfried kept Sanderson at bay. He had sent out thirty form letters to coaches inquiring about job openings. He coveted one more than all of the others combined. It was irrational, because he had no direct connection to UCLA or Jim Harrick, but he believed there would be no better place to begin a coaching career than Westwood.

Gottfried was with a Pistons squad in the 1988 NBA Summer League at Loyola Marymount, near LAX, when he called to check in with his mother in Moblie, Alabama. She relayed a message from Harrick. Gottfried raced to the Morgan Center to introduce himself to Harrick, who understandably was more concerned about filling his top three posts than the bottom-feeder spot. Harrick had had the job for three months. Gottfried sat in Harrick's office as the boss opened a file drawer jammed with four hundred letters from assistant prospects.

Alabama was on the semester system, and Sanderson wanted an answer. Gottfried needed to hustle to enroll in graduate school in Tuscaloosa. He stalled. UCLA was on the quarter system, which didn't begin classes until late September. Sanderson would be angry with Gottfried for years about what unfolded. "I felt it was a risk worth taking," Gottfried says. After a few weeks, through Jim Harrick Jr., Gottfried reached Jim Sr. at a Veterans of Foreign Wars post in West Virginia. "How'd you find me?" Harrick said. "Don't worry about that. I just want you to know I'm waiting for you to call."

A week later, Harrick rang and properly offered Gottfried his volunteer graduate assistant's gig. Gottfried eagerly accepted. Harrick had hired former UCLA guard Brad Holland, who played three NBA seasons and earned a championship ring as a rookie with the Lakers in 1980, and Tony Fuller, who had played for Harrick at Pepperdine and in the NBA, as his full-time assistants. Paul Landreaux, Harrick's former assistant at Morningside High, became the Bruins' part-time assistant. Gottfried was right where he wanted to be.

Landreaux, who had also assisted Jerry Tarkanian at Long Beach State, left Harrick's staff after a season to take the top job at St. Mary's, in the San Francisco Bay Area. Harrick bumped Gottfried to the part-time post. Ken Barone came on as GA. At the 1990 Final Four in Denver, where UNLV would dismantle Duke, Gottfried arranged for former AIA teammate Lorenzo Romar to formally meet with Harrick as a coaching prospect for the future.

When Barone left in 1991, Harrick tapped an unknown quantity with a gift for gab—in Steve Lavin, whom all would call Lav—for the lowest spot on his staff that had been renamed restricted-earnings coach. The youngest of six children to beloved Bay Area English teacher Albert "Cap" Lavin and wife, Mary, Lavin had been reared in a rich cultural environment. He had read Thoreau, Shakespeare, Graham Greene, and Marshall McLuhan—"the medium is the message," who foresaw the Internet and its ramifications—in grade school, *The Natural* (whose characters he would one day envision as figures in and around UCLA) in junior high. He would become a fan of Malcolm Gladwell, a popular author whose sociology and psychology studies posited, among much else, that narcissistic personality types were more likely to climb company ladders, and how a person's environment and drive affect his chances for success.

Cap took Steve to Saturday matinees at the Four Star Cinema that featured Charlie Chaplin, Humphrey Bogart, Edward G. Robinson, and James Cagney. Steve knew about tragicomedy and the Theatre of the Absurd long before his peers, prepping him well for some entertaining times in Westwood. The idyllic childhood included milkshakes at Bill's Place out in the Avenues. One weekend Steve tagged along with Cap to San Quentin, the maximum-security prison where Cap taught classes in English and poetry. Guards wanted Cap to carry a gun, but he eschewed firearms. "Give me a whistle," he said. "If I blow it, get your ass in here." Some prisoners became so endeared to Cap they wanted his address, to correspond. "But, you couldn't, you just didn't know which ones … " Steve says. "We ate with chefs, on their best behavior in the mess hall. To me, 'Wow, this is San Quentin!' To him, he was just teaching."

Steve was a stringer for the sports page of a local paper in high school. He and boyhood pal Jim Saia would sit in the top row of Candlestick Park and switch, every three innings, the play-by-play and color duties of makeshift radio broadcasts with a microphone and bulky cassette recorder. Lavin was a self-described "slow, thick-legged" guard, first at San Francisco State and then at tiny Chapman College in Orange County, who knew his future wouldn't be as a player. Purdue coach Gene Keady and Indiana coach Bobby Knight both answered his letters, the former bringing Lavin into the system as a volunteer assistant and the latter letting Lavin and Saia observe a season.

The duo headed east. In Bloomington, they stopped for gas. Lavin asked the attendant for directions to Assembly Hall. The guy laughed. Uh, you're in Bloomington, *Illinois*, he said. They continued heading east to watch the Hoosiers. Lavin sharpened an appreciation for defense—which had been instilled in him via

Menlo College coach Bud Presley, a family friend whose teams were known for their defense—in the Big Ten Conference. At Purdue, he also honed his sense of humor with Keady. Lavin witnessed an explosive coach who owned one of mankind's funkiest comb-over hairdos. "Pull your *asses* outta your *heads!*" Keady screamed at his Boilermakers. Lavin would subsist on a salad bar at the local Wendy's, a Boilermakers sponsor that fed endless coupons to the coaching staff.

He would bring a Stance drill to UCLA that was more of a football exercise; he'd crouch, hands up, before two or three rows of players, and they would mirror his every lateral slide, dive, twist, and turn. It began early in the season, for a minute or two, and would progress to where they could do it for twelve or fifteen minutes, before thousands at NCAA Tournament open practices. Fans gaped at the proceedings. A senior or two would sometimes run that show, especially when Lavin tweaked a knee that required surgery. When Harrick assembled his seventy-one-page Guidelines, STANCE occupied the top spot of five keys to success—followed by CONCENTRATION, QUICKNESS, BALANCE, and PLAY HARD—on page three.

Harrick went against his religious and matrimonial tendencies—which many head coaches consider grounded, stable characteristics in underlings—in hiring Lavin. Gottfried and Romar were married and devout. But Harrick had been won over by how sharp, enthusiastic, and passionate Lavin seemed to be about basketball if not life. "I certainly saw all that in Steve," Harrick says. "He could talk to anybody. He could talk an Eskimo into buying a refrigerator ... he could *talk.*" If a guy was enthusiastic and wanted to work hard, Harrick knew he could shape and mold to his specifications. Harrick had no idea that the father of the guy he had just hired had played for Hall of Fame coaches Pete Newell and Phil Woolpert at the University of San Francisco.

All Harrick knew, a few months later, was disappointment in his new hire when Lavin—coffee cup in hand, strolling down a Pauley Pavilion aisle oblivious to any timepiece—showed ten minutes late to his first official practice as a UCLA assistant coach.

After Indiana's total destruction of UCLA in 1992, both Brad Holland (to Cal State Fullerton) and Tony Fuller (at San Diego State) bolted from Westwood for their first head-coaching positions. Harrick stopped at Gottfried's cubicle and said, *I'm movin' you up. Let's go!* Gottfried acted cool, but he shook inside because in three legitimate seasons as an assistant he had never recruited for UCLA; that was reserved for the top two sidekicks and Harrick.

Harrick didn't deem Lavin ready for the other full-time post, and he had an inkling about Lorenzo Romar, whom Harrick first saw as a tenth grader at Pius X when Harrick coached Morningside. "I *knew* him," Harrick says. A late bloomer, Romar played junior college ball for two seasons before going to the University of Washington.

The Bruins went to Seattle in late February 1979 to play the Huskies when Harrick was a UCLA assistant to Gary Cunningham. Harrick played racquetball with a UW assistant coach and, being Harrick, boasted that the Huskies had no chance against UCLA because their guards were too slow. Romar always spelled starting guard Donnie Vaughn. That night, however, UW coach Marv Harshman—after consulting with a certain assistant coach—started Vaughn and Romar, the two quickest Huskies, together. UCLA had been the top-ranked team in the nation, but Washington won, 69-68.

A seventh-round draft pick by the Golden State Warriors, Romar played five seasons for three NBA teams, including a tour in Milwaukee with Marques Johnson. In pre-game lay-up lines, the six-foot leaper proved to be an attraction as he unveiled an array of dunks, including reverses, and one after catching the ball in mid-flight after having slammed it off the court. A seven- and eight-year-old Bob Myers, whose family lived in Danville, California, enjoyed Romar's warmup antics for the Warriors. I did, too, during my senior prep year and first year of college.

UCLA usually scheduled an annual exhibition against AIA, so Harrick and Romar steadily grew on each other. But when Harrick rang with the job offer in April 1992, Romar hesitated. He had a deep affinity for his AIA responsibilities, especially with thirty-two kids in Cincinnati who needed direction and focus. Romar believed he was impacting those kids' lives. He told an AIA colleague that he questioned the timing of a move to UCLA. The man told Romar, "Do you know if you become a head coach one day the kind of platform you can have to impact lives?"

Romar accepted Harrick's offer. Neither Romar nor Gottfried had ever recruited, and now they were the top two talent evaluators at UCLA. Their chief priority became Charles O'Bannon, about to start his senior season at Artesia High. Unlike those always-clumsy telephone discussions between Tony Fuller and Ed O'Bannon, Madeline and Ed Sr. heard unending boisterousness and laughter, like schoolgirls, when Romar and Charles talked on the phone.

Harrick's assistants were three active, effective guards. The eldest—Romar—was about to turn thirty-six, but he was the one who had logged NBA time and would sting all comers with fancy H-O-R-S-E shots. He never lost. They often beat any trio of Bruins in three-on-three matches. With a proper group of coaches, and talented, resolute, and rugged players, an *esprit de corps* would develop on that Pauley Pavilion maple wood that none of them would ever again experience.

126

Chapter 6

FINALLY, THERE WERE actual, although unofficial, games to be played before actual—although more than a few insufferable—fans. The intra-squad scrimmage and two exhibitions loomed. The Bruins could take out some frustrations from the droll weeks of practice in contests that at least would be played at night and with paying customers under those banners.

Many aficionados, alums, and armchair fanatics had long been used to winning, nothing less. They'd snip and bark at lesser foes, humiliate those opponents as they were getting humiliated by their boys. The moment a game or season turned sour, many "faithful" likewise would turn on its own. That occurred often during John Wooden's era—"nothing short of juvenile," reported *Sports Illustrated*—so it should not have surprised many that such vaingloriousness would carry over for years and be handed down, generationally, as if a birthright.

The discontent bubbled before him and behind him after Wooden retired. He left coaching. He couldn't leave the game. Wooden heard and smelled the rancor. He could touch it from his third-row seat, farthest from the aisle and against a big metal railing, behind the UCLA bench in his golden years. As those ten banners up there faded, the folks craning their necks as they gawked at them grew crustier.

The living legend, having just celebrated his eighty-fourth birthday, snarled, too, when he first viewed UCLA's new uniforms for the 1994-95 season. Ed O'Bannon had taken command of this squad, and he also took responsibility for how his team would *look*. In the offseason, O'Bannon asked Jim Harrick about a uniform re-design. Ed O'Bannon, a player-of-the-year candidate, amateur astronomer and budding thespian, proud papa, the ultimate locker-room lawyer—Michigan State coach Tom Izzo's lingo for the key figure of any team with championship aspirations—and now fashion diva?

The main request was for longer silky shorts. The Fab Five of Michigan had indeed rubbed off on O'Bannon and the Bruins, if not all of college hoops. "The catalyst, leader, and designer," says Harrick, who agreed to O'Bannon's accouterment alterations. When five-foot-nine guard Tyus Edney donned the new duds in the intra-squad scrimmage, the long shorts looked more like short pants. Seven-foot center George Zidek's looked like a pup tent that could house a few kids.

John Wooden cringed, as he did in January 1991 when Harrick somehow allowed UCLA to wear yellow shorts and jerseys in a home game—Harrick called them gold, but many viewed the hue as the yellow from a school bus. Wooden told Harrick the extended shorts looked like *bloomers*. Wooden would berate Harrick for allowing the inmates to have such run of the asylum, or something to that effect. "I took the brunt of all of Coach Wooden's venom," Harrick says. "He killed me, just *killed* me."

Jim Harrick kept a white dry-erase board off to the side of the court. He occasionally whistled his guys to it for a brief rest and tutorial about a drill, review some aspect of a plan, or a nugget on an opponent. After experiencing many of these "lessons," Kevin Dempsey turned to a teammate and whispered, *He gets everything from Wooden. None of this is original.* The guy next to Dempsey shushed him.

The UCLA hoops leader most often directed practice wearing tight blue shorts—anti-bloomers. Harrick refused to limit media access, feeling he had nothing to hide, and he could keep tabs on those keeping tabs on his program. Which writers would actually show regularly, *religiously*, to observe his players and how he taught, which ones were getting it and which ones were lagging, who would actually ask a pertinent question about the system, about basketball strategy, why they cut this way or did something another way?

Many years later, Harrick reveals what drove him regarding work ethic. "Dammit, you better work at your craft or I'm not gonna respect you," he says forcefully. "Work at your craft. I don't care what it is ... that's a weakness of mine. I don't give a pass on that. Think I'm kidding? No, no."

Another tendency became evident to regular observers of those practices as every three of four minutes, like clockwork, Harrick would touch his crotch with a tap or flick of a finger, or knuckle nudge. Clockwork. Many years later, reclining on a couch, all those practices flashed back when Harrick started bellowing about Pete Dalis, and he began stabbing at, or nudging, his crotch, every three or four minutes. Clockwork. It was a tic that seemed to signal he was in his element, on a roll and in control, and gaining momentum.

When irritated or heated, Harrick would lock those beady pupils on his prey. He punctuated certain words for effect. He would unleash his temper in a flash, a trait many would also note in his middle son, Jim Jr. Those who knew the family saw much calmer personas in eldest son Monte and Glenn. The two Jims, however, could be irrational and hotheaded, rash and reckless, often acting without thought. The Jims could get into jams.

Harrick could also be a showman. Part of the job, he said. Some of that had to have been passed down from his father, the small-time hustler with big-time dreams. When Harrick recruited Tracy Murray, he capped a speech at the talented player's Glendora High School auditorium with, "When you play for me and someone asks you how you are doing, you will answer in one of only five ways; good, great, terrific, fantastic, or sensational." He had borrowed that line from a Crystal Cathedral pastor. Speaking to a lunch group in Chicago before playing DePaul, Harrick revealed how he sensed this trip had been a set-up because the limo that took him from his hotel to this engagement arrived with a greeting card that read, *Courtesy of Stephen Howard and David Booth.* Those were two of DePaul's top players. But there had been no limo and no card; Harrick wanted to humor the crowd, which laughed. UCLA lost to the Blue Demons.

The coach particularly enjoyed poking at others—"pimpin' 'em," he called it—by relentlessly calling attention to them, especially if they had erred or made him look bad. Steve Lavin was a regular target, which Lavin despised. Harrick also enjoyed pimpin' beat writers, by slightly tweaking their surnames. Thus, Kawakami (Tim) became *Kamakawi* ... Wilner (Jon) would become *Wilmer* ... he called me *Minch*. I once showed late to a weekly press conference, which Harrick noted by stopping in mid-sentence and saying, "Rob *Minch* and his Band of Renown!" Yes, Harrick is a fan of Les Brown, a versatile musician and leader of a big band that he formed while attending Duke in the mid-1930s and headed until his death in 2001. The band still travels the world with Brown's son at the helm. A colleague once pointed at me, looked at Harrick and said, *You know his name is Miech, like Michigan, right?* Harrick paused. He looked confused. Then he smiled, pointed at me, and said, "Minch!"

"I do that on purpose," he says with a sly grin, "just to get a rise outta you."

When a lawyer became famous from a latest Trial of the Century, Harrick busted up those around him by always calling him Johnny *Cockring*. On occasion that's how Harrick addressed reserve center Ike Nwankwo, who had an interest in law school. At his pleasure, Harrick would tinge some of those comments with a drawl straight from the Blue Ridge Mountains. Most Harrickisms were humorous. *Holy Canorsi!* is a favorite, but he isn't sure of its origin. Harrick laughs. "I don't know, I got a million of those kinds of things. I think that's a West Virginia thing." He'd use *ball burner* to describe an upcoming game that promised to be tight and testy. He once asked Wooden what singular quality players from his title teams possessed. Insatiable pride, Wooden responded. But Harrick turned the adjective into at least five syllables—*in-SAAAAAAY-sheeee-uh-bull*. In his Guidelines it became *in satiable*—just a typo, sure ... but downright punchy to assume Harrick might think it's two words. To Harrick, the Achilles tendon is an *Uh-key-leeeez* tendon.

Harrick was also beyond generous. Mark Gottfried and his growing family spent every holiday meal, when the Bruins weren't on the road, at the Harrick household. When dining with assistants, anywhere, he always paid the entire tab. Always. (In my few occasions breaking bread with Harrick, he never allowed me to reach for my thin wallet.) That rote behavior, without a moment of thought, would end up costing Harrick dearly.

Some of the routine was definitely tasteless. In one weekly press conference, before a gaggle of media, I asked him about a groin injury that had shelved Mitchell Butler. With a devilish grin Harrick slowly gazed over the room. "After this I'll inform you how we heal those things, *Minch*." With his wife beside him, he once approached a colleague and me at a Final Four gathering and said, "What're you slapdicks up to?" As I entered a Tucson hotel with a girlfriend, Jim and Sally Harrick stood right there in the foyer. As we approached, for introductions, Jim never took his eyes off my companion, slowly scanning her from crown to toes, and back up. Jim said, "Minch, I *laaaaaak* yer style!" Sally had to have long been accustomed to her husband's peccadilloes.

Harrick's comments could sometimes be far from amusing; they could be downright unforgivable.

In the intra-squad clash, Kristaan Johnson looked comfortable in the new silky bloomers, which was evident by his performance. He led the blue team with eighteen points—and grabbed a game-best thirteen rebounds, with nine under the offensive glass thanks to his grit and girth—against the white squad. George Zidek was relieved that none of that damage had been inflicted upon him, since he was on the blue team, too. The white team, powered by a combined fifty points and eighteen boards from the O'Bannon brothers, won 81-78.

Whatever hype surrounded the Bruins—the respected *Blue Ribbon* college basketball yearbook rated them seventh in its national preseason ranking—fans weren't buying into it at the beginning. With a crowd of 4,477, barely a third of Pauley Pavilion's seats were filled. Was that a hangover effect from the Tulsa debacle, a commentary on what many thought about Jim Harrick's coaching abilities, or the growing mean streak of cynicism and doubt about a twentieth season coming and going without a piece of blue fabric joining the ten already up there in the rafters?

Johnson added twenty-eight total points in the two ensuing exhibitions, against Perth Australia and Athletes In Action, giving him forty-six in the preseason. Of the four newcomers that had received heaps of hype, it appeared Johnson might have an edge. His agility and craftiness belied his heft. His bullishness and backside under the boards reminded some of a poor man's Adrian Dantley, who cleared an NBA interior with a half-stoop.

Instead, injuries that included a stress fracture and a complex, explosive temperament limited Johnson. He would score a total of fifty-four points during the entire season. He'd barely average six minutes in twenty-one games, all off the bench. By March 1995, the only Bruin with bloodlines to the program's incredible history would become known more for his bench antics than for anything he did on the hardwood. He was so peeved during a seventeen he ran directly at Harrick. At twenty feet, Harrick saw Kris wide-eyed and heading straight for him. Then it was ten feet. Then five ... at the very last moment, Johnson averted Harrick. Prepared to hit the court or rolled-up bleachers hard, a braced Harrick instead exhaled. But to this day, Harrick adores Kris Johnson.

In a theater class Kris relished a soliloquy he gave as Neptune. A dramatic tear he shed won kudos from classmates and earned him a top grade from his professor. That acting ability would always confound teammates. He had inherited some of his father's charisma and elocution gifts. But when Kris is polite and accommodating and engaging, his former UCLA teammates invariably cringe. Even today. They believe Bad Kris is only a perceived slight or misinterpretation away from inflicting some serious verbal or physical harm. Some teammates call him Staany Loco Uno, an alias Kris promoted in a study hall.

It wasn't difficult to determine the origin of that anger and hair-trigger antagonism. In May 1987, Kris was eleven when he was told to keep an eye on fifteen-month-old brother Marques Jr. Senior oversaw a gate issue with an electrician at his Bel Air home on Stradella Court. A video game distracted Kris. Little Marques eked through a sliding glass door in the master bedroom, fell into the kidney-shaped pool, and would die the next day, from cardiac arrest, at UCLA Medical Center.

That was the linchpin to confusion, guilt, and violence. Kris attended more than two dozen schools—in Atlanta with Sabrina

Sheran, his mother, and in Los Angeles with his father or grandmother. A glare would become a fight. A comment would be answered with an elbow. He once ran from someone with a gun. He associated with Crips, wore their midnight blue, and stayed out until all hours. "Didn't care," he told a reporter. "Thought I had nine lives." UCLA teammates called him an Oakland Raider, whose NFL team and fans had a menacing image. He told his fellow freshmen about the passing of Marques Jr., in vivid detail, in another study hall. The Bruins knew Kris Johnson had issues, which made them sympathize with his plight.

Kris shut his eyes and always saw little Marques grinning at him, his little hands on that sliding glass door. Kris wanted to die. Marques Sr. did not recognize his son's guilt because he was so stricken with his own sadness and grief. Upon his father's advice, Kris transferred from the mostly white and private Montclair Prep to edgy Crenshaw High for his junior year. Like his father, Kristaan helped the Cougars win a state championship. After his freshman year at UCLA, Kris spent the summer in Atlanta with his trainer-mother who guided his training and diet, which included Ester C, on a strict schedule. He had shed nearly fifty pounds when he showed for practice in the fall of 1995. Kristaan promoted the supplement with such ardor he should have starred in infomercials.

In Westwood he was becoming well known as the angriest Bruin. He admitted being emotional and having thin skin. "Sometimes I snap, which I need to control," he said. Michael Jordan intervened when Kris and Ike Nwankwo exchanged punches in a pick-up game on a Warner Bros. studio lot, during the filming of *Space Jam*. Kris would lead the conference in scoring one season but not receive all-conference accolades. "I told him, 'You can't cuss out [Stanford coach] Mike Montgomery ...' Mike told an official to watch Kris throwing elbows. Kris was right there, taking the ball out, and he said, 'Fuck you!' to Montgomery," says Marques Johnson. "Another time my parents were sitting behind the UCLA bench, and Kris was coming out of the game with his head down. A fan yelled, 'Kris get your head outta your ass!' Kris said, 'Fuck you, you mother fucker!' Blah blah blah." Marques shakes his head.

Kris would be suspended at UCLA for fighting and using drugs. He avoided one imbroglio by enrolling in violence-intervention and alcohol-abuse programs. He claimed counseling sessions helped him finally exorcise the vision of little Marques smiling at that sliding glass door. That it doesn't anymore only one person can say.

Many years later, we watch UCLA inside the new Pauley Pavilion. Kris sits next to a daughter, Khalilah, one of his three children by two women. He was married once, for two months. He shakes his head, frowns, and says the marriage thing was not and is not for him. Kareem Abdul-Jabbar and A.C. Green sit in front of us in padded baseline chairs. The former Los Angeles Lakers teammates are antagonists tonight, as Abdul-Jabbar's Bruins play host to Green's Oregon State Beavers. They tease each other all evening. Kris plucks his smart phone out of a jacket pocket and snaps a photograph of the back of Green's dome ... Kris being Kris.

When his overseas pro career ended a few years earlier, Kris says he became depressed, that he smoked too much pot and drank too much booze. He put on weight. But he had pulled out of it, he says, and he was enjoying working for an online scouting service and occasionally providing color analysis for West Coast Conference television broadcasts. He wanted to get into coaching.

I ask Kris about dropping that tear when he played Neptune. Even for a seasoned actor, it's a formidable task to pull off on cue. He says he can become lachrymose anytime, anywhere, because he can enter a dark place in an instant. I ask him, Because of what happened to Marques Jr.?

He slowly nods.

Jim Harrick started both of his point guards—Cameron Dollar and Tyus Edney—in UCLA's exhibitions against Perth and AIA. They didn't count, so Harrick could conduct an experiment without ramifications. If outsiders complained, it would be no different than what Harrick had been hearing for six years, anyway.

Dollar had spelled Edney in all twenty-seven games the previous season, so Harrick believed Dollar had at least earned a chance to show what he could do, as a sophomore, among the first five. With two skilled ballhandlers in the fold, maybe this wrinkle would make the Bruins that much more dangerous? The new freshmen were talented, sure, but what had they earned? A pecking order would likely produce spirited practice runs and, in the long run, strengthen the squad.

That Dollar had displayed the character to warrant a spot among the starters was indisputable, that's something he showed the moment he stepped onto UCLA's campus for his official recruiting trip. Perturbed that he won nothing of significance at St. John's Prospect Hall in Maryland, Dollar insisted to roommate and future Duke Blue Devils forward Nate James that he, Dollar, would win a title in college. He did not matriculate through Douglass High School in Atlanta—where he played for his father, Donald, and his mother was murdered (in 1980, when Cameron was four) in a vexing cold case—and two Maryland prep schools to ultimately attend a college that did not have a reasonable shot at winning a national championship.

Dollar was going to sign early, with Temple University and veteran coach John Chaney, in the fall of 1992. Dollar was onto something, since the Owls would fall a victory shy of making the Final Four in a few months. *Blue Ribbon* would tab Temple fourth in the nation in its 1993-94 preseason annual. However, one of

Chaney's assistants visited a Prospect Hall practice to take a closer look at Dollar ... and promptly fell asleep on the bleachers. Dollar laughed and thought, *Man, that dude don't like me. I can't go there.* He would wait to pick a college in the spring.

Mark Gottfried scouted another Prospect Hall player—likely Nate James, but Gottfried declined to name—during a Christmas tournament when this pesky guard from Atlanta grabbed his attention. Gottfried talked with coach Stu Vetter on Dollar's behalf alone, and Dollar visited UCLA over the first weekend of March 1993. It would only be for a brief vacation, a little getaway from the harsh Eastern winter. He'd have some fun, then return to Maryland and decide where to take some serious visits.

The plane landed at LAX. Dollar met Gottfried at the gate, trudged outside, and immediately shed his thick winter coat on the seventy-five-degree evening. "It's like *this* every day out here?" Dollar said. Many years later he harkens back to that trip and his naivete, and laughs. He seems to laugh as often as he breathes. "It was like a hidden gem. I knew of it, but I never *knew* of it. Palm trees all over, you walk into the gym and see the banners. You've heard about Wooden but when you're in Pauley Pavilion, UCLA and John Wooden come to life. I was sold after I met the guys."

He was impressed by Ed O'Bannon's tranquility. He met Shon Tarver. Tyus Edney was Dollar's host. Don't buy the aloof tourist routine, though. Southern California winters always lured Eastern recruits. Dollar says he wanted a brief vacation, but that is not entirely accurate. He had done his homework and visited Westwood with purpose. Through his network of contacts, and library visits to scan Southern California newspaper microfiche rolls, Dollar knew there was some tension between Pete Dalis and Jim Harrick. He discovered Dalis's past as a student football manager and that he had risen through the athletic-department structure to run it. "I knew enough to know I needed to go talk to

[Dalis]," says Dollar, who also heard recruiters from other schools use the alleged ill will between Harrick and Dalis against the Bruins. Dollar had to gauge Dalis's relationship with his basketball coach for himself. "To … see how tenuous it was," Dollar says.

> Even if it was tenuous, how sharp is [Dalis] to get someone else? I weighed all that. Wherever you go, even though you go play for a coach, you want to make sure that the organization is sound and people around it are sound, too. Things change all the time. I just wanted to meet with him and ask him straight up about it. I felt at the time I was a pretty good judge of people. I just wanted him to see me, I see him, and we go from there. I'm a kid. For me, all that matters is me. You don't have to cater to me, but acknowledge me and respond, ask and answer questions. He did that, and then some, and I felt he was straight up with me about Coach Harrick and his situation. He didn't flower it; he didn't talk negatively about him, either.

Having knotted a royal blue silk tie, Dollar donned a charcoal suit and shiny cap-toed Oxfords on Friday, March 5. He trudged up that flight of metal stairs to Pete Dalis's corner office in the Morgan Center. The name on the office building that Dalis strolled by every day paid homage to perhaps the most powerful force in UCLA athletic history, the guy who laid the foundation for John Wooden's juggernaut. Dalis had a Sisyphean task, and some say he knew it. That name wasn't passed lightly. Dollar strode by it with veneration. Dalis greeted Dollar and showed him a seat opposite an august mahogany desk. Exactly what was the true nature, Dollar said, of your relationship with Jim Harrick? A laser beam seemed to connect Dalis's eyes with Dollar's.

Dollar remembers Dalis being unflinching in his candor. He told Dollar that Harrick *is our coach and he's doing a good job*, but *things can change*. He didn't anticipate making any changes. However, *the reality of coaching [is], they can change*. They talked for an hour. When Dollar departed, Dalis made a beeline down to the assistant coaches' cubicles. He asked Lorenzo Romar, Who is *that*? "No kid has ever asked to talk to me during a recruiting visit. I hope we get him." Retorted Romar, "So do I." While that might not have been the start of a beautiful relationship, Dollar says that meeting created a strong bond between him and the top UCLA athletic figure, a man many viewed as cynical on a good day. A Mona Lisa grin would qualify as all-out exuberance from Dalis, which Dollar understood. "I sensed that over time," he says. "But, man ... I think he's just straight. He'd counsel when I needed counseling, and he'd chastise if I did something I wasn't supposed to be doing. He was good. I really appreciated knowing him and our relationship."

Dollar flew back to Maryland wondering how he would sell his father on UCLA. That's *a loooong way away*, Donald Dollar said. Cameron visited the University of Miami, in Florida, to appease his pop, but he again became enchanted by palm trees, sunshine, and the coeds. That, however, was a football school. He could have visited Hawaii, to complete a kind of paradise trifecta, but Dollar quit taking trips to keep out of trouble. "UCLA had everything I was looking for," he says. "Academically, it was phenomenal. Athletically, even socially, it was just big time."

He returned to Los Angeles, attended summer session and played pick-up ball in the B.O. Barn and Wooden Center. In Los Angeles, there was no better place to find top-flight competition in the dog days. Dollar impressed many after only a couple of runs. Tyus Edney, who had established himself as UCLA's motor as a sophomore, sat out with several ailments. And he heard all the talk. *Cameron who? Where's he from? That guy can play! Russ had better watch out! UCLA's got a new man at the point!* Edney didn't flinch. He did simmer. In fact, he did most everything without fanfare. Calm and serene, Edney would produce several senior moments that UCLA fans would recall fondly for decades, if not forever.

When Edney was cleared to play in the summer of 1993, he dominated Dollar despite yielding almost four inches and twenty pounds to his six-foot-one, 170-pound opponent/teammate. Edney was quicker, smarter, better. He squashed any sentiment that the starting point guard position at UCLA might be up for grabs. Dollar didn't back down, either. Edney started every game his junior season, despite various issues (clavicle, knee, thigh, and back) that affected him until the end of the season, at the Oregon schools and against Tulsa in the NCAAs.

In practice and pick-up games for two seasons, Dollar and Edney—according to many veteran witnesses—staged some of the most heated and entertaining point guard battles in the program's history. Edney was a product of a Southern California athletic system that John Wooden knew would expand and excel as the population exploded, making the competition fierce.

Edney's father, Hank, had played football at Long Beach State. A knee injury led Hank to fencing, as part of his rehabilitation, and he quickly handled an epee as if he were a Musketeer. When Hank and Barbara Edney lived in Compton, Tyus and brother Russell were fixtures on the Victoria Park basketball courts, where they often played with and against Ed and Charles O'Bannon in games and tournaments directed by Izzy Washington. Tyus learned to compete and treat teammates with a stern but positive edge, instead of bitching or griping at them. "A switch flips," Edney says.

You can be friends, but when you're gonna play, it's time to go at it. Can be friends afterward. And I might get a little frustrated at times, but for the most part I've always felt that I get the most out of my guys when their confidence is up. If I can keep their confidence up, they're gonna play better. I felt like I'd get more out of them when they feel good, even if stuff is goin' bad. Each guy is different. You can snap 'em out of it by saying certain things to certain guys. For the most part, I'm usually a guy trying to get you back to that peak level that I know you can be at.

Hank, a longtime human resources manager for TRW, moved the family to the Bixby Knolls section of Long Beach, about five miles south of Artesia High in Lakewood. Tyus played prep hoops for coach Ron Palmer at Long Beach Poly. The Jackrabbits had a renowned football program that supplied the NFL with an inordinate number of players. But they did well in basketball, too, and boasted of a fine alumni group of guards that included Chris and Tony Gwynn, and Morlon Wiley. Arizona, Washington State, San Jose State, and Colorado coaches had earmarked Edney as a prized recruit.

Jim Harrick was dispassionate. He drooled about the top-shelf senior prep point guards in the West who were graduating in 1991, including Jason Kidd in the Bay Area, Damon Stoudamire in Portland, Jacque Vaughn in Pasadena, and Kevin Ollie from Crenshaw High. Edney, however, was not such an unknown quantity; *Blue Ribbon* didn't list Tyus Edney among its top forty-four national prep players, but he did make its next hundred stars of the future.

Hank Edney treasures videotapes of Tyus's high school games. Tyus ran the show, but Poly forward Willie McGinest— who would star in football at USC and play fifteen NFL seasons at linebacker—and Ed O'Bannon Jr. of Artesia staged tussles for the ages. After one, Hank told Ed Sr., "Do you realize Ed scored fifty points?" Senior had been caught up in the intense action of every play and just shook his head. In August 2013, Hank rang Senior after having watched that tape for maybe the two hundredth time. "Man, that was the best individual effort I've ever seen!" Hank again told Senior. "Ed just refused to lose!"

Other schools might have been eager to land the exiguous Tyus Edney, who barely tipped the scales at 145 pounds as a high school senior, but the player had always fancied UCLA, the way Jim Harrick and his assistants appeared to treat their players with dignity and respect. If UCLA got Tyus Edney, the ties that can bind would be substantial since the Edneys were not only related to Marques Johnson, but a cousin of Madeline O'Bannon had married one of Hank Edney's cousins. (It would have been truly preposterous if a Bruin's family tree could be traced to Prague.)

Harrick, though, was not exactly sold on Edney. That required some persuading by Ed O'Bannon Sr. The O'Bannon patriarch knew Darrick Martin's eligibility was extinguishing in 1992, knew UCLA needed a fill-in at floor general. Madeline O'Bannon was there, in 1990, when Senior told Harrick, "You need to check out this kid Tyus Edney!" Upon Harrick's official visit to the Edney household, Hank Edney conveyed to Harrick that his usual tantalizing pitch with all the hopeful hooks would not be necessary here, that Tyus wanted to attend UCLA. Harrick closed his notebook. He opted for the guy who wanted to be there rather than continuing to chase the blue chippers.

(Harrick had pined over Ollie, but the outstanding guard wanted to flee from the Fort Crenshaw area. He would attend Connecticut, play thirteen NBA seasons, and take over the Huskies' coaching reins from Jim Calhoun in September 2012.

But the collegiate careers of Kevin Ollie and Tyus Edney would intersect in a major confrontation in Oakland.)

Edney's production doubled, across the statistical board, in 1992-93, after he had started those four times in the NCAAs. John Wooden saw Tyus early in his collegiate career, in practice, and raved about his vision. Cap Lavin, Steve Lavin's father, also liked Edney, saying his moves were balletic and comparing him to a latter-day Fred Astaire. However, Edney had made the fateful decision against Michigan in Tucson in the NCAAs. And Edney was a junior when he led UCLA into the ambush against Tulsa in the Golden Hurricane's backyard in Oklahoma City.

Starting Edney and Dollar in the exhibitions had turned in lukewarm results. Against Perth, the guards recorded eleven points and eleven assists. Dollar had made only one of his five shots. The pair tallied fourteen points and seventeen assists versus AIA. This time Edney connected on only one shot. Could Jim Harrick afford to play both of his point guards at the same time if one would always shoot so poorly?

The undeniable aspect of the Bruins' last tune-up was that, fresh off being tabbed number one—Arkansas was rated second—in the *Sports Illustrated* college basketball preview issue, they definitely were not ready for prime time. AIA had dropped all ten of its previous games, and it had lost by twenty-six points in Cincinnati the previous evening. Robert Sewell, a six-foot-five Canadian postman who had played at Florida Tech, blistered UCLA for twenty-four points. Shon Tarver, the former Bruin who had originally wanted to go to UNLV with Ed O'Bannon, chipped in with fifteen points. The visitors had a five-point edge at halftime, and the Bruins struggled all night before a barely half-filled Pauley Pavilion. It took a pair of free throws by Ed O'Bannon, with six seconds remaining, to gain a one-point victory that was secured only when AIA guard David Daniels missed a three-point attempt over Edney at the buzzer.

Jim Harrick moaned about the top billing by *Sports Illustrated*—"I mean, Arkansas returns *fiiiiive* starters from the national champions!"—his team's lax defense, and that his players had been reading their press clippings, with some of that West Virginia twang for flavor. Ed O'Bannon had scored sixteen points, but he made less than half of his shots. Tyus Edney collected five points and seven assists.

AIA, however, might have been the most adroitly scheduled opponent by Jim Milhorn, since its older players combined to sink fifty-two percent of their shots. Only two UCLA opponents would hit at least half of their attempts all season, and only one would be sharper than AIA. Now his teammates knew why O'Bannon's clampdown demands were so vehement. Harrick heard dissension from the stands, and the modest output by two seniors on whom he depended made him nervous. "Those guys have to play or we're in a world of hurt."

Perhaps an abundance of what Harrick scribbled on that dry-erase board wasn't original, but sometimes it revealed a clairvoyant proclivity. He might have bellyached about that *Sports Illustrated* ranking, but he twisted it to his benefit about this time when he wrote, for all of his troops to see, *PLAY AS IF YOU'RE PLAYING AGAINST ARKANSAS.*

Chapter 7

AS J.D. MORGAN had done for John Wooden, Jim Milhorn did for Jim Harrick. Pete Dalis made a wise move when he charged Milhorn with assembling UCLA's basketball schedule. The Pacific-10 Conference fraternity amounted to more than half of the slate, so Milhorn would typically line up about ten annual games, generally about eighteen months ahead of a particular season. His dexterity setting up foes matched his touch on the racquetball court when he lined up that AIA tilt.

Harrick neither advised nor consulted Milhorn about his schedule desires, and their regular racquetball confrontations afforded Harrick many informal opportunities to do so. But Harrick never mentioned that he'd like to have a light start to a certain season, or test his guys with a string of tougher opponents in another campaign. Years later, Milhorn says, "I didn't even let them know [whom] I was talking with. It was a good schedule that [1994-95] season, a lot of solid teams."

That didn't exactly pertain to the season opener on November 26, a Saturday afternoon in which more than three thousand Pauley seats were empty for UCLA's 83-60 victory over Cal State Northridge. The Bruins put it away during four early minutes. Fueled by the famed two-two-one zone press, they rattled off fifteen consecutive points that had been ignited by Tyus Edney's three-pointer and coast-to-coast layin.

Northridge was one of a host of area colleges whose hoops programs could only fantasize of having a tenth of the success that UCLA had experienced. Occasionally, the Bruins—Milhorn—allowed those minnows entrée to Pauley. These were almost always easy efforts for UCLA and golden opportunities for those other guys to take some nifty photographs in the cathedral of college basketball for the following season's media guides.

Six-foot-seven junior Ruben Oronz acknowledged that playing inside Pauley made him nervous, but after he hit his first shot he calmed down en route to scoring fifteen points. He believed UCLA's top billing in *Sports Illustrated* was justified, although the Associated Press voters checked UCLA in at fifth. Northridge coach Pete Cassidy raved about the Bruins' size and depth, saying, "They're just terribly talented."

Harrick had so much depth nobody logged more than twenty-eight minutes. He played all thirteen guys on his roster, and he gave Toby Bailey a boost—exactly what he had sought in that informal meeting with Harrick—by starting him in the second half in place of Cameron Dollar. George Zidek led the Bruins with fourteen points and admitted that it would be difficult for Harrick to play this many Bruins regularly. "We'll benefit from it," Zidek said. "The season is real long ... with injuries, you never know what might happen."

Jim Milhorn had an auspicious sense of the enthusiasm that would be generated by UCLA's second game. What started as dinner conversation between Orange County businessmen Randy Ryan, a former John R. Wooden Award executive, and J.T. Visbal in August 1993 became reality in March 1994, when they announced the inaugural John R. Wooden Classic, a doubleheader of premier programs in the coach's honor. Kansas would play Massachusetts, and UCLA would go up against Kentucky at the Anaheim Arena (now Honda Center). It became an annual event, and by November 2013 it would expand into an eight-team tournament format and be rechristened the Wooden Legacy.

Kareem Abdul-Jabbar, Bill Walton, and Mike Warren joined John Wooden on the dais for the 1994 revelation. The frail Wooden said he was flattered, proud, and honored. You always have to "keep your ego in the proper perspective," he said, but he was grateful that area charities would benefit from the event. NBC would broadcast the initial doubleheader to eighty countries.

The featured attraction pitted two of college basketball's blue bloods against each other. UCLA had its ten national titles, while Kentucky, like Indiana, owned five—and four of the Wildcats' crowns were earned before 1960. Kentucky, which had been experiencing a drought of sixteen seasons without a new piece of hardware, could take solace in that the Bruins' bling blight was three years longer. Two of the most magical names in the game, said Kentucky coach Rick Pitino. "Such a big event, such a wonderful matchup," says Milhorn. They hadn't played each other since March 31, 1975, when Marques Johnson helped send John Wooden into retirement in style.

Pitino had been athletic director C.M. Newton's choice five years earlier to return the Wildcats to prominence, to pass those Hoosiers and make the Bruins sweat about being caught in the arms race. The Wildcats had a powerful roster, which included juniors Tony Delk, Rodrick Rhodes, and Walter McCarty, and sophomores Jeff Sheppard and Anthony Epps. *Blue Ribbon* ranked Kentucky third on its preseason chart.

Charles O'Bannon took a look at Lexington, for its Midnight Madness extravaganza, in the fall of 1992. A packed Rupp Arena crowd of twenty-four thousand fanatics serenaded him with chants of *Charrrr-ulllz! Charrrr-ulllz!* He inked autographs for kids and said, "I'm telling you, that's why you play basketball—

for that type of atmosphere. Words don't come to mind to describe how it was." Playing college ball before family and friends, and alongside his older brother, had won him over, he said, by a fifty-one/forty-nine split.

Jim Harrick had been unsure about securing the services of Charles O'Bannon, who waited until the spring of 1993—very late in the process—to announce his decision. Harrick had told many that he had placed *all his eggs in one basket* in regards to recruiting; hoping the egg yolk would sway Charles's decision. That could have been a two-man class, consisting of Cameron Dollar and walk-on forward Bob Myers, who passed Steve Lavin one day in the Morgan Center en route to inquiring about the club crew team and was diverted to hoops by Lavin. That fortuitous convergence put Myers, who would earn a scholarship as a junior and senior, on a most gratifying career path.

However, in Japan many years later, Charles O'Bannon admits that the odds of him becoming a Bruin were more like eighty/twenty in favor of the Bruins, if, in fact, it had even been that close. He said the UCLA pull was just too strong. "Wearing the blue and gold was something that was just in my blood. I was coming to UCLA, without question."

Ed O'Bannon wouldn't have known how to prepare for it had Beagle-Beagle gone to Kentucky. "The one person I don't like playing against," he said. "For some reason, he gives me everything he has, and everything he has is a lot." Kentucky's 124-50 rout of Tennessee-Martin a few days earlier had stunned O'Bannon. He couldn't recall Artesia beating anyone by such a spread when he was in high school. "If they beat us by seventy-four, they better be able to beat some pro teams, too." Charles O'Bannon predicted a high score in which UCLA's press would trump Kentucky's. "A lot of threes, and not much defense," he said. "If they can press Arkansas, they can press anyone. At the same time, having Cameron Dollar and Tyus Edney bring it up, myself and Ed on the wings, and George Zidek on the post, I think we can do some big-time damage."

Jim Milhorn wanted to avoid damage, too, so he dodged veteran broadcaster Dick Vitale at the Wooden Classic dinner the previous night. Vitale sat across from Milhorn at the same table. A bulldog's feistiness typically embodied those who made the grade to play for John Wooden, and that coursed through Milhorn. He earned his jersey by pressing the front-liners in practice. That synergy helped create a dangerous program for fourteen seasons. Jim Harrick knew about the former guard's energy and passion from all those racquetball duels. Eventually, according to Milhorn, Harrick got pretty good at swatting that little rubber ball around that court.

Milhorn didn't care much for Al McGuire, either. McGuire had said UCLA's string of seven consecutive national titles being broken in 1974 was good for college basketball. After the coach won his lone NCAA title with Marquette in 1977, he retired into broadcasting and said UCLA would never win another championship after John Wooden retired; too much pressure from people living in the past. *That's a bunch of baloney*, Milhorn thought. *That won't happen.* Milhorn crossed paths with McGuire on occasion, in airports or hotels, but Milhorn kept quiet. McGuire's prognostication was becoming more authentic by the year. Milhorn promised himself to keep exchanges with McGuire pleasant.

He did the same with Vitale, whom Milhorn believed always showed allegiance toward Eastern schools, especially in the Atlantic Coast Conference. Especially Duke. Milhorn grinned when told the broadcaster was called Duke Vitale in certain circles. Milhorn took the high road at that Friday night dinner and kept his words with Vitale to an extreme minimum. "I didn't want to get into it," Milhorn says years later. "I think he's probably a good guy. A lot of people like him. I just think he shows favoritism. He's got his love for the [Mike] Krzyzewskis, [Bobby] Knights, [Jim] Valvanos. I don't have a problem with any of those people. I shouldn't say that. I'm not a big Bobby Knight fan. [Vitale] was at the opposite end. He was always questioning whether we'd win it, and he was always picking against us. We didn't have a whole lot to say to each other."

(In December 2013, working UCLA-Duke from Madison Square Garden for ESPN, Vitale was effusive in his admiration of Wooden and beyond grateful for being one of four honorees for the inaugural Pyramid of Success Awards, in Wooden's honor, in 2009. Duke had been ranked in the top ten of the weekly AP rankings for a 120th consecutive week; the only program with a longer top-ten run was UCLA, with a string of 155 weeks under Wooden. But that Blue Devils' streak would soon end.)

Vitale sounded golden in the first half, for UCLA held the lead for only fifteen seconds—on a fifteen-foot hook shot by George Zidek. The Bruins controlled the start of the second half, until Charles O'Bannon got tagged with his fourth and fifth fouls, earning him a permanent spot on the bench next to Harrick. More fouls sent Kentucky to the line, Ed O'Bannon committed a turnover and missed the front end of a one-and-one free-throw situation, and Walter McCarty drilled a fifteen-foot jumper. The Wildcats led by ten points. Waves of applause and cheers exploded from the Anaheim crowd of 18,307. Many were Kentucky fans, whose support is legendary. The Wildcats secured ten-point edges three more times, but it disappeared when McCarty fouled J.R. Henderson on a drive. Henderson sank both free throws to cut UCLA's deficit to single digits.

Zidek converted a layup, a three-point play, and a five-foot hook shot to get UCLA to within a point with eighteen seconds remaining. He had connected on hook shots with both hands, causing the UCLA coaches to shoot mystified looks at each other. *The Sweeper*, they said in unison. That was the moment when Jim

Harrick believed this big kid from behind the Iron Curtain might finally produce.

Three ticks later, Mark Pope turned it over and Harrick called for a timeout, setting up a play in which Tyus Edney would look for Ed O'Bannon first and J.R. Henderson as the fall-back option. O'Bannon had scored twenty-six points and logged thirty-eight minutes, both game highs. But the Wildcats draped him. So Edney drove the lane and found Henderson. McCarty was whistled for hacking the young, thin Bruin with six-tenths of a second left on the clock.

Henderson coolly sank both free throws to give UCLA a thrilling 82-81 victory. Afterward, he admitted his teammates call him Mr. Excitement because just the opposite is true. Semi-comatose described his usual demeanor. "I just take it smooth and easy," he said just above a whisper, his normal tone.

J.R. Henderson had been raised in the verdant central farming valley of California. At East Bakersfield High School he played ball for his father, Milton Sr. Charles O'Bannon and Artesia High popped into Bakersfield and put on an electrifying slam-dunk show for the farmers. "Lob City," says Milt Jr., shaking his head. "We'd never seen anything like that in our gym." Henderson led his squad to a state title that spring.

Proud to call himself a country boy, Henderson knew zilch about the recruiting process or scholarships or college ball. His father kept all correspondence from collegiate coaches at the high school, but Junior never showed interest in any of it. Senior is as low key as Junior. J.R. took a token recruiting visit to Cal, in Berkeley. He committed to UCLA. When he went to Westwood in the fall of 1994, he didn't unpack his suitcase for two weeks. He wanted to return home. This city life was not for him. Everything and everyone moved way too fast. His mother forced him to stay.

Jim Harrick and his staff had been curious about Henderson's lethargic court countenance. They were accustomed to his neutral facial expressions and penchant for minimal words, but a routine pre-season physical revealed that Henderson had asthma. He would be treated with a medicated inhaler, which bolstered his energy and stamina, but his quietude was part of his DNA.

Teammates would learn that three words from Henderson qualified as a dissertation. He was unassuming, with the pulse of a rattler. He soon clashed with Ed O'Bannon. In a pick-up game, the six-foot-nine Henderson swatted Ed's shot. Ed howled, "That ain't happenin' again!" It didn't happen again. "I guess he and I clashed," Henderson says. "I didn't mess with him. I didn't block his shot again. He didn't let me; it's not like I didn't try. I didn't think anything of it. I guess he was just trying to mark his territory." Years later, Ed O'Bannon refers to Henderson's skills and with reverence.

Henderson is a light-skinned image of his father, who played hoops at West Texas State (now West Texas A&M) with Maurice Cheeks, who helped Philadelphia defeat Marques Johnson and the Milwaukee Bucks in the 1983 Eastern Conference finals en route to beating the Los Angeles Lakers for the NBA title. Senior and Avis Henderson also had twin boys Damon and Dernell, and named their other son Lendl; yes, they are also tennis fans. Those three boys have darker skin, like their mother.

Kimikazu Suzuki was visiting during that time. He always made several annual trips to Los Angeles. In his mid-twenties, Suzuki sort of resembled the actor John Cusack. Suzuki ran the Pauley stairs—every aisle—after every practice he observed. His passion, to this day, is coaching. Like Marques Johnson and Ed O'Bannon, Suzuki consumed every book he could obtain in his native Japan about John Wooden. Suzuki deplored the heavy-handed methods of Bob Knight. Jim Harrick, a longtime consultant to the Japanese pro team Mitsubishi, gave Suzuki an open-ended invitation to visit Westwood and soak up the UCLA way. Suzuki examined everything. He jotted down notes, insights, and tips relentlessly. "Jim Harrick is good coach," Suzuki says. "But before him, John Wooden make this college the most famous in the world."

Suzuki would play a major role in the life of Milton Henderson Jr.

After Henderson's two free throws had beaten Kentucky, Ed O'Bannon called everyone into a locker-room huddle. The five student managers were waved into the scrum, too. O'Bannon forgot nobody. Tony Luftman recalls how Ed O'Bannon, the star of the team and the most influential athlete on a campus full of elite sports figures, regarded him so kindly when Luftman was just a lowly freshman gofer, to other players and an assistant coach.

After one practice, everyone showered and changed and bolted for a team dinner at a Westwood restaurant. O'Bannon, always the last Bruin to leave Pauley, saw Luftman and inquired about the dinner. As soon as I haul the dirty gear to the laundry room, Luftman said. He was about to manipulate a four-foot-tall duffel bag, jammed with soiled shorts and jerseys and towels, into a large cart, which he would push into an elevator, then ... let me carry it up, O'Bannon volunteered. No, Luftman giggled, that's not necessary. O'Bannon insisted, and he hauled the thing up the 70 stairs and outside Pauley to the industrial washer.

Luftman made small talk next to O'Bannon the entire way. Once there, O'Bannon insisted on giving Luftman a ride up a short hill to Luftman's vehicle in a dorm parking lot. Luftman and O'Bannon became such good friends, so quickly, that other young UCLA basketball players envied their relationship. *Doesn't talk to us the way he talks to you*, a jealous Bruin once lamented to Luftman.

O'Bannon swiveled his head around the Anaheim Arena locker room. In his own sulky corner, Toby Bailey pouted. The previous evening, in the team's Anaheim hotel, Bailey could not have been more excited. He couldn't sleep. The Kentucky game would be broadcast on national television, so the freshman would be able to show the country, from coast to coast, what he was made of. Saturday morning, Bailey watched close friend Ricky Price win player-of-the-game honors in Duke's 70-65 victory at Illinois. The six-foot-six swingman scored fifteen points and grabbed seven rebounds. Price's father, Rick, and Bailey's dad, John, were also tight, so John Bailey had received several spirited calls—*Ha! See my boy?*—from Rick Price. John Bailey, a UCLA graduate, would get a chance to trump Rick depending upon Toby's performance against Kentucky.

It did not happen. Unlike Northridge, Toby Bailey did not start the second half against the Wildcats. He played only ten minutes. He had a steal, an assist, one point, and three rebounds. He missed both of his shots from the field. He felt he was now competing for minutes with the ultra-talented J.R. Henderson, not Kevin Dempsey. Bailey moped in that corner as if his scholarship had just been revoked. Ed O'Bannon ran up to him, nostril to nostril, and snapped him to attention. O'Bannon tossed a folding chair or two around the narrow room. "I ever see you poutin' or cryin' after a game again, I'm gonna fuck you up! This is a team game! This is a team victory! No one player is less or more important than the next one! Get over there!"

The vehemence of O'Bannon's delivery immediately sobered Bailey. Years later he frowns over his indolence. "I snapped out of it. I understood what was important. When you're young, you need someone to pull your coattail like that. You're so absorbed in yourself. I don't think I was a selfish player; I had goals. I knew what I wanted to do. I felt like I wasn't contributing or that I wouldn't be able to contribute … [but] that was an important turning point."

It didn't provide total salve to Bailey, however. That would require several visits to a little old man's condo in Encino.

Chapter 8

FRESHMEN WERE OFF-LIMITS, sort of. Jim Harrick had produced that edict after omm'A Givens, the much-heralded black post player from Aberdeen, Washington, told a reporter that he avoided dating black women because they have *attitude* issues. That quickly got back to Bill Bennett in sports information and Harrick, who muzzled the newcomers.

After J.R. Henderson's two free throws had beaten Kentucky, Henderson spoke to a swarm of media. The neophytes weren't restricted from talking after games, when only a few quotes or sound bites were needed. To talk with a freshman at any other time—after practice, say, for an in-depth feature—was forbidden. Unwisely, for Harrick's sake, he relaxed his own moratorium when Tim Kawakami of the *Los Angeles Times* pressed him to speak with Henderson for a feature. The piece would undoubtedly be positive, about the cool and quiet kid who had slayed mighty Kentucky, and run in the largest-circulated newspaper in Southern California. For a guy who so frequently received disparaging, negative press, this was a no-brainer for Harrick.

Kawakami is a scribe of Asian lineage, educated at Northwestern University, who shed no tears when the Los Angeles Rams sacked coach John Robinson. That wasn't unique; the fourth estate has had a penchant for agitating, from its bunkers and in numbers, since Bi Sheng first formed those fragile clay characters. Kawakami also covered boxing for the *Times* and

156

penned a book about Oscar De La Hoya. Unlike its half dozen or so competitors, his paper nearly changed its UCLA basketball beat writer annually—Kawakami was the next man up. This was his first season covering the Bruins, so he couldn't have been prepared for—and certainly didn't deserve—what awaited him as Harrick led him down those three flights of concrete stairs to the floor of Pauley Pavilion.

Harrick guided him past center court to the opposite rim. Still riding the elixir of having dispatched Kentucky, Harrick approached Henderson, who was shooting free throws. Steve Lavin and Tony Luftman stood on opposite sides of the basket, rebounding the ball for Henderson. Assuming his Vegas showman persona, Harrick said, "J.R., this is the great beat writer of the *Los Annnnn-ju-liss Tiiiiimes ...* Timmmmm *Riiiiiiiiice.*"

The gaffe instantly registered with the diminutive Kawakami, who wore a baseball cap, tilted up, with his bangs showing under the bill. He lowered his chin to his chest, leveling the bill with the court. Lavin's eyes widened. He pursed his lips. Luftman bit his tongue. Henderson, calm as a plastic surgeon, swished another free throw with no regard to what had just transpired. Henderson nodded at Kawakami, shook his hand, and the two dispatched to the side to talk. Harrick slightly swaggered during good times and stretches of success, and that's how he had approached Henderson at the free throw line. After the slur, Harrick's demeanor did not alter, apologetically or sympathetically, to any degree. He wore an oblivious expression much like Mr. Magoo, one of Steve Lavin's pet sayings for someone unaware of a palpable event that had just taken place before his very eyes.

But this had been no casual, comedic *Kamakawi* line. Luftman and Lavin registered the appropriate impertinence, an egregious slip not easily forgiven or forgotten. (To his cool, calm credit, however, Kawakami today does not recall the incident. He could be instantly forgiving, levelheaded, and professional in many situations.)

Someone close to Harrick, who requested anonymity, likened the coach to John Forbes Nash Jr., the subject of Sylvia Nasar's excellent 1998 book *A Beautiful Mind*, whose 2001 movie of the same name starred Russell Crowe as the brilliant mathematician who struggled in many other areas of life.

Demanding that his guys play every game as if they were battling Arkansas—because the Hogs were the elite standard, the defending champs, what UCLA aspired to be—on the dry-erase board so early in the season was sheer precognition. Harrick could call out a play, a "back-end third reversal to get Bob Myers an easy layin," and it would work to perfection. Some likened Harrick to the former chess master Bobby Fischer, who seemed to scheme a few moves ahead of a foe. Harrick was a master hoops tactician that many failed, or declined, to recognize. So often, however, in those other areas of life, he was his own worst enemy.

People in higher stations than college hoops coach have been prone to verbal slips, mistaken identity, or other such faux pas. A cottage industry gorged itself on seemingly every other line spoken by President George W. Bush. In his epic *The Best and the Brightest*, about the people and events, lies and deceit that all figured into America's role in Vietnam, eminent author David Halberstam wrote of LBJ anecdotes that enlivened the White House press corps and made for jocular after-dinner banter ... later, however, "they would not seem so amusing."

In the aftermath of the conquest of Kentucky and the ensuing locker-room incident, Toby Bailey was still drifting. Ed O'Bannon's pointed review had hit its mark, between Bailey's eyes and ears. Bailey knew there was more to address. He sought the counsel of Michael Warren, Wooden's former guard who had starred in the television series *Hill Street Blues*. Bailey knew the Warren family well and would date Mike Warren's daughter Koa.

Warren saw confusion etched across Bailey's face, and he suggested an initial meeting with John Wooden in his small condo in Encino. That started a somewhat irregular and informal series of discussions, over oatmeal, scrambled eggs, and pancakes, between Wooden and Bailey that would affect Bailey's freshman season and the rest of his life.

That Warren served as the conduit between the elderly coach and the new Bruin who believed he could be an immediate impact player was deeper than Bailey could have realized. In his youth, Warren clashed with Wooden. A five-foot-eleven point guard from South Bend, Indiana, whom teammates had nicknamed Flea, Warren's guile was the glue, with Lew Alcindor and Lucius Allen, of the UCLA squads that won national titles in 1967 and '68. Warren served as the team's lone captain both seasons, in which the Bruins were 59-1.

He also drew some of Wooden's wrath when he dated a white girl. As detailed in *The Wizard of Westwood*, Wooden told Warren he had received threatening phone calls and would discourage anybody from interracial dating. "I imagine whites would have trouble dating in an Oriental society, too," Wooden said. "It's asking for trouble." Wooden told *Sports Illustrated* he never told a player whom he could or could not date. "But, man, how about telling me my life is in danger? How's that for a hint?" Warren said.

His relationships with blacks have no meaning. The coaching staff was seriously interested only in us playing, studying, and keeping out of trouble. Our individual progress in terms of maturing as black men

Rob Miech

was of no concern. It's superficial, the same kind of dialogue every day.

Wooden believed he'd had constructive dialogue with black players. He had tried to understand and adapt. He recalled hearing Wilt Chamberlain say he couldn't be *handled*, that only animals were *handled*. Wooden admitted having used that term, but not since Wilt's revelation. "I learn more every year," Wooden told a reporter. "But there are some things I have to stand upon."

Kareem Abdul-Jabbar later apologized for some charged comments he had written in a scathing *Sports Illustrated* feature about Wooden in the magazine's issue dated November 3, 1969. Warren, too, had made amends with the coach and knew conversations with him would comfort and encourage Bailey. "He has one of the best relationships with Wooden, of all the coach's former players. Kareem, too," says Bailey.

Wooden's domicile could not have been more than eight hundred square feet, with a roll-top desk and sitting area, next to a nook that contained a counter, sink, and basic kitchen utilities. A modest bedroom and restroom were just a few steps to the right. Bailey saw the 116 letters, tethered by a yellow ribbon, Wooden wrote to his late wife Nell on the twenty-first of every month and carefully placed on a corner of his bed. That's the date she died, at seventy-three, in March 1985. In 2003, per Wooden's request, the Pauley court was christened *Nell & John Wooden Court*. (Tony Luftman once asked Wooden, Why not *John & Nell* ... to which Wooden recoiled, and softly said, "Gracious sakes alive, Tony. Ladies first!")

Warren, Bailey, and Wooden went to Vip's, one of Wooden's favorite dining spots. Wooden listened to Bailey explain his frustrations about not starting and not playing many minutes.

Coach Harrick told me I had to beat out Kevin Dempsey, Bailey told Wooden, but now there's J.R. Henderson. I worked on my shot all summer, I'm shooting well ... but there's no reward, no recognition of my work. In his measured tone, Wooden told Bailey he needed to be an all-around player, an overall threat. Nobody can survive on just one aspect of the game. Strive to be a solid teammate, too, whether on the floor or sitting on the bench. Wooden also threw in the crucial stuff about not getting too high or too low, having balance on the court and in life. *Keep working*, Wooden said. *Keep asking coaches questions. Always strive to be better than you were yesterday, and be better tomorrow than you were today.*

It started Bailey on a path of clear thinking, with perspective, and lifted his spirits. "Coach has a way of putting you on the right track and making you feel that you can't have this woe-is-me attitude, that everything happens for a reason," Bailey says. "If it's not working out, you have to dig down deep, within yourself, to figure out what you need to do to get on the floor."

Bailey likens Wooden to Gandhi or the Dali Lama, whose words are simple yet profound. Bailey says so many Wooden sayings, stories, and anecdotes had depth and texture, and directly related to his world. Then again, Bailey grew up attending Wooden camps and first met him when he was eight. Still, these intimate meetings were surreal. "He talked to me not like I was a camper," Bailey says. "He'd say, 'Toby, nice game [last night or recently], just need to do *this* or *that.*' "

Basketball was Bailey's entire life, his sole purpose for being on the planet. He thirsted for stardom. It was all hoops, hoops, hoops ... until he actually conversed with Wooden. Bailey began noticing the world around him. He began to develop a personality, a soul. "That's when I knew I needed to branch out in life and look into other interests," Bailey says. "Missing a shot didn't become as important to me. [Before] I'd be crushed for days. He gave me the perspective that kept me from going into a dark place."

When Bailey returned to UCLA after his collegiate career, he was impressed that Wooden would always call him by his first name. Wooden never forgot. "I've only been star-struck by a couple of people, and he's one," Bailey says. "I got a thrill every time he called me by my name." Ed O'Bannon, though, regrets that he never tapped the sage figure for advice or insight. Rehab, returning to form, keeping his teammates in line, a little bit of academic work, and fatherhood demanded all of his time. With Wooden, such relationships formed on an individual basis, which he never initiated.

The last time they shared eggs, oatmeal, and stories, Wooden was in his nineties. A man, maybe in his mid-eighties, approached the table and glared at Wooden. In mid-sentence, the outsider paused and looked crestfallen. He had forgotten what he wanted to say. Wooden shook his head slightly as the man turned and walked away. He told Bailey, "That young feller has got to take care of himself."

Bailey laughs at the memory. "Still sharp," he says. "Awesome."

Jim Milhorn's scheduling of Cal State Fullerton, a week after Kentucky, was meant to be a reunion for Titans coach Brad Holland, who had starred for UCLA and assisted Harrick when he accepted the powder blue baton in Westwood.

However, Holland had moved on to the University of San Diego in late September. Bob Hawking, who had coached Don MacLean at Simi Valley High School, was promoted from within to take over the Titans. Hawking might have been geared up for the confrontation, since a coveted assistant's gig under Harrick never materialized, but his rotation took a hit when six-foot-seven swingman Darren Little was declared academically ineligible. Winston Peterson, a six-six senior, shouldered all of his team's burdens with twenty-six points and nine rebounds against UCLA.

It had started at 5 P.M. Not until six-thirty did the Bruins finally run away from the Titans, when Ed O'Bannon ignited a run of twelve consecutive points. Harrick cleared his bench in the final minutes, which allowed Kevin Dempsey to drill a long three-point shot beyond the top of the arc and shift a nifty no-look pass to Toby Bailey for a strong left-handed tomahawk dunk. Ike Nwankwo hit a jumper. Marquis Burns banged in a long three-point shot. Pauley Pavilion had been barely half full, but Harrick faulted little in the 99-65 victory with a full week until the Bruins played again, against Louisiana State in Baton Rouge.

When LSU visited Pauley Pavilion for the first time, the building burst at its five-year-old seams. Tigers coach Press Maravich, who called John Wooden *Padre* or *Saint John*, had brought a famous troupe to Los Angeles in December 1969. Make that a famous son, senior Pete Maravich. "This gangly kid with the Age of Aquarius look and the Ringling Bros. sideshow," is how the *Los Angeles Times* characterized the ace shooter known by all as Pistol. The old man allowed his mop-topped and floppy-socked kid free range, which inspired Pistol to want to win badly for his pop. Said Pete, "He's taken such a terrible beating [at LSU] for what he lets me do. I've seen what it's done to him, how it's changed him."

A throng of 12,961 crammed into Pauley, a record that stood for more than twenty-two years, to see Pistol Pete and the Bayou Bengals play the Bruins, winners of the previous three national championships. Lew Alcindor had moved on, but Sidney Wicks,

Curtis Rowe, and Henry Bibby kept UCLA formidable. Indeed, the Bruins racked up sixty-nine points by halftime en route to a 133-84 pasting of LSU.

Maravich made only fourteen of forty-two shots, and he turned the ball over eighteen times. "Pete ... was horseshit," wrote Mark Kriegel in his definitive *Pistol: The Life of Pete Maravich*. It had been the Tigers' fourth road game in six days, a junket that Press had arranged. "He's a damned tired boy," Press told the press. Pete averaged forty-four points in his collegiate career, without a three-point line or shot clock. LSU coach Dale Brown once examined every shot Pete sank and concluded that he would have averaged fifty-seven points had a three-point arc existed in his days.

LSU, however, never played in the NCAAs with Pete Maravich wearing a purple and yellow uniform or with Press Maravich coaching it. The Padre recognized that the Pistol had wonderful talents and was a great attraction, but admitted that the six-foot-five hot shot could never have been a Bruin, from those socks to that hair, to the gunner mentality. Wooden said, "His style would not cut it with me."

Dale Brown featured nobody like that on his current LSU squad, although Randy Livingston and Ronnie Henderson gave the Tigers a potentially lethal backcourt. The Pete Maravich Assembly Center held nearly fifteen thousand rabid Cajuns, and a caged Bengal tiger would be wheeled out to further incite pandemonium. Livingston was a two-time *Parade* All-America selection in high school in New Orleans who had suffered a serious knee injury a year earlier, so his freshman season—a la Ed O'Bannon—was delayed a year. Henderson played prep ball in Gulfport, Mississippi. The six-five guards had been friends, too, before landing at LSU.

But the Tigers had no chemistry on Saturday, December 17. Livingston still wasn't in prime shape, and he scored only four points on two-for-thirteen shooting. Henderson tallied twenty-two points, but his only help came from the twenty provided by Ukrainian forward Roman Rubchenko. Tyus Edney and Cameron Dollar led a sticky defensive effort that forced LSU's guards to turn the ball over nineteen times. Ed O'Bannon had been too strong. He led everyone with twenty-eight points, on nine-for-thirteen shooting from the field. Charles O'Bannon (seventeen points) and Edney (sixteen) complemented Easers. Dollar had seven assists and only two turnovers, but he made only one shot in six attempts. And Toby Bailey chipped in with eleven points and seven boards off the bench. John Wooden's wisdom was calming the precocious freshman.

The LSU arena was rambunctious, and Jim Harrick had been slapped with a technical foul. But UCLA won knockouts in both halves. The 92-72 victory proved to be a warm-up for a track meet that awaited the Bruins a few days later. When the Bruins returned home, Ed O'Bannon posed with Larry Pierce for pictures, by a formal photographer, on the Pauley Pavilion floor. The wheelchair-bound Pierce suffered from muscular dystrophy, but he had unlimited admiration for UCLA basketball. He attended most practices. Every player knew him. O'Bannon, honored to spend time with Pierce, patiently sat through the tedious photo session.

Paul Westhead brought his George Mason squad into Pauley Pavilion on December 22 with a grand reputation of runnin' that had no precedence. He had coached the Lakers to an NBA title in 1980, but he was soon replaced by a slick assistant named Pat Riley either by Earvin "Magic" Johnson's insistence or a vision by Dr. Jerry Buss, the team's owner; the scale of truth tips to the latter scenario, with at least a trace of influence from the former. The "Showtime" Lakers were born.

Westhead showed up at Loyola Marymount in 1985 and initially played a conventional brand of hoops. He and Jim Harrick, at Pepperdine, were West Coast Conference combatants for a few seasons. Westhead disappeared into his laboratory. Blue chippers Hank Gathers and Bo Kimble, who led the NCAA in scoring in 1988-89 and '89-90, respectively, left USC to experiment with Westhead. They added panache to what evolved as Paul Ball. He authored a running system—which Westhead had artfully dubbed The System—that relied upon possessions lasting no more than five seconds, earning him the Guru of Go alias. It was disorganized chaos. Anarchy.

To sustain such mayhem, Westhead ran his charges relentlessly. Part of the workout routine included grueling hauls up a steep sand hill in Manhattan Beach. That enabled the Lions to make their Gersten Pavilion resemble the Brickyard in Indianapolis. In January 1989, Loyola beat US International University 181-150—Gathers scored forty-one points and hauled in twenty-nine rebounds—in the highest-scoring game in Division-I history. Paul Ball earned large-type headlines, but it turned tragic when Gathers collapsed and died during a West Coast Conference tournament game at Gersten on March 4, 1990. LMU played on. In the NCAAs Bo Kimble, a righty, shot his first free throw of every game left-handed in tribute to Gathers. LMU belted Michigan, 149-115, in the second round in Long Beach, California, to slip into the Sweet Sixteen. The Lions advanced by squeaking by Alabama, 62-60.

Loyola was a national heartbreak story and a victory from earning a spot in the Final Four in Denver. UNLV, however, blasted LMU, 131-101, in Oakland. Westhead's fairytale had run into Jerry Tarkanian's locomotive. The Rebels won two more and the national championship. Larry Johnson and Stacey Augmon and Anderson Hunt and Greg Anthony had put on a dazzling show whose siren song would captivate seventeen-year-old Ed O'Bannon.

Westhead's chapter at Loyola fizzled in a flurry of lawsuits. He took over George Mason in 1993. And he brought the show to Pauley to test it against a supercharged UCLA squad. What Westhead called The System had been christened The Disease by Jim Harrick. The Patriots never had a winning campaign in Westhead's four seasons. On Thursday, December 22, fans filled Pauley to about three-quarters of its capacity for what promised to be a cherry-picking carnival.

Anyone interested in seeing what happens when UCLA is challenged to sprint might have gleaned some precious insights. Must have been bowling night in Connecticut and Arkansas. The Bruins pressed back. After they made shots, the Bruins—especially Tyus Edney—did not hustle back to defend the other basket. Edney picked and poached passes from Patriots, accumulating eleven steals that still stand as UCLA's single-game record. The frenetic pace helped the under-manned Patriots stay within single digits into the first five minutes of the second half, but the O'Bannons put GMU away. Before the midway point of the second half, Jim Harrick had put omm'A Givens, Ike Nwankwo, Kevin Dempsey, and Marquis Burns into the track meet.

Burns slammed in a miss by a teammate to give UCLA a 101-78 edge with ten and a half minutes remaining. That would be Burns's third basket of the season and his last as a Bruin; a severe lack of playing time would compel him to leave UCLA. He transferred to New Mexico State, where for the first time Neil McCarthy enjoyed some windfall from Westwood. Some teammates would forever refer to Burns as The Fifth Beatle. Even Bob Myers registered on the stat sheet with an assist in the 137-100 victory.

Harrick had given his squad a goal of keeping GMU to double figures in points. The Patriots hit triple digits thanks to a pair of Curtis McCants free throws with twenty seconds left, but not a point more. A compromise, said Ed O'Bannon. Didn't matter to Harrick. For allowing the other guys to hit a hundred, the Bruins would spend an abundance of their next practice bolstering their lungs. Seventeens.

Edney rang up a fantasy box score with twenty-eight points, nine assists, and the eleven steals. The Bruins were learning to defend as if their lives truly depended on it. They could thank AIA, and Ed O'Bannon did not let them forget that exhibition lesson. He had twenty-three points, fourteen rebounds, and four assists, while Charles tallied twenty points, six assists, and seven boards. Toby Bailey poured in twenty-two points in twenty-five minutes, and he had two assists and steals, while turning it over only once.

The Disease didn't disappear when the Patriots left the arena. Jim Harrick believed the herky-jerky nature of that style would carry over, detrimentally, to UCLA's final game of the calendar year. He wasn't mistaken. UCLA had to claw a bit to improve to 6-0 by defeating North Carolina State, 88-80, on Wednesday, December 28. Center George Zidek scored thirteen points, on six-of-nine shooting, and grabbed eight rebounds. Would he truly be a legitimate factor in his final tour of the Pac-10? His coaches were seriously beginning to think so. He no doubt felt good with his father, Jiri—a famous basketball figure from a stifling era of Czechoslovakia—watching him play in a UCLA uniform for the first time.

This wasn't the Wolfpack of Jim Valvano, who had burnished one of the all-time defeats onto Jim Harrick's resume when Harrick was at Pepperdine. Les Robinson had succeeded Valvano—after he was sacked in a hailstorm of allegations, many of which were investigated and found to be false—at his alma mater in 1990. (Many years later, Mark Gottfried would take over at North Carolina State.) Against UCLA, the Wolfpack cut a thirteen-point deficit almost in half eight minutes into the second half. But Tyus Edney put it on ice by scoring eight of his team's final ten points, which included hitting all six of his free throws down the stretch. It was a weeknight game, but the natives seemed to be warming to this UCLA team as Pauley was only a few bodies shy of a sellout.

Jim Harrick, for one, wasn't too excited. His team would head to Oregon for the start of league games the following week. The Bruins were undefeated, but Harrick recalled the midway point of the previous season when they were 14-0. His uneasy feeling had been warranted as the calendar flipped to 1995. Having called a practice for mid-morning New Year's Day, Harrick turned his back to Kevin Dempsey, an opening Dempsey used to flip off his coach with the middle finger of his right hand. He was red-faced and panting. Harrick had been whipping his charges. Seventeens. They were about to run some more. Dempsey didn't like any of it.

Then again, Dempsey told me, he was still drunk; he had had a rollicking New Year's Eve that had only ended a few hours before the start of practice. That wasn't a first. Teammates said when Dempsey felt sluggish and woozy, he would get them to give him an elbow in the gut or back, to give him a viable excuse to step aside and miss a few drills, to rest on the sideline, sometimes to even sit out the rest of a practice.

When he gave Harrick the bird, however, Steve Lavin saw that I had observed Dempsey. Lavin would rebuke Dempsey for disrespecting Harrick with media lurking. Keep that up, Lavin told Dempsey, and you'll be driving a FedEx truck. Never mind that the patriarch of the O'Bannon family made a good living and raised his family in such a vocation. Lavin could slip, too. When he first met John Wooden and informed him that his father, Cap, was *just a teacher*, Wooden cringed. He viewed himself as just, ahem, a teacher, and he never let Lavin forget the slight.

Harrick would always talk about Kevin Dempsey in glowing terms. But the vulgar act was only a warm-up to what was waiting for Harrick, and his team, in Oregon.

Chapter 9

PLAYING A MERE BASKETBALL game in a two-tiered cauldron that basted, simmered, and burned every unsuspecting University of Oregon opponent wasn't about to make Jiri Zidek Sr., or his namesake son, nervous.

A few days earlier Senior had seen his youngest boy play in a collegiate game for the first time, on friendly turf. Jiri Sr. tagged along with the Bruins up the coast. He had played before more than eighty thousand fiery, frothing Greeks once, so this one against the Ducks would be mere child's play for perhaps the most famous basketball player from the former Czechoslovakia. His son, who preferred to be called George, knew about true danger, too, in his young life. George neared the end of his prep studies in Prague with the very real prospect of having to defect—leaving his father, older brother, and the love of his life—to attend a college in the States.

Vague light from shops and street lamps gradually assumed illumination duties in the late-afternoon dusk on the corner of Perlova and Narodni, not far from the northwest entry to Wenceslas Square in Prague. At 3 P.M. on that icy Friday of November 17, 1989, a student celebration to commemorate International Students Day had kicked off at Vysehrad. The tenth-century castle south of the city center is the final resting place of famous Czech poets, writers and statesmen, and its imposing twin-spiered basilica stands sentry over the Vltava River to the west.

The pack crawled north, attracting more participants, resentment, and hostility. On the outskirts of Wenceslas, it had swelled to at least fifteen thousand—some say more than thirty thousand—and became a demonstration against the Communist regime that had kept a knee on Prague's throat since 1948. People were shouting anti-Communist slogans, demanding their freedom, and singing the national anthem. As George passed the National Theater at Narodni trida 16, well-known actors and actresses stoked the crowd with waves. A large copper block featuring hands—some waving, some signaling, with index and middle fingers, V for victory—and 17.11.1989 would later be permanently affixed at eye level by the theater's entrance.

An ominous feeling overwhelmed George Zidek. Riot police and armed guards surrounded the group and slowly tightened their noose around the demonstrators. Shields protected the faces of the authorities. They had batons, grenades, and automatic weapons at the ready. With interlocked arms, they took half-steps inward. Plainclothes StB, or secret police, officials lurked in the shadows.

At nearly seven feet tall and weighing about 220 pounds, Zidek was an easy target. He begged two cops to unlock their arms, pleading that he had to meet his older brother, Jan, at a train station. The officers finally released their grips. Zidek tore north down a cobbled medieval alleyway—where a Czech Geppetto would one day offer wooden marionettes of Barack Obama and Lionel Messi, the global soccer star for FC Barcelona, for the equivalent of forty bucks. George heard the whistle. The heavy army boots clumped as one. Years later, the guilt still pervasive about preserving himself, Zidek says, "Just an eerie feeling. I did not stay. I admit that."

The Velvet Revolution had begun.

Eight days earlier, the Berlin Wall had started crumbling. East and West Berliners chipped away at it with sledgehammers and picks. Still it was absurd, for anyone who lived behind the Iron Curtain, to believe the rest of it would crumble, too. Zidek says, "Nobody believed the system was going down. On seventeen November [1989], who would have thought the Communist system would disintegrate? They had a firm grip. They had the army, the police, the media ... they were in complete control." He points to an archway, where police allowed demonstrators to flow into the northwest entrance of the square. The militia swung its batons and truncheons, injuring hundreds. A female classmate ended up in a hospital with a blood clot in her brain. "They just beat the shit out of everybody," Zidek says.

They didn't care. Usually you could walk off. Not this time. They closed it off. I didn't want to get caught by the police. I feared it would be the end of my life. I don't want to make myself sound like I was some kind of a political activist. I was very much going to practice in the morning, then to individual studies ... I was very much a part of the junior national basketball team, but my family got kicked in the ass by the Communists. The StB, the guys who didn't wear uniforms, they were the biggest bastards; plain clothes, always spying on everybody.

Later that night he returned to Wenceslas with Jan to find bloody cobbles. Shoes and jackets were scattered all over the square. Had he remained, he might have been detained, his passport confiscated. He envisioned being booted off the junior national hoops team and kicked out of Arabska Secondary School. An extremely bright student who would weave *disquieting* into his everyday vocabulary, and correct a visitor who believed a building was Gothic—"No, I think that's baroque," he says—Zidek believed something was odd about the spark to the revolution. He felt there was a bit of stagecraft involved, that it was contrived.

In his impressive *The Atlantic And Its Enemies,* on the Cold War, author Norman Stone detailed how the StB, by order of the KGB, had filmed a supposed "student" getting shot in Wenceslas in a hail of bullets. The camera kept rolling and caught the student "walking away, once his 'death' had been recorded." Radio Free Europe reported the death of student Martin Smid as fact. Supposedly the revolution was being expedited by very influential Geppettos. Another demonstration drew half a million locals.

Zidek and many of his countrymen believe in conspiracies. They believe Communist brass knew the end of their reign was inevitable, that the closing of this chapter in Czechoslovakia would enable them to either control or purchase public utilities and property that was about to become privatized, eventually making them rich, or flee across the border to safety in their homeland. Some of them hoped to replace the old, hard line with "reform Communists" that would be acceptable to the West and keep them in the picture. In December 1989, a Czech Cabinet was installed that, for the first time in forty-one years, put Communists in the minority. But Zidek bristles that the party was never outlawed.

After the melee of Nazi Germany occupation during World War II, the Soviets ruled Czechoslovakia. The Communists became popular by parading as democratic, anti-Fascist bodies. In the early summer of 1947, at a conference in Paris, the country's fate was sealed when Soviet leader Joseph Stalin denounced the

Marshall Plan as an imperialist plot and restricted Czech involvement. Sixteen countries would adopt the plan, which revitalized their economies. West Germany thrived with the aid.

Czechoslovakia had already gone the way of Poland, Hungary, East Germany, and the Balkans. Her heavy industry, and large working and middle classes were operating on behalf of the USSR. George Zidek can talk for days about the *spheres of influence* that were divided among Winston Churchill, Franklin D. Roosevelt, and Joseph Stalin, as if Zidek himself had been at Yalta in February 1945. That doomed Czechoslovakia. After World War II, the West wasn't about to tangle with the Soviets. "Unfortunately," Zidek says, "we fell to the wrong territory."

Historians have documented that Czechoslovaks had largely welcomed the shift from Fascism, and subsequent surface stabilization, that the USSR provided. But peace and prosperity were replaced by the one-party regime. In February 1948, just after Jiri Zidek Sr. turned four, the Czech Coup hit full stride during a terrible winter. Barbed wire, Dobermans and German shepherds, watchtowers, minefields, and searchlights became ubiquitous across the land. The Iron Curtain of Churchill's prediction had descended.

Zidek's great grandparents and grandfather, on his mother's side of the family, had every bolt of linen, silk, and other fine cloth confiscated from their Zlin fabrics store. They were forced against a wall as commoners, drunkards, and beggars looted their business, swiping the gold and silver, and framed paintings. Nationalism would strip capitalists of their materials, energies, and lifetime earnings. The trio was put on trial in Zlin's largest theater, to accommodate their many peer protestors. They were given prison sentences of five to nine years. Zidek's grandfather was forced to mine uranium with bare hands.

Zidek's mother, Marie, was in the first grade when a teacher pointed to her in a classroom and said, "Look at this person; part of the bourgeoisie that's taking advantage of the working class." George becomes enraged at the mere thought of a teacher talking to his six-year-old daughter Ela that way today. "Unbelievable propoganda," he says. "I cannot imagine anyone going through this shit." Zidek's elder relatives, all of who were ultimately released early from prison for good behavior, would have been familiar with life in a normal, democratic Czechoslovakia before 1938.

The Prague Spring of 1968 provided Jiri Sr. and Marie with a glimmer of false hope about a future without a Red Star on buildings, neighbors informing on each other, or ever-suspicious StB spies sitting next to them on a trolley. On April 4, Senior—wearing number ten, reflecting his star status—tallied thirty-one points in a losing effort for Slavia Prague in a Cup Winners' Cup basketball finale against AEK Athens. An estimated eighty thousand rabid fans set a Guinness World Record that lasted for decades when they crammed into the white-marbled, hairpin-turned Kallimarmaro Stadium, home to the first modern Olympics in 1896, for the night game. Another forty thousand raved outside the stadium. The Boston Celtics made a bid for Senior's services, but defecting wasn't an option for him because of his devotion to his family.

Stalinist abuses and political oppression were hot topics on radio and television shows. Victims confronted their torturers on live broadcasts. In August, however, two hundred thousand troops and two thousand tanks from Warsaw Pact members Bulgaria, Hungary, and Poland joined Soviet battalions to occupy, and further silence, Czechoslovakia. Pete Dalis, a young UCLA athletic administrator, had been in London on holiday with an airline ticket to Prague, but he heeded strong advisories against visiting Czechoslovakia and made other plans.

It became verboten to even mention the Prague Spring. "My parents were twenty-four in 1968," George says. "They had a chance, a shot, if this thing in 1989 happens in 1968, to have a different life. Unfortunately, it did not." Meanwhile, Jiri Sr. continued collecting his monthly stipend at the factory that sponsored Slavia's soccer, ice hockey, and basketball teams. The athletes were conspicuous in their sharp slacks, dress shirts, ties, and suit coats, and they hauled in as much as four times the amount—roughly the equivalent of a hundred bucks—that the threadbare factory workers collected.

In January 1969, student Jan Palach set himself on fire, to protest the freedom-crushing Communist regime, near the National Museum. He fell in a heap near the majestic Monument of Saint Wenceslas at the south end of the square. Atop a powerful steed whose head points north, the caped and helmeted Wenceslas, chain mail covering the back of his head from ear to ear, holds a narrow flag on a pole in his right hand. His perpetual glance is to the right, or east; a swivel might have been more poetic. Not far from the monument's base a plaque commemorates Palach and Jan Zayic, another student who protested the Soviets by committing suicide via self-immolation.

Eva Zidkova, George's aunt (Czech females add "ova" to their surnames), studied languages at Charles University, the main university in Prague that was established in 1340, where she met Palach. She had been a student leader and suffered a leg injury from the treads of a Soviet T-54 tank during the snuffing of the Prague Spring.

On October 28, 1988, Eva and fifteen-year-old George observed state police—shields down, batons up, saliva dripping off the fangs of riled-up German shepherds—surrounding the Wenceslas monument during a celebration of a pre-war Czechoslovak holiday and the forty-ninth anniversary of the Nazis' killing of nine students. Several thousand demonstrators sang the national anthem and bellowed anti-Communist chants. George laughs about the authorities' desire to protect Wenceslas, as if the students would have damaged such a sacred symbol. Water cannons dispersed the demonstration after an hour, when police screamed through bullhorns that it had turned into an illegal gathering. George supported his gimpy aunt as they hobbled away. "You could feel the oppression, that you had no chance," he says. "You were against the system, but you felt so powerless."

In a classroom of about thirty students at Arabska, an instructor asked for a show of hands from those who hoped to pursue university studies. Half of the pupils responded. And who wanted to consider studying abroad? Zidek's friends sniggered. George, they told her, was thinking about studying abroad. Oh, really? He's thinking of the United States, they giggled. The teacher was not amused. "Not possible!" she responded with cold authority as she stared at Zidek. "Only Moscow!" The two Zidek boys learned any dissent against the government was best voiced, quietly, under their own roof. Their parents made them clearly understand that neighbors were not to be trusted, that StB officials prowled everywhere.

Marie Zidkova, a general physician, was a skinny six-foot athlete, a fine skier and adept on a basketball court. She wanted her two sons to lead exceptional lives so she raised them on additional strict academic regimens in their home, apart from school, that included English and Russian. She demanded excellence. She'd test them often and "slap them around," George says, when they goofed off or did not fare well on an exam. Jan Zidek became a doctor.

Bach, Beethoven, and Mozart—his mother's albums—echoed throughout the wood-floored home that Jiri Sr. built with his own hands. George outgrew his peers and, unsurprisingly because of his genes and father's guidance, started getting a feel for basketball. He joined the popular club team Sparta Praha, with whom he traveled to Italy, Spain, and West Germany. Due to his father's status with the national team, the Zideks were also allowed to vacation in other parts of Western Europe. George immediately noted how Spanish supermarkets were clean and well stocked, how petrol stations offered so much more—snacks, drinks, and household items—than petrol; at home, only petrol could be had at the petrol station.

He was deeply affected by how Italians, and everyone else in those foreign lands, never looked over their shoulders. They were relaxed and outgoing, smiling, and seemingly happy. At home, shopkeepers and attendants were reserved, annoyed at the slightest request, scowling and suspicious of any small talk. Zidek, like his family and teammates, often kept his head down and his mouth shut.

Senior enjoyed fishing, so the family always had a freezer full of pike-perch (or zander) and trout. Fruit consisted of in-season apples and pears. He never saw a banana or orange in his youth. Coca-Cola was available, but expensive. George and his pals considered a bottle of Coke, Sprite, or orange Fanta a rare treat. He ponders his diet then and concludes that it wasn't so bad. "There were no [fast-food] restaurants, junk food, or cheap sodas. We had little variety, ate simple ... but in the end it could have been healthier than most stuff we eat on the go now."

Jan and George grew to truly despise the Communists after a thousand-ton seal cap blew off Reactor 4 at the Chernobyl Nuclear Power Plant, eighty miles north of Kiev, on April 26, 1986. Marie Zidkova had been sunbathing along the Adriatic Sea coast on a three-week holiday. She was diagnosed with cancer two months later. That fall she was pronounced clinically brain dead, and she died after four months on life-support machines.

George and his family firmly believe his mother was one of the many victims of Chernobyl's nuclear fallout, which littered parts of Europe, Asia, and North America. In her critically acclaimed *Voices From Chernobyl*, Svetlana Alexievich reported how, "the Soviet system had taken a poorly designed reactor and then staffed it with a group of incompetents ... [then lied] about the disaster in the most criminal way." Marie had a low immune system, but there was no trace of cancer in her family. George and his family learned about the Chernobyl disaster through an illegal radio broadcast. "It was the worst *fuckeeen* thing that the Communists didn't tell us about it," he says.

> Then it was, "Oh, there was a minor accident in the Soviet Union. Nothing to worry about." The Voice of America talked about this thing happening. "Watch out, the radioactive cloud goes all the way to Sweden." I think that was the worst kind of crime. At home we spoke about how things were bad and what the government had done to the family. At the same time, we never did anything to express ourselves in the open. She would have been scared for me [in November 1989], and maybe that I was wrong for taking part in this ... my future could have been crushed in one demonstration.

Zidek's youth seemed perpetually gray—the sky, the ground, the rows upon rows of five-story buildings along the main thoroughfares of Vinohradska and Sokolska, his mother's death. Coal was used for heat. "You just cannot understand," he says. Now those apartment complexes and shops and restaurants are fudge brown, pea-soup green, or peach. Zidek scans down Vinohradska in April 2013 and acts as if he's viewing the flamboyant pastels of South Beach in Miami. BMWs and

Mercedes-Benzes zip over the cobbles. A man cruises by in a burnt orange Toyota 4Runner, windows down. He whistles along to "Bird Dog" by the Everly Brothers, blaring from his stereo, as if it had just hit the airwaves. He steers with his right hand. He taps the outside of the door with his left hand in time with the tune.

Zidek gazes around and still seems shocked at what has happened to his homeland in the course of his life. His father kept a newspaper from the old days. He gave it to George, who grins at headlines and stories that boast about their excellent political system and how *the Soviet Union, big brother, is taking care of us.* "You read that and can only think, 'Those people were out of their minds,' writing that and reading that," Zidek says. "Things have changed so much. It's really hard to remember and recollect … but I think it just gave me so much more motivation and hunger to succeed, because I felt it was a lifetime chance to go to the United States."

Some aspects of life, perhaps, don't change. When a meteor crashed into Russia in February 2013, many residents had radiation fears. Officials said they had measured radiation levels and determined that all was okay. "But we didn't believe them completely," a college student told a journalist.

The break of Zidek's life occurred when Peter Schultz showed a VHS tape to Jim Harrick. A former lawyer in Bratislava who had escaped the Iron Curtain, via Vienna, in 1974, Schultz settled in Orange County with his wife, Olga, and young daughter. Olga Schultz would not see her mother again. Peter boxed groceries and performed other odd jobs, and he enrolled at Cal State Los Angeles to study accounting. He landed a fine job with the Big Eight accounting firm Arthur Andersen. He set out his own shingle, representing a single client, and became rich through their real estate ventures and other business deals.

An avid basketball fan, Schultz had befriended Jiri Sr. in Czechoslovakia. A friend in Los Angeles knew Harrick and brokered a meeting. Schultz showed Harrick the VHS tape that highlighted Julius Michalik, a supposed seventeen-year-old Czech wunderkind swingman who played for a club team in Brno, a hundred miles southeast of Prague. Schultz's tape showed Brno against Sparta Praha, whose top two centers were saddled with foul trouble. Harrick liked Michalik's skills, but a sixteen-year-old reserve center for Sparta intrigued Harrick. The skinny seven-footer was cloddy and mechanical, even kind of clumsy, but he banged in a few baskets. "Who is he?" Harrick said. Schultz told Harrick, "That's the son of legendary Czechoslovak player Jiri Zidek Sr." Harrick asked Schultz. "Can you get him here?" Schultz smiled and nodded.

Schultz returned to Prague to explore investment opportunities in his newly freed homeland and meet with Jiri to discuss George's future. George had visited Boston College, but that program was too disorganized. When Schultz visited the Zidek household, Jiri warned him that his son had fallen in love. Schultz informed George about UCLA. Wearing tattered Adidas sweat pants that barely covered his knees, George explained that he had a big test coming up ... he had to prepare to get a driver's license ... excuses flowed.

In reality, George did not want to leave Martina, who would become his wife. He did not want to waste any more time visiting another American college. Schultz shifted his tack. "Look, George. You don't have to visit UCLA. But if I were you, they pay for the trip. You go there, take a look. And if you don't like it, go home and forget it." George sips an espresso—he cannot function without a couple of morning super-caffeine jolts whose cups look like upside-down thimbles in his fingertips—outside his favorite café on the corner of Italska and Anglicka. "You have to understand, my hormones were flying high," he says. "My dad had enough. One day he said, 'What are you gonna do, get married at seventeen? What the hell are you thinking? This is stupid!' He saw through it. Peter laughs about it now."

Schultz's challenge inspired Zidek to visit UCLA. Schultz arranged everything. Harrick lieutenants Tony Fuller and Brad Holland accompanied Schultz when he picked up Zidek at LAX. Arrangements were made for Zidek at a hotel on Century Boulevard, but he didn't spend one night there. When Schultz took the trio to his elegant Palos Verdes Estates home with the ocean view, an orange tree in the frontcourt drew Zidek like a magnet. Could I take one home to Martina? Schultz smiled and nodded.

Peter Schultz had done very well. He and Olga had recently moved into the new 6,374-square-foot home, with six bedrooms and five bathrooms, on Paseo Del Mar. Inside the front gate, a Jacuzzi, and lap and swimming pools tempt visitors to the left. Both stories flaunt a brilliant bluff view of the Pacific out back. In a 2013 appraisal, it was valued at more than three and a half million dollars. As Zidek toured the plush home beside Olga Schultz he asked her, *If I go to UCLA could I come here on weekends?* Of course, she said. That's the moment Peter Schultz knew George Zidek would become a Bruin. "He's sold," Schultz whispered to the two UCLA recruiters. "When he starts asking questions like this ... "

The following day, Zidek and Harrick sat for brunch at the Bel Air Sands (now Luxe Sunset Boulevard Hotel), where the Bruins stayed on the eve of home games during Wooden's era. Zidek inhaled two rib-eye steaks. The recruit's bottomless pit of a stomach entertained Harrick, but he also enjoyed George's stylish clothes, sharp intellect, and grasp of English. George felt as if every minute of the trip had been planned, that Fuller and others had gone out of their way to keep him busy, show him the school, and inform him about UCLA's rich hoops history.

"I mean, it was such an accident," George says. "[Sparta vs. Brno] was the only game of the whole series that had been televised, and I got to play. I was sixteen and almost seven feet tall, so I had good potential. Peter came to Prague and told me of UCLA. I decided on Los Angeles because Peter was there. He played a role; if I had not met him, I would not have gone to UCLA. No way."

Zidek returned to UCLA with his life savings of three hundred and fifty dollars and a bicycle. He would never attend a social gathering with teammates or peers. When Rich Herczog, a UCLA official in charge of compliance, met with the basketball players and other Bruins athletes in the fall of 1991 to review the NCAA's litany of rules, Zidek thought, *I am back living under the fuckeeen Communists!*

For his first road trip he wore a pinkish-violet three-piece suit. His teammates thought Zidek had just stepped out of that Steve Martin Wild and Crazy Guy skit in *Saturday Night Live*. They fell off chairs, laughing. "It was the shit!" Zidek says in his staccato Slavic monotone. "It was a customary style for older Czech businessmen. It was completely unbelievable for the States. The guys asked if I was gay. I only wore it once."

He felt as dispensable as that suit as a freshman and sophomore, when he did not register a combined three hundred minutes of floor time. But teammate and fellow Czech native Richard Petruska and he did meet Vaclav Havel, the dissident who had spent much time in jail after the Prague Spring, when the first president of the Czech Republic visited UCLA to give a speech in November 1991. In their powder blue cotton sweats and long-sleeve sweatshirts, Zidek and Petruska towered over Havel as they shook his hand on a podium. Zidek says, *"Nervous?* "Of course!"

184

In flight to a summer tour of Italy in 1992, Shon Tarver stopped in the aisle at Zidek's seat and playfully pulled at his headphones. Tarver curdled when he heard "The Well-Tempered Clavier" by Johann Sebastian Bach. Thinking of his mother, Zidek smiled. He enlightened his teammates that the ornate St. Peter's Basilica in Vatican City is the grandest example of Renaissance architecture. He called attention to a bronze door by Antonio Averulino, Michalengelo's marble Pieta, the Chapel of the Sacrament by Bernini, and an equestrian statue of Charlemagne by Comacchini. Jim Harrick had no idea he had recruited an expert European museum tour guide.

Zidek mostly spent those first few seasons as the butt of Don MacLean's unmerciful athlete's-foot jokes. He had some initial reservations in the classroom, since English wasn't his main language. "As far as school, I was so nervous going to my first lecture. I thought, 'Shit, am I going to understand what the professor is talking about?' " That first class was computer science, administered by an Asian-American woman in an auditorium that accommodated more than two hundred students. Zidek comprehended maybe every third word, relying on the chalkboard for notes and direction. He relaxed as he discovered that he had already learned most of those lessons at Arabska.

His heart panged for home, and Martina. He'd count the days until he'd see her again. They exchanged frequent letters, because of the exorbitant cost of long-distance calls. When UCLA returned to LAX from a trip to the East Coast, where the Bruins played Indiana in Springfield, Massachusetts, coaches were stunned to see Martina—her flight from Prague having landed at the same time—in the baggage-claim area. George slept on the floor of his dorm room as Martina snoozed in his bunk. Coaches stayed mum. Martina would babysit to earn spending money during her visits.

The summer between his sophomore and junior years Zidek considered getting a one-way ticket back to Prague. He had not developed on the court. His father was coaching in Europe and knew the owner of a professional club in Finland who was starting to throw some serious money at promising players. Jiri Sr. believed his son could get a spot on that team and begin earning a good living.

Jim Harrick had not been thrilled with his Sparta project, either. Harrick had referred to Zidek as *a lummox*, said he "couldn't walk and chew gum" when he first showed up. He questioned if Zidek could become a dependable player. At a junior international tournament in Canada, Harrick served on the staff of the US team. Zidek played for the Czech Republic and all but tripped over himself. Mark Gottfried's father Joe asked Harrick about Zidek. "What about George?" Harrick sarcastically quipped. "He was *awwwwwwwful*! He's *nevvvvvver* gonna help us play!" The elder Gottfried teases Harrick with those fateful words to this day.

Later in the summer of 1993, Mark Gottfried and Lorenzo Romar, and roommate Tyus Edney, all convinced Zidek to stay at UCLA, that it was common for a player to bide his time, learn the system, and hit the weights, in order to become productive as an upperclassman. With renewed confidence, George attacked workouts. Most days he met reserve center Ike Nwankwo before 7 A.M. at the Wooden Center or Pauley, for sessions that pressed and prodded both big men. They warmed up for twenty minutes. They'd go at each other for fifty or fifty-five minutes. "A battlefield," Zidek says. "Physical hell. We crushed each other, but never any cheap shots. What better way to start the day?" Nwankwo never backed down because he wanted to prove he deserved to play, too. Nwankwo forced Zidek to hone those ambidextrous hook shots that he would unveil against Kentucky.

Moreover, Malek Abdul-Mansour—who went by Fred Warren when he attended UCLA, and had pushed friends Lew Alcindor and Marques Johnson in individual workouts—often ran Nwankwo and Zidek through a program of demanding drills. Zidek often stayed after practice, too, for further personal instruction from Romar or Gottfried. They all watched Zidek begin to blossom in 1993-94, when he averaged more than eleven points and seven rebounds, and almost twenty-five minutes per game. He made more than half of his shot attempts. He was dependable at the free-throw line. "It was unexpected of me to play," Zidek says.

> It was a pleasant surprise to everyone, including me. It was starting to be expected that I'd be a factor. The tall guy with the funny accent on UCLA's bench was getting notoriety. I started to feel the pressure of unexpected performances [becoming expected], and I did not want to let my teammates or coaches down. And I didn't want to let any chance slip between my fingers.

If he worked out for six hours today, he'd put in seven tomorrow, then eight the following day. Tony Luftman would rebound for Zidek as he jacked twenty-foot jumpers—from a baseline corner, to the wing, to the top of the key, to the other wing, to the other baseline corner … and back—in relentless succession. Those were shots he'd never take in games, but Luftman was impressed by the big man's long-range accuracy and that he moved at full speed in the middle of the summer.

Zidek would work odd jobs in scant spare time. On Christmas Days, when nobody wanted to sweat, Zidek would put in four hours cutting grass or washing the windows of some building, sometimes the B.O. Barn, on campus in the glorious warmth. It paid him eight or nine dollars an hour at a time when his father was making about a buck an hour coaching in Prague. Zidek saved every penny, eventually sending nearly two thousand dollars to his brother for their first real-estate venture.

His constant need to work out, to improve, drove Zidek batty. He slept less than two hours a night. The malady would stick with him the rest of his life. Tests at UCLA Medical Center only gave him a prescription for sleeping pills that worked only for a short spell, until his system became accustomed to the medication. He was about to be part of a three-pronged senior nucleus for a team expected to contend for a national championship. He had one amateur season left to prove he might belong in the NBA. "I came from a country where people could not play professional sports," Zidek says.

> Nobody could tell me, "You'll be a professional basketball player," because it did not exist. When I did have it in my head, it was somewhat difficult. I focused on it so much; it only led to over-training. Communism was my biggest advantage. I appreciated things because I had it very tough when I was growing up. I knew what it was to be oppressed. I really wanted, badly, the freedom. I earned it when I was sixteen. I didn't grow up in some rich country, where I wouldn't be so hungry. It gave me a hunger, a work ethic.

Zidek shakes his head as we wend over more cobbles, past countless red Coca-Cola signs and billboards. The symbol of the American Dream and global imperialism and excessive marketing for a universal panacea, according to author Marcus Gray, is plastered all over Prague as if it pummeled Pepsi in a landslide city election. Zidek's refrigerator in his rural home on the Western edge of the city, on an unlit narrow gravel road, contains those red cans with the familiar white-script lettering. He avoids relating to his three kids how the product was considered extravagant in his youth, possibly because drifting back to that era would lead to other realities, all of which would only make six eyes roll.

We pass a tiny, narrow L-shaped Levi's store that offers a pair of jeans for the equivalent of one hundred and twenty US dollars, to the Old Town, Zidek's favorite section of the city. He enjoys strolling through here in late January, after the vacationing Russians have departed. It's quiet. The snow-draped Prague Castle looks like a fantasy. Next to Martina, he shows his children the Italian restaurant where he began wooing their mother and first kissed her.

Peter Schultz is immensely proud of George, who thought Schultz was hurt that he did not establish roots and raise his family in Southern California when his professional career ended. Ridiculous, Schultz finally told George. "It's a free country. You can do whatever you want."

Chapter 10

THE FIRST TWENTY MINUTES in Eugene should have left every UCLA basketball fan drenched in a cold sweat. The Bruins were dominating, on paper, which didn't translate to the scoreboard as the visitors only led by four.

That happens frequently on McArthur Court, the venerable building on 1801 University Street that had been built in the mid-1920s. The facades of Mac Court's two top tiers only seemed to hover directly over the benches. Cheers and jeers rained down upon the participants in the tight quarters. Since top-ranked North Carolina had lost the previous day, a couple of victories in Oregon would give the second-rated Bruins the top spot in the AP poll come Monday.

The Bruins, however, were in trouble at the intermission. They had made fifty-four percent of their shots; the Ducks had only connected at a thirty-one-percent clip. But Oregon was onerous on its own wood, in its own madhouse. It needed to be, because UCLA built a 56-43 lead in the first five minutes of the second half. But it was fools' gold. The Ducks, bolstered by more than ten thousand raucous fans that registered the program's first sellout in five years, took ten minutes to eke back into it and led, 68-67. After a timeout, Tyus Edney slipped inside to gather an inbounds pass under his own basket. His layup gave UCLA the lead with about five minutes left, but the Bruins would not sink another field goal. Sophomore guard Kenya Wilkins sailed inside

190

for a scoop shot twenty seconds later, and the Ducks poured it on to win by ten points.

The ignominy of the defeat arrived with thirty-seven seconds left, when Edney was whistled for a traveling violation on the right wing, in front of the UCLA bench. A spring-loaded Jim Harrick flipped out. He hounded official Steve Wilson, who had called the foul on Edney. Lorenzo Romar and Mark Gottfried and Steve Lavin could not have possibly formed a barricade to defend Harrick against himself. Wilson immediately blew his whistle at Harrick and formed a T with his hands—technical foul. Nothing could have stirred the locals into a more frenetic state, except maybe another technical. Harrick didn't let them down. Wilson charged to the official scorer's table to report the initial offense and technical. Harrick, yapping all the way, charged after Wilson. Catering to the rabid fans, Wilson hit a zombie-eyed Harrick with another technical foul, earning Harrick an ejection and police escort from the premises.

Senior guard Orlando Williams sank all four free throws (each technical warranted a pair), and Oregon retained possession of the ball, turning it into another free throw. Six-foot-nine Ducks senior Jeff Potter would crow that the technicals and ensuing free throws didn't matter, that Oregon had UCLA whipped.

The Ducks rubbed it into the nose of the UCLA leader, to boot, at the end. Perhaps fed by the deranged decibel level, Oregon senior forward Darryl Parker sliced in for a right-handed jam to finish a fast break and then pointed at Ed O'Bannon, taunting the safety valve of the UCLA defense. Parker was called for a technical foul. O'Bannon thought, *Why are you pointing at me? Got something against me, or the uniform? Do you hate us cuz you ain't us? What does that mean, you pointing at me after you dunk the ball?* O'Bannon says today, "High school shit, quite honestly."

The scoreboard read 82-72 seconds later when the final buzzer blared. The wild crowd tidal waved onto the court after its team's ninth victory in ten games. A sea of screaming maniacs engulfed UCLA players. The green mob ruled. Ed O'Bannon feared that tiny Tyus Edney would be knocked around. He was. "Cheap shots," Edney said. O'Bannon had never been more enflamed leaving a basketball court, and afterward he said, "They need to celebrate something; they didn't win the Rose Bowl." Three days earlier, Oregon's football team had lost to Penn State, 38-20, in the Rose Bowl in Pasadena, California, the Ducks' first appearance in the Granddaddy of all bowl games since 1958.

Jim Harrick hadn't exactly followed the script of the seventy-one-page manifesto—*discipline, self-control, poise*—he would pen as he reacted to Steve Wilson's calls. An intrepid writer asked Harrick if he had sought those two technicals *on purpose*, as if that, too, might be a wrinkle somewhere in his Guidelines.

Tim Kawakami somewhat blistered Harrick in a feature that ran in the *Los Angeles Times* two days later, the Saturday of the Oregon State game in Corvallis, Oregon. *As is his custom, and curse, Jim Harrick has given life once again to all of the niggling, nagging doubts ... his career continues to be dotted with odd and disturbing moments of disarray.* Was Harrick's meltdown yet another indication of someone *who sometimes gets lost in the habitual chaos of pressure-cooker basketball*, and was his players' *disjointed performance down the stretch ... reflective of [their] coach?*

Kawakami included a qualifier; *A little warily, but to his credit ... without much posturing* Harrick [on Friday] answered more questions about the game, and *with some justification he argues that it is patently unfair to draw conclusions about his mental discipline or that of his team—or the future of his program—from random scenes in a long career.*

The piece perhaps flirted with the fine line between reporting a story and dispensing opinion—even antagonism—something normally reserved for a columnist. But the paper had not sent one to Oregon, so Kawakami wearing two hats in that situation was understandable. He certainly knew how to push buttons, as did Harrick. But Kawakami also possessed tact. Moreover, the game had not been televised to Los Angeles; only bars with appropriate satellite transponders picked up the local Eugene TV feed. UCLA's first defeat of the season had been rich theater for anyone chronicling it.

Nearly twenty years later, however, Kawakami reveals the trigger to that follow-up piece—a Friday morning call in which his boss, *Los Angeles Times* sports editor Bill Dwyre, instructed Kawakami in no uncertain terms that he had the ability to suggest, in print, that Harrick's actions in Eugene were fireable offenses. Kawakami took Harrick to task, for sure, but he tempered the tone and was utterly fair in assessing blame for UCLA's first loss, and in allowing Harrick his review of the events. Kawakami says Dwyre wasn't so thrilled that he had spared the rod.

Harrick had known Steve Wilson for twenty years and said he had never seen Wilson call a technical foul. Harrick claimed during the 1988-89 season he watched another coach walk from his bench to the other foul line and call Wilson the "worst names I'd ever heard in my life" ... and Wilson did not slap a technical foul on that coach. "But I take full responsibility ... whether it cost us the game or not, you'll never know. Pure speculation." Harrick did not appreciate the gray area of the follow-up piece. "Ostensibly a news report, but it has much more commentary [than] reportage," Harrick wrote in *Embracing the Legend*. "It was beginning to look like another season of serious scrutiny."

If not for the judicious approach of a writer for one of the nation's largest newspapers, however, it could have been far more scathing.

Sally Harrick would have some choice words for her husband—she had lived through all those episodes at Pepperdine and the constant criticism in Westwood that her husband certainly did not need to fan—as would Pete Dalis. Harrick expected both. He admitted having acted out of line when he wrote, "You don't want to let those things happen. But getting a technical at UCLA seems to generate a lot more heat than I see happen to coaches at other places. Maybe that's because Coach Wooden never got any … [but] I felt the resulting attention and inferences made about me were out of proportion. Suddenly, I was a coach whose ability was suspect again. It's always somethin'."

At UCLA, it always reverts back to John Wooden.

In reality, with the number one position in the AP poll waiting for them, Ed O'Bannon and the Bruins had been kind of full of themselves. Such a ranking meant absolutely nothing, and he and his veteran teammates had experienced the false sense of security and value attached to such attention, yet they still yearned for it. When they landed on that slippery slope in the second half against the Ducks, in the crucible of an arena locals called The Pit, they couldn't think straight and dropped to 6-1.

O'Bannon boiled inside the tiny visitors' locker room. He had his lines all prepared before a swarm of media. *Not only are we gonna beat Oregon when we see them next, but if we don't beat them by twenty points you can count it as a loss!* He was going to give it to those Ducks, ensuring that everyone within the Eugene city limits would know of his decree and about imminent reciprocation, to hell with jinxes or bulletin-board karma.

Ed O'Bannon played it out and, leaning toward discretion, believed Jim Harrick would not have appreciated how those comments would look in ink and how Southern California media would have skewered him and his words. "But that's how I felt," O'Bannon says today. "They stormed the court after they won. Obviously, it was a big game for them and their program, their school. I was just so upset after that loss. Those words were on the tip of my tongue. I wish I had said it, as a psychological thing to tell them ... to ensure that it would be on their chalkboard before that [next] game [at UCLA]. I wanted them to know that we expected to blow them out next time.

"But I didn't."

Chapter 11

PUBLICLY, JIM HARRICK spoke about the events that led to his guys absorbing their first loss late that Thursday night in Eugene, even into the following day, with reporters. Dealing with the media earned him part of his paycheck.

Privately, his assistants rarely saw fourth-estate issues distract, perturb, or upset Harrick. Peripheral drama did not connect with him, by design. All that was fodder to Harrick. His lieutenants marveled at Harrick's ability to parry such superfluous appraisals and reviews. Harrick exulted in victory just as infrequently. "He just stays the course," Mark Gottfried says. Harrick always invited input from his assistants, and he'd just as frequently wind up telling them, "Holy *Ca-norrrrr-si*, you guys think you know *evvvvv-reeeee-thangggg* about coaching. Wait til you get your own team one day."

The deputies had all learned from Harrick. They saw him deal with the media as easily as if he switched a water spigot on and off, although they did hold their breaths on occasion. In the aftermath of the late fade at Oregon, after his accusers were finished, it was all about his players, his assistants, and plans for Oregon State. Those assistants saw a laser focus. "The Ducks played out of their minds. Unbelievable. It happens," Gottfried says.

You learn from it and move on. He didn't go crazy about it. He told me after that ["Always a Question"] article ... actually, he always said, "I'm never gonna let these [media] people get to me, never gonna let these people get to me. I'm gonna beat them. I'm gonna win." I tried to encourage him to leave a couple of times; Tennessee was one, Ohio State another. I said, "Jim, you need to go." I didn't think Pete was very supportive. "The wind is not at your back here," I'd tell Jim. He would always say, "I'm *noooooot* gonna let them run me outta town. Not gonna do it." He had an even keel. Just coached his team. Amazing. With all that, he never had the real support inside [in administration]. Never.

Harrick reviewed his squad after Eugene and tweaked the rotation. Cameron Dollar had attempted only one shot, a three-pointer, against Oregon. He missed it. In seventeen minutes, he hadn't recorded an assist. He turned it over three times. J.R. Henderson had come off the bench to spell Dollar, and he scored five points and grabbed five boards. Henderson had also turned the ball over four times. But for rebounding purposes, and to confuse opponents into their own matchup and switching snafus, Harrick put the six-nine Henderson into the starting fold in place of the six-foot Dollar against Oregon State. Harrick abhorred the way his squad had been pushed around under the glass in Eugene.

Toby Bailey would not take kindly to the switch.

Late the morning of Saturday, January 8, Harrick informed Henderson that he'd be starting for the first time. Henderson nodded. Barely. If Harrick never allowed anything written or said by the media to affect him in any manner, Henderson followed that line about life itself. The sole emotion that seeped out of Henderson on a basketball court was a pouting tendency, which did not endear him to some collegiate coaches, recruiters, professional scouts, and fans; he would still display that trait in Japan in 2013.

Harrick asked Henderson about shadowing Brent Barry, a savvy six-six senior who was Oregon State's best shooter and among the league's top-ten returning scorers. Barry had just torched USC for thirty points in an overtime victory in Corvallis as UCLA came unglued at the end against Oregon an hour's drive south in Eugene.

"Can you guard that guy?"

"Coach, I can guard anyone."

"Okay, pal. He's all yours."

Switching Henderson for Dollar empowered the UCLA starting lineup as each of the Bruins' first five registered double digits in points for the first time all season in Corvallis. Trailing by six at the half, the Bruins became physical in the second and made seventeen of twenty-one free throws. The Beavers went to the line only four times, missing all of them. And UCLA shot seventy-one percent from the field, marksmanship it severely required because OSU hit fifty-seven percent of its shots, Only one other Bruins opponent, a most memorable one, would connect on at least half of its attempts the rest of the season. It had been a strong bounce-back from the events in Eugene. Henderson tallied sixteen points, the most he had rang up in a UCLA uniform. That effectively neutralized Barry, who went for seventeen. Six-seven senior Mustapha Hoff led everyone with thirty-one points, but the Bruins had shared the sugar, as Steve Lavin liked to say. UCLA also beat Oregon State decisively on the boards.

All of which masked the turning point. UCLA held only a two-point edge with two minutes left. Harrick had J.R. Henderson and Toby Bailey on the court. Charles O'Bannon and Cameron Dollar were on the bench, and neither was in foul trouble. Edney snaked into the lane to feed Bailey for an easy layup, serving as the catalyst to UCLA tallying ten of the final twelve points. Edney sank six free throws, and Henderson drained two with twenty-three seconds left to seal the 87-78 victory.

The Bruins returned to Los Angeles relieved to have been inflicted with only one loss in Oregon. After a practice, a clump of players hiked up two long sets of concrete stairs to the Treehouse, the area of the Ackerman Student Union where a host of culinary options awaited UCLA students and staff, as did what looked like half of the Bruins football team. The large open eating area featured a large-screen television set. It was nearing the appointed hour.

Another session of *Jeopardy!* was about to commence, six-foot-eleven sophomore Ike Nwankwo against any footballer. World capitals for five hundred, Alex. Fruit or Vegetable, for a thousand. The game show separated the room, several hoopsters on this side, a few more footballers over there. It was all in fun, but there was always heat. Players settled in as fans with Styrofoam containers of orange chicken, Mongolian beef, and a heap of fried rice or chow mein from Panda Express, smoothies from Tropix, sandwiches or burgers, and French fries. Ed O'Bannon savors fries the way some connoisseurs delight over Almas beluga caviar or a 1966 Dom Perignon Oenotheque.

O'Bannon was also Nwankwo's loudest cheerleader and the football team's greatest Treehouse nemesis. Ikenna Chukuemeka Nwankwo was quick and clever, with a biting sense of humor. His parents were from Nigeria, and he had four siblings. Nwankwo often told teammates he hailed from the tough Fifth Ward section of Houston. They laughed. They knew his family resided in a stylish upper-middle-class suburb. Before his junior year at

Cypress Creek High School—about fifteen miles northwest of the Fifth Ward—the right-handed post player severed the ulnar nerve in his left arm when it slipped, slicing through the glass, as he opened a pane on a sweltering day. He disliked talking about the injury and avoided it at all costs.

Decades later, Nwankwo runs a popular youth basketball academy in Bangkok. Kids flock to him, and the silver whistle his Hungarian girlfriend Agnes Nemethi gave him as a present dangles from a powder blue UCLA lanyard. He has no sensation in the two outside fingers of his left hand and he can't straighten the others. After learning about the injury UCLA and Indiana continued recruiting Nwankwo, but Duke, Georgetown, Kentucky, Michigan, and Syracuse all stopped calling. His long overseas career lends an indomitable hue to Nwankwo's desire and diligence. He peeks at his left arm, and says, "I'm finally at peace with it."

Nwankwo was in his element in the Treehouse. Copper ... What is the Statue of Liberty made of? To the living we owe respect ... Who is Voltaire? Ed O'Bannon always believed that was a show for nerds. He couldn't get into it, until he traipsed up there one day with Ike and came away impressed by the depth of his acuity. First person to win an Emmy, Grammy, Oscar, and Tony. Who is Richard Rodgers? His basketball teammates gawped at Ike. He could holler the questions before teammates were finished reading the answers. Ed led furious charges— standing and pointing, with crazy eyes—at the football players. *Take THAT! Yeah, Ike!* O'Bannon howled as he high-fived his teammates. *Give it to 'em!* Those sessions always ended with the football players capitulating, dispersing, bowing their heads, and filing out to study hall or night classes. All of those challengers left vanquished. Nwankwo never lost.

He dropped the most sweat in the packed living area of his dorm suite, evenly divided between the two sides for a titanic showdown. In the other corner stood Jonathan Ogden, the outstanding six-nine, 340-pound junior left tackle whose bust would adorn both the college and professional football halls of fame. Twenty minutes into the half-hour show, Nwankwo grabbed control when the answer related to seismic activity. Ogden blurted, *What is plate tectonics?* Wrong. Nwankwo correctly posed a question about continental shift. Once again, Ike was victorious. "Hero for the night," he says. Years later O'Bannon beams about regularly trying to catch *Jeopardy!* and always thinking of Nwankwo.

Maybe those game-show battles had worn out the basketball players, because they sleepwalked through the first half of a weeknight matchup against Washington inside Pauley Pavilion.

Tyus Edney ran the new-look starting quintet, with three forwards (the O'Bannons, and J.R. Henderson) and George Zidek at center. In only his second season coaching the Huskies, Bob Bender was not completely responsible for the UW roster. For a newish coach that is a critical justification, a priceless fallback if the first few seasons don't go well. Just wait, such coaches can tell superiors, till I'm responsible for every player in the program. If his bosses aren't receptive, or pressures real and imagined keep him up at night, the end of a coach's run will appear in the headlights. Jim Harrick's five predecessors were familiar with such scenarios.

About four minutes into the second half, the Bruins ran away from the Huskies by rattling off thirteen consecutive points, ignited by Charles O'Bannon's bullet pass inside to Ed O'Bannon for an easy layup. Pauley was a couple thousand shy of a sellout, but it sounded like a full house. The faithful began stomping and clapping and yelling for the Bruins during their roll. Every player heard the racket. Seven days earlier, it had fueled a dismal finish in Eugene. Now the noise implored them. UCLA sailed to the finish of a 75-57 victory, improving to 8-1 overall and 2-1 in the Pac-10. "When you're on the road and that happens, you hear it and feel it," Ed O'Bannon told reporters of the commotion. "It makes the [home] team get going. It was a nice change to hear it here. I appreciate it, that's for sure."

Washington made only one of its twenty-two attempts from beyond the three-point arc, establishing a program record for long-range futility. Bender admitted that his guys got impatient, for which the Bruins punished the Huskies by turning their quick, off-target shots into running opportunities. When the footrace started, the visitors could not keep pace. The O'Bannons combined for thirty-three points and nineteen rebounds. Tyus Edney continued a strong pattern with fourteen points. He had tallied 103 in a five-game skein in which he had shot better than sixty percent from the field.

Edney was feeling very good. Less than forty-eight hours later against Washington State, the five-nine sparkplug turned a mundane afternoon into a gilded memory by converting his first dunk as a collegiate player. Charles O'Bannon had slapped the ball out of Isaac Fontaine's grasp and rifled it to Edney. A dribble later, he scaled high on the right side to slam it through the rim with his right hand. "A statement," said center George Zidek. "He's a big fellah now. He's not five-ten now, he's six-ten." (UCLA provided Edney with an extra inch in the program, which teammates promoted.) Charles O'Bannon had never seen his longtime friend dunk a ball. Ed O'Bannon vaguely recalled one in a Wooden Center pick-up game and said, "Everybody kind of stopped and said, 'Where did that come from?' " Edney vividly remembered missing one his freshman year. "I've wanted another chance," he said. "I knew I was up there, so I dunked."

The exclamation point occurred with eleven minutes, fifty-eight seconds remaining. It pumped UCLA's lead to thirty points and ignited a thunderous response from the crowd of 10,632. The audience roared again six seconds later when Jim Harrick took Edney out, allowing him to bow to his adoring fans. Washington State cut its deficit to 91-78 by the final buzzer because of Harrick's mass substitutions.

UCLA capitalized on a weakened WSU squad, since coach Kevin Eastman had suspended starting point guard Dominic Ellison and forward Taveras Mack for missing curfew Thursday night after playing USC. It also represented Harrick's two hundredth game as UCLA's coach. Only Walt Hazzard, of Wooden's five previous successors, had registered triple figures (with 124) in games. However, it was no time for Harrick to celebrate. Not with a trip to Arizona on the docket.

Chapter 12

LUTE OLSON HAD BEEN DUBBED Midnight Lute by Jerry Tarkanian, because of Olson's penchant for purloining commitments from top-notch schoolboys when it appeared they were definitely, most certainly, undoubtedly headed elsewhere. As if, within a minute of the start of commitment period, a kid would realize, with total clarity, that he had to be in Tucson, stunning "expert insiders" from coast to coast. Others called the Arizona coach the Silver Fox for his lustrous locks and the stealth with which he operated.

Olson likely had a few other names for Tarkanian when the Shark brought his UNLV team to Tucson for the opening of the 1991 NCAAs. Arizona had a jumbo leather basketball on display in the foyer of its locker room that each Wildcat traditionally patted before dashing out to the McKale Center court. The Rebels were given Arizona's locker room for the tournament. Of course, being Rebels, every one of them autographed the historic ball in ink, ruining it and the tradition, before a second rounder against Georgetown. If not for a slight twist in his plans, Ed O'Bannon's name would have been scrawled on that ball.

After four seasons at Long Beach City College, Olson replaced Tarkanian at Long Beach State in 1973 and went 24-2. That led him to Iowa, where he shaped the downtrodden program for four seasons. The Hawkeyes then played in five consecutive NCAAs. Olson jumped to the University of Arizona in 1983, and the payoff arrived much quicker. After a mediocre season, the Wildcats went to twenty-three consecutive NCAA Tournaments before Olson retired in 2007, five years after he was inducted into the Naismith Basketball Hall of Fame. In 2001, in tribute to the passing of his wife, the McKale floor was christened the Lute and Bobbi Olson Court. Lute left the profession having won forty-six NCAA games, one fewer than John Wooden.

Some didn't consider Olson such an endearing figure. Kevin Dempsey, the UCLA junior from San Jose, California, averaged more than twenty-six points his final prep season. He was rated the 112th-best senior in the country by one scouting service. Dempsey would one day execute a runaway dunk in a big victory over Arizona and all but flip off Midnight Lute, whom Dempsey had charged with reneging on a scholarship offer. Dempsey told the *Daily Bruin*, "I hate the man ... a low-class individual."

On Thursday night, January 19, UCLA cruised into McKale and the Bruins were not thinking about vandalism or disdain. Concentrating on anything other than hoops would have played into a rabid crowd of nearly fifteen thousand and Olson's considerable tactics. The eight Pac-10 programs outside Arizona—Washington and Washington State, Oregon and Oregon State, Cal and Stanford, and UCLA and USC—could not expect to have success upon visiting the Grand Canyon State. They had combined to make eighty-eight such trips with Olson running Arizona, and only six swooped in to defeat the Wildcats and Sun Devils on the same jaunt. Three of those sweeps belonged to UCLA. Jim Harrick had been irked to learn that Olson had said the Bruins couldn't do it on this journey.

Odds were in Olson's favor. Arizona was coming off a Final Four season in which it had dropped a national semifinal to eventual titlist Arkansas. The Wildcats went into the UCLA game having won 112 of their past 115 games in McKale. Many years later, Ed O'Bannon sat with two of his three children in the living room of their comfortable home in Henderson, Nevada, and a game from McKale aired on their big flat screen. Ed smiled when the intensity of the Arizona fans shocked his kids. He casually mentioned that he had played on that floor. Jazmin and Edward III focused their bugged-out eyes on their old man. "One of the most difficult buildings I ever played in," he told them.

"Really? You played there?"

"Yeah. That place is crazy. They all scream at you."

That Thursday night in early 1995, Harrick and fourth-ranked UCLA fine-tuned their calibrations to hush that crowd in an 81-71 victory in which the eleventh-ranked Wildcats never owned the lead in the second half and fell to 12-4. The only other double-digit defeat Olson suffered at home had come in his first season in Tucson, against Tennessee. Tied 26-26 out of the final TV timeout of the first half, the Bruins blitzed their foes by scoring the final nine points of the opening twenty minutes. That Toby Bailey figured into the roll showed the power of John Wooden's words. As Tyus Edney strolled to the foul line, Ed O'Bannon pulled out his mouthguard, threw a fist into the air, and yelled, "Yeah, baby! Yeah! Yeah!" Grinning courtside, Marques Johnson noted the phrase.

UCLA thwarted anything Arizona tried to muster in the second half, and the Wildcats connected on less than forty percent of their shots. Early in the last half, Ed O'Bannon fouled Ben Davis under Arizona's basket—no dunks, no layups, no prisoners—and immediately called his four teammates into a motivational huddle to reinforce not letting down, not giving an inch. No matter the score. He did it two more times. He was taking over in a very vocal, public manner.

Damon Stoudamire only went six-for-twenty-one from the field, a golden tribute to the viscid defense of Tyus Edney. Bailey and Cameron Dollar also helped out on Stoudamire, who found Ed O'Bannon on patrol if he did sneak by the first or second lines of defense. "They just flat-out beat us," Stoudamire told reporters. Unlike O'Bannon in Oregon, though, the salty Stoudamire's savoir faire would escape him after this one. Ed O'Bannon led everyone with twenty-one points and eleven rebounds. Edney delivered nineteen points, and his nine rebounds again belied his stature. The guy who raised Harrick's eyebrow, however, had been Toby Bailey, with nine points and twelve boards in twenty-three minutes. He had started the second half in place of J.R. Henderson, who missed all four shots he attempted in twelve minutes of action.

For twelve years, Tennessee had owned the biggest victory over a Lute Olson team in Tucson, at twelve points. The Bruins didn't match that, but they did join Tennessee in getting a double-figure win at McKale thanks to the cold-bloodedness that was empowering Ed O'Bannon. Reggie Geary had yanked a teammate's air ball and tossed it into the rim to get Arizona to within 69-61 with one point four ticks remaining. Except for Ed and Charles, everyone else on the court slumped his shoulders, angled toward his bench, or rejoiced. Game over. The Wildcats were humiliated. Their fans had long ago filed for the exits. Ed nonchalantly let the ball slip through the net and into his mitts. A rule started the previous season that stopped the clock on a made basket inside the final minute. Ed inched out of bounds and gazed down the court. He and Charles, at the center circle, glanced at each other. Ed slightly nodded at his younger brother.

Charles casually skipped behind everyone. He bolted for the rim. Ed lofted a seventy-foot changeup at Charles, who let it bounce. He grabbed it in stride and tossed down an emphatic dunk a tenth of a second before the blare of the final buzzer for the ten-point edge. Ed had thoroughly enjoyed hushing the crowd of 14,257. "I've never heard it that quiet. Our objective going in was more or less to keep the noise to a minimum." As Harrick left the floor, a fan derisively yelled, *Thanks for making it interesting again!* As if, finally, someone had the talent and temerity to give Arizona a good run on its own wood. Harrick didn't let the comment pass without notice. He sighed at the fan, waved his rolled-up program at him, and quipped, "Oh, you can afford it!"

Arizona had stockpiled pantries of goodwill at home, and its run to the Final Four—with sharp-shooting senior guard Khalid Reeves—the previous season had been impressive. But it had bowed out of the first round of the NCAAs in 1992 and 1993, as a three seed (to fourteenth-seeded East Tennessee State) and a two seed (to fifteenth-seeded Santa Clara), respectively, prompting some local levity ... *been to the new bar in town, Lute's Place? One round and you're done.*

In the afterglow of the impressive victory, Bill Bennett called for Ed O'Bannon to join Tyus Edney for an interview on the national television broadcast. As soon as the red light blared on the camera, O'Bannon, hands behind his back, slinked a half step to the right and out of the picture. He strolled back to UCLA's locker room. Ed believed Edney deserved every watt of that spotlight.

Harrick pored over the stats and the tape, and discussed Bailey's role on the team with his assistants. On the dry erase board in the UCLA locker room after the Bruins had improved to 10-1, the team's intentions were clarified in blue magic marker— *We came to win 2.*

Up Interstate 10 in Tempe, a gambler awaited UCLA. Sun Devils coach Bill Frieder was the colorful Division-I hoops character in the state, the guy with the unkempt gray mop who so perfectly played off the dry Lute Olson—whose glorious locks were always combed to the side *just right*—in a series of popular TV commercials to promote a state bank. Frieder was an ace card counter and admitted that his name was in several black books, barring him from casinos, in Reno and Las Vegas. "If you're just lucky, they tolerate it because they know they'll get you later," he said in 1987. "If you're cheating, they'll catch you and arrest you. But if you count cards, they'll eventually bar you."

I once happened by a Las Vegas blackjack table on which Frieder sat at the far left. To his right sat Steve Fisher, who had famously taken over for Frieder at the University of Michigan before the 1989 NCAAs. Ticked that Frieder had already accepted the ASU post, Wolverines athletic director Bo Schembechler had wanted *a Michigan man* to coach Michigan. (Frieder had graduated from UM in 1964 and earned a master's degree in business administration from the institution, but he was officially an ASU man, in Schembechler's view, the moment he signed the deal with the Devils.) Fisher guided UM to six consecutive victories, capped by an overtime victory over Seton Hall in the NCAA finale at the Kingdome in Seattle.

Fisher played blackjack for the table minimum, three bucks. He fumbled with his chips and looked like he wanted to chew his fingernails as the dealer flipped the cards, the natural rouge in his cheekbones flaring. Normally frenetic and fueled by cases of Coke and Pepsi, Frieder stomped sidelines with a towel over a shoulder. He thrived with numerals. He did very well in the stock market, real estate, and ponies.

Frieder played more than thirty times Fisher's wager per blackjack hand, but Frieder was calm and patient, his Deep Blue brain calculating the cards that had been played and the odds of what was likely coming up. He once played between two recruits. NCAA rules forbade him from talking with them, so Frieder communicated via the dealer, whom he told, "Now, I can't talk to them but I want you to know that I'm going to recruit the heck out of those two and I'm not going to stop until I get them." The players laughed and high-fived each other behind Frieder's back;

he got Richard Rellford and Butch Wade. Frieder, as usual, won at that table. "That impressed them, too," he said.

Bill Frieder and Lute Olson also counted thoroughbreds as a common interest, joining Jerry Tarkanian, Pete Newell, Pat Riley, Rick Pitino, Bob Boyd, Henry Bibby, and Dan Issel as former collegiate or professional players or coaches who could talk equine with any jockey, trainer, or owner in the country. (Olson and Tarkanian couldn't exactly be bitter enemies with horses as a mutual hobby.) Many of them met regularly at the short Del Mar meet, where the turf meets the surf north of San Diego, every August.

Over the course of an ASU tenure that would cover eight seasons, this thirteenth-ranked squad would be Frider's finest. It featured the athletic Mario Bennett in the middle, and Ron Riley, James Bacon, Isaac Burton, and Marcell Capers. The Sun Devils were 13-3. They had defeated all five ranked teams they had played so far, which included Michigan and Maryland en route to the Maui Invitational championship in Hawaii.

Frieder jiggered with the probabilities and percentages, and tried to avoid ASU's twelfth defeat in a row to UCLA by attempting to beat the Bruins at what they do best, by pressing and running with them. Jim Harrick kept Toby Bailey on the bench at the start. Harrick did settle Bailey, telling him, "You're a starter on this team; your name just won't be announced at the beginning." (Harrick was not aware of Bailey's counseling sessions with John Wooden.) J.R. Henderson had laid an egg against Arizona, but Harrick decided against a knee-jolt reaction. "I'm not going to change my lineup every time a guy has a bad game."

It was a knockdown, drag-out affair before 14,287 in the bowl-shaped University Activities Center (now Wells Fargo Arena). ASU turned the ball over twenty-four times, a season high; as did UCLA, with twenty-six mishandles. They ran at each other and pressed and pushed. The first twenty minutes ended 42-42. The Bruins peeled away by scoring twenty of the first twenty-five points in the second half. It teetered, but they regained control to win, 85-72.

In the first half, Ed O'Bannon received a technical foul when he bolted to the defense of teammate Cameron Dollar, who was being taunted by Quincy Brewer. Jim Harrick had heard O'Bannon say the magic word. Tyus Edney sort of returned to earth after a strong few weeks that included the first dunk of his collegiate career. His shot was off (three for nine), he tallied only nine points, and he nearly registered as many turnovers as assists (six to seven). But Edney found solace that UCLA could turn the ball over so much and still win.

UCLA kept ASU from shooting forty percent from the field, and the Bruins' hounding defense was especially effective in a second half in which the Devils made only eight of twenty-five shots. The Bruins were nearly twice as efficient over the final twenty minutes. Frieder had doubled down, and lost, by playing into Harrick's strength. Five years earlier Frieder had so badly wanted to see Ed O'Bannon wearing a Sun Devils uniform. And there he was, as a fifth-year senior, turning the Bruins into a terror. Frieder said this was the best UCLA team he had ever played, that the Bruins were even better than *his* 1989 championship squad. "They shoot the ball better, and they can go bigger and smaller easier ... they were deeper than we were, and they got more out of their guys. They're a team that's going to be there when it's over. They know they're that good. What they did this week is proof of that."

The Bruins became the seventh Pac-10 team to sweep the two Arizona programs, in Arizona, since Lute Olson went to Tucson, and four of them now hailed from Westwood. Charles O'Bannon, who gathered nineteen points, was pleased about improving to 11-1 but advised his teammates, and fans, not to get ahead of themselves. It lets us know, he said, that we can play with anybody, anywhere. Reserve guard Cameron Dollar aptly noted that the Bruins were in the driver's seat, "but it's not a comfortable seat."

Others believed the Bruins were starting to dominate. If some wasn't paying attention, especially down in Fayetteville, Arkansas, that was their problem. "Congratulations to UCLA," said CBS commentator Billy Packer, who played guard for Wake Forest when it lost to UCLA in the 1962 national third-place game in Louisville, the following day during a national broadcast of Michigan State's victory over Michigan. "They made the finest breakthrough in any conference so far." In addition, Jim Harrick served some notice about Ed O'Bannon, who was in the top ten in the Pac-10 in scoring, rebounding, and free-throw, field-goal, and three-point shooting. "I don't want anybody to get any misconceived ideas that he's not the best player in the league right now and a first-team All-American. I don't see anybody in the country playing better than him."

Harrick limited an ineffective George Zidek, who made his only shot attempt in fewer than ten minutes on the court, and replaced him with the active Toby Bailey to start the second half. Bailey tallied nineteen points, a career high, on eight-of-twelve shooting. He had logged more than thirty-five minutes. He was easing into a groove. He was playing with a freedom and strength that was unmistakable to his teammates and the UCLA coaches. He had bided his time, just how John Wooden had counseled him, and was turning in quality minute after quality minute, not worrying about beating out Kevin Dempsey or J.R. Henderson, or Lew Alcindor for that matter, for *burn*. He was about to force his coach's hand.

Ed O'Bannon, meanwhile, had analyzed the tape, over and over, of the Oregon defeat with Steve Lavin. They noted how the

Bruins had unwound toward the end, when it mattered most. O'Bannon had vowed to make changes. His huddles in Tucson and his immediate retaliation against Quincy Brewer in Tempe showed O'Bannon was acting on his convictions. Plenty of previous UCLA wannabe captains had talked about leading, and talked, and talked ... Ed O'Bannon was *doing*.

"No matter what the time is or the score is, if you're still together and you still have your heart and your pride, everybody on the team will know that," O'Bannon told me after UCLA's next practice. "The only way you can win or stay in the game is to stay together, and that's what I've been trying to get our team to do."

Chapter 13

A NEAR-SELLOUT CROWD settled into Pauley Pavilion the evening of Thursday, January 26, to watch UCLA play Stanford. The Bruins had climbed to fourth in the AP poll by virtue of five consecutive victories, those previous two in the stunning sweep in the Arizona desert.

Mike Montgomery was the professorial mentor of the Cardinal who started out wearing spectacles and tweed jackets, and was called *a bit of a curmudgeon* by the guy who had hired him in Palo Alto. Monty, as the Bay Area scribes called him, might have had more of a direct link to the legendary figure sitting three rows behind the Bruins' bench than anybody else in the building.

When John Wooden arrived in Los Angeles in 1948, Jack Montgomery was on the faculty of UCLA's physical education department. He and his wife had both attended UCLA, and Jack had played on the Bruins' football team with Jackie Robinson, in his second season with the Brooklyn Dodgers. Jack Montgomery and Wooden struck up a friendship, and Wooden often cradled the infant Mike Montgomery in his arms.

Dr. Jack Montgomery became the first athletic director at Long Beach State, where Mike would play basketball. Mike was in the middle of an eighteen-year run coaching Stanford in 1994-95. He was still a favorite of Wooden's because of the smart, tough, and fundamental style that was his standard. Monty was a few years from being considered, quite informally, for yet another vacancy in Westwood. Montgomery, though, would remain in Palo Alto, where expectations, pressures, and other surprises were as mundane as Montgomery's mile-and-a-half commute from his home in Menlo Park to campus—although he would eventually cover that distance of about twenty-five football fields in a silver Porsche Boxster, showing, yes, he did possess some flair. A later move to the NBA would enable him to obtain a fleet of Boxsters.

This version of the Cardinal would not be Montgomery's fastest, or finest, but that didn't mean it wasn't fierce. Stanford had a 12-2 record, and a top-notch backcourt of five-foot-ten sophomore Brevin Knight (who would play twelve NBA seasons) and six-two junior Dion Cross. The footwork, passing skills, and shooting touch of seven-one freshman Tim Young were improving with every game.

Most of what the Cardinal tried in the first half, however, was nixed by a UCLA defense that allowed only nine baskets. Knight, playing with a damaged right shin, and Young didn't register a point in the first twenty minutes. The Bruins had a 45-31 edge at the intermission, but Jim Harrick knew Mike Montgomery squads rarely let down in both halves. Harrick was correct. Stanford chipped away at UCLA. Knight and Young scored. The audience gasped, as is its wont. And the Bruins found themselves trailing by a point within the final minute.

Stanford usually is physical, and UCLA played into the wrestling match. Fifty-four fouls were whistled, and one of them was shrieked at Young, who grasped at his Czech counterpart. George Zidek sank both free throws to give UCLA a one-point edge. Another whistle was soon blown on David Harbour, a gritty and versatile left-handed player who had severed his right thumb in a 1992 water-skiing accident, for lowering his shoulder on a drive by Cameron Dollar, who canned both of freebies.

But the always-demanding crowd could not rejoice until Dion Cross's desperation heave at the buzzer missed everything but the ground. J.R. Henderson and Toby Bailey were ineffective and on the bench at the end. Harrick relied on his senior triple threat; Ed O'Bannon, Tyus Edney, and George Zidek had combined for fifty-four points and eighteen rebounds. It had not been a convincing end-to-end effort, which augured that the return game against Stanford on the Cardinal's trampoline-like court promised to be tough, perhaps even a *ball burner.*

No Bruin could have foreseen the circus coming to town. In about seventeen hours, the drama that would unravel in Pauley Pavilion would challenge some of the far-out propaganda to which George Zidek had become accustomed growing up under a Communist umbrella. Fingers would be pointed and heated allegations would be levied. Charles O'Bannon's tears, however, would require no exaggeration.

Todd Bozeman took over the California program, from the deposed Lou Campanelli, in a strange set of circumstances in 1993. Bozeman had an edge, a scowl that he cultivated in his players. In a telephone interview he once asked me not to reveal, in a profile of him, that he had asthma. I pressed, trying to convince him that maybe a kid out there who suffered from the ailment might receive some inspiration from Bozeman. That requiring the assistance of an inhaler need not inhibit dreams or achievement.

Bozeman would not relent. His affliction embarrassed him. He viewed it as a weakness. His way worked, everything and everyone else be damned. Be patient, his cancer-stricken father Ira on his deathbed would tell Todd, more about life than hoops. It was a hard lesson.

In 1993, he gave Jason Kidd free rein and the Golden Bears beat Louisiana State and Duke in the NCAAs, only Cal's second appearance at the Sweet Sixteen level in thirty-three years. Pete Newell had taken the Bears to grand heights, as the 1960 championship-game twenty-point defeat to a balanced Ohio State squad—which included John Havlicek and John Lucas, and a reserve named Bob Knight who missed his only shot—in San Francisco had occurred a year after Cal beat West Virginia and Jerry West (who had tallied twenty-eight points) by a point in Louisville for the NCAA title.

At twenty-nine, Bozeman became the youngest coach to direct a team to that stage of the tournament. The administration had made him the permanent coach when Cal won nine of its final ten regular-season games, which included a victory over third-ranked Arizona in Berkeley.

Kidd departed after his sophomore season of 1993-94, but these Golden Bears still had an arsenal. Bozeman's charges included senior center Ryan Jamison from Los Angeles, freshman forward Tremaine Fowlkes out of Crenshaw High, freshman forward Tony Gonzalez (who would fashion a sterling NFL career as a tight end) from Huntington Beach, and Jelani Gardner, a freshman guard from St. John Bosco High School in Bellflower whom many supposed recruiting insiders had pegged for UCLA. It was through recruiting Gardner that Jim Harrick and Lorenzo Romar met Andrew Pruter, Gardner's Bosco backcourt mate who would become a manager for the Bruins.

With those rich Los Angeles ties on a team from Berkeley, this one would be unusually personal. One of them would play an ignominious role in Bozeman's downfall.

The actual game took place on the afternoon of Saturday, January 28. The mental games began a day earlier in the seconds leading up to 2:50 P.M. Cal players were finishing a practice session inside Pauley. UCLA players, assistant coaches, and student managers ambled out of their locker room in the northwest corner of the arena. Cal had reserved the court for 1-3 P.M. The Bruins practiced at three o'clock, and they always strolled onto their floor about ten minutes early. Managers prepped the court. Players lollygagged, exchanged jokes. Which is what they did on this particular Friday. They spoke to each other in murmurs. Cal players decompressed, stretching, sprawled on the floor around the egg yolk. Some Bruins thought that was odd; stretching *after* practice? The Golden Bears also had nylon straps, to use as resistance for leg stretches.

Someone suggested that Tony Luftman and Andrew Pruter lay down two long lines of white tape and three short ones. Harrick had managers tape the court, to further instill defensive principles, when conference games started. A long line was taped from the middle of a baseline, under the basket, to the top of the key; another one stretched from sideline to sideline at the top of the key. That formed a big T, reinforcing the boundaries of help defense and area responsibilities. Three lines were laid down in front of the basket, marking a square maybe six feet long and eight feet wide, to highlight UCLA's Red Zone defensive area. It reinforced Ed O'Bannon's no-dunks directive. Step into that zone, risk decapitation. Steve Lavin capitalized on the theme by printing T-shirts—BRUIN DEFENSE on the front, RED ZONE on the back—that were all the rage among the players. An initial model involved a Master Lock theme, but copyright or trademark issues made UCLA's legal beagles nervous. Lavin executed a swift transition.

Lavin hatched the garment idea, hoping to drill it into the Bruins to become their hallmark, when San Francisco's football team finally beat nemesis Dallas for the NFC championship, in which the Cowboys had defeated the 49ers in 1992 and 1993. The tone of the Niners' victory was set on the third play, when cornerback Eric Davis picked off a pass from Troy Aikman, a former UCLA quarterback, and ran it in for a touchdown. The 49ers turned two more Dallas turnovers into touchdowns. Defense.

That was January 15, before the Bruins ventured into the desert to take on Arizona and Arizona State. Harrick gave his blessing on the tape and the T-shirts. The players completely bought into the inducements, from Ed O'Bannon's invectives to the T-shirts to the results in Arizona, to the tape that was starting to be applied to the court, for practice this Friday, to further instill the Red Zone philosophy. Luftman and Pruter, rolls of tape at their hips like John Wayne's Colt revolver, followed the order. Cal players lay around the egg yolk. Luftman and Pruter lined across the top of the key, from sideline to sideline. The nearest Cal player would be maybe twenty feet from them. Luftman held the edge of Pruter's tape roll on one sideline as Pruter unraveled it, walking backward. Pruter held the edge when Luftman backtracked from the top of the key to the baseline. Both heard an irascible voice. *Uh, naw man! Hell no! Fuck that!* Luftman and Pruter continued. They thought that was an exchange between Golden Bears.

It had been Todd Bozeman.

The Golden Bears stood, gathered for a few words, and shuffled off to the southwest corner of the arena. Up that ramp awaited a bus to haul them back to their hotel in Marina del Rey. The Bruins practiced, just a glorified walk-through because it fell between conference Thursday-Saturday home games. That episode ignited a soap opera that would build until UCLA had suffered its first defeat of the season on its own court. Thespians came out to play afterward.

This rivalry had always been laced with the unique anger and resentment that can fester within kin. Cal began, by law, in 1868, and the Berkeley campus was opened in 1873. It adopted a southern branch, California State Normal School, in 1919, and that campus became UCLA in 1927.

Two years later those fertile bean and barley fields were scraped away for the new campus. Then John Wooden arrived in 1948. Cal won that one national basketball championship in 1959. Wooden had a string of difficulties against Pete Newell's deliberate tactics. Newell retired. Wooden then rattled off those ten titles in twelve seasons. UCLA's hoops shadow from the south engulfed that imperial campanile to the north in Berkeley.

Bozeman took those feelings of ill will and contempt to a new level. Cal had another chance at redemption, with a little extra manufactured impetus. Coaches have forever developed slights, real or imagined, to spur their players. Bozeman just added a new wrinkle to the playbook. The game, played before another national television audience, was damaging enough to the Bruins, but the games didn't end at the final buzzer.

The Golden Bears took control on three-point shots by Jelani Gardner and Monty Buckley in the first half. The sellout crowd of 12,203 became sullen when the whistles cascaded onto the Bruins, and long-range shots kept falling for Cal. The Golden Bears led, 52-45, at halftime, and they snuffed out every Bruins' attempt at rallies in the second half. Less than four minutes remained when a dead ball signaled the last television timeout. Tremaine Fowlkes was giving Charles O'Bannon some lessons, and Monty Buckely had dunked on Beagle-Beagle. A ball flew out of bounds. Richie Ballesteros, a short, wispy referee with grayish hair, trumpeted his whistle. Both quintets shot to their benches.

Jim Harrick, as usual, trudged in front of his bench to confer with his assistants. Ed O'Bannon stomped to the bench but remained on his feet. He made a beeline at Beagle-Beagle and glared at him. Charlie took an embarrassed seat.

In a flash Ed thought of Tulsa, with shades of Indiana at the Pit and Oregon in Eugene. Ed O'Bannon saw a near-total letdown, but he saw the most significant lack of effort, motivation, and passion in his younger brother. Charles was not fighting back. All of the Bruins were at fault, but a large portion of the blame had funneled directly onto Charles. "Motherfucker, I raised you better than this!" Ed yelled at Charles, almost eyelash to eyelash. "You're out here playin' like a bitch!" Charles bowed his head. "If anybody in this gym right now knows how I'm feelin', it's you! What the fuck is your problem! What are you doin'?"

The rest of the Bruins were slack-jawed. They knew they were just as culpable. Many thought, *Damn, if he's gonna go at his brother like that none of us is safe!* Some shouldn't have been surprised; when Charlie was a freshman he danced and pranced and dunked against a pick-up team that included his older bro. Ed insisted he shelve the punk attitude, that he'd put Beagle-Beagle on his ass the next time he attempted a showboating dunk. Charlie did it again. Ed describes the ensuing few seconds of that pick-up game as the last fight in which he had ever been involved. No punches were thrown, but Charlie still ended up on his behind from an extremely forceful shove in the chest by Ed. Ed says he would never have actually thrown a punch at his little brother, but smoke was spewing out of Ed's ears, nonetheless, and Charles clearly understood the point.

That moment in Pauley Pavilion against Cal, Marques Johnson heard the barrage from his broadcasting roost maybe thirty feet away. Ed verbally leveled his brother. Ed's teammates froze. Charlie's eyes became red, tears dribbled down his cheeks. "Ed was just bustin' [Charles's] ass," Marques says. "Ed had seen that Charles had a tendency to lay down in tough situations ... Ed insisted that [Charles and every other teammate] show the same fight that Ed demanded of himself."

The elder O'Bannon had long ago made a promise to himself and his teammates—his band of brothers—that he wasn't going to stand there and let something like that happen again. Not Tulsa. Not again. If others were going to backslide and be okay with losing, Ed was adamant that he wanted nothing to do with that type of behavior or person. Ed always screamed at them, *If you can't figure out a way to stop somebody put them on their ass! See if they get up off the floor!* Spittle flew out of Ed's mouth that afternoon against Cal. He never took his eyes off Charles. Decades later Ed recalls every beat of that scene. "Nothing personal," Ed says.

> It was about getting your shit together on the fly, right then and there, and going back out there to handle your business. If I had said those things to anybody else, on national TV, I don't know that they would have handled it as well as he did. I knew he could handle what I was gonna give him, and it wasn't one hundred percent at him; it was to everybody. But I knew he was gonna be the victim.

Cal recorded a 100-93 victory. It shot fifty-one percent from the field as a team, on UCLA's floor. No UCLA opponent would make half of its shots the rest of the season. Whatever statistics any Bruin tallied didn't matter to Ed O'Bannon. They had all let him down, all laid down on him.

Most coaches would have praised Tremaine Folkes's twenty-four points, Jelani Gardner's eighteen, or his team's strong effort under its own glass. Todd Bozeman instead seethed to reporters. He lambasted the Bruins for gross and negligent acts of disrespect at Friday's practice, hissing at the alleged gall of the two student managers. Bozeman even blamed the Bruins for laughing when his guys missed free throws. Bozeman said he and his players "owed a lot" to the Bruins. "Something I've never seen before in my life. We were right in the middle of practice and they just walked right through our practice," he said. "It was a ridiculous sign of disrespect and my guys took offense to that." Randy Duck said, "What goes around comes around ... our whole team was like, 'This is garbage. We'd never do this.' "

Steve Lavin laughed at was, to him, pure fiction. If we wanted to do some *Mission: Impossible* type stuff, he said, we would have hidden tiny cameras in the rafters and placed pinhead microphones by the Gatorade cooler and towels. Tony Luftman and Andrew Pruter believed the Golden Bears had long run through their paces and that enough distance separated the two groups to where they wouldn't disrupt, or disrespect, the visitors. Lorenzo Romar had always implored the UCLA student managers to accommodate and welcome their opponents, to heed their every desire or demand. *Do unto others*. It had flabbergasted, and embarrassed, Luftman and Pruter that their actions, in part, would wind up in newspaper stories as motivation for the enemy. That it had been a defeat for the Bruins grated on those two managers; they wondered how it would have played out had the Golden Bears lost.

Tyus Edney and Ed O'Bannon firmly discounted Bozeman's accusations. "There was no disrespect on our side," O'Bannon said. "Everybody gets fired up for different reasons. They just flat out beat us, that's all." Decades later O'Bannon confirms that there was *no doubt* that Bozeman had grossly blown Friday's actions way out of proportion to give his players a boost, to make UCLA look even worse after losing on its own maple wood.

In fact, that victory would be overturned. Todd Bozeman had arranged for Jelani Gardner's parents, Tom and Linda, to receive fifteen thousand dollars a season, enabling them to watch Jelani play as a freshman and sophomore. *Sports Illustrated* reported that the cash was sent to the Gardners, via overnight mail, from Milwaukee Bucks assistant coach Butch Carter, a former Indiana University star with connections to Bozeman. Tom and Linda taped a conversation with Bozeman about the payments, were ticked about a drop in Jelani's minutes as a sophomore, and delivered the tape to the NCAA. Bozeman subsequently lied about the payments to authorities.

Cal canned him to cap a forty-three-month run of drama and conflicts that started with the ouster of Lou Campanelli and ended with the illicit-payment revelations. Penalties were exacerbated due to Bozeman's deceit. The Golden Bears were slapped with scholarship cuts, probation, and a ban from postseason play in 1998. Bozeman was smacked with an eight-year show-cause penalty, effectively barring him from coaching in the collegiate ranks during that period.

Pete Newell, Cal's Hall of Fame coach whose tactics had so frustrated John Wooden, told *Sports Illustrated* in 1996 that cheating would not be tolerated in Berkeley. Momentary glory would be washed away in the long run. "See, at Cal, the alums don't want a national championship every year, or even every decade. They want to be proud." Lou Campanelli, coaching in Japan, was not subtle about being ousted when Cal not only had a winning record but had just drubbed UCLA in Pauley Pavilion, too. "They carved out a piece of my heart. Let them just bury themselves. They've made their nest. Let them lie in it. As you sow in life, so shall you reap."

Morgan State University, in north Baltimore, hired Bozeman, a native of Washington, DC, in 2006. A crowd at American University serenaded him with chants of *Thir-tee thou-sand!* "Some of them were saying, 'Hey, Bozeman! Loan me thirty thousand!' Hey, at least they did their homework ... I made a bad mistake, but I'm not a bad person," he told the *Washington Post* on one occasion. On another, he said he understood that some people would never forgive him. "I admit what I did. I've paid the price." At a Morgan State football game, he happened to run into a former Morgan State football player—Tom Gardner, Jelani's father. They barely acknowledged each other.

As for the UCLA defeat to supposedly practice-maligned California that was ultimately overturned in ensuing NCAA sanctions, Bruins forward Kristaan Johnson refused to recognize a loss that could be erased, turned into a victory—UCLA officially lists one more win, and one less defeat, on its 1994-95 record than actually occurred—so antiseptically after the fact.

"They still beat us on the court."

Chapter 14

NINE AND A HALF MILES separate the USC campus from Westwood. In hoop terms, light-years separate the two programs. At least Cal didn't compete with UCLA for column inches in the local newspapers or airtime on Southland TV channels. USC basketball could be found back on the agate page. The enmity compounded over generations. USC's early dominance and John Wooden's stunning reversal were mere figures, numbers in black and white.

The colors and blood surface whenever athletic teams from the two universities meet. In basketball, magnify it by ten ... championships. "Much as I hate to lose, especially to USC ... " wrote Wooden in *They Call Me Coach*. Unhappy with his minutes as a young Bruin, Gail Goodrich admitted thinking about transferring to USC ... then he did call it *that other school* before hundreds of UCLA faithful at an awards banquet and received a marvelous round of applause. UCLA fans accosted USC supporters with UNIVERSITY OF SPOILED CHILDREN signs, and USC fans sometimes hung little powder blue bears in effigy.

Former USC player Bob Boyd took over coaching his alma mater when Lew Alcindor became eligible, as a sophomore. A photograph of Boyd, wide-eyed and open-mouthed, hung in his office under which someone had written, *Oh, My God! Is THAT Alcindor?* Some USC fans had nicknamed Alcindor "Godzilla." The man who would become Kareem Abdul-Jabbar hooked and bank-shot his way to scoring those then-school-record fifty-six points, against USC, in 1966.

USC had dealt UCLA its first defeat in fifty-two Pauley Pavilion games, on March 8, 1969. Ernie Powell's jumper rolled around the rim and fell through, with six seconds left, in USC's 46-44 victory. The previous evening UCLA had squeaked out of the Sports Arena with a double-overtime victory. In a sweat-drenched blue dress shirt, the tie-less Boyd howled in the tiny Pauley visitors' locker room that the Bruins were *damned lucky* they hadn't lost the previous evening, too. *Who's coach of the year?* Boyd yelled to his carousing players in a jab at Wooden. *Who's coach of the year?* Days later Wooden shook his head at the madness that ensued after his building had received its first stain. He said, "When winning becomes *that* important, I'm getting out."

Boyd's water-torture slow-down tactics infuriated Wooden, but he would owe Boyd some gratitude when the Bruins defeated a similarly structured New Mexico State squad in their opener of the NCAAs. That launched UCLA to its third consecutive championship, which it secured by beating Purdue—the boss's alma mater—in the finale in Louisville. Wooden had claimed five of six national titles. Complaints raged in Los Angeles, from the USC faithful, that the Trojans could not dethrone UCLA. But Jim Hefner, one of Boyd's assistant coaches, said that wasn't the correct perspective; "No one in the United States of America could beat UCLA at that time." Boyd had to match wits with Wooden in nine of his thirteen seasons coaching USC. "Right place, wrong time," Boyd said.

The temperature inside the Sports Arena, opened by Vice President Richard M. Nixon in July 1959 just a short walk east from the Coliseum, and Pauley Pavilion escalated when USC and UCLA fans had to co-exist for a couple of hours. Streaks, stalls, controversy, and fisticuffs were all a part of the rivalry. The life-size Tommy Trojan and the two-ton, ten-foot-long Bruin bear, the bronze monuments on each respective campus, were always threatened by a few gallons of cardinal or powder blue paint from the other side. The figures often get tight plastic wraps— protection from ill-willed enemies—as USC-UCLA clashes approach. Provocations sometimes spilled from the seats onto the court, no matter where the Bruins and Trojans played, providing additional bang for patrons' bucks.

In 1951, Bobby Pounds of the Bruins duked it out with Bob Kolf of USC, only to be upstaged several minutes later when Bob Boyd, the player, threw the ball at Dick Ridgway's noggin and knocked him down; Ridgway had tossed the ball at Boyd, who caught it and returned the favor. Officials made the two shake hands, which ignited another exchange. Sheriff's deputies and the band, playing the national anthem, restored order. At the Pan-Pacific Auditorium in 1958 players from both sides exchanged jabs and punches. Jim White of USC showed the bobbing and weaving skills of a natural pugilist. But Jim Steffen, who also played football at UCLA, got in some good licks, too.

A game at the Sports Arena in 1960 might have provided the most entertainment. Referee Al Lightner scooped the ball into the air for a jump between two players with twenty-three seconds remaining. They let the ball hit the court, then wailed on each other. Fans jumped into the mayhem. Someone in the UCLA band smacked a trombone onto the head of USC's John Rudometkin, whom broadcaster Chick Hearn had called "The Reckless Russian." Hearn was about to begin a legendary career doing Lakers' games. John Wooden, on his hands and knees, scurried away from the brawl. His nose was bruised and cut. His glasses were gone. USC coach Toogie Twogood saw someone aim a fist at Wooden, but as Twogood intervened an elbow caught Wooden's cheek. Wooden said, "If a player lacks desire for one of these games, there's got to be something wrong with him."

Strangely, sometimes it was difficult to tell who was rooting for whom. Bill and Helen Gillette, who held Pauley season tickets for its first twenty-one years, ventured into the Sports Arena for an epic encounter on March 8, 1975, a Saturday. Their six tickets were way up in the last row, up where the cigarette smoke clouded. Their notoriously negative seatmate Al, a presumptive UCLA supporter, constantly denigrated the Bruins. UCLA won, 72-68. It represented a seismic shift because it gave the Bruins an 80-79 edge in the series, their first advantage since the Trojans had thumped them so severely in those early decades. UCLA has led the rivalry ever since this game. Some of its fans, though, never knew satisfaction. Afterward, a USC fan at the end of the Gillettes' row told Al, "You, sir, are one of the most consistent people I've ever been around—a consistent asshole!" Al left the arena speechless, the first time all day he had nothing to say.

The Sports Arena did not age gracefully. When Ed O'Bannon entered it for the last time as a collegiate player, it had played host to a few too many circuses and dog shows; a urinal stench seemed permanent.

UCLA strode into the building the evening of Thursday, February 2, having won only one of its previous five games on USC's court. George Raveling had directed USC to win six of its past ten against the Bruins. From 1964, when UCLA won its first national championship, through 2014, that matched USC's most successful five-season stretch against the Bruins.

A fervent reader who always trudged through airports carrying a stack of newspapers and books, Raveling had guided the Trojans to four consecutive postseason berths—but only one victory in the NCAAs. He had turned down a mid-summer offer to take over at Seton Hall, which could have planted him near his

Philadelphia roots. He cited his love for Los Angeles in remaining at USC. Two months later, his Jeep Cherokee was involved in an accident with a BMW on a Sunday morning at the intersection of 39th Street and Arlington Avenue. He suffered nine broken ribs, a broken collarbone and pelvis, and a collapsed lung. Two months after that near-fatal collision, in November, he retired from coaching.

Raveling—known to all as Rav—had effectively dissuaded son Mark, who had played club ball as a teenager with Ed O'Bannon, from the coaching profession. Rav said, "People only care if you win ... unfortunately, the real victories come off the court."

Assistant coach Charlie Parker was named the interim boss and USC struggled, going 7-11. Stais Boseman, a six-foot-four sophomore out of Morningside High, and six-seven senior Lorenzo Orr needed to produce for USC to have any hope against the Bruins. In addition, Cameron Murray was a hot-shooting newcomer out of Glendora High, the school about thirty miles due east of Westwood which had produced older brother and former Bruins forward Tracy. Recruiting expert Bob Gibbons regarded Cameron Murray and Allen Iverson, from Hampton, Virginia, as the two best point guard prospects in the nation. Cameron Murray went to USC to play for Raveling; he would leave for Louisville and Denny Crum, whose system mirrored UCLA's, at the end of his sophomore season largely because of Rav's departure.

As much as the Trojans had been struggling, UCLA went to the Sports Arena without one of its main weapons when Tyus Edney's highly contagious flu virus kept him under the sheets in his dorm suite. That gave the Bruins' steering wheel to Cameron Dollar, who had started the first seven games of the season next to Edney. It would be a keen test in a very hostile environment, where belligerent fans had again spilled onto the court in recent seasons. Weathering this predicament would enable UCLA to remain atop the Pacific-10 Conference, half a game in front of Arizona.

UCLA did start as if something were missing. The Bruins made only one basket in the first eight minutes, and the crowd of 7,273 sounded twice its size. USC led by as many as seven points in the first twenty minutes and settled for a 35-31 advantage at halftime. Dollar had three fouls and no assists. "Our team is a lot different team without Tyus," Ed O'Bannon said. "He's a defensive stopper and he penetrates on offense. He's the leader."

Jim Harrick retreated to the locker room and told his guys to keep Lorenzo Orr in check, not to foul, and to be patient. USC's trips to the free-throw line were nearly cut in half, from fourteen in the first half to eight in the final twenty minutes. The Trojans burst out of the break with a flurry of three-point shots to take a 49-41 edge. Charlie Parker switched his guys from a pressing, man-to-man attack to a two-three zone, which informed Ed O'Bannon that USC was tiring—Trojans were catching their breath on defense by generally defending an area rather than a person.

The Bruins took advantage by being patient with the ball and exploiting the Trojans. A couple of slam dunks by Charles O'Bannon, and two jumpers by George Zidek and a dunk by the seven-foot Czech kept UCLA close. With about five and a half minutes left the Bruins took control on a layup by Ed O'Bannon and, after Brandon Martin traveled, another dunk by Zidek. Ed O'Bannon sank a short jumper. Parker called for a timeout.

When play resumed, Toby Bailey slipped inside for a tip-in. UCLA missed three of five free throws to give USC some hope in the final minute, but the Trojans couldn't capitalize. Ed had been perceptive; the Trojans were tired. Toby Bailey sank two free throws, and Ed O'Bannon made one to cap a finish that was sloppy on both ends. The O'Bannons totaled thirty-two points and fifteen rebounds in a game that was very personal for them. Zidek contributed fourteen points and seven boards, and Bailey had eight points and nine rebounds. Dollar registered nine points and five second-half assists, and he was a main reason why UCLA committed only twelve turnovers, a low for the season.

Jim Harrick noted that the 73-69 victory had not been pretty, his guys had hung in there, and the outcome had been a gritty defensive effort. Since that travesty against Cal and Ed O'Bannon's insistence, defense would be an absolute premium for the Bruins the rest of the way. In addition, for the first time in his collegiate career, O'Bannon never took a seat on the bench. He had never played all forty minutes of a college game.

Three days later Notre Dame visited Pauley Pavilion for the latest of a traditional series whose history had been laced with shock. That record winning streak of eighty-eight games that UCLA rattled off between January 1971 and January 1974? The loss before that first victory and the defeat that ended it both took place in South Bend, Indiana, against the Irish. This Sunday matinee at Pauley, though, would only be interesting for about twenty-five minutes. Then it got very interesting for a national television audience.

Ed O'Bannon gave the Bruins a nine-point lead with a twenty-foot jumper out of the first television timeout in the second half. Notre Dame turned it over, and Tyus Edney raced in for a fast-break layup. Perhaps frustrated that it was getting away, six-foot-seven Irish freshman forward Derek Manner came down hard on the point guard's shoulder as he sailed into the right side of the east basket.

Edney landed with a thud. He slid to the anchor of the basket and sat with his back against the thick pads. Two beats later Ed

O'Bannon entered the picture, having raced from seventy feet away. In full fury he bumped chests with Manner and gave him a forceful shove. O'Bannon hollered, "What the fuck is wrong with you!?!" As officials debated the situation at the scorer's table, O'Bannon stalked to the center of the court, spittin' mad at Notre Dame, defiant of anyone who would attempt to harm one of his teammates so blatantly.

These were officially the Fightin' Bruins. Nobody came within twenty-five feet of him. Nobody dared. O'Bannon stood huffing and puffing atop the egg yolk. Reserves on the bench saw his sweat-soaked jersey, the specific area of his heart, pounding. A vein in the middle of his forehead throbbed. An audience of 11,617 shrieked and howled, threatening to blow the roof off the thirty-year-old building; O'Bannon heard nothing.

He was hit with a technical foul, his third of the season—the first arrived two minutes into the season opener when he hung on the rim too long after a thunderous two-handed slam, the second against Arizona State when he rushed to the defense of Cameron Dollar against Quincy Brewer. Jim Harrick always yanked a player who had committed such a transgression, because another one in the same game would earn an ejection and suspension from the next game. Harrick never delayed in pulling a player who had just been slapped with a technical foul. Never. It was immediate. That guilty party went to the bench for an earful or a lesson or to calm down, most often all three.

However, for what might have been the only times in his twenty-three seasons as a head coach, Harrick never pulled Ed O'Bannon when he got a technical as a senior. He left O'Bannon on the court. Harrick knew how to battle, too. Sure, it had been a hard foul. That's part of the game. But, "[Manner] put a hurt on the little guy, and we need that guy," Harrick said. He let the rage build and burn within O'Bannon.

Ed O'Bannon had heard enough jibberish, from teammates, in his four seasons at UCLA. All talk. No action. Cocky. Not confident. At this point, Ed O'Bannon defined confidence. No Bruin dared to approach O'Bannon to settle him, or high-five or fist-bump him. They fed off his rage, scoring thirty-eight of the next fifty-one points to seal an eventual 92-55 victory.

UCLA players, assistant coaches, and managers would vividly recall the scene, the flash of O'Bannon confronting Manner and the statuesque image of O'Bannon lording over the court, for decades. It was the countenance of a career. Notre Dame coach John MacLeod, who had spent seventeen seasons in the NBA, told reporters that O'Bannon's antics were uncalled for, over the top, that his kid was just learning the ropes. However, MacLeod also recognized that the Bruins "are an awesome club ... their defensive pressure was incredible. Once they got rolling, we saw just how strong they are."

The Bruins were buoyant about their supercharger. Fired us up, said Edney, whose bruises and nicks were taking a toll. Charles O'Bannon said his older brother looked out for others. "He's always been protective of his family or his teammates. When he sees someone is hurting or about to get hurt, he steps in."

Tim Kawakami of the *Los Angeles Times* quoted Harrick saying O'Bannon needed to control his emotions, that that type of reflex could prove costly in a tight one on a bigger stage. And Kawakami couldn't resist ... noting that Harrick *drew two technicals of his own at the end of UCLA's loss at Oregon.* Inkwells run deep. From his vantage point Ed O'Bannon believed Manner's foul looked quite intentional. Just sticking up for my friend, Ed said. "That's something any friend would do, whether you're on the street or on the basketball court."

Or on a mission.

Chapter 15

THE CHARTER BUS hauled the UCLA basketball team from Pauley Pavilion to LAX early the afternoon of Wednesday, February 8. United Airlines shuttled it to San Francisco and Seattle-Tacoma International Airport (Sea-Tac). The top two figures on the Bruins were eager to tend to some business affairs in The Evergreen State.

For Ed O'Bannon, it's where some of the first leadership embers had sparked him approximately two years earlier, when the rotation of a Northwest trip matched this one—first the University of Washington in Seattle, then Washington State on the other side of the state, in the Palouse, two days later. It was O'Bannon's third-year sophomore season, the first in which he had participated in the season opener. Mitchell Butler and Shon Tarver were other upperclassmen.

In the winter of 1993, Washington pounced on UCLA, 81-67, in Seattle. Washington State followed with a 67-56 conquest. O'Bannon scored six points and didn't grab a rebound in the former, and he had eight points and nine boards, with five turnovers, in the latter. When the Bruins returned to their hotel in Moscow, Idaho, seven miles east of WSU's campus in Pullman, Washington, Lorenzo Romar corralled O'Bannon. They repaired to a conference room.

Romar enjoyed basketball immensely, but he cherished relationships. During all those years playing ball on the asphalt jungles of Los Angeles, the late bloomer swam upstream and continued battling, making a niche for himself in the NBA. He became adept at reading people and situations. He didn't speak often; when he did, it was softly. Romar confronted O'Bannon. "What's goin' on?" Romar was disturbed. He wasn't angry, but he was forceful. The floodgates opened for O'Bannon, who wept within moments. Romar's eyes also became dewy.

That road trip had presented O'Bannon with a major hurdle. Harrick considered it one of the two lost weekends of his UCLA career, the other being a thrashing by the Arizona schools in the desert in the winter of 1989. O'Bannon shouldered all the blame. He felt as if he had let down every teammate, all of his coaches, the UCLA campus, Los Angeles, and anyone who had ever worn a Bruins T-shirt. "A huge, big issue for me," O'Bannon told me. "I didn't feel comfortable at all. I didn't perform well, and it was almost like, when I was playing, I didn't care. I've never felt like that before. It was tough to take and tough to swallow."

Romar quickly registered O'Bannon's devastation. Romar saw that nobody could be tougher on O'Bannon than himself, so Romar treaded softly. O'Bannon said, "This [trip] was fucked up." Romar was impressed that O'Bannon would assume such ownership. "He really got it out," Romar said. "It was very good for him. He could get on with his life. That wasn't the end of his life."

Jim Harrick had no idea that O'Bannon had broken down before Romar, who kept it confidential. "I hope he did cry over the way he played," Harrick said a year later. "That tells me how involved and serious he is about his game." Harrick could rebuke any player, any time, with a sting. Heading into one NCAA Tournament, he had told me how a player needed to *cut the umbilical cord* to be genuinely respected by his teammates, to actually be a man on the court, to be considered a leader. But those Bruins lacked chemistry and direction. Cocky. Not confident. Jim Harrick did not disagree with Neil McCarthy's indelicate assessment. In the winter of 1994, UCLA beat Washington State by two points and Washington by twenty in their arenas. In the winter of 1995, Ed O'Bannon returned to the area with the results of 1993 still fresh like an open wound. He would do everything in his power to avoid repeating that farce.

Jim Harrick had another excursion atop his Emerald City itinerary after the Bruins' noon shoot-around at Hec Edmunson Pavilion on the UW campus. The driver of the coach steered the beast west on State Route 520, south on Interstate 5. Harrick interjected. The driver pulled off the highway at James Street. Players gawked at each other and at gloomy, overcast Seattle. After a soft right on Yesler, the driver made a hard left on First Avenue, and another hard left on South King Street. To the right sat the gray hulk of the Kingdome, site of the Final Four in two months. Toward the end of the summer, Harrick had found a color photograph of the eighteen-year-old eyesore (let's be truthful) and had a manager tack the photo high up on a wall in the Bruins' locker room inside Pauley. Every day, those players saw the goal of the season. Now they would touch it, get a whiff of it. They would also get a guided tour.

Several hundred recreational vehicles were lined up inside for a weekend show, like Matchboxes in a gray, dank, circular Mattel carrying case. Vern Wagner told Harrick not to worry, that he would give the guys perspective on the magnitude of the grand event that would take place under her roof. The six-foot, 240-pound Wagner had a firm handshake and an unmatched diligence in his post—like a border guard—as the Kingdome's director of operations. Harrick first met Vernon Walter Wagner at Morningside High; Harrick coached ball, Wagner taught science and physical education.

The bus pulled up to the largest domed concrete structure in the world. Built with twenty-five thousand tons of concrete, its forty vaulted exterior ribs stuck sixty feet into the ground and were reinforced by a concrete ring tightened to 8.8 million pounds of tension. Players bitched and moaned. Pipe down, Harrick said. This won't take long. They walked inside and saw the RVs.

When Wagner explained how the basketball court would be laid out, where the benches would be placed, and how the stadium seats would be arranged, Harrick saw each player daydream about competing inside this building for a national semifinal and, hopefully, for an NCAA championship. Charles O'Bannon drifted to the Final Four in seven weeks. "Whatever message he was trying to send us, it registered. I got a taste of it, now I want the whole thing."

The springboard worked, at least for the first twenty minutes against Washington inside Hec Ed. UCLA connected on almost sixty percent of its shots, while the Huskies were half as efficient. The Bruins led, 43-28, at intermission. They stretched their edge to seventeen points in the first few minutes of the second half. Six-foot-one junior shooting guard Bryant Boston boosted the Huskies, and they cut their deficit to three points with less than nine minutes left.

But Ed O'Bannon and George Zidek sank key baskets; they'd tie for team-high honors with seventeen points. O'Bannon also blocked four UW shots, gave out four assists, and didn't turn the ball over once. He was warming to playing in Seattle. He wasn't about to have any repeat performances of his disastrous trip here as a sophomore. Zidek thrived against man-to-man defense in which he often had an advantage of three or four inches. He made eight of his ten shots. He said it was imperative for him to "make them pay for single-covering me, no doubt."

Charles O'Bannon had soaked in every syllable with which his older brother had chastised him in recent weeks, if not months— years?—by blocking five shots, more than any other Bruin had deflected so far in the season. Still, Washington had dominated UCLA on the boards by grabbing a ridiculous twenty-six under its own rim. But controlling rebounds wasn't proving to be the most critical aspect of the Bruins' defense; it was about badgering the other guys, getting a hand in their faces when they shot and in the lanes when they passed.

Jim Harrick noted Tyus Edney's weak stats; three points, one-for-six shooting, one-for-five at the line, four assists, and three steals, with three turnovers. Perhaps, Harrick said, the flu that had zapped the little guy more than we all figured. Edney acknowledged that he needed a bit more time to get his sea legs back, but it was reassuring to know that his team could keep the lead and secure the victory without his usual productivity. Seattle would most definitely have an unsettling effect on Tyus Edney.

J.R. Henderson took one look at the Bombardier Dash 8 sitting on the Sea-Tac tarmac Friday morning and stopped cold. Teammates need not inquire. The twin turbo-prop airplane, a puddle jumper to frequent flyers, nearly induced Henderson to lose his breakfast on the runway. His special strain of aerophobia—*propellophobia?*—was kicking in.

In high school Henderson had boarded a prop-powered plane to return to Bakersfield from LAX. He sat near the front, the propeller spinning right there in front of him out the window. That became his own personal hellish mix of *Vertigo* and *The Twilight Zone*. When he finally got home he laid down in his bed, stomach churning and head dizzy. "Bad experience," said Charles O'Bannon. "He hadn't been on a prop plane since."

That had been a much smaller aircraft than the Dash 8, so at Sea-Tac he finally inched along as Toby Bailey assuaged him with calming words and coaxed him to slip one foot in front of the other. There ya go. Easy does it. Teammates saw Henderson panic when the bird took off. His stomach knotted up. Ed O'Bannon swears he saw Henderson turn blue. "Looking real scared. He had a straight face, and it looked like he was in a zone." The Dash 8 could carry forty passengers, and Henderson endured the ninety-minute flight to Pullman-Moscow Regional Airport—a building the size of a 7-Eleven in the middle of gently rolling hills of golden wheat, when snow doesn't blanket the topography—with a beige sick bag in his lap that he thankfully did not employ.

A wholesome facial hue returned once he returned to terra firma, and the Bruins were all jovial during a practice run at Friel Court, at Washington State, that amounted to a light shoot-around session. Laughter echoed off the arena walls. Several Bruins launched half-court shots, their usual comedic cap to a road practice. Just to see what the view was like, Ed O'Bannon hiked up to the highest point in a corner of the gym. A couple of teammates followed. Mark Gottfried trailed the trio. The two teammates drifted away. O'Bannon and Gottfried chatted about the June NBA draft, revealing that Ed O'Bannon had far more on his mind than just the next UCLA opponent or ensuring that tiny Aaron's diaper was dry and he was sleeping soundly. O'Bannon had been pondering the draft. To him, it was a foregone conclusion that he had been putting together the type of numbers and displaying the leadership becoming of a prospect that would surely be selected with one of the top three picks. "I'm playing pretty well," he told Gottfried. "Why wouldn't I be in the top three, [or] top five, at least?"

Gottfried had been culling information from NBA coaches and front-office personnel. The coach shocked the player. Right now, Gottfried said, you're projected to go in the top twelve or among the top fifteen. Ed thought, *What? Are you kidding? THAT is what they're saying about me?* Gottfried continued, "But I think if we win the national championship and you play great, your stock will rise. One would think that it would rise." O'Bannon descended those concrete treads much slower than he had ascended them.

Toby Bailey and J.R. Henderson roomed together on the road. Once Bailey muffled the volume on the music videos he watched that Friday night, Henderson finally drifted into a coma of a sleep. At Friel on the afternoon of Saturday, February 11, Henderson and Bailey slipped into another zone to power sixth-ranked UCLA in a 98-83 victory over Washington State.

The Cougars unwisely chose to play as fast as possible, which nearly enabled an opponent to hit triple figures in scoring for the first time since February 1976, when the Bruins beat them, 104-78, at Pauley Pavilion. Capitalizing on the pace, Tyus Edney doled out eleven assists, stole four passes, turned it over only once, and tallied eighteen points. He was feeling well again. A vociferous crowd of 11,463 watched its Cougars lose for the first time in eleven home games.

Jim Harrick might have caught WSU by surprise by using the two-three zone defense, which enabled the Bruins to rule the boards, poach perimeter passes, and conserve some energy for sprints to their own basket. However, six-one junior Shamon Antrum exploited the boxed-in defense for a career-best twenty-nine points; he had bombed away from three-point land fourteen times, nailing six. If someone hoped to beat the Bruins, outside marksmanship might be essential.

Henderson inflicted the most damage with twenty-eight points, a career high, on ten-of-twelve shooting. Many of those baskets came close to the rim. Perhaps the Dash 8 brought out the best in the country boy? The six-foot-nine freshman often contended with six-four sophomore Isaac Fontaine, as WSU mostly employed three guards. That left Henderson with a felonious size advantage, which he exploited. "In the low post, I have a few moves ... no turning back. I'm not going to slow down at all," said Henderson, who dispensed with even fewer words than usual because that twin-propped flamingo was waiting for him at that dinky airport. Jim Harrick saw how Henderson played so naturally so close to the rim, often with his back to it, and made some mental notes.

Bailey had propped up his buddy for the flight to Pullman, and he pumped up the Bruins with fifteen points in twenty-five minutes off the bench. "When he's helped us is when we've really needed him," said Harrick. "When you're on the ropes, boom, there's Bailey for you." Harrick's noggin was churning with thoughts about Henderson playing inside, Bailey outside. Charles O'Bannon added fifteen points. Ed O'Bannon recorded eleven points (on three-of-ten shooting) and eight boards; had he missed just one of those three field goals, he would have failed to etch his name atop a vaunted UCLA chart. But the two victories were all that mattered. The Great Northwest had become a much more welcoming destination to Ed O'Bannon.

Chapter 16

JIM HARRICK AND HIS three assistants had highlighted this stretch of the schedule before the season had begun. Five games over eleven days—the Arizona schools in Pauley, at the Bay Area programs, Duke in Los Angeles.

UCLA football coach Terry Donahue once responded to inquests about a rough stretch, possibly not endurable by mere mortals much less winnable, by lamenting to media, *Folks, it's not the Bataan Death March*. Harrick wasn't so sure about what awaited his squad. "A prelude to the most critical part of our schedule, the 'mini-tournament,' designed to test our willpower as much as our talent," he wrote. Harrick admitted pondering past late-season swoons. His team's heart, soul, character, and moxie—and postseason viability—would be revealed to him here and now. All that was at stake was Ed O'Bannon's legacy as a Bruin and Harrick's reputation as an elite Division-I coach.

Every other team in the country, except for the Ivy Leaguers, played in conference tournaments. Not the Pac-10, not yet. So Harrick told his players to view this next set as their league tournament. Towel-shouldered Bill Frieder and Arizona State entered Pauley Pavilion with an 18-5 record, and Frieder would continue to gamble by turning a press on the Bruins and an offensive scheme that, surprise, relied on three-point marksmanship. It nearly worked for the Sun Devils, who lost in overtime but would go on to win twice in the NCAAs until running into Kentucky in the Sweet Sixteen.

UCLA led by five at halftime, and ASU hadn't attempted a free throw. Mario Bennett went for twenty-one points and nine boards, and his layup with eighty seconds remaining boosted ASU's lead to 66-63. It was the first of the five challenges, and the Bruins were already on the ropes. Twenty-eight seconds later, Charles O'Bannon knifed through the left side for a little scoop shot. Bennett fouled him, and O'Bannon's subsequent free throw tied it. Isaac Burton tried taking Beagle-Beagle solo at the other end, but Charles got a fingertip on the flip shot and it rolled out of the rim. Ed O'Bannon embraced his little brother. His admonishments had not been taken lightly. When it mattered most, Beagle-Beagle would not disappear.

Ninety seconds into overtime, Ed O'Bannon curled around a double screen and drilled a twenty-four-foot shot from the top of the key to pump UCLA's lead to 73-68. It ended 82-77 before a packed crowd of 12,318. Something was building. The fans were paying attention. The Bruins could breathe.

San Francisco had slammed San Diego in the Super Bowl, in Miami, so Steve Lavin sauntered around on the balls of his feet for a couple of weeks. Animated and spirited, anyway, he was always imagining motivational tools, ways to convey certain messages to the players that would click, or manifest, in desirable methods and outcomes on the court.

He had devised a doozy for Arizona, visiting Pauley on the afternoon of Sunday, February 19. For a practice before the game, Lavin and video coordinator Ken Norris assembled a *Rocky*-themed clip that Harrick played for a couple of minutes in the darkened locker room. Limiting the other guys to forty-percent shooting, reinforcing the prohibition of layups, dunks, and uncontested shots, and remaining in fifth gear for all forty minutes were the messages. Finishing with a bang, a sassy side-view photo of Damon Stoudamire was displayed, with his guarantee that the Wildcats would win at Pauley at the bottom. "It was about doing everything—helping down low and shutting that down, and getting back to snuff the perimeter—asking them to do the impossible, but they did it," says someone who was in the room. "The refrain was, 'Get beat over the top, not around.' The graphics were crude, but it was the first time we'd done that. Incredible."

Get beat over the top, by long-range bombs. Nothing easy. Nothing in the middle. No layups. No dunks. No prisoners, either, by Ed O'Bannon's mandate.

Arizona was 19-5 and nearly did waltz out of Pauley making Stoudamire look prescient. UCLA shot less than forty percent, but it was strong on the glass and played smart with the ball, committing only seven turnovers. The difference in the Bruins' 72-70 victory was Ed O'Bannon, who tallied thirty-one points, more than he had ever scored in college. Ed and younger brother Charles, and Toby Bailey, were the only Bruins who scored in the second half, which they had gone into with a seven-point advantage.

When Arizona knotted it, Ed O'Bannon answered and UCLA did not trail again. Bailey provided some highlights with a dunk in traffic, a twenty-foot straightaway shot, and a twenty-three-footer from the left wing. Bailey also spelled Tyus Edney in the second half and bothered Stoudamire, who led the Wildcats with twenty-seven points in an effort to back up his guarantee but scored only three baskets in the final twenty minutes. John Wooden had been connecting with yet another UCLA basketball player.

The Bruins had weathered the two Arizona schools, both of who went back to the desert trailing UCLA (18-2 overall, 11-2 in the Pac-10 Conference) by two games in the league standings. "I felt it," Ed O'Bannon told reporters. "I'm not out there counting points or anything, but if it feels good, I'm shooting it. I'm not the type of guy who wants to go out and get fifty points a game. I just want to help the team win. If my scoring helps, that's fine." Cameron Dollar went to him whenever the Bruins were stuck and needed a basket. Ed O'Bannon wasn't going to disappear.

Jim Harrick expounded about Ed O'Bannon being a legitimate candidate for national player of the year. UCLA had shown itself to be one of the country's most consistent teams, and all of that credit went to O'Bannon. "From that moment on, I thought Ed O'Bannon became the best basketball player in America," Harrick wrote. "Finally, after nearly five years, he was back in every way: mentally, physically and emotionally. Ed just wasn't going to let anything stop him, or his team. Make no mistake. In many important ways it was his team. Just as I'd wanted it to be for quite some time ... he was no longer just a real good player. [He had] ascended to a whole different level. He was thoroughly dominating games."

Ed O'Bannon, however, still insisted that Tyus Edney was the most important Bruin. For a second consecutive game, knee tendinitis had limited Edney's minutes. But Cameron Dollar logged twenty-five minutes, and he stole four passes while committing only one turnover. That Dollar got such rich experience against a tough opponent was a development that would be looked upon favorably.

For now, Harrick was on the verge of making another decision that would alter the makeup of his rotation and further affect his team's fortunes.

As the Bruins left Los Angeles for the San Francisco Bay Area— fortunately, for J.R. Henderson, twin turbo propellers weren't powering them—on Monday, February 20, Jim Harrick scratched and searched.

In a somewhat related event, top-ranked Kansas lost that evening at Oklahoma. Two victories in the Bay Area—in an unusual Tuesday-Thursday alignment—and a win over Duke at Pauley Pavilion on Sunday could propel second-ranked UCLA to the top spot in the AP poll. Would that even matter to the Bruins? That Monday night inside the Marriott Waterfront in Burlingame, where patrons could watch and always hear jumbo jets landing a few hundred yards across the water to the east on Runways 28R and 28L of San Francisco International Airport, Harrick carried out his plan.

Harrick told Mark Gottfried, *I need to make a change. If I put Toby into the starting lineup, I'll be able to rotate J.R. through George and Ed in the post.* Henderson's recent success down low had convinced Harrick that he would be the perfect relief for George Zidek *or* Ed O'Bannon.

At the Bruins' Tuesday morning shoot-around on the bouncy Maples Pavilion court, Harrick told Henderson that Bailey would start that evening. "But you're still a starter in my mind," said Harrick, repeating an oft-used line, "we just aren't going to announce you as one." That's a delicate discussion with any player, because of the egos involved. But with true freshmen it could mean deflation; Bailey knew how that went. Harrick believed Henderson took it like a man, a team player. Harrick was confident the switch would improve his team, overall, and it could likely confuse the Cardinal.

"That changed our whole year," Gottfried says many years later. "Our team took off."

Bailey, who thought he had only had to better Kevin Dempsey to get burn, had taken it personally when Harrick picked Henderson to start a few weeks earlier. Bailey was a natural shooting guard, and he had spent months perfecting his shot. But breakfasts with John Wooden were settling Bailey. Wooden convinced him to keep working hard, but not just on his shooting touch. Don't slack in any areas of your game, Wooden said. Play defense as strenuously as you do offense. Don't let down. Your time will come when you least expect it, but you had better be ready when it does come.

"I soaked up as much as possible," Bailey says decades later. "It wasn't even just what [Wooden] said, it was his presence; the way he was so positive about everything. He told me life stories and life anecdotes." Wooden conveyed what balance meant, in basketball and life, to Bailey. Basketball wasn't life, just a small part of it. "I really needed to branch out," Bailey says. "I looked into other interests. A missed shot wasn't as important; it was important, but from then on it wouldn't crush me for weeks. I had gained some perspective." Which would allow Bailey to undertake a career abroad without trepidation, but that was several years away.

After the practice, Ike Nwankwo trudged across the Stanford University campus—*the Farm*, to the Malbec-sippin' sophisticates of the area—to check in with the Stanford Law School for a third consecutive year. Heeding the desires of his professor father, Nkem, Nwankwo would keep abreast of admission requirements and costs, and LSAT timetables, for decades, even after his professional career abroad ended and he was running a basketball academy in Bangkok. On that cross-campus jaunt in 1995 he picked up a copy of *The Stanford Daily*, the school newspaper, and smoldered as he perused a feature that, he believed, had disparaged the UCLA hoops team, discounted its lofty national standing, and doubted its chances for a long run in the NCAAs.

Nwankwo related the supposed slights to his teammates. They barely acknowledged him. The three seniors had heard and

248

read it all, anyway, in previous seasons. They told Ike all that was hearsay, hokum, rubbish. The charges were especially futile in the wake of the pre-Arizona video, actually seeing a photo of Damon Stouadmire above his guarantee—which he nearly pulled off, too. The main figures had enough on their minds with the precise offensive sets and bruising defensive tactics of Mike Montgomery.

Jim Harrick tinkered some more. UCLA trailed nineteenth-ranked Stanford, 47-44, at the half, and Harrick had noted how some of his guys had had trouble, on defense, navigating through the thick screens of six-foot-eight junior Darren Allaway, six-seven senior Andy Poppink, and seven-one freshman Tim Young. Charles O'Bannon crumpled to the floor like a rag doll when he collided with Allaway's well-placed shoulder, allowing Dion Cross an open look at the rim; he drilled a three-point shot. Toss in a rambunctious sellout crowd of 7,500, and Harrick was pressed to search for options to prevent a repeat of Oregon. So he reverted to the two-three zone defense for the second half, to keep his guys from getting ensnared in multiple screens and Stanford's infamous gauntlet of elbows, shoulders, and torsos.

It worked. UCLA turned its three-point deficit into a five-point advantage early in the second half. The zone helped snuff Stanford—making its players shoot over the Bruins, and enabling the Bruins to poke at passes and ignite fast breaks—and a three-point shot by Charles O'Bannon kept UCLA's margin at five points with five minutes remaining. The Cardinal uncharacteristically folded. Poppink and Cross, who combined to score thirty-one points in the first half, totaled only eight in the second. The Bruins won going away, 88-77. Ed O'Bannon swatted away a career-best five shots, and he had three steals, five assists, nine rebounds, and twenty-two points—his third consecutive game scoring at least twenty-two. Charles O'Bannon, like his older brother, played thirty-eight minutes.

Tyus Edney recorded fourteen points and ten assists, and Toby Bailey had twelve points and six rebounds. Both of those Bruins logged thirty-seven minutes. J.R. Henderson thrived off the bench, tallying nineteen points in twenty-seven minutes. Starting center George Zidek experienced foul trouble, but Henderson capitalized against Tim Young despite yielding four inches to his opponent. "When I have a big guy [defending him], I can take him inside, get in a few moves, then I take him outside and they don't know what I'm going to do," Henderson said. "That's when I have him where I want him."

Those were settling in as the main Bruins, and they were running—and staying—in high gear. Mike Montgomery was impressed how UCLA could shift speeds, too, and he called the second-half zone defense Harrick's checkmate move. "UCLA's playing with great determination," Monty said. "The way they slowed us down in the second half … is something they've been doing whenever they've needed it against everyone."

UCLA did not show up for a practice or shoot-around inside Harmon Gym in Berkeley only to have Cal players intrude upon it near the end, clown on them and cause a ruckus, or witness Golden Bears student managers disrespecting them with taunts or tape. There were no post-game accusations about disrespect or chatter about the Todd Bozeman-fueled carnival elements of their first confrontation of the season back at Pauley Pavilion. This was purely a business trip for the Bruins, and for Ed O'Bannon in particular.

O'Bannon continued rolling with twenty-seven points, which included seven of nine three-point shots, to power UCLA to a 104-88 victory over its northern cousins. A sellout crowd of 6,578 jammed into Harmon's little bandbox of a gym, only to watch their Golden Bears drop a seventh consecutive game on

Pete Newell Court. Cal seemed to be psyched out on its own hardwood. Tremaine Fowlkes—who had been so effective against UCLA inside Pauley, causing the elder O'Bannon to induce tears from his little brother—made only four of eleven shots from the field and six of fourteen at the foul line, for a hard-earned sixteen points.

George Zidek excelled in the hostile environment, nailing eleven of thirteen shots, ringing up twenty-five points, and leading UCLA with eight rebounds. Tyus Edney dished out eleven assists, and Charles O'Bannon gave out eight on a night when the Bruins set a school record with thirty-two. The Golden Bears could not retreat fast enough, and UCLA kept them off-balance with its unselfishness.

Moreover, no previous Bruins team had ever shot more accurately than the 66.7 percent (forty of sixty) with which UCLA had burned the nets against Cal. In the second half, UCLA connected on a gaudy seventy-nine percent of its shots. Ed O'Bannon and his troupe had gotten even with Cal in a blistering way. Steve Lavin had been so impressed he told brother John, one of his five older siblings, over dinner, "I think we're gonna win the national championship. When you come to the Bay Area you might get swept, or you might split. If you win two games, you'll labor through them. But the fact that we just blitzed those teams, just dismantled them ... wow! We are really good."

"Simply awesome," wrote Harrick. The talk about settling a previous score came later. In his book, Harrick put it succinctly; *Payback time.* Bozeman was gracious after the defeat. UCLA could have beaten the Lakers tonight, he said. Eighteen months later, Cal officials asked for and received Bozeman's resignation in the midst of the NCAA investigation that would reveal the shady payments to Jelani Gardner's parents. The coach opposite Bozeman that night ultimately would not be deigned a dignified or graceful departure from his program, either.

Jim Milhorn might not have approached Jim Harrick about every potential scenario of foes as he arranged schedules a year or two in advance, but Harrick did advocate a regular series with Duke. In 1992 and 1993, that hadn't worked out so well for the Bruins. But they were only one of the many punching bags the Blue Devils were slapping en route to becoming an elite program.

Mike Krzyzewski had played for the demanding Bob Knight at the US Military Academy, and he continued learning under Knight by assisting him at Indiana University. Krzyzewski took over Duke, in Durham, North Carolina, in 1980, and he guided the Blue Devils to national championships in 1991 and 1992. Krzyzewski became the first coach since John Wooden to win consecutive NCAA titles, but Wooden's adoration of Coach K had been grounded in far more ways than basketball victories; the character and class in which Krzyzewski ran his program and carried himself impressed Wooden more than anything the Blue Devils did between the lines.

Duke was the featured attraction on the afternoon of Sunday, February 26, and drew a crowd of 12,857, the thirteenth-biggest audience since Pauley first opened its doors. However, a prominent figure—Krzyzewski—wasn't in the building. Exhaustion and a back injury, which required surgery, forced Krzyzewski out of action for the rest of the season in January. Pete Gaudet, a loyal, longtime Blue Devils assistant, tried to replace Coach K, but that was an impossible feat. The Blue Devils were 12-14 when they visited Westwood. It had been to the previous ten NCAA Tournaments, but it would miss that grand stage in two weeks.

(In 1996 Duke would return to the NCAAs, and would do so nineteen consecutive times, through 2014, which would include two more national crowns for the lobby at the entrance of Cameron Indoor Stadium. Krzyzewski, who had his own private elevator up to his office, would also restore full glory to the US national team. When Wooden spotted talent, he rarely erred.)

Still, there was plenty to play for that Sunday. It would mark the end of the much-ballyhooed run of five games over eleven days that Jim Harrick and his staff believed would mark their squad as a contender or a pretender. Plus, Cherokee Parks would be in uniform. Harrick had seen the six-foot-eleven center at many UCLA football games, wearing flip-flops and surfer shorts, when he was attending Marina High School in Huntington Beach. Harrick had not been certain that Parks would pick UCLA, but he felt damn good about the prospect. Instead, Parks went to Duke, where kids spend nights in the pup-tented Krzyzewskiville outside Cameron for prime seat locations. First come, first served. Coach K sent pizzas to those tents.

Had Parks chosen UCLA, the Bruins wouldn't have pursued a seven-footer out of Prague. Harrick was annoyed that Parks didn't even bother to call him with his decision. Parks was annoyed that the boss of UCLA basketball could be so petty. When Blue Devils freshman guard Steve Wojciechowski bounded onto the court to warm up, the crowd serenaded him with *Roooo-deeeee, Roooo-deeeee* chants; the 1993 award-winning movie *Rudy* had starred Sean Astin—a dead ringer for Wojciechowski—as Daniel Ruettiger, an underdog figure who overcame obstacles to play football at Notre Dame. The Pauley crowd could be demanding, even target its own, but it would never whiff on a silver-screen reference.

Dick Vitale provided analysis for the national ABC telecast, and Jim Harrick made a point to tell him during lay-up lines to watch Ed O'Bannon. Maybe he didn't start the season so well, Harrick said, but just watch him now. "He's been dynamic. Just watch." Jim Milhorn stayed out of Vitale's path.

After a tight first half, in which the Bruins nursed a 40-37 lead, Kris Johnson, after asking for and receiving Ed O'Bannon's blessing, told his teammates in the locker room that they were performing as if they didn't want to lose instead of playing like they genuinely wanted to win. The freshman's sour practice deportment (Harrick had tossed him from a couple of recent sessions) and sulky courtside behavior had become issues, but O'Bannon praised the young Johnson for his salient words about his teammates' listlessness in the first twenty minutes against Duke. Harrick had agreed. He thought the Bruins looked heavy-legged, even slow, maybe due to this demanding stretch of the schedule.

Those thoughts were extinguished midway through the second half. Ed O'Bannon took over and dominated. Duke guard Trajan Langdon and Parks were keeping the Blue Devils in it; Langdon's three-point shot from the right corner cut Duke's deficit to 65-62 almost ten minutes into the final frame. That's when O'Bannon and the Bruins ignited their afterburners, which coincided with Jim Harrick slipping them back into the familiar two-three zone. UCLA scored seven consecutive points, then thirteen in a row to knock Duke out. O'Bannon converted a three-point play, powered a banker inside, and put in another close shot after snatching a rebound. Jim Harrick pointed at Dick Vitale, who grinned and gazed back at Harrick. O'Bannon nailed a three-point shot along the left baseline. Harrick again pointed at Vitale, who laughed into his microphone.

O'Bannon recorded thirty-seven points, another personal best. He had taken flight during the five-game stretch of his life, and he wasn't thinking only of himself. Harrick urged him to go for forty. Ed had other ideas. The Bruins led by nineteen points, with a bit less than four minutes remaining, when Ed fed Tyus Edney on a breakaway. On UCLA's next possession, Ed dished the ball to Beagle-Beagle for a rim-rattling jam to make it 90-67 with three minutes, twenty-four seconds left.

Fifteen seconds later, Duke turned it over. Harrick used the lull to slip Ike Nwankwo in for Ed O'Bannon. A hail of applause fell on Ed as he strolled to his bench. "Ed wouldn't shoot," Lorenzo Romar says. "He said, 'These guys [seldom-used reserves] don't get to play. Let them shoot. They're at practice every day, too.' Coach took him out. 'Not gonna shoot, I'll take you out.' But that's how [O'Bannon] led all season."

Ed O'Bannon had made fourteen of his twenty-two shots, including four of seven three-pointers, and he yanked down a game-high thirteen rebounds, gave out three assists, and stole a pass. In thirty-five minutes, he didn't register a single turnover. Toby Bailey saw the same forceful player in high school. "Ridiculous," he said. Charles O'Bannon recognized his brother's impressive return to form, too. "This is it. Stepping out for threes, working hard underneath, playing defense, that's the way Ed played in high school ... everybody has focused on showing that we're for real, that we can end [a season] better than we started."

Dick Vitale interviewed Ed O'Bannon afterward, heaping accolade upon accolade onto the UCLA leader; O'Bannon dodged every plaudit, instead praising his teammates at Vitale's every attempt to single him out.

During the five-game onslaught, all O'Bannon did was tally 139 points, for an average of 27.8. He connected on forty-eight of eighty-two field-goal attempts, which included a lethal sixteen of twenty-five makes from three-point territory. And he thought about the back-up Bruins, who challenged and tested the main players so frequently in practice, when he could have gone for forty against Duke. "We ran through that stretch," says Mark Gottfried. "That's when I believe our guys poked their chests out, to say, 'We're for real. We might be good enough to win it all!' That string of games changed our mentality. We knew we were good."

Harrick was elated. In the toughest stretch of the season the kid who some doubted would even play ball again after that horrible knee injury in 1990 had become a man, the toughest player in the nation. Confident. Not cocky. "Bring your attitude?" Harrick wrote. "Ed had branded his attitude—on anybody who'd dared to get in his way ... a twenty-three-year-old fifth-year senior who was hungry, focused, and a veteran of the wars. He'd seen adversity. Now he was inflicting it."

Their run of success ensured the Bruins of the top ranking. Bataan was conquered. Ed O'Bannon only looked to the immediate future. Feels good, he said, but we have to move on. To be the last team standing in Seattle in a few weeks, he said, is what matters.

Chapter 17

AT UCLA PRACTICES Jim Harrick had been resting Ed O'Bannon like clockwork, sidelining the team's inimitable general for stretches of drills and runs of weaves. Scant practice time was another benefit to the recent schedule. The Bruins rested weary legs and restored energy in between the parade of formidable foes. Harrick and O'Bannon also knew it would be a proving ground, prep work for what promised to be a grueling NCAA Tournament in which how a team handled itself in the single day between games determined who kept playing and who went home to view the rest of the action on television.

Harrick had started pulling O'Bannon to the side, even before that rough stretch, to preserve him, to protect him. Marques Johnson visited practices frequently. The infant he had hoisted to the stars as a UCLA undergraduate had blossomed into a force that was terrorizing the enemy, and some of his teammates. O'Bannon demanded that his peers match, or try to equal, his own drive and determination. Marques saw Ed sitting to the side. Ed would slip a blue sleeve down his calf, and massage his left knee. Marques wondered if Ed was even aware of what he was doing, as if it were as subconscious as breathing.

Johnson knew not to inquire about it. "I didn't know if that would be used as an excuse, or if that reminded him of the injury ... I didn't want to go there," Johnson says. "But it looked like it was causing him a lot of pain. That kind of played into this aura ...

he had the appearance of a guy like Atlas, with the weight of the world on his shoulders. He was carrying so much."

Having delivered for John Wooden and those relentless legions of fans, Johnson knew all about inordinate pressure and unhealthy expectations, and what all that can do to a player's psyche. Johnson viewed a hangdog expression on O'Bannon as the victories piled up. Johnson rarely saw satisfaction. O'Bannon had prepped himself, physically and mentally and emotionally, for more than four years. This was no time to take it easy or bathe in the afterglow of a win. Too many predecessors became content with small achievements, personal accolades. Immediately after a game, there was another that would again demand all of O'Bannon's concentration and effort and ability. For Johnson, it was a reflection.

Johnson started a routine in which he would pass by O'Bannon after a game and tap him, on a shoulder, arm, leg, or back of his dome. At the start of that five-game assessment, UCLA had nine remaining in its regular season. An NCAA championship would require six victories in the tournament. Every Bruins fan, player, and coach aspired to have fifteen more games on the schedule. Nobody could have wanted them more than Johnson, except for one person. Johnson tried to simplify Ed O'Bannon's burden by telling him, after beating Arizona State at home, *One down, fourteen to go* ... or in the aftermath of winning at Stanford, *Three down, twelve to go.*

It was shrewd encouragement. After Duke, Johnson tapped O'Bannon and said, "All right. Come on, man. You can do this. Five down, ten to go. And it's over. Destiny. National champs. You're the one that has to carry this. Only ten more, then it's over. Done."

Few people on the planet could have conveyed that to Ed O'Bannon and had it resonate, actually seep into O'Bannon's synapses. Marques had been in Ed's position, poised to add to UCLA's illustrious reputation. Marques delivered. Could Ed? He didn't need to hear any speeches or boring diatribe, but those few words from Marques Johnson would help O'Bannon retain cold blood.

"Marques is the man," O'Bannon says years later. "I love Marques. There are certain guys that you don't have to see every day or talk to all the time to feel a connection with. He's one guy I genuinely love to see. I genuinely like to embrace Marques Johnson. Just being in his presence … not necessarily because of what he means to UCLA but because of his history with Los Angeles basketball players. He is one of the greats."

Ed O'Bannon's teammates finally broke him. Made him quit. Well, to be accurate, one did. Six-ten, 235-pound center omm'A Givens had arrived from Aberdeen, Washington, with some prestige as a McDonald's All-America and third-team *Parade* All-America selection. The Bruins soon discovered that Givens, whose Choctaw Indian father Roger had hatched his first name by combining the Hindu mantra for the sound of the universe ("ommmm") with an apostrophe'd "A" for uniqueness, was raw, all glares and elbows and flailing arms.

His rage stemmed from losing his father to AIDS, kidnappings in his youth, and racial incidents and pressures. He was the first black basketball player at tiny coastal Aberdeen High School, where he became something of a local hoops legend. He had size-18 feet and more natural ability than any young UCLA center since Bill Walton, according to Jim Harrick. But those words were delivered before Givens first slipped on a UCLA jersey. His teammates would learn, the hard way, about his savagery.

UCLA's conductor was accustomed to pain and punishment, but when a Givens elbow found Ed O'Bannon's ribs the Bruins' leader exploded. He yanked his blue mouthguard, from between his incisors and molars, and chucked it a hundred feet. O'Bannon howled, *This is bullshit! Fuck! I'm tired of this, motherfuckers!* Teammates shuddered. O'Bannon implored to all that he quit, that he was done with this band of hooligans. He stormed off, banging the metal locker-room door open and slamming it behind him. Tony Luftman retrieved the piece of polyethylene and acrylic resin whose origin was another L.A. story with a UCLA twist. Los Angeles dentist Rodney O. Lilyquist is considered the father of the modern mouthguard, first used by UCLA guard Dick Perry in his lone season as a Bruins basketball player in 1946-47. Perry modeled the Acrylic Splint at tradeshows for the good doctor.

Luftman handed the thing to Lorenzo Romar, who washed it and would return it to its owner. Cameron Dollar, Kristaan Johnson, and other Bruins would recount that scene to Romar for years, with ample laughter to make it seem as if Romar were O'Bannon's lap dog. Romar isn't too embarrassed. Just doing the polite thing, he says, which he would do anytime, anywhere, for anyone. Many players were furious with Givens for his carelessness. *Damn, omm'A, why'd you have to provoke him?* They questioned why he would jeopardize not only their chances in the upcoming NCAAs but even risk injuring O'Bannon with the NBA draft just a few months down the road.

"You didn't want Ed mad at you," says Toby Bailey. "It was more of a father-type thing. We weren't afraid that he'd hurt us or spank us ... you just didn't want to disappoint him, like you don't want to disappoint your parents. He was so feared, that's why it was, 'I'll take this charge ... don't want to disappoint Ed.' We never wanted to stop hustling. We'd dive onto the floor ... didn't want to disappoint Ed. All the young guys feared him, and he treated all of us the same."

Romar gave O'Bannon ten minutes to cool down before joining him in the locker room. Of course, O'Bannon didn't quit. He blew his radiator cap over Givens's swipe, but he would forgive the negligent rookie. Nearly twenty years later, O'Bannon recalled being more angry with the lean center's demeanor than any physical indiscretion. "He was that dude, he'd hit you and have no idea that he'd hit you. He had no clue, the elbow he hit me with ... I can take a punch. But you hit me; at least *know* that you hit me. No clue. That's what upset me. But he's a good kid. I like omm'A ... a cool cat."

The first day of March, a Wednesday, brought UCLA's bitter crosstown rivals into Pauley Pavilion, and the Bruins and Trojans could not have been in more disparate positions.

USC had not recovered from the shock of George Raveling's retirement. The Trojans traveled to Pauley in total freefall, having lost their previous eleven games—the fifth defeat in that string had been to UCLA at the Sports Arena. Interim boss Charlie Parker had no answers. They had dropped thirteen of fifteen in the league and were 7-18 overall. At the other end of the spectrum, top-ranked UCLA (21-2 overall, 13-2 in the Pac-10) would become the first team in the country to secure a spot in the upcoming NCAAs with a victory. The Bruins had a two-game edge, over Arizona, in the league with three conference games to play. All UCLA had to do was defeat the Trojans because it held the tiebreaker—in head-to-head play—over the Wildcats.

The league had staged a tournament from 1987 through 1990, but fan disinterest led to coaches getting their wish to preserve the value of the regular season, so conference executives scrapped it. Only the Pac-10 and Ivy League did not have a league tournament. "We don't want co-champs ... we want it outright," said Toby Bailey. "We've already talked about that."

Charlie Parker believed fans might see his squad's best performance of the season and compared it to a popular basketball documentary at theaters. "If we're ever going to get motivated to play, this is an ideal situation; playing the number-one-ranked team, the number one player in the country, and have it [be] against your rival school ... they oughta call it *Hoop Dreams II*."

Jim Harrick certainly empathized with all the distractions and uncertainty that had plagued USC and Parker. However, Harrick knew that narrative all too well. He could try to get his guys to keep George Mason from reaching triple digits, but that was a long time ago. Parker's problems would easily become Harrick's with a defeat to the Trojans. When referee Mark Reischling hoisted that ball up into the air for the opening tap, neither Harrick nor his players wanted to give the Trojans anything less than their full attention and effort.

Which did not translate into a scintillating first twenty minutes. Jaha Wilson (ten points, seven rebounds) and Lorenzo Orr (eight points, six boards) powered the Trojans to a 39-38 lead at the half. Having sunk only four of nine free throws kept USC from creating more of a pad. Unfortunately, for Parker, the second twenty minutes had to be played, he had no bench, and of his regulars only point man Cameron Murray (ten points, five assists) played unselfishly.

The Bruins scored the first dozen points of the second half. Game over. UCLA enjoyed a 47-27 second-half advantage, and its 85-66 victory gave Harrick only his second sweep of USC since his first season in Westwood. Public-address announcer Chuck White informed the jubilant crowd of 12,608 that UCLA became the first team in the country to earn an NCAA berth. Nice, said Cameron Dollar, but that's just one of our many goals. "We have to move on. It's in the past." Ed O'Bannon slightly grinned; those comments fit his script.

When the Trojans threatened, having cut their deficit to single digits just past the midway point of the second half, Tyus Edney lobbed a fast-break lob that Toby Bailey finished with a flourish, and UCLA kept USC at bay. Bailey tallied twenty-four points, a career best, in his fourth consecutive start. "You're always going to have to stop our runs," he said. "When we play defense and rebound and fast break, we all follow. We're an explosive team." Like a match striking sandpaper to ignite dynamite, said Cameron Dollar.

Ed O'Bannon cooled off, tallying only fourteen points. But he had two of his team's three three-point shots, and he highlighted efforts by Toby Bailey and J.R. Henderson (fourteen points off the bench), strong rebounding by his teammates, and USC's tenacity, since every starter hit double figures in scoring. "They don't get enough credit," O'Bannon said. "They play hard, at least against us. It's tough to play against that team."

Harrick had made the final tweak of his team—starting Toby Bailey—during its mettle-testing stretch of five games, and that gave him a core unit of seven players on which he would depend. The last missing link in making this team exceptional, Harrick wrote. That also gave him immense flexibility, on defenses to which he could resort and players who could assume different roles within those concepts. They had weathered a first-half pelting by USC, and they dramatically turned it around in the second half. The past had taught Harrick, his assistants, and his senior players that the Bruins could never relax, and a game at Louisville would provide further reinforcement.

Denny Crum had played for John Wooden and served two stints as an assistant to the master tactician, the second of which took place during the seasons that ended in national titles in 1969, 1970, and 1971.

Crum, a native of the San Fernando Valley, was aggressive and strong-willed, sometimes too headstrong. He once told a UCLA reserve to prepare to enter a game, which made Wooden exclaim, *I'm the coach of this team and don't you tell me how to coach my team!* Wooden threatened to force Crum to sit at the far end of the bench. That was akin to making Crum stand with his nose in the corner. Crum left for Louisville in 1971. He would coach for thirty years, win two national championships, and land in two halls of fame.

Tony Luftman, the rookie student manager, often took girls he dated by Wooden's condo. Luftman was either trying to gain the approval of the elder statesman, or show off; likely both. This one, Luftman said, might be a keeper. (That was a common Luftman line.) Wooden would cross his arms and tell Luftman, very matter-of-factly, how much he reminded Wooden of Crum, a skirt chaser of some renown. It took Luftman a while to comprehend that that did not exactly qualify as a glowing endorsement from Wooden.

Between the lines, Harrick believed Denny Crum was one of the few candidates—maybe the only one—who could have immediately followed John Wooden at UCLA and not been intimidated or overwhelmed by all that awaited him. Those intense expectations and pressures drove the amiable Gene Bartow out of Westwood after only two seasons. Crum had been intimate with UCLA, its hierarchy and system, the pathology to which Steve Lavin had referred, but he left for Louisville for the long haul—perhaps because of that pathology. And he brought glory to the Cardinals using much of John Wooden's system, which helped Cameron Murray resuscitate his enjoyment of the game.

On the gray, brisk afternoon of Sunday, March 5, Crum had just celebrated his fifty-eighth birthday. He had already won his NCAA titles, in 1980 and 1986. His Cardinals were 16-12. They would reach the Sweet Sixteen the following season, and the Elite Eight after that, but Crum's run in Louisville would end in 2001. (That would coincide with Rick Pitino's exit from the Boston Celtics, but Louisville wouldn't secure Pitino's services until Pete Dalis instigated a messy escapade with Pitino.)

Freedom Hall, which opened in 1956, held nearly twenty thousand people for the first time. As it turned out, the crowd of 19,872 still constituted a record. All of them and every Cardinals player walked away impressed by the Bruins, who slammed Louisville, 91-73. They had witnessed a UCLA team hitting full stride. It shot higher than sixty percent in the first half, and better than fifty percent in the second. Jim Harrick relied on six players, and Ed O'Bannon had led the way with twenty-five points. He made two of three shots from beyond the three-point arc. He had five rebounds and two steals. He didn't commit a turnover.

When Louisville threatened the Bruins twice in the second half, with the din of the crowd redlining, Ed O'Bannon took the life out of the Cardinals. Toby Bailey had been the object of taunts before and during the game, but he had won over his critics by scoring seventeen points, grabbing eleven rebounds, and doling out seven assists (with seven turnovers). Afterward, fans begged him for his autograph; he even signed a one-dollar bill. Bailey said his coaches know turnovers could come along with his high level of energy, but that they had confidence in him. "They know I'll do something like Jason Kidd. I'm not comparing myself to him, but he also has a lot of turnovers when he plays."

George Zidek (eight points, five boards) and J.R. Henderson (four points, three rebounds) had performed under par. But Charles O'Bannon and Tyus Edney supported Ed and Bailey. Harrick was feeling more and more sanguine the less he went to his bench. But Harrick hoped the disappearance of Cameron Dollar—who turned it over three times, collected two personal fouls, and tallied only one free throw—wasn't be an omen. The Cardinals were suitably impressed. Sophomore forward Jason Osborne said Michigan State had been his team's strongest opponent of the season, until that Sunday. Of the Bruins, he said, "They deserve to be number one."

Chapter 18

TONY LUFTMAN HAD LUGGED a case of orange juice from a storage area into the UCLA locker room. He plopped it in front of a refrigerated unit with sliding glass doors, poked some holes into the clear plastic covering with an index finger, and ripped it open. He bent over, grabbed a few warm containers.

A dozen feet away, Ed O'Bannon sat at his locker. He changed into his practice uniform. Nobody else was in the room. On a television screen high in a corner, Jim Harrick sat across from Chris Myers, who had taken over *Up Close* duties from Roy Firestone. The popular ESPN interview show aired in the early afternoon on the West Coast.

Neither O'Bannon nor Luftman paid much attention to the TV. They had been listening to Harrick's voice for months. It was as if he were actually in the room, as if they could never escape that twang, part of their perpetual background hum. But Luftman froze as Harrick praised Ed O'Bannon. Luftman slowly glanced to his left, at O'Bannon, who didn't pause as he slipped his jersey over his head. "Ed O'Bannon," declared Harrick with some insistence, "is the *best* basketball player in America."

Luftman's eyes widened as he stared at O'Bannon, who shifted his eyes over to Luftman. O'Bannon slightly raised his eyebrows, feigning surprise—as if he were hearing sports-related praise for the first time—with a slight grin. Again, hot air.

Mere words. Meant nothing. He grabbed his high-tops and strolled into the trainer's room to get his ankles taped.

Classic, Luftman thought.

If only college hoops games were two-on-two contests, even three-on-three. Then maybe Oregon State would have been able to hang with the Bruins at Pauley in the next-to-last game of the regular season.

The Beavers featured Brent Barry and Mustapha Hoff, and not much else. With Gary Payton as a catalyst, Jim Anderson had coached OSU into the NCAAs in 1990. Since then the team's victory total had slipped annually, and the bald fifty-seven-year-old coach had announced his imminent retirement after this season. He was coaching his final collegiate games. Would the Beavers rally to send the boss out on a positive note? That it fell on the night of Thursday, March 9, could have benefited OSU, too, since Oregon would visit the arena Saturday—that's the game Ed O'Bannon had circled on his calendar for two months.

Would O'Bannon's focus and fire regarding all those indignities from the Ducks transfer to his teammates, and would they take Oregon State for granted and possibly give the Beavers an avenue to an upset of the nation's top-ranked team?

That appeared to be the case, as Oregon State guard J.D. Vetter nailed a jump shot five minutes into the second half to slice the Beavers' deficit to 48-43. The visitors were not going to lie down before one of the country's powerhouses. A sellout crowd of 12,682 again sat on its hands and worried. Jim Harrick sat Charles O'Bannon and George Zidek, for Cameron Dollar and J.R. Henderson. Brent Barry had rung up fifteen points in the first half, and most of those had been against Toby Bailey. Bailey didn't appreciate Harrick giving that defensive assignment to two other Bruins, but Harrick told him not to worry, that Bailey would get more chances to snuff Barry.

After Harrick's substitutions, though, he had Bailey play the back line of the two-two-one zone press, with Henderson and Dollar up front, and Ed O'Bannon and Tyus Edney in the middle. A main goal of that scheme is to hogtie an opposing dribbler in the back half of the court, to make that guy stop dribbling and panic as the ten-second clock winds down. The next objective is to trap the guy just past the midcourt line, near the sideline; the ball can't go backward, and the sideline acts as another defender to suffocate the poor foe. That gives the Bruins myriad angles and opportunities for thievery.

Within a minute that transpired, resulting in an easy layup for Ed O'Bannon. OSU cowered, and O'Bannon dunked the ball over Stephane Brown for an eleven-point lead. UCLA scored fourteen of eighteen points in one stretch, and followed that by slamming the Beavers with a 10-1 run. Barry led a spectacular fast break, capped by a sleight-of-hand pass that set up Hoff for a dunk. But that only got OSU within nineteen points, and UCLA eased to the finish line with an 86-67 victory. Barry finished with twenty-one points, eight rebounds, and seven assists, and Hoff had seventeen points and ten boards.

Charles O'Bannon had disappeared, but he avoided a public shaming by his older brother. Ed registered twenty-one points and nine rebounds, and Tyus Edney (thirteen points, eight assists), reserve forward J.R. Henderson (sixteen points, nine rebound), and Toby Bailey (fourteen points, seven rebounds) complemented their fearless leader well. Bailey was grateful that he wouldn't have to tangle with Barry again on a college court. "He's sweet. He has one of the quickest shots off the dribble that I've ever seen."

UCLA (24-2) was atop the national poll, the champion of its conference with a league record of 15-2, and the victor of twelve in a row. It was steaming into Ed O'Bannon's vendetta with Oregon, and it was confident a victory over the Ducks would garner it the top seed in the West Regional in Sunday's NCAA selection show on CBS. Jim Anderson praised the way the Bruins finished and predicted that they would do well in the tournament. Ed O'Bannon refused to gloat, saying, "As long as we keep it going, we'll be fine."

Not only did all twelve Bruins play against Oregon State, but walk-on, six-foot-six sophomore forward Bob Myers converted a layup with twenty seconds left to get into the scoring books for the first time all season. The future wunderkind general manager of the Golden State Warriors said, "Incredible ... things are going so well. We're the number one team in the country, and we're just having fun."

Myers and Ike Nwankwo often recorded the highest grade-point averages on the team every quarter, which they turned into duels. Both had clever wits, too, which helped when a week or two passed without their numbers being called by Harrick. Myers once told Nwankwo that sometime, way down the road and when he least expected it, Nwankwo would be sweating and swatting away butterflies as he waited outside the door of some executive's office for the job interview of his life. As Nwankwo strolled inside, he'd be stunned to see Myers sitting there, waiting to grill Nwankwo with the heels of his wingtips resting on an antique Louis XIV desk.

Nwankwo was almost certain that, in Myers's vision, he was also toking on a double corona Cohiba from Cuba, grinning like a revenuer. En route to dropping me off at the Bangkok airport, Nwankwo laughs. After the airport, he would be heading to an important meeting with a potential promotional client for his academy. Myers was less than a year into his post with the

Warriors. No way Myers could be laying in wait for Ike inside that corner office. Absurd. Asinine. But Nwankwo always walks into any meeting thinking Myers will be sitting on the other side of the desk. Always.

The schedule makers inside the league offices up in Walnut Creek, California, could not have fathomed what they had mustered once they inked Oregon in the regular-season finale against UCLA at Pauley. The messy technical fouls, and ejection, of Jim Harrick in the conference opener in Eugene had provided ample grist for his many critics and detractors. Here we go again, they wrote in columns disguised as features and bellowed on the talk-radio circuit. Harrick alone kept the airwaves hot, and certain bellicose broadcasters employed, for years.

After that meltdown in the final minutes, Oregon students rushed the court and just about ran over the Bruins. Ed O'Bannon wanted to take on all of them—*in this corner, fighting in the powder blues* ... Somehow, he bit his tongue when surrounded by media in the Mac Court visitors' locker room. He had so badly wanted to reveal to the world how that had not accurately represented who the Bruins were and what they could do, and, well, if we don't beat them by twenty points when they come to our house we will consider it a loss. Yet, in a typhoon of emotions O'Bannon—unlike Damon Stoudamire—had retained his diplomacy.

On Saturday night, March 11, Ed would let his actions speak volumes. The Brothers O'Bannon were plenty pissed. The Bruins were about to finally finish these Pac-10 preliminaries. Los Angeles responded, as more than thirteen thousand fans packed into Pauley for only the second time in the building's history. They had missed that mark by thirty-nine fans when Pistol Pete Maravich and LSU visited in 1969. And the 13,037 bodies eclipsed the arena's previous max—when Coach K and Duke and Christian Laettner visited in 1992—by fourteen. For a change, a UCLA basketball team was receiving overwhelming and unbridled support from a fan base that had always been as fickle as it was demanding and spoiled.

The seniors were introduced. Tyus Edney strolled out with his parents, Hank and Barbara, beside him. George Zidek towered over Peter and Olga Schultz. The Schultz's orange tree had been Zidek's first genuine inducement to attend UCLA, and the couple's nourishment had comforted him in ways they'd never know. But the combustible combination of a flu virus and Senior Night festivities discombobulated the Czech big man's inner workings that were as delicate as a Swiss timepiece.

Wanting to go out on a high note, to thank so many fans for their years of support, Zidek missed all four shots he attempted. He did grab six rebounds, but he turned the ball over twice and committed three fouls, and Harrick only played him twenty minutes. Sitting on a picnic bench inside a large dining hall near his Prague home many years later, Zidek's embarrassment hadn't dissipated. "I just had one of the worst games. Clearly, the self-imposed pressure got to me. My routine was broken up a bit with everyone walking out to mid-court before the game. I just did not score a point. That was pretty heavy stuff on your Senior Night." Administrative assistant Doug Erickson relentlessly chided Zidek with *goose egg* taunts for years.

Ed O'Bannon, surrounded by Ed Sr., Madeline, and Rosa Bravo, shuffled out to the center of the court. He plucked Aaron—wearing a tiny UCLA jersey with LIL O'B on the back—out of Rosa's arms. Ed smiled and raised his tiny son nearly to those banners. Thunderous applause initially shocked the lad, but he quickly smiled. Twenty-five feet away, Marques Johnson grinned, too; twenty-two years earlier, Marques had hoisted a tiny Ed Jr. the same way out there on campus.

Oregon tried to upstage the festivities by scoring five of the first seven points, but the Ducks were quickly euthanized. The Bruins scored the next eight points and never trailed again on a night when their devastating defense limited Oregon to shoot thirty-five percent. Kenya Wilkins was psyched out, missing all ten shots he attempted. Darryl Parker hit four out of ten, and Henry Madden connected on only five of thirteen off the bench. Parker had no reason to point at Ed O'Bannon this time. UCLA led, 43-30, at halftime, and coasted to a 94-78 victory.

The O'Bannons led the way. Beagle-Beagle didn't require any saliva-addled cursing from his older brother as he led everyone with twenty-five points and eleven rebounds. After Oregon's shoot-around in Pauley the previous day, Charles found a wide green Ducks wristband by the bench. He wore it, between the elbow and biceps on his left arm, during the game for special inspiration. He thought it would be humorous to defeat Oregon wearing its own colors. He says, "Especially because we owed them." Ed tallied twenty-four points and yanked down ten boards. The brothers combined to make eighteen of their thirty shots.

The *piece de resistance* was reserved for Ed O'Bannon, when Jim Harrick took him out of his final Pauley Pavilion game with less than five minutes remaining. O'Bannon had just slammed home a lob from Tyus Edney to make it 78-54. Ten seconds later, finely tuned to the tenor of the evening, Harrick sent omm'A Givens in for O'Bannon when a ball rolled out of bounds. O'Bannon bowed to the student section. Wild applause enveloped him. He angled to the center of the court, to the four gold block letters on each half of the powder blue donut, and bent down. That was the midpoint of all those hundreds of seventeens he had rattled off over the years. On that court, in his words, he had experienced so many ups and downs, and fights, and love.

Ed O'Bannon knelt down and smooched the egg yolk. The night and the career and that injury, so long ago, and tonight's foe ... it all flooded O'Bannon with an emotional well that made him tingle. "It hit me this was my last game in Pauley," he said, "that five years were coming to a close, and it seemed like the right thing to do." He loped to his sideline for a long exchange of hugs, and he reserved the longest one—tears and all—for trainer Tony Spino, who to Harrick was *Spiiiiine Dawg*, the man who had put in so many hours with O'Bannon in his recovery process and would tend so delicately to an infirm John Wooden in his final months.

"Ed owes a lot to this program, and the program owes a lot to Ed," said Charles O'Bannon. That this opponent had been Oregon was not lost on Jim Harrick or Ed O'Bannon, or many Bruins; it had been against the Ducks that O'Bannon finally appeared in his first UCLA game, Oregon had zapped UCLA on Mac Court in the regular-season finale a year earlier before the Bruins visited that slaughterhouse in Oklahoma City, and then there was that horrible ending nine weeks earlier in Eugene that left Ed tongue-tied. Moreover, his number thirty-one would be retired, along with Marques Johnson and his number fifty-four, at halftime of another Oregon contest.

UCLA didn't win by his predicted margin of twenty points, but the one-sided victory was just as rewarding to O'Bannon. The Bruins would not count it as a defeat. They had secured Jim Harrick's second conference championship in seven seasons. Amid the celebrations on the court, Marques Johnson tapped O'Bannon on his shoulder and whispered, *Nine down, six to go.*

Chapter 19

WHILE FLORIDA INTERNATIONAL coach Bob Weltlich ran his Golden Panthers through their paces, in preparation for UCLA in the first round of the NCAAs, his boss—athletic director Ted Aceto—interviewed candidates to replace Weltlich. A stern and demanding figure on the court, Weltlich fit the template of a Bobby Knight disciple. He even passed a few of those eighty-three prospects in the halls of the FIU campus in Miami. That was not appropriate, Weltlich admitted, but he did not care, either. Weltlich passed his eventual replacement when he walked by Marcos "Shakey" Rodriguez, a Cuban-American who at fifteen had been tagged with the nickname by a coach because of his hyperkinetic body language. Rodriguez would become Division-I basketball's first Hispanic head coach.

Weltlich had been an assistant to Knight at Army, and he was on Knight's Indiana staff when the Hoosiers went 32-0—and defeated UCLA and Marques Johnson in the Final Four—in the 1975-76 season. Weltlich had announced in January, during a desultory regular season in which the Panthers would win only eight of twenty-six games, his intention to bow out at the end of the campaign. He didn't care about coaching or the university. Fans barely filled the arena to ten percent of its 4,661-seat capacity.

However, the fifty-year-old balding Weltlich would bring a biting sense of humor to Boise. He likened FIU, against UCLA, to a convicted felon sitting on death row. *You wanna see us die by lethal injection, the gas chamber, or the electric chair?* (A form of that phrase would portend UCLA's next game.) Somehow the Panthers awoke in the Trans America Athletic Conference tournament to beat Stetson, Southeastern Louisiana, and Mercer, snatching the league's bid to the NCAAs. The selection committee looked at FIU's 11-18 record, slapped it with a sixteen seed, and sent it to Boise as the bottom-feeder to meet top-ranked and top-seeded UCLA.

"Most of us were just hoping to get the season over with," said senior guard Matt Tchir. "Now look at us. My God, we're playing UCLA!" Star forward James Mazyck said it didn't make sense, and he confirmed that he was a big dreamer, "... but I could never be crazy enough to dream this stuff up." When FIU's draw was revealed, its players locked arms and bellowed, *We want UCLA! We want UCLA!* Assistant coach Clarence Flournory interjected, *No, you don't! No, you don't!* He had reviewed the Bruins and knew the Golden Panthers were in trouble.

The last team to play in the NCAAs with a worse record than FIU had been George Washington, at 9-16, in 1961. Only two other squads had poorer seasons than the Panthers and still managed to get into college basketball's marquee event, and they played each other in 1955, when 7-19 Bradley defeated 9-17 Oklahoma City. Bradley upended Southern Methodist before losing a Final Four spot to Colorado.

Panthers senior guard Marc Dozier didn't concern himself with the tremendous odds stacked against his team. He was a fan of Ed O'Bannon, so at the very least he would be able to watch his favorite player up close. "You don't think I'm going to be loving life?" Tchir believed he and his fellow Panthers would not get tossed around Boise State Pavilion (now Taco Bell Arena) and lose by fifty points, but they weren't exactly figuring on an upset, either. He said, "I mean, it is UCLA."

The Bruins arrived in Boise on Thursday, March 16. That night twelfth-seeded Miami of Ohio defeated Arizona in a first rounder in Dayton, Ohio. As soon as it ended on TV, every Bruin heard a commotion out in the hotel hallway. Doors opened. Heads peered down the hall. Ed O'Bannon was running, jumping up and down, pumping his fist, hollering as if his Powerball numbers had just come in. "I *hate* those guys!" he yowled in his excitement. Lute's Place was open for business, once again, in Tucson. (Ed O'Bannon and Kevin Dempsey weren't the only UCLA figures who abhorred Olson or his program; many associated with the Bruins would despise Olson for, they believed, wielding his considerable influence—with other league coaches, who vote for the award—to have Damon Stoudamire share conference player-of-the-year honors with O'Bannon, whose national cachet was only rising. In two years, Olson would win his lone national championship.)

Missouri defeated Indiana in the third Boise game on Friday, March 17. In the last one, given prime-time status because of the Bruins, FIU did not lose by fifty. UCLA won, 92-56. A clump of FIU players encircled the Bruins, namely Ed O'Bannon, for autographs. Every player on UCLA's roster played and recorded at least one basket, compliments of Jim Harrick sitting his starters about five minutes into the second half. Charles O'Bannon had fourteen points, on seven-for-nine shooting, and J.R. Henderson scored sixteen. George Zidek rebounded from that poor performance against Oregon to make four of eight shots, for eight points, and grabbed six rebounds in sixteen minutes, but he was nearing two months without having logged thirty minutes in a game.

James Mazyck scored twenty-one points for Florida International. That's the extent of its highlights. Unless, that is, Bob Weltlich is factored into the Boise experience. "That's what you call an ass kicking," said Weltlich, who wore a shirt bearing a phone number and scrawled with I NEED A JOB and LEAVE A

MESSAGE, at a press conference. Someone called; he coached South Alabama to three twenty-victory campaigns, including the NCAAs in 1998. He taught middle school in Alabama. And he penned a novel, *Crooked Zebra*, about a referee who fixes an NCAA final. A reviewer liked the plot but wrote that Weltlich has *virtually no writing style.* He joked about only being able to coach again under an assumed name, since every ref would give him two technicals and eject him at the start of every game.

A goal of limiting FIU to forty points was trashed by Harrick, who didn't want to embarrass anyone. However, Harrick did not exactly like what he saw on his bench in the final minutes. Players smiled and laughed, horsed around "a little *too* much." Harrick felt uneasy, too, about his senior point guard. Tyus Edney had tweaked his left ankle at some point in the first half. Near midnight back at the hotel, Edney needed to be carried off the bus. Ice was wrapped around the swollen ankle. Hank Edney was prepared to employ the healing method, based on heat, he had learned from a Jamaican tiler. Jim Harrick glanced at Hank as he told trainer Tony Spino, "*Spiiiiine Dawg*, don't let him [Hank] do *that treatment* on Tyus." Hank said, "Coach, do you need him tomorrow or in two weeks?" Resigned, Harrick said, "Go to it; do your thing."

Years earlier Hank Edney was experiencing excruciating back pain. He lay on a tray of ice as a Jamaican man—Hank thinks his name was Johnny—placed and secured tiles on a bathroom floor in his Bixby Knolls home. Johnny laughed at Hank, telling him heat was *da answer*, not ice. "In Jamaica, their joints and muscles would be hurting after a day of cutting sugar cane," Hank says today. "But they'd have to get back out in those fields the next day, to earn a living, and heat was the answer." Johnny prepared a scathing pot of water and another, which simmered. He'd dip tiles and place them on Hank's back. Since then Hank has had no back issues.

When sons Tyus and Russell sustained injuries playing ball in their youth, Hank always went to the hot tiles. He treated Tyus's ankle with as much heat as Tyus could bear that night, and throughout Saturday. Says Hank, "Without that, he wouldn't have been able to play in the next game."

In a radio interview many years later, Jim Harrick was asked what he recalled about his team's overall tournament run. He said, "I remember *evvvvv-reeeee-thangggg* ... we started out with Florida *Atlantic* ... "

UCLA coaches spent Saturday devising strategy—they would err, big time—for Missouri on Sunday afternoon. Iowa State and Julius Michalik had thumped the Tigers at the start of the Big Eight Conference tournament, but Missouri regrouped to get by Indiana, 65-60, in Boise to improve to 20-8. Senior guard Paul O'Liney was its motor, and Missouri had a few other talented players in its backcourt. The UCLA masterminds slipped when they placed too much attention on twin seven-foot juniors Sammie and Simeon Haley, and fellow postman Derek Grimm.

Ed O'Bannon studied. He roomed with Cameron Dollar. The Bruins slept in Saturday, had a team meal, and reviewed strategy—focusing on the Haleys, and Grimm—with coaches. Some reviewed texts for upcoming exams. After another team meal that night, players retired to their rooms. Hank Edney monitored Tyus's ankle, applying constant heat, for hours. Toby Bailey watched videos. J.R. Henderson toyed with a video game. Cameron Dollar slept.

Ed O'Bannon was bored and could not sleep. He had become the emboldened leader that he had set out to be. He had shown his teammates the proper way and only raised his voice when the situation demanded authority, or had he? At UCLA's last Pauley practice before it left for Boise, Jim Harrick had Bill Walton deliver some nasal-plugged, guttural words of encouragement to his players. "Play your best when your best is needed," said the verbose Walton, cribbing a few lines from John Wooden. A parrot shop, hawking birds that mimicked Wooden quotes, would do very well in Westwood. He told the Bruins to take care of their bodies, to eat and sleep well. George Zidek sighed about that last part.

Steve Lavin had nicknamed Ed O'Bannon Daddy Lion; when he snarled the rest of the Bruins—as if they were his cubs—responded and straightened up. They could screw around only so much. There was always a limit, which Ed would enforce and remind. They astounded him by paying so much for shirts, jeans, and shoes; he was simple, practical, and knew how to stretch thirty or forty bucks. To Ed, his teammates carelessly threw money away on expensive duds. He did not look after them twenty-four hours a day, ensuring that they were always tucked under the covers by a decent hour to get their requisite sleep and be fresh for the next day. He had his own apartment, with Rosa in Mar Vista on Sepulveda, to retire to at the end of each day, where his priority was tucking in his own infant son.

But late the night of Saturday, March 18, Ed was restless, keyed up. No way he could sleep. He strayed. Ed inched opened the door to his hotel room. He peered right, left, and right. He slinked to Deanna Cherry's room. He heard muffled laughter. She was talking with managers Tony Luftman, Brendan Jacobson, and Andrew Pruter. Ed lightly tapped the door. It opened. He sat on the far bed. Kevin Dempsey showed. Charles O'Bannon might have appeared, but he didn't stay long. They talked and laughed, just what Ed needed to alleviate some of the stress that had been accumulating with the advent of the tournament of his life, learning every day how to be a parent, and the uncertainty of the upcoming NBA draft. Ed even told his peers about his initial desire to attend UNLV and how that had disintegrated.

Years later, some of Ed's teammates playfully accused him of some shenanigans with Deanna. At a taco feast inside the home of Toby Bailey and his wife, a former UCLA soccer player, they teased Ed about that night, but he swore nothing untoward happened. That was confirmed by three figures in the room. They were just shooting the breeze. Ed was loose and relaxed. Pruter thought, *Man, it's kinda late ... the game is gonna be early ... but this is so much fun.* They only noticed it was 3 A.M. when they heard a rap at the door and glanced at the red glare of the clock radio on the nightstand between the two beds. All of their eyes widened, like a slapstick scene from a silent-era flick.

"Shit!" Ed said. "Three in the mornin'? What am I doin'? I got a game [today]!" Deanna eased open the door to find a UCLA official scowling at her; he had the room next door, and they were keeping him up with their loud banter. He thought the racket would quell. It did not. The man took a few steps inside the room and glared at everyone. He peered at Ed sitting on the edge of the bed nearest the window.

"What are *you* doin' here? You're all suspended!"

Ed's heart sank. *Holy Shit! I know this will get back to Coach Harrick. He'll kill me. We'll lose and it'll be blamed on me.* The guy who had become someone UCLA fans had not witnessed in a generation, someone that just might be able to take them back to the pinnacle of the game, was acting like a sailor on leave. "I thought that was it," Ed says today. "I was told [Cherry] got fired after that." Others confirmed her release. Harrick would eventually take his players to task for breaking curfew both nights in Boise. "I was so disappointed in myself, mentally disappointed in myself," Ed says. "I could not get into a situation like that again. Didn't need much of Harrick's riot act after that ... how I screwed up. I knew I had screwed up."

The Bruins were on their heels from the start. The Tigers played aggressively and confidently, hitting seven of eleven shots beyond the three-point arc in the first half and taking a 42-34 advantage into halftime. Tyus Edney was operating on that tender left ankle, but it was remarkable that he could even play. Missouri was having its way.

UCLA's plan that had emphasized the Missouri centers—the Red Zone—was being abused thoroughly by the Tigers' guards and forwards, who were striking from the outside. *Only get beat over the top.* That had been the Bruins' mantra, clogging the middle to deny layups and dunks. Woe to any trespasser. Missouri was beating UCLA over the top; Norm Stewart was foiling Jim Harrick.

In the second half, Harrick noticed his guys drooping their shoulders and noggins, some slouched. Tulsa, Michigan, Indiana ... Missouri? Ed O'Bannon snapped out of it. It wasn't about the past or feeling sorry for yourself, of which he had accused so many previous Bruins. He ignited fifteen consecutive points by UCLA. It's the heavyweight exchange of uppercuts and hooks for which he had been preparing since returning from Oklahoma City. To him the Bruins were up against the ropes, but the bell hadn't tolled yet. O'Bannon dropped in an eight-foot bank shot to give the Bruins a 73-72 edge in the final minute. Again, though, the Tigers showed they did not possess glass jaws. Cameron Dollar got whistled for fouling Jon Sutherland with forty seconds left. A new thirty-five-second clock began. Missouri could almost whittle that thing down to nothing.

It nearly did just that. Julian Winfield connected on a short banker for a 74-73 lead with four point eight seconds left. Harrick was grateful for the rule that stopped the clock on a made basket inside the final minute. That probably saved him at least a tick. He called for a timeout—he always preferred to have one in his back pocket for the end, just in case. A head coach and his three assistants, who were most fortunate to retain their jobs twelve months earlier, needed to come up with some magic, right now, to very likely remain employed.

Harrick did not wait for Tyus Edney to reach the bench. He approached Edney on the court. Fresh in Harrick's mind were Michigan and Jimmy King. He told Edney this *will* be *his* play. He will receive the inbounds pass and take it all the way. Harrick clarified himself. *You take it. Do ... you ... understand .... me?* Edney nodded. *Ty-russ, do you have a crystal clear understanding of what I said?* Yes, Edney responded, you want me to shoot the ball. *Absolutely. I want you to shoot the ball. You understand that, don't you?* Edney nodded.

Michigan was fresh in Edney's mind, too. Although he had told some reporters the nightmare of King picking off his interior pass to Ed O'Bannon in Tucson had long faded from his memory, that wasn't true. Edney had told me how Jimmy King, at the damnedest of times, kept popping into his thoughts and dreams over the previous 728 days.

Harrick turned to his bench to find Lorenzo Romar exclaiming, "the long ball! We have to throw a long pass! We have to ... " Harrick told Romar to shut up and sit down. Harrick had already made the call, on the court, to Edney. Harrick and his assistants had botched this one by focusing so heavily on the seven-foot, 230-pound Haleys; they had combined for only two baskets and five boards in twenty-nine minutes. Derek Grimm had thirteen points and four boards. The Tigers had connected on twelve of nineteen attempts beyond the three-point arc.

If the Bruins had looked like they were scrambling on defense, it's because that's exactly what they were doing. Now they had one chance at redemption. "We are NOT going to lose this game!" Ed O'Bannon demanded in the huddle. "We're NOT losing!" Harrick knew exactly what he wanted. Cameron Dollar inbounds the ball to Edney, Harrick said. The others will spread the court. Edney will go all the way, "and they're NOT going to foul you," Harrick told Edney.

In a similar scene his first season as UCLA's coach, Harrick watched UC-Irvine beat the Bruins the exact same way. Harrick knew his team couldn't afford to foul the Anteaters' guard. He also envisaged Jerry West's dash against the Celtics more than thirty years earlier. Plus, he knew Edney could circumnavigate whatever defensive tactics the Tigers threw at him. Moreover, Edney was the best Bruin in a seldom-used practice drill of Harrick's in which five seconds were put onto the shot clock, by Tony Luftman, and a random player had to go full-court against another random player. The big guys were the worst, always flailing sixty-foot rainbows generally in the direction of the other rim. Others could cross mid-court but were left with prayer heaves, too. Edney was the only one whose opposition never altered, and Cameron Dollar always tried to force Edney another direction, to make him turn. But the super quick Edney always ended up with a layup at the front of the rim. They ran that fire drill maybe four times a season.

Out of the huddle, Ed O'Bannon told Edney to look for him, that he would be in the left corner. Edney heard, but he didn't listen. He had resisted testing his sore left ankle on drives into the paint. He stayed on the perimeter. He deferred. Now he will depend upon that ankle—and all that heat from his pop—for the play of the game, perhaps the play of his life.

In the stands, Hank Edney closed his eyes. He had seen Tyus navigate such full-court situations in his youth, weavin' and zig-zaggin' through and around all comers, twisting and turning, only to miss the shot at the very end of the ordeal. Doesn't matter how good you look, Hank told Tyus, if you don't hit the shot. Tyus made a couple but missed a lot of them. His eyes still closed,

Hank thought about how difficult that plane ride home was going to be, having lost this thing by a single point. *A single point!*

Dollar, whom Norm Stewart chose not to defend, easily tossed a ten-foot pass to Edney from under the Missouri basket. Jon Sutherland tried to guard Edney, who zipped up the left side to the mid-court line. Julian Winfield tried to deflect Edney's thrust, but Edney executed a nifty wrap-around dribble behind the left side of his back. The ball bounced to the right, Edney controlled it knowing it would be right there in his right palm, and he sped by Sutherland and Winfield. Edney darted into the right side of the lane. Derek Grimm, a six-foot-nine sophomore, inched up on the tips of his toes, hands high in the sky. A foot shorter, Edney lunged into the air and ensured that he leapt up, not forward, as he closed in on the rim. He took the ball far out in his right hand, and he kind of scoop-hooked it barely over Grimm's fingernails.

The ball gently kissed off the backboard and fell through the bottom of the net as the final buzzer blared. Hank Edney only opened his eyes in time to see the ball fall through the bottom of the net. He nearly fell over the seats in front of him. Marques Johnson screamed into homes and automobiles all over Southern California, *Yeah, Baby! Yeah, Baby!* Near a tunnel Jim Milhorn bear-hugged and high-fived John Dolak, an assistant to Bill Bennett. The crowd of 11,886 exploded. Next to me in press row, mild-mannered columnist Randy Hill sprung out of his seat like a jack-in-the-box, screamed, and grabbed me as if he had just won the big stuffed elephant at a fair. He might not have matched that enthusiasm at any of his weddings.

On the same days the Bruins played, defending national-champion Arkansas had squeaked by Texas Southern, 79-78; Randy Bolden, Southern's best free-throw shooter, missed the third of three consecutive attempts with 6.1 seconds left. Then the Hogs beat Syracuse, 96-94, in overtime after Lawrence Moten called a timeout when the Orangemen had none at the end of regulation. The Razorbacks would meet Memphis in the Sweet Sixteen.

UCLA had a fifteenth consecutive victory, its longest winning streak since it had rattled off that NCAA-record eighty-eight in a row in the early 1970s. It would meet Mississippi State on Thursday night in the Sweet Sixteen in Oakland. "Just *glad* to be going," Jim Harrick said when asked about the Bulldogs. "I haven't thought about that, but I will ... give me a minute to enjoy this."

Ed O'Bannon had been clapping for the ball in the left corner. "I wanted it ... but he just kept going. At the free-throw line, I knew he was going to take it. Then your mind starts racing ... unbelievable." Toby Bailey lurked under the rim for any tip chances. Dollar trailed the entire play. Charles O'Bannon was sitting on the bench, beginning a pattern that would spur a clash between him and Jim Harrick.

J.R. Henderson stood, like a statue, in the right corner. "I'm the only one he could have passed it to, but I'm thinkin', 'Man, don't pass it,' " Henderson says in January 2013 in a tiny diner in Kariya, Japan, where we eat a late-night meal with Kevin Young. Born in Jamaica, Young played center at Missouri, and he is Henderson's teammate on the Aishin Sea Horses of the Japan Basketball League.

"Ain't nobody want the ball at that time," says Young, whom Henderson calls Big Boy. "Yeah, you don't want the ball at that time," says Henderson, who has become a naturalized Japanese citizen and changed his surname to Sakuragi. I retained his birth name throughout this project because that's what he was called at UCLA. "I had been in pressure before, in the Wooden Classic, but I'm thinkin', '*You* [Edney] have got to get this shot, man. Somebody has to get it ... just not me.' " Young shakes his head.

He played for the Tigers in the mid-2000s, and he says Edney had performed a lobotomy on the good citizens of Columbia, Missouri, and Tigers fans everywhere. "It broke the community's heart," Young says. He did not like hearing that Hank Edney's wonder tile healer had also been a Jamaican. Seven years later Julian Winfield told the *St. Louis Post-Dispatch*, "I still have, like, an eternal flame burning from that game."

Derek Grimm wondered aloud about not fouling Edney. Afterward he said, "You keep saying, 'What if? What if? What if?'" More than seventeen years later, Grimm had long retired and was living in his native Illinois, where a writer caught up with him. "It's nice to be part of history, [but] I wish I was on the other end of it," said Grimm. He still wished he had been more aggressive in defending Edney. "I don't think you ever really get over it ... I'm not so sure we ever bounced back the way we needed to."

With a balding pate and a hawk nose, the crusty and edgy Norm Stewart resembled an eagle. He had beaten cancer, and he would retire in 1999 having coached more than eleven hundred college games. He was curt after being stung by Edney; "Obviously, I've won a hell of a lot of games like that."

Ed O'Bannon had made amends, somewhat, after his curfew violation by leading everyone with twenty-four points and hauling in seven rebounds. Paul O'Liney had been grand, tallying twenty-three points on nine-of-thirteen shooting, which included five of six from three-point range. In the afterglow of Edney's triumphant dash, O'Liney crumpled onto the court. Jim Harrick praised Cameron Dollar for consoling O'Liney instead of joining his happy teammates.

Many years later, however, Dollar admits that neither courtesy nor humility had compelled him to approach O'Liney. Dollar hugged O'Liney, told him, "Great game." Inside, Dollar had other thoughts. He says, "I thought, 'Man, you're going home. I feel bad for you, but you're going home. It sucks that you had to play us ... you didn't think you'd win, did you? Well, it's time to go. Gave a helluva effort, but we're winning this deal. But, hey man, you gave a great effort.' That's probably a little arrogant. But I did feel bad for him."

Those weren't exactly Christian thoughts. Faith played a major role with the Bruins, and Jim Harrick talked about fate after beating Missouri. He always declined to discuss his Mormon beliefs when he was coaching, knowing how religion could be so polarizing. That his top two assistants were deeply religious, however, exemplified Harrick's priorities.

I once posed the recruiting aspects of religion to Bruins for a feature. Some declined to talk about the subject. Others said a few words. In airports, during delays, a pocket or two of Bruins could be found studying scripture. Cameron Dollar scrawled JESUS IS THE REASON and the Christian Ichthys symbol on his ankle tape. When your team is built around spiritual things, Dollar once said, "you can't be broken down by outside influences." Center omm'A Givens explicitly picked the Bruins over Arizona because, "The UCLA coaches are Christian and more down-to-earth than the staff at Arizona." The O'Bannon brothers often praised the Lord, and Tyus Edney and other Bruins taped Bible quotes on their lockers.

Nearing the twentieth anniversary of his drive, it was clear that UCLA faithful would salute Tyus Edney as a hero for many, many years—Jamaica Johnny deserved some recognition, too. In November 2013, Tyus was beginning his fourth season as the Bruins' director of basketball operations. He had had a long, successful career in Europe, primarily in Italy. But once he returned to Westwood it was crystal clear to him how he had etched a nook of his own in a place already steeped in lore.

He had heard tales from countless people about where they were and what they were doing as he drove coast to coast in Boise to keep the Bruins alive in the NCAAs. A gaggle of revelers at a wedding reception gathered around a TV set in the San Fernando Valley; a superb celebration ensued. Nuptials in Southern California on March 19, 1995, had some extra zing. The richest scene might have been at the hospital in which a woman was delivering a baby. She craned her neck, just so, to catch Edney's drive on a wall-mounted television set. Many hesitate when approaching him. They don't want to bother Edney. But he makes them feel welcome and conveys that he genuinely enjoys hearing every memory. They are so constant he is considering writing a book about what so many were doing, and stopped doing, in those few moments.

"I've heard so many stories about The Shot," Edney says in his usual low-key tone, just above a whisper. "A thousand stories, maybe more. Crazy stuff. They broke things in their homes." He laughs. "They say, 'Oh, I remember The Shot.' I say, 'Tell me the story.' It's fun to hear them. I love it."

In Japan, Big Boy rubs the corners of his red eyes deeply.

Chapter 20

THE BRUINS RETURNED to Los Angeles having been handed a reprieve from the governor, in the always-colorful lingo of Steve Lavin, by way of Tyus Edney's mad dash. With four point eight seconds until midnight, the stay of execution had arrived, just barely, in Boise.

That did not mean they had dodged punishment for multiple curfew violations in Idaho. As in seventeens, if one missed curfew they all missed it. But this was different, because it involved the undisputed captain. Ed O'Bannon hadn't been the only tardy Bruin, as it turned out. The penance? Seventeens, along with some pointed words.

Jim Harrick gave his players Monday off, to rest and heal. Nobody needed more downtime than Tyus Edney, who had a long list of aches and pains. They had been tentatively scheduled to fly to Oakland on Tuesday, but Harrick postponed the departure by a day. He wanted more time at home, to remain on familiar turf and allow his players the luxury of an extra night sleeping in their own beds. In addition, that allowed for a regular afternoon practice session on Tuesday, March 21, rather than a hasty morning run and afternoon getaway to the Bay Area.

Harrick arranged his locker-room chairs in a semi-circle. Since his practices were open to media and certain fans, huddling in front of the lockers was a way to get some private words with his guys. Some of them believed they were about to hear strategy chatter, inspiration, or words of concern about Mississippi State, whom UCLA would play Friday. The semi-circle nature of the set-up, though, was a give-away. The chairs were never orchestrated like that. Harrick had prepped just exactly how he would blister them for their lack of focus and direction and responsibility in Boise, for busting curfew, for being so extremely fortunate that Tyus Edney had come through, bailing out all of them, against Missouri.

Harrick's voice boomed off the walls. He informed them a security guard would patrol their floor in The Claremont, nestled in the hills of Berkeley with a postcard view of the San Francisco Bay. He excoriated them, ranting how his 28-0 Morningside High team had so royally fucked up in the playoffs in 1973, absolutely ruining what should have been an unforgettable team and season. He named Ed O'Bannon and listed his grievances with the team's star. He moved on to Charles O'Bannon, with whom more issues would bubble in Oakland, and George Zidek, and Toby Bailey, and J.R. Henderson, and Cameron Dollar. "Trouble," one of them says many years later. "We were in trouble." They recalled the grilling as the most thorough asschewing they would ever receive from Harrick.

"He challenged us," said Ed O'Bannon. "He said if we didn't come out [against Mississippi State] and do battle, everything we'd worked for would be gone." Needing to include all of his main players, Harrick hollered, "Edney!" But Harrick was momentarily stumped. The guy had just rescued UCLA's season, just as the pilot light was flickering to and fro, with a drive and basket that just might go down in the thick annals of the program's all-time highlights ... and Harrick struggled to think of anything remotely negative about the water bug who might, just might, tip the scales at 150 pounds while dripping wet after one of those mega-feast barbecues with the football team. Plus, Edney, as usual, had that list of ailments.

"That fourth foul!" Harrick implored. Yeah, that's it. The fourth foul. "That was the stupidest thing you've ever done since you've been here!" It had been an ill-advised foul, for sure. But Harrick just turned it "from a misdemeanor to a felony," he wrote in *Embracing*. It had been imperative to include everyone in his harangue. In the practice, after several seventeens, the Bruins executed sharply, with focus. Harrick saw all business. Mike Warren, John Wooden's former guard who had served as chaperone to Toby Bailey for his introduction to John Wooden, spoke to the players about the program's mystique.

Everything worked in a one-sided first half against Mississippi State in the Oakland Coliseum Arena (now Oracle Arena). The Bulldogs tried to play man-to-man defense against the Bruins, but Tyus Edney zapped them for thinking their guys were head-to-head better than his troops. He pushed the ball into the middle and scored on six-foot-eleven center Erick Dampier. Forced into playing a zone defense, MSU got burned by UCLA jump shots.

Bulldogs coach Richard Williams had no options. He did have the bearing of a high school math teacher, which he had been. Bespectacled and stringent, brown hair parted in the middle and feathered back, he chafed at media overkill that came with being a head coach in the Southeastern Conference. He had been elevated to the main chair when Bob Boyd, the former USC coach who had so frustrated John Wooden, resigned in the mid-1980s.

Dampier's stock rose considerably a year later when he helped Mississippi State get to the Final Four in East Rutherford, New Jersey, where the Bulldogs would lose to Syracuse. Williams quit two years later. He coached in lower pro leagues and in high school, and became an assistant to John Brady at Arkansas State. Dampier would play sixteen NBA seasons and earn almost a hundred million dollars.

Against the Bruins, Dampier disappeared. He hit all of his shots but attempted only four. He scored eleven points and had four rebounds, none under his own glass. The Bulldogs shot themselves out of the game by making only thirty-two percent, for nineteen points, in the first half. UCLA led, 40-19, and it wasn't threatened in an 86-67 victory. Bulldogs junior guard Darryl Williams had twenty-two points, but he had scored only seven when he finally sank a three-point shot with a bit more than seven minutes remaining. By then, the crowd of 14,399 knew the outcome was academic.

With two minutes left, Jim Harrick exchanged some words with Richard Williams on the sideline for about twelve seconds; Williams had instructed his players to foul, which only delayed the inevitable. "I was just wondering how the weather was in *Starksville*," said Harrick. The Mississippi State campus is in Starkville, Mississippi. Said Williams, "Just two coaches complimenting each other on the play of their teams."

George Zidek had fretted about the heavyweight matchup all week. On the previous Sunday in Boise, Dampier had burned Utah for twenty-one points and ten rebounds, and he blocked eight shots. For four days, Zidek's imagination ran roughshod with visions of Dampier thoroughly exploiting him. Zidek logged more early-morning hours shooting and working on his footwork with assistant coaches and managers inside Pauley Pavilion. He hit five of his eleven shots from the field, and hauled in two offensive rebounds against the Bulldogs.

Afterward, Zidek was as mentally exhausted as he was physically drained. "He's dog-tired," said Ed O'Bannon. "I think he's ready for bed." O'Bannon had twenty-one points and eight boards, Tyus Edney recorded ten points and eight assists, and Toby Bailey tallied a dozen points. For neutralizing Dampier, Zidek was yanked to the post-game media conference by Harrick, but Zidek was the only one of three Bruins that did not have his name placard before him on the long table draped in white cloth. Quipped Harrick, "After that performance he should have a card."

Williams always disdained media and the abundance of time he had to devote to that aspect of his job. Many years later, he admitted he should have had a better attitude in dealing with the press, that he finally recognized it was largely out to fairly report the news. In Oakland, he despised the fourth estate's constant criticism of Jim Harrick. "That's a well-coached basketball team, believe me," Williams said. "They know what they're doing ... they have great talent, but I've seen coaches screw up great talent. Some of you guys need to walk in his shoes and see what it's like, maybe coach a team and see what it's like."

UCLA had only a day to prepare for Connecticut, a 28-4 squad that liked to run, too. On that off day, Arkansas defeated Memphis, 96-91, in overtime in Kansas City, Missouri. Memphis held a one-point edge with eleven seconds left in regulation, but a questionable foul sent Arkansas to the line; another extra session for the Hogs, another victory.

Marques Johnson delivered some words of inspiration to the Bruins, in the ballroom they used for a walk-through session, about staying together, remaining on the same page, supporting each other, helping each other on offense and defense, and being a good teammate.

That night at The Claremont Hotel, UCLA's luxurious headquarters in the Berkeley Hills, Ike Nwankwo called Marquis Burns in Las Cruces, New Mexico. Burns—the Fifth Beatle—had been Nwankwo's roommate in the Hitch suites, and he had kept paying rent since he left UCLA in January because a replacement tenant couldn't be found. One had just been tapped, though, and Nwankwo rang Burns about his wallet relief. Burns and Nwankwo talked about the Bruins' good fortune, being just a victory away from the Final Four in Seattle. Tyus Edney eventually got on the line. You'll go as far as you take them, Burns said. He had been a Bruin for two and a half seasons, and before he said goodbye he told Edney to wish everyone good luck from him. "My boys are gonna get 'em," Burns told his fellow Aggies when he hung up the phone. They did not disagree with him. "The tradition," Burns says years later. "They were rooting for the Bruins, too."

UCLA radio engineer Lew Stowers was thoroughly entertaining a small, convivial troupe by perpetuating haunted tales of the grand hotel when he exacerbated a creaky floorboard and drafty windowpane into paranormal activity—to this day, Stowers swears that that supernatural stuff was genuine. Unusual activity had occasionally been reported in Room 422, where the ghost of a little girl who had died in a laundry-chute accident was supposedly seen, and especially heard, engaging in playful tricks with visitors for decades. In 2014, some San Antonio Spurs freaked out at the same spooky events in the hotel and at that room.

In George Zidek's room, he was lost deep in a two-year-old maze in his mind, a beguiling restlessness that would plague him the rest of his life. Zidek drove himself zany thinking about a fast pace that would be an ultimate test of his conditioning and stamina. The Huskies were sprinters. Could he keep up? He heard noises in his sleep. He saw demons, wearing Huskies uniforms, swatting his hook shots and stemming the full fulcrum of their weight against his hips, forever keeping him away from rebounds.

Somewhat like Zidek, fifty-two-year-old Connecticut coach Jim Calhoun was also tossing and turning under a down-feathered comforter in his room. He'd win three NCAA championships by the time a spate of health issues would force him to retire in 2012. But by 1995, the gruff and tough Calhoun had had rosters of outstanding players but not one crown to show for his efforts. Against the Bruins, he would feature senior point guard Kevin Ollie, the Fort Crenshaw product whom Jim Harrick had wanted so badly at UCLA; Israeli sophomore shooter Doron Sheffer, whom Harrick also recruited hard and was twenty-three; and senior forward Donny Marshall.

That's a solid crew. The jewel, however, was guard Ray Allen, a sophomore from South Carolina who would play only one more season for Connecticut. In June 2013, Ed O'Bannon would marvel over Allen's professional career. He had just nailed a huge three-point shot against San Antonio that would fuel the Miami Heat's drive to a second consecutive NBA championship. Allen had collected more than twenty-six thousand points in nearly fourteen hundred NBA games, including playoffs, and earned more than $180 million. He'd make another $3.3 million for the 2013-14 season. In August 2014, as this went to press, Allen was contemplating playing one more NBA campaign.

Allen gave a preview of what was coming when he bombarded UCLA for thirty-six points. He made twelve of his twenty-five shots, and he had nine rebounds, three assists, and four turnovers. The Bruins knew what was coming because Lorenzo Romar had always had his way against them in halfcourt pick-up games and those H-O-R-S-E contests. Jim Harrick told his guys to act as if Allen were Romar; *that's* what's coming at you, to give you some personal history that you can relate to, just don't let anyone else have a career day. Limit everyone else. A dusty-old hoops axiom holds that the first squad to a hundred points wins, and that was UCLA, who hit triple digits for the fourth time.

A bevy of East Coast media believed nobody could run with the Huskies. They had hit triple figures four times. Jim Calhoun knew better. Tyus Edney led a devastating attack with twenty-two points and ten assists; his twenty-five-foot jumper just beat the first-half buzzer, swishing through the net to give the Bruins a 48-41 lead at the intermission. Edney stood like a successful gunfighter, hands—like six-guns in each holster—at his hips. He glared at Cameron Dollar and coyly arched his back.

Those last few seconds of the half provided an ember that would threaten to sweep into a brushfire between Jim Harrick and Charles O'Bannon. Ray Allen had nailed a three-point shot to cut the Huskies' deficit to four points with three seconds left … and Beagle-Beagle signaled for a timeout. Harrick had been fine with the small advantage, although Connecticut would surely dash into its locker room feeling bubbly.

Instead, Harrick blew an internal fuse when O'Bannon seemed to squander one of UCLA's three precious timeouts. *We don't want to waste one here*, Harrick wrote. *What in the world is he thinking? We're up four, we'll take that. WHAT IN THE WORLD?! OHMYNO!* Harrick coveted timeouts like Krugerrands, which—surprise—came from Wooden, who called his timeout-hording a fetish. An entire calendar year once passed between Wooden timeout calls. That had saved Harrick and the Bruins against Missouri. He glared at O'Bannon, who required no words to decipher that Harrick thought he had pulled a boner. But Edney had struck back before the halftime buzzer. When the Bruins had settled in their locker room, Harrick found Charles and said, "That was a nice call, son." O'Bannon knew otherwise.

UCLA never slowed down en route to a 102-96 victory. Ed O'Bannon was off, missing eight of thirteen shots. The pace was indeed too great for George Zidek, who played only twelve minutes but still managed nine shots. He made four, for eight points, and had three boards. Toby Bailey and J.R. Henderson made the Huskies pay for daring them to run. When Connecticut got within seven points midway through the second half, Bailey and Henderson remained in sprint mode to help boost UCLA's margin to 82-68 with eight and a half minutes remaining.

Bailey poured in twenty-six points for the first time as a collegian, and he had nine rebounds. Henderson added eighteen points, on nine-of-twelve shooting. Edney, the only guy on either squad who played all forty minutes, connected on UCLA's only pair of three-point shots as the Bruins focused on getting high-percentage baskets. Ed O'Bannon didn't have to be Superman, said Lorenzo Romar. O'Bannon almost laughed at Connecticut challenging UCLA to run. They didn't know that we've got the fastest basketball player in the country, he said. "You try and run? Fine. But don't say that we can't run. That's like shooting yourself in the foot." Marques Johnson strolled by O'Bannon, leaned into his left ear, and whispered, *thirteen down, two to go*.

Kristaan Johnson, who did not play in Oakland, began getting face time on the bench from CBS cameras. Marques Johnson had been trying to convince his portly son about being a supportive teammate. Injuries and attitude issues had shelved him after a promising start. He carved out a niche role, as only Kris could conjure, by fashioning white hand towels into his own masquerade. Among his personas was the Lone Ranger, with a cowboy-style kerchief hanging like a triangle below his nose, and some type of turbaned desert nomad that he dubbed The Terrorist, something that resembled the logo of the Dakar road rally.

In the history of the NCAAs there has not been a more constrained group of players cutting a net from its rim after having just won a spot in the Final Four. They were not done. Much more work lay ahead, which emanated from their leader who feared nothing and nobody. I found Ed O'Bannon Sr. on the court, and his bearhug surely bent a few ribs and bruised a lung.

Jim Milhorn made sure he attended the post-game press conference. He eagerly anticipated hearing Jim Calhoun's thoughts about the game. *Run against UCLA? Not* this *UCLA squad*, Milhorn thought. John Wooden's former guard had earned the title of hoops oracle in the UCLA basketball offices. Lorenzo Romar would never work anywhere else where such an administrator knew so much about the game. Milhorn didn't boast, either. But when he visited the coaches, strategies and counters were always within his grasp. His reviews were so sharp his boss, Pete Dalis, copied them.

Milhorn leaned against a wall, in the rear of the cavern-sized media room in the Oakland Coliseum Arena. He heard Jim Calhoun explain the trepidations and dangers of playing the Bruins. Calhoun had known, going in, that this would be trouble and admitted, "I have to be very honest with you, UCLA was the one team we did not want to play." Milhorn grinned. "When I heard him say that … " Milhorn says many years later. "He said the Bruins had the kind of team that would cause them problems. They had hoped to avoid us. We didn't win by a lot, but we had control throughout the game."

Not everyone in powder blue was happy. Inside the locker room, with parents and other outsiders milling about, Charles O'Bannon was in full fury. He had played twenty-two minutes against Mississippi State, twenty-four against Connecticut. In those forty-six minutes, he hadn't committed a turnover; he scored nineteen points, shot the ball only eleven times (making five), got to the line (where he made nine of twelve free throws), hauled in ten rebounds, and he showed discipline, having launched only one three-point shot.

With outsiders around, he exchanged some choice, heated words with Harrick about how he was being used. Harrick became as pissed at Charles as O'Bannon was at him. Some witnesses froze. As quickly as the two geysers erupted, though, they extinguished. O'Bannon believed he had crossed a line. He was nervous for days that his indolence would affect his playing status in Saturday's national semifinal against Oklahoma State in Seattle.

In New Jersey, the Cowboys had defeated Wake Forest. In the East Regional finale, they soundly beat Massachusetts. OSU had not reached such heights since the years following World War II, under famed coach Henry Iba. In Kansas City, Arkansas coach Nolan Richardson's kids had played well, too. They beat Virginia and six-foot-eight senior forward Junior Burrough, 68-61. Burrough would log several years in Japan, where his career would take an abrupt detour when J.R. Henderson showed up. The Razorbacks, like the Bruins, were headed to Seattle.

Chapter 21

AS OKLAHOMA STATE sealed its 68-54 victory over Massachusetts on Sunday, March 26, an interested observer turned away from a small black-and-white television set in Westwood. The avalanche of hype about his pending personal matchup would make UCLA's world-class seven-foot insomniac fidget and squirm on the too-short mattress inside his tiny solo room in the Saxon Suites dormitory. The molecules of George Zidek's mind raced around an elaborate, exit-less labyrinth.

He had to wait more than six twenty-four-hour chunks until meeting Bryant Reeves, Oklahoma State's seven-foot, 292-pound senior who went by Big Country. Zidek would spend every moment of every one of those hours in pitched mental battle with the big dude from some place called Gans, out in the sticks of Oklahoma. (It's where Reeves would retire from the NBA, having made more than $60 million, and live in a fifteen thousand square-foot home, on a three-hundred-acre cattle ranch, with his wife and three kids. When former teammates saw that he tipped the scales at about 350 pounds, they redubbed him Big Continent.) Zidek would be tabbed Foreign Country or Big Czech on the billing. Reeves had dispatched Antonio McDyess of Alabama and Tim Duncan of Wake Forest, and he had just sent Marcus Camby of UMass on spring break with twenty-four points and ten rebounds in a runaway East Regional final.

A resume that included Big Eight Conference player of the year as a sophomore, in which he became that league's first player to lead it in scoring, rebounding, and field-goal percentage since Wilt Chamberlain in 1958, was thoroughly inspected by Zidek. The next three mornings, he slipped inside Pauley by six-thirty. Lorenzo Romar showed a few minutes early only to find Zidek nervously sitting atop the concrete staircase in the northeast corner of Pauley. Romar saw Zidek in anguish. It was as if hundreds of versions of the game had played out in his mind, and none favored him. "Just paralyzed," Zidek says years later. "That's my trademark." Peter and Olga Schultz would be watching inside the Kingdome, too. How could George disappoint his two immensely proud benefactors?

He had nearly slinked back to Prague after two seasons, but he stuck it out to become a viable weapon for Harrick. The Sweeper could now gnaw on brisket and walk at the same time. Mark Gottfried chuckles when recalling that Zidek once told him he wanted to be the strongest basketball player in the world. "Not just on his team or in the conference, or in college basketball, but in *all* the world." Ed O'Bannon recalls Zidek and Ike Nwankwo arranging their own weight-lifting sessions over and above what they participated in with their teammates. "George is a great man," Ed says. "He has a very big heart. I loved when he had big games."

Reeves had appeared in Stillwater, Oklahoma, and from the start—like Zidek—struggled. Reeves could barely curl a fifteen-pound dumbbell. Every thousand feet of two-mile conditioning runs made him pause to regain his breath. A Cowboys strength coach recommended that the chubby kid wear a bra. Like a certain Bruin, Reeves feared airplanes—and not just little ones with propellers. However, he hustled and worked on his own hook shots and quickly learned how to use his bulk against opponents to become an immovable rebounding force in a red zone of his own. He might not have vowed to his coaches that he wanted to become the strongest basketball player in the world, but he bettered himself annually and became veteran coach Eddie Sutton's foundation.

Zidek saw visions of that large number fifty, in the black and orange uniform, gambolling around him, and laughing, in the snippets of sleep he could catch at night. Earvin "Magic" Johnson called the Bruins, in their Pauley locker room, from Hawaii to give them a boost after a practice, but there was nothing in that call that could cure what ailed Zidek.

On Monday, March 27, Jim and Sally Harrick attended the Academy Awards ceremony at the Shrine Auditorium, across Jefferson Boulevard from the USC campus. The most important game of his career awaited Jim Harrick, in Seattle in five days, but he and his wife viewed the Oscars as another once-in-a-lifetime event. They were guests of Wendy Finerman, Dr. Gerald Finerman's daughter who had co-produced the popular *Forrest Gump* film that starred Tom Hanks. The Harricks strolled by Clint Eastwood, Jodie Foster, Sylvester Stallone, Robert DeNiro, Paul Newman, and Dustin Hoffman, trying to act as if it were just another bingo night back at the VFW post in Charleston. Finerman's movie won best picture. At the ensuing Governor's Ball, Wendy Finerman smacked her golden statuette into Jim Harrick's right hand and said, "Next Monday night is your turn!"

The Bruins flew back to Sea-Tac on Thursday, March 30. They settled into the Airport Marriott. Steve Lavin handed out new T-shirts, one blue and one white, that excited the players—RED ZONE IN THE DOME on the front, NO DUNKS, NO LAYUPS on the back. They shuttled to the Kingdome, for a shoot-around and media interviews, late Friday morning. The bus stopped inside a huge portal that they all recognized, and a giddy Vern Wagner guided the UCLA contingent through a door, around a few turns, and into a locker room. The Bruins joked with each other, trying to convince themselves that this open practice before thousands of fans would be nothing unusual, nothing special. Jim Harrick scribbled a few objectives on a dry erase board. They slipped back through hallways to the huge media area.

Harrick brought his starters. It was the first time George Zidek had scores of interviewers interrogate him about Prague, the Communists, the Velvet Revolution, and Big Country. Word trickled in that someone had just shattered a backboard, that UCLA's practice would be delayed about thirty minutes. Zidek's mental funk hit a new low when he discovered that Big Country had caused a big mess. The Cowboys were dribbling and pick-switching through their session when an assistant coach lobbed a ball off the backboard. Bryant Reeves, stepping in through the right lane, caught the ball with both hands as his body twisted 180 degrees to the right, enabling him to execute a two-handed reverse jam in one motion. The tension was too much. The backboard shattered into a thousand pieces. Teammates giddily extracted small shards from Big Country's jersey, shoulder, neck, and short hair.

The Big Czech's mind spiraled. Finally, they were shown the way to the court. They were nearly winded when they dropped into the first-base dugout. The journey wasn't over. The RV-less Kingdome overwhelmed them. Ed O'Bannon was stunned. A huge set of double doors was opened. Ed could see clear across the court, to the other side of the dome. *Wow*, he half-whispered. The Stance drill hushed much of the huge Kingdome crowd that might have thought it had stumbled into a Seahawks' tryout. The news of Big Country's smashing practice reverberated from coast to coast. Tyus Edney falling on his right wrist at some point was hardly even noticed by some of his own teammates. Then again, he had been so banged and and battered over the previous weeks, months, and seasons, one more bruise didn't seem noteworthy.

Upon returning to the Airport Marriott, the Bruins changed and attended a team meal. Like a foam-mouthed hound dog, a hotel administrator trailed them inside a ballroom carrying a new basketball. The guy attached himself to Tony Luftman. The man insisted that every player sign the ball. It would be featured, presumably forever, in a glass encasement between the hotel's elevators and lobby. The request rapidly turned desperate. He pressed Luftman.

Tyus Edney overheard the employee's rising outrage and took umbrage on Luftman's quandary. As affable as he was quiet, Edney told Luftman, "No sweat," and asked for the ball. Edney smiled and signed *Russell Jenkins, #43*. Every Bruin followed Edney's mischievous cue. Not one signed his correct name. Charles O'Bannon wrote, *David O'Neil, #13*. George Zidek inked *T2*, in tribute to the *Terminator* sequel that starred Arnold Schwarzenegger, whose Eastern Euro accent fellow Bruins had so closely associated with their seven-foot center. Zidek says, "Kind of stupid for us to make hard time for this fella." Players signed *#71* and *#88* underneath pseudonyms. Luftman would grin every time he passed that trophy case.

Many players do not recall what nom de guerre, or number, they had inked onto the ball. "Silly kids," says Toby Bailey. "Sorry brotha, I can barely remember yesterday. LOL," writes Cameron Dollar, now the head coach at Seattle University, in a text message. The glass encasement, and ball, disappeared from the hotel two renovations ago. A chef who has worked there for decades has no clue about the ball. If someone still possesses it, he or she might be interested to know a *Jenkins, Russell* is not listed on the all-time UCLA basketball roster.

Six nights of forceful and frightening images of Big Country slamming him off every concrete wall inside the Kingdome reached a climax for George Zidek late the afternoon of Saturday, April 1.

Bryant Reeves took sixteen shots, more than any other Cowboy. He made half. He sank all nine of his attempts from the foul line. He finished with twenty-five points, more than anybody. He grabbed nine rebounds, five under his own glass. All he didn't do was break another backboard. Zidek scored six points, rang up more personal fouls (three) than rebounds (two), and didn't even play twenty minutes. But it stayed tight, thanks to the smallest guy on the floor. Tyus "Russell Jenkins" Edney had led two breakaways for UCLA, but Oklahoma State and Reeves—with eighteen first-half points—kept it tight.

With about three minutes to the half, Edney was the only Bruin back on defense as three Cowboys charged to their hoop. Edney correctly read a pass and drew a charge, but he wound up in the air and came down hard on that right wrist. He flexed it as he sat on the court, his back against the padded basket anchor. Hank Edney, sitting high up in the dome, instantly thought of Jamaican Johnny. It was 37-37 at the break. Tony Spino wrapped Edney's wrist in gauze and tape, and Edney continued amped on adrenaline.

With Zidek in foul trouble and on the bench, Jim Harrick shifted to the fail-safe gambit, the two-three zone defense with Ed O'Bannon defending the Red Zone. The strategy clogged the Cowboys' interior and made it a half-court slugfest at both ends. UCLA threatened to run away, but Oklahoma State punched back. With about five minutes left, Harrick, his assistants, and just about every Bruin on the bench barked *Take him, Tyus!* at Edney. He breezed by Chianti Roberts for a layup. Edney's wrist was throbbing so badly he had only one option to score; get as close to the rim as possible. *Take him, Tyus!* Edney barely heard those chants over the crowd of 38,540, but his drives led to points.

Big Country cut Oklahoma State's four-point deficit in half with a reverse layup, which Edney answered by getting fouled en route to the hoop and sinking both free throws—to this day he has no idea how he made them, with such pain pounding his wrist. Randy Rutherford eked the Cowboys to within a point with a three-point shot along the left baseline. Again, though, Edney answered with a scoop shot—*take him, Tyus!*—to give UCLA a 64-61 advantage.

Eddie Sutton called for a timeout to regroup and recharge his guys, with two minutes, nine seconds left, but they were done. The Cowboys missed their next five shots, and they immediately fouled the Bruins to dare them to secure passage to the national championship via free throws. In that flurry, however, was Cameron Dollar's swipe of the ball from Big Country. Dollar felt as if that had zapped the Cowboys' will. "That's what I look to do out there," said Dollar, whose court time in the final minutes before tens of thousands in the cavernous building would prove crucial.

UCLA did not falter at the line. Dollar hit all four of his freebies, and Edney, Zidek, and Charles O'Bannon all sank two to give the Bruins a 74-61 victory. Edney led the Bruins with twenty-one points, Ed O'Bannon had fifteen, and eight rebounds. Marques Johnson found him in the locker room. *Fourteen down, one to go.*

Charles O'Bannon emerged with nineteen points, on seven-of-nine shooting, six boards, two assists, and a steal in thirty-seven minutes ... he was back in Jim Harrick's good graces. Beagle-Beagle made a timely dent, too, for J.R. Henderson and Toby Bailey combined for only four points in forty-eight minutes of action. Henderson had seen a serious look on Charlie's face in the locker room and knew Ed's little brother was due to inflict some punishment. As UCLA athletic director Pete Dalis left his seat, he told a friend, "Let's hear them now say Jim Harrick can't coach ... he goes to that zone, sticks Ed O'Bannon in the middle, and that game is over." No doubt Jim Milhorn had thought, likely even spoken, those same sentiments.

Edney showed his taped wrist to the post-game media horde and declared "this is just preventative." But he knew it was much worse. Harrick believed the little guy would battle through it. *A day off and treatment*, Harrick thought, *and he'll be fine.*

Arkansas and North Carolina followed the UCLA-Oklahoma State game. High up in the rafters Dr. Michael Shapiro and eight-year-old son Marcus rejoiced after the impressive Bruins victory. Hank and Barbara Edney, and their relatives and friends, sat in front of the Shapiros. Throngs of Bruins fans whooped and hollered about UCLA advancing to the finale. Hank was even-keeled, anxious to see his son. Marcus Shapiro was a bit more exuberant than the rest of them. When he settled and his father gathered him to slide out of their row, a man wearing a plastic cardinal hog on his head turned to Marcus and told him he wouldn't be so happy Monday ... the Razorbacks would defend their championship in style, he insisted in an urgent tone.

Marcus paused. His father, who had mended Ed O'Bannon's badly damaged left knee in October 1990, stood still, curious how his son would respond. "Well," Marcus told the guy, "at least I'm not wearing a red pig on my head!" The man turned crimson. Didn't say another word.

On the floor, Lorenzo Romar became subdued when Ed O'Bannon Sr. informed him that he believed Romar's father, Davis, was having a heart attack in the stands. Lorenzo rushed to his dad's side. Davis Romar, in serious condition, was taken to Harborview Medical Center, where he would be diagnosed as having suffered a stroke. He underwent two operations. Davis Romar did not walk again; he would pass away, at sixty-seven, in 2001.

On the half-hour bus ride back to the Airport Marriott, Kris Johnson mutated into Staany Loco. He sat behind Tony Luftman. The rookies would partake in a national championship game.

Luftman had walked onto that bus barely able to contain his exuberance. He had predicted to Jim Harrick, in his managerial interview, that the Bruins were about to win several titles. They were already in position for the first. Yet, as the wheels of the bus rolled, some unknown force provoked Johnson to thump the back of Luftman's noggin, like a whip, with the fingertips of his right hand. The bus was loud and rollicking. Laughter abounded. Players and coaches were giddy about having diffused Oklahoma State. Below that glee, tears poured out of Luftman's eyes as he muted his mouth with his right hand.

Inside the hotel, pockets of UCLA alumni, boosters, and fans watched Arkansas defeat North Carolina, 75-68. Those wearing red plastic pigs in the dome were in hog heaven. Having so many months ago implored his guys to compete, every time out, as if they were playing against Arkansas ... well, Jim Harrick once again resembled John Nash. The quick consensus in a hotel bar produced a sorrowful sigh, a mixture of bad feelings about the injury to Tyus Edney's right wrist and the 30-2 Bruins having to play the 32-6 defending national champs in the finale Monday night.

"God, how will we match up?"

"What will we do against Arkansas?"

"Arkansas is so good."

Jim Milhorn entertained none of that negativity. He told them, "Now wait a minute! I am SO happy! The best thing about tonight was Arkansas beating North Carolina! You can't imagine what we're talking about here. Defending national champions? I don't care about that. As a matchup, we can win! We're as quick as they are. They're not overly big. We're better than them!" Some nervously sipped white wine. A few frowned and gazed at the carpet. A guy in the corner glumly pulled at a can of beer. "I would have been worried about North Carolina, and [Jerry] Stackhouse, and [Rasheed] Wallace! We're gonna win this thing!"

He was on a roll. Milhorn recalled UCLA's difficulty with Kentucky, in Anaheim, as if that had transpired yesterday, and he watched on television when Carolina handled the Wildcats, 74-61, in Birmingham, Alabama, to earn a ticket to the Final Four. He knew Tar Heels coach Dean Smith was in the top tier of his profession. Milhorn had seen fifty-seven-year-old John Wooden guide Lew Alcindor and the rest of the Bruins to a twenty-three-point shellacking of the thirty-seven-year-old Smith and Carolina in the 1968 finale at the Sports Arena in Los Angeles. That was the second of three consecutive Final Fours for Smith, who was just getting started. He had won two championships, and this was his tenth Final Four appearance.

Milhorn wanted his Bruins to avoid all that, so he was ecstatic that the Heels were sent home by Arkansas. Fans weren't so sure. "The best thing is we [didn't] have to play North Carolina. I was worried about Dean Smith," Milhorn says. "Not to take anything away from Nolan Richardson, but Dean Smith is a better basketball coach."

Several outsiders leaned in to hear this white-haired man seem to believe every word he was discharging about the upcoming title match. Some had no idea he had played guard for John Wooden. He had no clue about Tyus Edney's status. He was certain about another Bruin. "They will not overpower us," Milhorn insisted in that bar. "They like to run, but we have ball handlers to handle whatever kind of press they want to throw at us. The matchup is perfect."

The watering hole, not far from the trophy case that housed a basketball bearing some funky names, did some solid business that Saturday evening. In another part of the hotel, Jim Harrick began poring over videotape, notes, statistics, and other nuances of the Arkansas Razorbacks with assistant coaches Mark Gottfried and Lorenzo Romar. This was the huddle of their professional lives. They'd exchange ideas and discuss plans until 4 A.M. Steve Lavin, whom Harrick had tabbed The Cup o' Coffee Kid for being late to his first official UCLA practice, was nowhere to be found.

Chapter 22

ONCE ARKANSAS BECAME a national player again, grizzled broadcasters and scribes began reaching for the aspirin and earmuffs. Coach Nolan Richardson and his Razorbacks are feeling persecuted again, media members thought, spoke, and wrote—uh oh, here come the lectures and indignation.

Richardson had guided the Hogs to the Final Four in 1990, when they lost to Duke in Denver. It had been twelve years since Arkansas, under Eddie Sutton, had played in a national semifinal. The Razorbacks won their first NCAA hoops title in 1994, and at every stop along the way Richardson's spiel was met with tilted noggins, yawns, and headshakes. He preached at every stop, wrote an East Coast writer accustomed to the show; "The audience, a cynical bunch by nature, was not entirely receptive." By the end, the day before the championship against Duke in Charlotte, North Carolina, Richardson's audience was "downright hostile."

He had long railed against the stereotype of the black head coach being viewed so frequently as a strong recruiter and motivator, but lacking in tactics, according to veteran *Philadelphia Daily News* writer Dick Jerardi. Richardson was confrontational and bombastic with a microphone, high above his audience. Richardson was in top form as the Hogs battled out of a ten-point hole early in the second half to beat Mike Krzyzewski in its own backyard. Few criticisms were lobbed at Coach K after his players had lost their composure against that stifling Arkansas defense. What would have the fallout been like if it had been Richardson's guys, the supposed superior athletes, who had lost their poise? We'll never know, Jerardi wrote, "but we can imagine."

Richardson had battled out of the hardscrabble Segundo Barrio section of El Paso, played ball for Don Haskins at Texas Western—whose all-black starting five had upended Kentucky's all-white starters in the landmark 1966 NCAA title clash and is now known as Texas-El Paso—and was forced into separate lodging and eating arrangements from his white teammates due to Jim Crow laws. He coached kids of all shapes, sizes, and colors. He won. He started hanging his Stetson on defense, forcing the other guys out of their comfort zones. He won some more. He saw discrepancies.

If he were white and achieved all that he had, Richardson said, statues of him would have been built. Had Bob Knight or John Wooden been black, Richardson said, *they'd be nobodies*. He referred to Knight and Mike Krzyzewski as *great white hopes*. In 1994 he told *Sports Illustrated*, "When I was playing running basketball, it was called niggerball. When Rick [Pitino] did it, it was called up-tempo. If I lose, I can't coach. If I win, it's because my athletes are better." (In a 2007 Olympic qualifying tournament in Las Vegas, Krzyzewski coached the US team against Mexico, mentored by Richardson. Coach K gave his band of all-stars a history lesson and enticed them to thank Richardson for paving the way for them. Krzyzewski said he understood Nolan Richardson and some of the barriers he had to overcome, and he overcame them "in magnificent style.")

The fifty-three-year-old Richardson, whose prodigious, cratered forehead resembled the moon, didn't even wait to get to Seattle to begin slicing into UCLA. In Kansas City, at the previous weekend's Midwest Regionals, Richardson said some get confused about the 1960s. Don't wanna take anything away from

UCLA's glory days, he said, "but it's over, those days are over. They've been over so long." He mocked having to win only four games to win a title. Today that just gets a team to the Final Four. He belittled Wooden's Bruins playing so often on the West Coast, trumpeting that his teams played all over the country.

College basketball was certainly parochial through the mid-1970s. Only conference winners, and select independents that fit the regional format, received NCAA Tournament berths during Wooden's stellar run. USC got especially stung when some of the best teams in that program's history didn't make the NCAAs. The Bruins did benefit from some home cooking, winning two of their crowns in finales at the Sports Arena in Los Angeles. Two others were obtained by advancing through regionals inside Pauley Pavilion. The other six all began in Western cities; only 1967 and 1969 (both in Louisville), and 1970 (College Park, Maryland) finished west of the Mississippi River. The only year that required Wooden to win five games to win a title was 1975, when the tournament had expanded from twenty-five to thirty-two teams.

Any modern-day coach can whine about an era from days of yore, the challenge is not sounding nonsensical. UCLA simply dominated when its taskmaster, detail-driven coach ripened, and his assistants were able to woo some top-flight talent (and more than a few lesser-rated players whom Wooden polished) from his own increasingly fertile backyard and other regions.

Give Richardson a platform, though, and hold on tight.

That the 1995 finale would be staged in Seattle was of no small significance. The Emerald City had launched UCLA to its title run in 1970. The Kingdome had also been the Final Four host in 1984, the last one that John Wooden attended with Nell, his wheelchair-bound wife. She died in 1985, after spending a hundred days in intensive care, and John Wooden slipped into a funk. Month by month, Jim Harrick observed the sullen Wooden opt for isolation; "[He] still had that marvelous intellect and gentle soul, but his heart had left him."

A few new great-grandchildren lifted Wooden. He had always been aware of being a role model. His *A little fellow follows Me* poem is framed in Harrick's home. In 1991, Harrick helped arrange a special honor to recognize Wooden in his native state when the Final Four was played in Indianapolis. But Wooden didn't stay for the championship. He was unsure if he could get to Seattle on the first Monday in April 1995, he told Harrick. The UCLA hoops patriarch had committed to attend the McDonald's All-Star Game in St. Louis on Sunday, April 2. He made no promises, but he told Harrick he would try to get to the Northwest.

X-rays on Tyus Edney's right wrist weren't available until late Sunday afternoon, and UCLA medical personnel restricted anyone from ministering to the injured joint until those results were confirmed. They were negative; no bones were broken. Of course, the extent of ligament or tendon damage could not be determined. But the optimal, immediate healing window had been missed, says a frustrated Hank Edney. Saturday night and a big chunk of Sunday were gone. Finally allowed to tend to his son Sunday night, Hank saw a weak and swollen wrist. It was too late for the heat to be effective. Be ready, Tyus told Cameron Dollar that night. Tony Spino administered an electro-therapy gadget, ice, Novocaine, cortisone, and a brace. Marques Johnson was tempted to remind Jim Harrick that Kristaan was a capable dribbler, that he knew every teammate's moves and nuances. But Marques resisted, not wanting to meddle in Harrick's affairs.

Interviews were conducted at the Kingdome. Players had their own tables. George Zidek was a main attraction. Media salivated over the Communist oppression of his youth, and sprinkled in some inquiries about this Corliss Williamson character for Arkansas who went by Big Nasty. One writer noted how the English *w* sounds like the Czech *v*, and the Czech *w* sounds like the English *v*. "It is good to rebel," the *Philadelphia Inquirer* quoted Zidek. "We had a very limited flow of information from the Western world," the New York *Daily News* quoted him, on knowing zilch about UCLA's hoops history when he first visited Westwood.

Williamson had averaged nearly twenty-three points and ten rebounds in the Hogs' five NCAA games. Instead of the six nights of fretful "sleep" he had to endure before meeting Big Country, Zidek would only battle a couple of nights of hook-shot-swatting and super-duper-dunking phantasmagoria before facing off against Big Nasty. Fortunately for UCLA, it had its own thick ball of nastiness in Kristaan Johnson. Zidek had been prepped well, by Kris's ruffian thuggery all season, for what awaited him Monday. That familiarity might have provided Zidek with the succor he required to doze for hours and hours, like a pooped puppy—his first fitful sleep in months, maybe years—that Sunday evening.

In the book he wrote after the season, Harrick was kind to Steve Lavin, having included the junior member of his staff in the overnight strategy meeting that bled from Saturday into Sunday. That was not the case, which Mark Gottfried and Lorenzo Romar also confirmed. What was Lavin doing? "Fuck, I don't know," Harrick says today. "It's my fault for not asking him. I don't have time to worry about him. If I got to coach you and worry about you, I don't need you on my staff. I don't know how he's not embarrassed and humiliated by that."

Harrick, Gottfried, and Romar decided to press the Arkansas outside shooters, with a caveat. But Zidek would receive an abundance of help on Williamson, whose strong spins, quick release, and rebounding ability always anchored the Razorbacks. Zidek would get help from whoever would be assigned to Corey

Beck; Harrick would gamble that Beck would have a cold hand. Beck had made only two of nine shots against North Carolina, had not made more than two baskets in any tournament game, and was only shooting at a thirty-three percent clip in the NCAAs. Everyone would protect the Red Zone. Business as usual. Ed O'Bannon had prepped his teammates for this all season. He had prepped himself all his life.

Harrick and his two lieutenants kept dissecting Arkansas tape. They knew the Hogs were going to open the floor and press and trap, "all the things they like to do," Harrick said. Which coincided nicely with how the Bruins liked to play, too. Richardson had a Forty Minutes of Hell philosophy in which his guys pressed and confused opponents, full court, for every second. It hadn't been such a total blanket attack recently, but Arkansas did win the previous national crown. Harrick thought his floor general would overcome his usual ailments and be ready for his final collegiate game. But Tyus Edney's right wrist had not sustained a usual injury.

The two national finalists got practice time behind closed Kingdome doors on that Sunday, but Harrick passed, as he did the day before playing Connecticut in Oakland. He had learned many years earlier from John Wooden that a team is hungrier and fresher the more it stays away from the court. That had benefited Ed O'Bannon and his left knee, too. Harrick wanted his players to have fresh legs and strong appetites. He had the managers tape the floor of an Airport Marriott ballroom. He conducted a walk-through of plays and reviewed videotape.

Harrick received a Monday morning boost when he learned that Wooden was on his way. Microsoft had booked him to speak at a function. He would sit next to Bill Gates, that company's founder. The players rose and lounged. They ate breakfast together. At Ed O'Bannon's table sat Tony Luftman, Kevin Dempsey, and Bob Myers. Talk was light, even funny, as they picked at scrambled eggs and bacon, sausage and pancakes. Ed was relaxed and carefree. A pause lengthened. Myers became introspective. "Wow. This is it. Our last team meal."

O'Bannon shifted from lighthearted and playful to taciturn. He stood, placed his dishes and utensils in a gray tub. Damn Bob, Dempsey said, why'd you have to go and say *that*? Ed had been in such a good mood, so loose. But UCLA's soul became solemn. O'Bannon retreated to his room. His amateur career, the knee injury, all those seventeens, and Indiana and Michigan and Tulsa, Oregon's arrogance, and the indiscretion he showed just hours before the close call against Missouri ... all of it rattled around in his brain.

UCLA's basketball contingent stepped off the elevator. That signed basketball smiled at everyone from the trophy case. Bruins fans, including UCLA football coach Terry Donahue, swarmed them. That spring football practice had started that day was not lost on several basketball people. Said one, "That's when it hit me, that this was the big time, if *he* was here." Donahue and alums and fans and cheerleaders, even Kimikazu Suzuki, roared and cheered for the Bruins, and Donahue led the group into an eight-clap—eight strong hand claps that lead to a *U-C-L-A go-fight-win* chant. Donahue always enjoyed witnessing how the behavior and posture of one of his players switched from a practice to a game, saying, *We'll see if he's a porch dog or a hunting dog.* He hoped the other guys tonight would be porch hogs.

The team bus was scheduled to leave the hotel at about 3 P.M. The opening tap would take place at 5:40. Tony Luftman boarded the bus early, as was his custom. He was always the first one on the coach. Luftman bounded up the three big stairs, turned left, and was taken aback. In the middle seat at the very back, Ed O'Bannon sat in his gold UCLA silky satin sweats with the four powder blue letters across his chest. His hands were clasped in front of him. Total peace. Light beamed from somewhere, bathing O'Bannon in an aurous shower, framed by total darkness. He gazed straight through Luftman, who didn't say a word.

On another bus, en route to the Kingdome, Sally Harrick fidgeted as she nervously stabbed her cream-colored high heels in the aisle and took her customary window seat in the middle on the left side. Nearly thirty-five years earlier, she left West Virginia as a newlywed. That seemed so long ago, her husband joked about some day titling an autobiography *Covered Wagons*. All roads led to this short trip up the gray freeway to the gray dome, where the forecast on the senior point guard was neutral at best.

Seattle, however, was awash in sunlight. Halfway to destiny, a ladybug fluttered inside the window and landed on the left lapel of Sally Harrick's midnight blue blazer. She grinned at it and relaxed. She reclined. Every ounce of nervous energy floated outside that window. That little orange-red beetle with the black spots convinced her that this evening would go her husband's way, that all of his strains and struggles would pay off handsomely in the game of his life. Most UCLA players were so close to the Bruins' basketball matriarch that all they needed from her was a hug to know that their own struggles would not be in vain, that everything Jim Harrick had put them through was meant to temper them, on and off the court. Few words were required to know that Sally Harrick—who had a latent feistiness—was in your corner, which made dealing with her husband on his worst days bearable.

The bus pulled into a dark recess of the Kingdome, where Vern Wagner hugged Jim Harrick, wearing a dark suit and a paisley-patterned tie that matched his suspenders. Throngs of fans greeted the Bruins. In the UCLA locker room, Tony Spino fitted a beige brace on Tyus Edney's right wrist. It received more injections. Harrick tested it by softly tossing a basketball at Edney; the ball thudded off the back of Edney's right paw. Uh oh.

Today, in his office on the second floor of the Morgan Center, Edney grabs a little orange plastic basketball with his right hand. He straightens his fingers, rests the ball in his palm, and turns his hand over. The ball drops to the carpet. Edney frowns. That's how little control he had of that hand in the Kingdome. Harrick would let him try to play, but both knew it would be fruitless. Cameron Dollar would be called into service. The rest of the Bruins, however, never believed Edney would not play and would not be effective.

Harrick offered some half-hearted words. Inside, he fretted about Edney. Harrick tried hiding his immense frustrations. However, as he neared the doorway he slammed the jamb with his right hand and yelled, "Fuck Arkansas!" His guys responded, hollering and hopping, and shot out of the room. When everyone had departed, only Jim Harrick and Jim Milhorn remained. Harrick cussed to the heavens; why me? Why now? Why does this have to fuckin' happen *now*? Milhorn, as he had the previous evening with scores of UCLA fans back in the hotel, tried to soothe the guy he had whipped so frequently on the racquetball court.

"What do you mean?" Milhorn said.

"Tyus isn't going to be able to play!"

"Jimmy, don't give up on this team! You got a guy on that team, remember, who can take over a game and win it!"

"What do you mean?"

"Ed O'Bannon can take over a game and win it! In this particular matchup, we're better than they are! We'll beat them!"

The Bruins sprinted through a tunnel. The Hogs were already out there, goofing off and jumping around and acting, quite frankly, as if they had never been in the middle of such a spectacle, with all the floodlights on them. A composed Ed O'Bannon pulled his guys around him and calmly said, "Fellas, this is just gonna be a pick-up game."

Nolan Richardson dazzled in dark cowboy boots and a pastel lime suit that would probably look good—at least, passable—on only one person. "He pulled it off. That's his thing," says Ed O'Bannon. Suited and booted, indeed. That Richardson had pulled it off was debatable. Was that the latest among businessmen in Prague? Frederick's of Monsanto had designed it, wrote *Orange County Register* columnist Mark Whicker. *Was it natural grass or AstroTurf?*

In the summer of 2013 I slip a DVD copy of the final game of O'Bannon's amateur career into a computer in an Italian restaurant in Henderson, Nevada. He is serious, as usual, and says, "I don't know that we ever questioned that we'd win or lose. I felt like, the whole time, that we would win the game. I never saw a look of doubt in anyone's faces or eyes." The CBS television production is so archaic it should have been aired in black and white, with a sketchy VIA SATELLITE at the bottom. The score is not on constant display. When it is shown, the time remaining rarely accompanies it. As if it hasn't been introduced yet, the shot clock is just as scarce. There is no scrawl at the bottom of the screen, but an infamous trial is about to change that forever.

(By contrast, a December 2013 broadcast of a UCLA game at Missouri—in which the Tigers exacted a smidgen of Boise revenge with a victory—constantly shows the score, the period, the time remaining, the shot clock, each team's free-throw status, timeouts remaining, and the direction of the possession arrow. The constant narrow line at the bottom flashes scores, updates, and breaking news. Play-by-play man Kevin Harlan ponders the perception of West Coast softness and Eastern players who supposedly have "more grit" to analyst Greg Anthony, a key UNLV player on its 1990 title team who was, for only several weeks, a teammate of Ed O'Bannon on the Rebels during the ensuing summer. The mettle of West Coast players had not been debatable during John Wooden's glorious seasons as the Bruins' coach. In late 2013, Anthony calls the UCLA gig "arguably" one of the "top five best jobs" in college hoops, as if it were a universal given that yet another change was imminent in Westwood ... and it was.)

Pat O'Brien anchored the stiff 1995 pre-game show, with Quinn Buckner and Mike Krzyzewski, whose back had sufficiently mended. John Wooden even joined the trio for some banter on the set atop a tunnel in a corner of the court. Whether Edney's injury would hamper the Bruins, Wooden said they should still play their game, their style. "Remember what got you here ... [but] naturally, I'd feel better if they were at full strength." O'Brien asked Wooden what any of the current Bruins might know about his legacy and all those banners in the Pauley rafters. "I don't know why they should; that was twenty years ago," Wooden said. "They have to establish their own identity."

Coach K said if Edney can't go, reserve point guard Cameron Dollar had better get the ball into Ed O'Bannon's hands. Wooden's departing words were about defense winning championships, "and Dollar is an excellent defender." CBS went to the benches for introductions. First up for UCLA was Ed O'Bannon. He smiled and winked his right eye ... at those living along the Strand in Manhattan Beach? "Could be. I mean, I wanted to be loose," he says.

> I wanted to appreciate being there. I didn't want to *look back* and appreciate it. I wanted to see that game as if I were watching a tape. I didn't want to have any regrets.

When your career is over you look at a tape and see what you should have done better and could have done better. I was kind of reliving that moment as it was playing out. I wanted to remember everything about that game, appreciate everything about that game. I just knew I'd never get back to that. For me, this was a once-in-a-lifetime deal.

Charles O'Bannon began the final forty minutes of the season by tipping the opening tap to Tyus Edney, who zipped it to Toby Bailey on the left side. Ed O'Bannon had already sped downcourt to the left corner. Bailey rushed the ball to him, and Ed O'Bannon sank a three-point shot just five seconds into it. At the start of every subsequent NCAA final, Tony Luftman sends Ed O'Bannon a text message; *Man, I'll bet you both kidneys and both testicles that nobody takes a three-point shot within the first five seconds of this game. Do you know how crazy that is? What possessed you? Why would you shoot that shot? Not only did you take it, you made it, as if it were a designed play.*

"Boom!" Ed says as he watches himself. "You can't think about it. It was just a straight reaction. I was just trying to get an open spot. If open, shoot it. If not, we'll get into our offense."

Big Nasty swerved, slid down, and went to work at the other end. He forced a quick whistle on George Zidek for fouling. He hit a basket. A bit later, Zidek faded out to Clint McDaniel as McDaniel zipped the ball to Corliss Williamson in the right post. Williamson slammed into Toby Bailey, arms straight up to take a charge, who fell to the floor backward. Williamson continued with his shot, only to have Charles O'Bannon soar high to spike the ball way out of bounds near midcourt. Charles flexed and hollered. "He went up and got that," Ed says, peering left at the computer screen, with his hands clenched on the table's red and white vinyl checkerboard cover. He sips an Arnold Palmer. He will let his chicken Parm sandwich get cold. "He surprised me. I knew Charles was on help side. I saw him comin'. I didn't know he'd get up and grab it ... I thought, *Ohhhhhh!* There's a method, a reason why I yelled at those guys; we're finally there, to put it all together and on display. That set the tone for us."

Tyus Edney favored his left hand as much as possible. When he went to that right appendage it was cursory, a mere flick. Arkansas guards reacted like sharks smelling blood, pressing his right side. After two and a half minutes it was obvious that Edney could not go. Clint McDaniel drilled a three-point shot. Ed O'Bannon inbounded the ball on one bounce to Edney, in the left corner of the Arkansas baseline. Senior forward Elmer Martin swiped the ball from Edney. Corey Beck hauled in Martin's pass and converted a close banker over O'Bannon.

Edney nodded to Harrick, the signal to take him out, but Harrick had already tapped Cameron Dollar to shed his sweats and check in at the scorer's table. Ed O'Bannon says, "Tyus can't dribble. Once he goes out I figure he's gotta be hurt."

Dollar had taken the switch from starter to reserve like a selfless veteran. He sat in on coaches' meetings, and when the discussion drifted to the guards—and him—he made sound, rational judgments. He would call prospects that could ultimately replace him, only asking Harrick, *Is he good?* He was all about the team, the program. By the end of his sophomore season, Dollar had earned immense admiration from every Bruin, including Ed O'Bannon, who gave Dollar the utmost sign of respect when likening him to Gerald Madkins. Dollar would shout directions at and chastise any teammate, O'Bannon included, for straying from strategy. Dollar didn't know how to back down. "It's all about just who wants it most," Dollar said. "And it's just hard for me to fathom that somebody would want it more than I do."

In scouting other teams and having a feel for how they play and knowing precisely what those guys like to run in certain situations, Dollar even told opponents that they weren't running their own plays correctly, that a certain player should be here or there. And he had convinced Nate James at Prospect Hall that he was going to win an NCAA title. "I'd been plotting and strategizing for that day for a long time. Seriously, [at that moment] I'm thinking, 'It's about god-damned time!' " Dollar says. The Chris Rock comparison is uncanny. Now he could affect that title. What would Arkansas say, or do, about that? Plenty.

Two minutes, thirty-seven seconds after the tap, Dollar walked onto the court and gave a slight nod to Edney, as he shuffled to the bench. Edney had told Dollar to be ready, to have his mind right for Arkansas. Still, Dollar paused. *This is surreal*, he thought. *Hey man, where you goin'? Hey man, fuck that! You can go! Yo, where you goin'? You can't miss this! You're not missin' this, man!* Dollar gazed around the dome. His mind wandered. *Damn, lots of people!* Clint McDaniel quickly swiped the ball from Dollar and cruised in for a layup.

George Zidek turned it over, and Arkansas bolted to a 12-5 lead. Corey Beck, the six-foot-two senior guard from Memphis, smiled and skipped around as if he were spending a sunny spring day in the park. The Razorbacks had tallied ten points off UCLA turnovers and were feeling very good. They hollered, "Keep it goin'! They're scared! Let's go. Here we go." Ed O'Bannon thought, *Really? It ain't a big deal. We just gotta relax. If we can run off a couple of buckets, stop them, run off a couple more buckets, we'll be fine.* Corey Beck fouled Dollar and yipped at Dollar, who stopped within a few feet of Beck. "You talkin' trash to *me*?" said a startled Dollar. "Awwww, okay. All right." That snapped Dollar to attention. That snapped every Bruin to attention.

It would become evident that Nolan Richardson, his staff, and his players had not done their due diligence in scouting the Bruins. Toby Bailey, in particular, would make the Hogs pay for taking him for granted. Steve Lavin always talked about Southern California players emitting a casual, smug swagger that he had dubbed California Cool, an image of superiority because of where they were from, not from any achievement. Cockiness. Not confidence. Plenty of pretender predecessors could have been poster boys for that slogan. New Mexico State coach Neil McCarthy had a profane label for the Bruins in 1992. Flimsy defense if not fortitude nearly cost UCLA against those Aggies, and did against Indiana. And Michigan. And Tulsa.

Arkansas had returned all five starters from its national championship team, so it had to believe it could show up at Monday's finale and punk these West Coast chumps without doing much homework. The Razorbacks had been mighty fortunate in this tournament. Why wouldn't that continue? As someone who fully comprehended attitudes in the South and East, since he grew up in Atlanta and played elite prep ball in Maryland, Cameron Dollar knew the plot, perspectives, and contexts of Monday, April 3. Dollar laughs when he recalls what turned it. "The hardest thing for Southerners and East Coasters to understand about the West Coast is … first of all, it is softer. Okay. Let's just call it what it is," he says.

But the level of skill and the ability to turn it up when they get pissed off … I played with a lot of dudes on the West Cost. I call it L.A. Cool. Yeah, you piss 'em off, in a game that matters, then all of a sudden [he laughs] … they're pros. Hey, man, that dude can handle it! He can shoot it! He can jump higher than you! That's just how the West Coast dudes are. It was funny to see [the Hogs] not handle that. See, the same thing happened to UConn when we played them. They thought they could just pressure us and they were gonna bully us. [He laughs again.] You have no idea ... they didn't know how skilled Ed, Charles, Toby, J.R. ... them dudes are thoroughbreds! They do that in their sleep. That's the last thing you want to do, but that's the way Arkansas plays. What are they gonna do, slow it down and milk the clock? They can't do that.

Hank Edney added to that theory, saying Arkansas must have felt so much better about itself, and the game, when UCLA's floor general was taken out, obviously for good, so early. "Cameron showed what he can do," Hank says. "It was an incredible game. That's just the way life is."

Arkansas led 14-9 and kept pressing. "We want them to press," Ed O'Bannon says with his elbows on the vinyl. Both teams switched from two-two-one zone presses to matchup zones to man-to-man coverages. The action often did look as if it belonged on after-school asphalt, as O'Bannon had forecasted. UCLA appeared to be playing some sort of Super Amoeba, the ultra-flexible defense devised by Jerry Tarkanian—which UNLV used so expertly to win its lone crown—that made it seem as if there were seven or eight defenders; everyone, everywhere, shutting down all options, inside and outside at the same time.

A close shot by Ed O'Bannon, Charles O'Bannon's follow of Cameron Dollar's off-target short jumper, a free throw by Charles, and a bank shot by George Zidek kept the Razorbacks from running away from the Bruins. The Hogs, and especially Scotty Thurman, responded with their mouths. He once told an official, *I'm gonna talk to you. I'm gonna talk to myself, and I'm gonna talk to other people. I'm not going to say anything vulgar. But I'm gonna talk. That's just the way I am.* Thurman & Co. mostly bleated at the Bruins when they turned it over or when they were at the foul line. *Don't miss! Aw, his asshole's getting' tight. He's gonna miss; his asshole's getting' tight!* "They said it to me," Ed O'Bannon says. "I stopped and said, 'What? C'mon man!' "

At the first television timeout the Hogs nursed a 16-12 advantage. Jim Harrick saw some disconnect on Dollar's mug and said, "You know why you're on scholarship, right? RIGHT?" Dollar straightened up. Harrick said, "To get the ball to Ed O'Bannon!" Dollar smiled and nodded. Tony Spino offered a hot pad to Tyus Edney, for his damaged wrist, but Edney declined. UCLA just had a shake-up, was turning the ball over, and needed to adjust to life without Tyus Edney. And Arkansas, the famed runners and pressers, had not raced away from UCLA. "That's what we wanted ... to keep it close," Ed says.

> We knew we were the better team. Just wanted to keep it close, see if *their* assholes would tighten up. We knew we could run off eight, ten straight points within a minute and a half. Even if they made their baskets, we got the ball up the floor so fast. Personally, I prided myself in getting the ball up the floor as fast as possible. [Even] when that ball comes through the net [on opponent shots], I'm grabbing it and sending it out there.

Zidek raised the ball above his chest and had it swiped by a Razorback. "Killin' me, George," Ed says under his breath. But UCLA kept its poise and knotted it, 21-21. Every Bruin says withstanding an Arkansas onslaught immediately after such a shocking development—the removal, very likely for good, of the guy who had directed them to this apex—was critical. The Bruins showed press then backed off. Or they retreated at half speed before suffocating the Razorbacks with a full-on press, turning their strategy back onto them. "We wanted them to see different looks, throw wrinkles in there sometimes," Ed says. Playgroundish? "Yep. It didn't feel like a national championship game, to be honest," he says.

> We were so loosey-goosey, so matter-of-fact, for the whole thing. Weird. Like an out-of-body experience. I think that's why I got a chance to see it from a different angle while I was going through it. I had a chance to appreciate where we were and what we were doing. We weren't tight. I almost felt like a spectator, just kind of watching myself. The whole experience was kind of surreal. First, I'd never played before so many people before. Second, we were in a situation where we could accomplish our goal *tonight. Tonight*, we can make it happen.

UCLA exploited a third foul on Corey Beck, who shrugged as he trudged to his bench, and pumped its advantage to as many as eight points, on a close basket by Toby Bailey. A dunk by Bailey made it 36-29, but Arkansas rallied. With twenty-four seconds left until halftime, six-foot-eleven, 255-pound sophomore Lee Wilson converted a close banker on the right side over Ed O'Bannon to give Arkansas a 39-38 edge. Charles O'Bannon had tried to help, but his swat attempt was late and off target; it appeared he was trying to shoo a big fly out of the dome.

Ed O'Bannon struggled to inbound the ball against the Arkansas press. But he found Toby Bailey, who dribbled twice. Four passes later, J.R. Henderson knifed down the middle of the lane and hauled in a return pass from Charles O'Bannon for an easy transition layup off the glass, on the right side, to give UCLA a 40-39 advantage with ten seconds left. Almost twenty years later, Henderson still plays professionally, in Japan, and says he owes his longevity to his penchant for executing layups instead of taxing his knees with flamboyant dunks.

The Bruins do not trail again.

As the second half was about to commence, Corey Beck strolled near the middle of the court. He rolled a shoulder. He slowly shook each leg, swiped at the bottom of each white Adidas hightop, grinned, and exchanged a few words with Cameron Dollar. They slapped right hands. Dollar detected nervousness. UCLA scored close baskets on three of its first four possessions. As Ed O'Bannon made a free throw to polish off a three-point play, Corliss Williamson looked concerned. Toby Bailey would inflict more worry on Big Nasty and the rest of the Hogs. Bailey grabbed his own rebound, went back up, had it deflected, gathered it again, and put it in on the right side for a 48-42 lead. The Bruins were pasting the Razorbacks in second-chance points, sixteen to nothing.

Near the first television timeout, a play unfolded that cemented itself in the memory bank of every witness. Ed O'Bannnon grabbed Corliss Williamson's miss in the left post and dribbled once while gazing toward his rim. Toby Bailey had sprinted away. Ed looked as if he were a six-eight starter, on the Dodger Stadium mound. His sixty-foot, six-inch strike found Bailey belt high. Bailey took flight, twisted, and threw down a two-handed reverse dunk that padded UCLA's lead to 55-45. The dome erupted. Today Bailey says, "Yeah, I traveled ... I had no nerves. I didn't know what was at stake. I took a hop ... a reverse, especially with a guy comin' down on my shoulder? But I was a freshman. Good, good times."

On CBS, play-by-play ace Jim Nantz said, "That was a bullet!" A camera caught another lefty, Dodgers' Hall of Fame pitcher Sandy Koufax, smiling in the crowd. CBS would use slow-mo footage of the super jam—Bailey seemed to crouch at the peak to keep from smacking his head against the Kingdome ceiling—out of a commercial before the end of its broadcast. It was one of O'Bannon's favorite plays. "I saw [Toby] leak out before the shot went up; you read it before it happens," he says.

> When we're in there boarding, someone can leak out because we normally get the rebound. A lot of times, in most games, we outboarded everybody. Toby, from his vantage point, can see all that's happening. He's thinking, "We get the board, I'm out." As I threw it I thought, "Don't throw it too hard" and "Don't put a spin on it." I didn't want him to have to dig it out of the ground.

In fact, opponents grabbed more rebounds than the Bruins twelve times during the season—although UCLA crushed Arkansas, fifty to thirty-one, on the boards in this one. What classified this version of UCLA basketball with its elite teams of all time was its efficiency on its own basket and its devilish disposition on defense.

The Bruins led by ten. It seemed to take the air out of everyone in the crowd wearing red plastic pig hats. UCLA felt good, "real good," Ed O'Bannon says. Arkansas players hushed. "I don't think they can say too much right now," Ed says. "But we don't want to get too excited or too comfortable. We needed to keep the foot on the gas pedal." Despite Billy Packer calling out some Bruins for grabbing their shorts—usually a telltale sign of fatigue—early in the second half, UCLA had pulled away from Arkansas. Stamina was no issue with Ed O'Bannon or any of his regulars. "No way," he says. "No possible way that we're going to get tired. I know I wasn't going to get tired."

Toby Bailey felt the same way. He stole Corliss Williamson's half-court pass, executed a 360-degree spin around his left side— by Corey Beck, who hit the wood when he bumped into George Zidek—and leaned in to push a shot over Williamson in the lane. The ball banked high off the backboard, Bailey snatched it, and in one motion lobbed it into the hoop to give UCLA a 65-53 pad.

At the other end, Williamson tried maneuvering for a shot but was banged onto his rump by Bailey. All that toughening up by Ed O'Bannon had worked, as did choice words from John Wooden. Sitting on the court, Williamson glanced up at Bailey, who reigned over Williamson as if inquiring whether Big Nasty just might like some more of that. No prisoners. As a teammate slowly helped him to his feet, Williamson grinned at the precocious Bailey. Ed O'Bannon moved in fast to remove Bailey from the scene, not wanting him to get hit with a technical foul but applauding his enthusiastic aggressiveness. He had done exactly what O'Bannon had tutored for months.

Eighteen years after that scene, O'Bannon acts as though he is witnessing it, moment by moment, for the first time. "Toby was standing over Corliss like, 'Yeah, motherfucker! Now what you gonna do?' I get goose bumps right now. He *got* it. The lesson was, '*This* is *our* land! We're playing defense on this half of the floor and for you to score you have to go through one of us, if not all of us.' I hate to point Corliss out like this, but he couldn't get through ... Toby put him on his ass!"

Officials Ted Valentine, Jim Burr, and John Cahill deserve credit for largely letting the action dictate and flow, for hardly ever becoming support players. When they were heard from, it was obvious, as in Bailey's thumping of Williamson.

The Bruins had to weather a stretch of about six minutes in which they only tallied Ed O'Bannon's strong hook-scoop shot after hauling in his own miss. UCLA continued to resemble an accordion, shifting zone defenses, daring Arkansas to make outside shots. *Only get beat over the top.* These were the critical moments. Dwight Stewart canned a couple of jumpers, and Corey Beck drilled a three-point shot to get Arkansas to within 67-63. A frenetic couple of minutes was filled with sloppiness, turnovers, and missed free throws. With five minutes, seventeen seconds left, George Zidek fouled Corliss Williamson near the Arkansas hoop. Williamson went to the line and made his first foul shot to get the Hogs within three points.

This was the final juncture for both coaches. For Nolan Richardson, his squad was a free throw from cutting its deficit in half. It could teeter either way. Would the Arkansas karma continue? Richardson was on the brink of guiding his guys out of another hole to earn a second consecutive NCAA crown. Since John Wooden, he and Mike Krzyzewski would be the only two coaches who could make that boast. For Jim Harrick, his players had stretches of control while playing without their senior floor director, the diminutive point guard who had doled out thirty-eight assists in the NCAAs and provided them with so many clutch field goals. But the Bruins had shown their resiliency and tenacity. If they could hang on, Ed O'Bannon would redeem five years worth of agony and angst. And a UCLA boss will have finally hurdled the high bar established long ago by Wooden.

Ultimately, however, neither coach would leave his current institution in a stylish or tasteful manner. For nine seconds a crowning achievement hung in the balance for both, until Ed O'Bannon struck as a CBS camera shifted from a crowd shot of Williamson's brother and father, exchanging guffaws, to the action.

O'Bannon rebounded Big Nasty's errant second free throw and dished it to Cameron Dollar. Williamson slid over to shadow O'Bannon, jogging backward to stay with O'Bannon down UCLA's left wing. Once Dollar crossed midcourt, he drifted left. O'Bannon planted a screen on Al Dillard thirty feet from the rim. Williamson shot up to trap Dollar. Dillard popped out on Dollar, too. Charles O'Bannon had been out on that left side, but he circled under the hoop to rid that area of traffic. Scotty Thurman had been denying Charles, but Thurman backed to the left post and did not go with Charles.

As the Bruins had most of the game, Dollar navigated around the turmoil of the Dillard-Williamson double team. Dollar dribbled left, once, then squeezed between Dillard and Williamson to deliver a two-handed chest pass to Ed O'Bannon, who had stepped back after setting the screen. O'Bannon dribbled hard, once, to his right (to the left post) and rose dramatically over Thurman to sink a no-doubt power lefty hook shot. Thurman, who never budged from a crouching defensive position, didn't have a chance.

The two-man play, called by Harrick, ignited the army of Bruins fans among the audience of 38,540. UCLA had a 69-64 lead. Dollar had not forgotten why he was on a UCLA scholarship. "Dollar was lookin' at me," Ed says. "He brought it to my side. I know we need a bucket. I was lookin' for it. Dollar knew exactly what he was doing. There isn't a whole lot of separation, at this point, but I felt we were in control."

Corliss Williamson again made only one of two foul shots, twenty-four seconds later, and during that lull Ed O'Bannon heard some gibberish from a Hog or two, hollering, "Come on! Let's go! Let's go!" Ed O'Bannon grinned, and steamed. He thought to himself, *Let's go? Dude ... what do you mean, Let's go? We're kicking your ass. You're gonna just turn it on now? All of a sudden, you're pissed off? No, I don't think so. This is our game. We're the number one team in the country. No, let's go. Not against us, let's go.*

Toby Bailey added to his highlight reel. Ed O'Bannon missed a pull-up jumper left of the foul line. Bailey—in front of Corey Beck, who reacted half a second too late, and Dwight Stewart, who failed to budge from his spot in the left post—launched high in front of the rim from the right side and softly tapped the ball through the net with his left hand to make it 71-65 with 4:31 left. "You're looking at a future star there," said Billy Packer.

Scotty Thurman would say UCLA's ability to use the Arkansas press against itself was impressive, that it repeatedly finished with that assassin's touch. Thurman believed Bailey shot the ball "extremely well" and "did some things they needed down the stretch, that's why they won the game." At the New Jersey Nets' preseason camp six months later, Thurman would make a stark admission to Ed O'Bannon; *Who was that Toby Bailey? We had no idea.* "He told me, 'The man [Bailey] wasn't even on the scouting report,' " O'Bannon says. In 2008, Thurman told an Arkansas online site that he occasionally thought about how the Razorbacks could have beaten UCLA, "some adjustments" they could have made; paying attention to Toby Bailey might have been a good place to start. All he did was punish Connecticut with twenty-six points the previous weekend. How did the Arkansas brain trust overlook that and not circle Bailey's name in crimson?

"I don't think they really knew much about us," Ed O'Bannon says. "I don't think they knew we ran as much as we did, that we could shoot as well as we did. Quite honestly, I thought they were a bit surprised at what they ran up against that night."

It marked the beginning of the end for the Hogs, who followed with a wild three-point shot by Dwight Stewart and an errant jumper by Scotty Thurman. They fouled at the other end, to stop the clock and try to stem the flow, but Cameron Dollar sank two free throws. Thurman missed a free-throw jumper, and Dwight Stewart fouled Ed O'Bannon on a rebound in the left post. Billy

Packer mentioned the five Arkansas players huddling, and Jim Nantz pointed out that Corey Beck had herded them together.

Packer and Nantz failed to recognize that Ed O'Bannon had gathered his own troops to jog to the other end of the court, where he would attempt two free throws. "It's still a tight game, and I'm telling the guys to run," Ed says. "We ain't gonna walk. Mentally, psychologically, I'm tellin' myself that I hope [the Razorbacks] see us. We ain't tired. We ain't slowin' down. Bring that Forty Minutes of Hell!"

In between Ed O'Bannon's two free throw conversions, a CBS camera found Ed Sr. and Madeline O'Bannon, in front of Bailey's father John and brother Moose, in the stands. Back from the final television-timeout commercials, Jim Harrick calmly sucked on a mint—he always carried a pocketful—as Jim Nantz said, "What a night this man is having. It's been a long journey to this championship game."

Thirty-five feet from the Hogs' basket, in front of the Arkansas bench, Ed tightened his defense on Dwight Stewart, daring Stewart to dribble. A flustered Stewart couldn't find an open teammate. As he lowered the ball, Ed swiped it from him. "I could see him lookin' away," O'Bannon says. "He was kind of careless with the ball. I told myself, 'I'll give it a shot. I'm gonna see if I can take it from him,' and he put it right in my face."

The Bruins patiently tossed the ball around. It made its way to a wide-open Bailey at the left elbow, and he drilled a jumper to give UCLA a 77-65 edge. The Kingdome again roared. At the other end, for what seemed like the hundredth time, Corliss Williamson struggled to lift a shot over George Zidek in the right post. Zidek stood with both hands high in the air. Williamson flailed on an attempt, and the ball flew on a weak line drive along the left baseline, five feet under the basket. "My guesstimation is [Zidek] is as big an opponent as they've seen all season," Ed O'Bannon says. "Not only is he big, he can move. He's light on his feet. He goes left. He goes right. Look at Corliss; he can't move. George hits Corliss on his tailbone ... watch [Williamson's] head bounce back. Boom! George just anchors our defense."

Williamson would say he got too caught up in the conflict with Zidek. When Zidek bumped him, Williamson's natural reaction was to bump back, to force the issue. That had most often served Big Nasty well during his three seasons as a Razorback. He would give UCLA, and Zidek, credit for psyching him into a strongarm competition.

When Zidek missed the first of two free-throw attempts with 2:35 left, a CBS microphone caught him saying an abrupt "Shit!" It was more like, *Sittttttt!* Billy Packer said, "Well, he's learned a little English, for you who heard that remark." Zidek missed his second, too. But whatever Arkansas did the rest of the way, UCLA matched. In a timeout with 1:25 left, Harrick drew up the same play he had concocted at the end against Arizona in Tucson to put the Hogs out of their misery.

Ed O'Bannon shuffled to the far baseline to inbound the ball. Charles O'Bannon—the Bruin farthest from Ed—casually inched up to the middle of the court, toward Ed, with Al Dillard a step behind him. Charles pulled a one-eighty and sprinted to his basket, Dillard trailing. CBS was lucky to capture the play, as it showed John Wooden gingerly descending a steel staircase to exit the building. Beagle-Beagle caught the bomb and sailed in for a rim-rattling dunk on the left side for an 83-71 lead. Billy Packer announced, "Jim Harrick has coached a brilliant game tonight."

In the final minute, Cameron Dollar stole a short pass Al Dillard had intended for Corey Beck, way out on the perimeter, and Dollar cruised in for an easy layup. For Dollar, the swipe and sail-in for an easy score was poetic retribution, occurring right about where he had gotten the ball pilfered from him just three seconds after he had replaced Tyus Edney.

The Razorbacks had failed to get the ball into Beck's hands. Foul trouble also hampered him. A year earlier, in the championship against Duke, Beck had fifteen points and ten boards in thirty-five minutes. Against UCLA, he was on the court for ten fewer minutes, he scored eleven points, on four-of-six shooting, and he yanked down three rebounds. Harrick had wagered, that his defenders could stray from Beck, and won. Scotty Thurman (fifteen points to five) and Corliss Williamson (twenty-three to twelve) had also experienced scoring shortages from Duke to UCLA.

Ed O'Bannon followed with an emphatic dunk. Packer said that play personified what this game was all about, "UCLA in the open court." Ed paused for a few seconds and raised both hands along the right baseline. He saw UCLA fans celebrating and yelling and jumping in the stands beyond the floor and up to the rim of the dome. He tried controlling his emotions. "It's hittin' me," O'Bannon says. "Every bone in my face, every muscle, I'm doing all I can not to smile. I'm saying to myself, 'Oh my god, we are going to win this thing ... the whole thing ... it's over. Nothin' they can do now.' It was perfect for us."

Charles O'Bannon lost his grip on the ball as he tried to dunk in the final seconds. The buzzer blared. Charles raised both hands and jumped up and down. Kristaan Johnson, looking like a bedouin with only a slit for his eyes under two towels fashioned like a shroud, danced toward his teammates.

UCLA had its eleventh national championship banner by virtue of its 89-78 victory. Charles O'Bannon (eleven points, nine rebounds, six assists, two steals, and two blocked shots) and Cameron Dollar (eight assists, six points, and four steals) had both played thirty-six minutes, and Toby Bailey (twenty-six points and nine boards) had logged thirty-nine. Bailey and Ed O'Bannon combined to make twenty-two of forty-one shots from the field. Corliss Williamson had made only three of his sixteen shots. He finished with twelve points and four rebounds; his Czech adversary had ended with fourteen and six, respectively. According to Nielsen Media Research, more than twenty-seven million viewers tuned in, a figure surpassed only once in the ensuing twenty years.

Mark Gottfried hugged Jim Harrick as they stumbled along the sideline to shake hands with Nolan Richardson, his staff, and the Razorbacks. Harrick stood on the tip of his toes to give Richardson a hug, but Richardson didn't reciprocate with the same glee. The Bruins encircled at the foul line in front of their bench, held hands, and rejoiced to a prayer by Lorenzo Romar.

Ed O'Bannon's happy wails can be heard over Romar's invocation. The leader of the Bruins had tallied thirty points and seventeen rebounds, and he never took a seat. Not on this canvas. Through 2014, the only other player to rack up at least thirty points and fifteen rebounds while playing every second of an NCAA title game for the champs was Clyde Lovellette, for Kansas in 1952. And the Emerald City had played host to both gems. The six-foot-nine, 240-pound terror from Terre Haute had thirty-three and seventeen, respectively, in the Jayhawks' 80-63 victory over St. John's at Hec Edmundson Pavilion. He had a nice hook shot, says Jim Harrick, who was thirteen at the time and recalls Lovellette. "A bit slow, but nobody had that size in those days." That was the lone national championship in the celebrated coaching career of Dr. F.C. "Phog" Allen.

UCLA's majordomo pared and polished the Bruins into a team for the ages, even by their lofty standards. They shot 51.3 percent as a team and held foes to 40.8 percent. Through 2014, the only other UCLA teams to match, or better, those figures at both ends of the court were the Lew Alcindor title squads of 1967 and '69, and Bill Walton's in 1973. The 1994-95 Bruins also established a school record with 312 steals. UCLA vexed the other guys with constant hands in their faces when they shot, at their midsections when they dribbled, and in passing lanes. O'Bannon's defensive demands paid incredible dividends.

Through 2014, he was also the last UCLA senior to average twenty points (20.4), and he was the first Bruin to tally double figures in scoring thirty-three times in a single season. While he was instilling everyone within earshot, including himself, to defend the paint, he delivered at the other end, too. He watches himself bawl on the computer screen. "Crying like a baby. Couldn't hold it in anymore. My emotions, they were bustin' out. It didn't get any better, to me, than that."

Jim Nantz tilted the microphone toward O'Bannon. "We stayed positive the whole time," O'Bannon told the CBS audience. "We put everything in God's hands. We walk by faith, not by sight ... He brought us here." O'Bannon's voice rose as he stared at the camera. "MVP goes to Tyus Edney!" Nantz pulled George Zidek into the frame. It was about 5 A.M. in Prague, and Zidek said nobody in his hockey-crazed homeland was watching. How'd you shut down Corliss? "I don't even know how I did it," Zidek said in his sharp Slavic tongue. "But I shut him down. We played hard and we showed everybody that we have heart ... we proved all critics wrong ... we showed what West Coast basketball is all about." Nantz pulled the mic away, but Zidek grabbed it back with his left hand. "We are the best team in the nation!" Someone out of the picture said, " ... this is a long way from Morningside."

A camera picked up Kristaan Johnson. Every Bruin either wore a white championship T-shirt, cap, and/or gold sweatsuit top; Kris has already donned a blue *Yeah, Baby!* T-shirt. Marques Johnson claimed to have had clumps of those shirts in Seattle and made *a pretty penny*. Through 2014, of the four father-son combinations to have won NCAA titles the Johnsons were the lone duo to have accomplished the feat at the same school.

UCLA athletic director Pete Dalis mugged with some players, and the blocky wood trophy. In the next several weeks, his office would be swamped with hundreds of letters extolling Harrick's performance and Dalis's fine, fine stewardship of the basketball program. A year earlier he had told his secretary to keep all the hate mail he had received after the Tulsa disaster. "Many people complained about Coach Harrick, and for whatever reason I told Judy, 'Let's keep all those ... we'll see what the outcome is,' " Dalis says. "I don't know why, because I normally didn't do that. Now people wrote about the great job Harrick did, and those were the same people who wanted him fired. *The same names.*"

Pat O'Brien mentioned the demanding nature of UCLA fans, that Jim Harrick had just won one title, now how about nine more? O'Brien couldn't resist going to the laziest of clichés when he yapped about Harrick having had a *monkey on his back.* "Well, there shoulda never been a monkey on his back, Pat," Krzyzewski said. "Jim Harrick showed, not just in this tournament but through the whole season, what an excellent coach he is. To lose Edney going into this game; their team had a chance to rationalize and say, well, we've come this far ... now we have an excuse. I think the leader of that team was Jim Harrick, and he never let them rationalize."

A floor-level camera showed Ed O'Bannon standing on a yellow ladder—with KINGDOME in blue down the side—topped by a blue platform. He handed a small video recorder to a teammate below him. He held scissors in his left hand and snipped away at the net.

A gracious Nolan Richardson told CBS sideline reporter Michele Tafoya that his Hogs had not been effective ... UCLA had neutralized Corliss Williamson ... and Jim Harrick and his crew should be congratulated for playing *lights out*. Before hundreds of media, Richardson admitted knowing little about the Bruins, that he had viewed *some* tape. UCLA made his guys look as if they were running in mud all night, he said. "The sun, we hope, will come up tomorrow." Half a minute later, he talked about tomorrow, "if I should live to see it ... I'm just happy enough today that I'm alive ... tonight the best team was UCLA." His grandstanding rants were for other days. Richardson grew melancholy as he alluded to true sorrow when he watched leukemia claim his fifteen-year-old daughter, Yvonne, in 1987.

Author Rus Bradburd barely devoted half of a small paragraph to the Razorbacks' loss to UCLA in *Forty Minutes of Hell*, a biography of Richardson published in 2010. Twenty-eight paragraphs described the Arkansas national championship victory over Duke, not including Richardson's quote in which he confirmed that he had *created a monster*. And that was after only one title.

Ed O'Bannon went out with several teammates that evening, but he avoided alcohol; he had been scheduled to appear on *Good Morning, America* at 4 A.M., his time, and he did not want to appear disheveled or sloppy. The group settled inside the now-defunct Fenix Underground. There was some rappin', and his teammates doubled over when George Zidek strolled onto the stage, grabbed the mic, and did his *Terminator* routine. Toby Bailey drank 7-Up, because he was underage, but he acted as if he were drunk.

Inside their room at the Airport Marriott, Madeline and Ed O'Bannon Sr. shared hugs and clinked flutes of champagne with Dr. Michael R. Shapiro. Parents, relatives, friends, and coaches blissfully shuffled in and out of rooms. In another room, J.R. Henderson and Tony Luftman played video games. Later Tuesday morning, Kristaan Johnson wearily slogged up to a Sea-Tac gate and declared that this was just the beginning; the Bruins were primed to rattle off a few more championships and add to that history.

They would not.

In fact, no program in the country would match UCLA in conflict and drama in the coming months. Many years later Kristaan Johnson says UCLA, in subsequent seasons, led the nation in games played while hungover. "Let's just say it was a great [time] after the championship," says Charles O'Bannon, who missed a flight to North Carolina, to play Duke, when he overslept after a night of birthday carousing. "We had a key to the city," says Toby Bailey. Rarely were they presented a bill for anything. Celebrated too much, says Jim Harrick. One player probably represents all when he says, "I don't know how many of those stories are fit to print."

Unlike the previous few months, UCLA basketballers of all ages were now welcomed into clubs like the Roxy on Sunset and Madison's in Westwood. Some rang up serial one-night stands, on occasion in the alley behind a Sunset Strip club. Coeds, strippers and suburban females dallied with the national champs. Witnesses' eyes bugged at the steady rotation of tens exiting one player's suite. Another admitted that he would not be shocked if he were eventually diagnosed with the AIDS virus. The entertainer Queen Latifah sent a bottle of Dom Perignon to every player on the championship team. Many players told me they had not opened their bottles, that they were dusty and packed away in a corner of their garage, or in the attic of their parents' homes. Those were improper extra benefits, according to NCAA rules. So what? The Bruins bacchanalia was on.

UCLA's commercial jet landed at LAX early the afternoon of Tuesday, April 4. A police-escorted coach whisked them up the 405 freeway. A TV station's helicopter hovered overhead. Motorists turned into the far right lane, parked their cars, and hailed the victors. At overpasses, fans cheered and waved as the bus slipped underneath them. It was eerily similar to another run up that stretch of highway, minus an old white Ford Bronco, ten months earlier. The resultant trial was barely into its third month. Every player chanted *The Juice! The Juice!* as that bus rollicked along the 405. "We were rock stars," Charles O'Bannon says today.

Streams of light blue and yellow balloons curled at corners of the Pauley Pavilion court. Confetti fell from the rafters, where an eleventh blue banner would be raised. Thirteen thousand fans celebrated with the team. Richard Riordan, the mayor of Los Angeles, roared, "They're going to do it again next year!" Jim Harrick quipped back, "Do you want me to vote for you or not? Easy." Afterward, John Wooden found Tony Luftman in the back of the locker room. "Well, Tony, how does it feel to win your first championship?" In Wooden's condo a few days later, Luftman was feeling very content as he sat at the roll-top desk. He couldn't resist popping off about the school-record thirty-one victories. No Wooden squad, obviously, had won that many games in one season. *Tony, how many did you play?* The icon emeritus said in his gentle, light-hearted way. "But he wasn't joking," Luftman says.

For someone born and bred in Los Angeles the timing of the title was poignant for Ed O'Bannon. His gargantuan role in restoring UCLA to prominence came during a dearth on the Southern California sporting landscape. His beloved Dodgers, and the Lakers, had not won championships since 1988. The Los Angeles Rams had played in the Super Bowl in 1980, and the Los Angeles Raiders had won the Lombardi trophy in 1984; both, however, left Southern California after the 1994 season. Wayne Gretzky's arrival infused an abundance of hockey interest in the Los Angeles Kings, but they were ousted in their lone Stanley Cup Finals appearance with the Great One, by Montreal, in 1993. USC football fans were slogging through a dry spell in which the

Trojans had not won a national title since 1978 and were in a stretch in which they would drop eight consecutive games to the Bruins. In the Southland, the only folks kicking dirt, once again, were USC loyalists.

After the Pauley celebration, Ed O'Bannon trickled back to an apartment where his infant son eagerly awaited his arrival, crown or no crown. A few weeks later, Larry Pierce died from cardiac arrest on a bus during his morning ride to work at UCLA from his Santa Monica apartment. He had suffered from muscular dystrophy for more than twenty years, and he was a fixture on the campus as a staff member responsible for ensuring it complied with the Americans with Disabilities Act. He made it a much better place for people like him. He often attended hoops practice. At a ceremony, Ed O'Bannon stayed longer than anyone else from the basketball program.

On the evening of Friday, April 7, O'Bannon won the John R. Wooden Award as the country's best basketball player. At the black-tie affair, in the stately downtown Los Angeles Athletic Club, John Wooden mimicked a line he had heard so frequently in his career when he turned to Jim Harrick and said, "Now, Jim, we the alumni expect another championship." The crowd liked that one. But Ed O'Bannon elicited the grandest reaction when, after he accepted the award, he stared at Harrick and said, "Coach Harrick, we the alumni expect you to do it again yesterday."

North Carolina coach Dean Smith mingled with Dr. Michael R. Shapiro. Wooden Award runner-up Randolph Childress (of Wake Forest) and third-place finisher Shawn Respert (of Michigan State) had also required surgery to repair knee injuries during their careers. Cocktail in hand, Smith saluted Shapiro and said the award that year was also a tribute to the country's fine orthopedic surgeons.

The recipient of Shapiro's expertise had descended from that Kingdome ladder and fell out of love with basketball. He didn't know it at that precise moment, but many years later he could point back to that ascension and admit, with absolute certainty, that those had been the penultimate steps of his sporting life. He would never again feel so elated about basketball. "Best time of my life," O'Bannon says. "No doubt about it. My guys. I didn't get one hundred percent healthy until my senior year. Once my senior year was up, that was it."

When he received his NCAA championship ring, Ed Jr. presented it to Ed Sr., who shows it off in his Cerritos home as if it's Christmas morning and he's seven years old. Junior glances back at the computer screen that shows Tyus Edney covering the length of the court against Missouri and a slow-motion Toby Bailey rising and twisting for the two-handed reverse dunk. There's Ed, atop that ladder. The view was tremendous. "That was it," he says. "It never got as good as that; the highest point of my mountain, right there. Yes, indeed."

Aftermath

HIS PERCEIVED PERSECUTION by Pete Dalis reached an endgame for Jim Harrick on Tuesday, November 5, 1996, nineteen months after he had guided UCLA its eleventh national basketball championship. Dalis and chancellor Charles Young fired Harrick for repeatedly lying about an expense-report irregularity from a recruiting dinner nearly four weeks earlier.

During the summer of 1995, Harrick had written, in *Embracing*, that he hoped to coach maybe eight more seasons at UCLA before calling it quits on a rewarding career. He had received a contract extension, and salary bump, through 2000. "We win the national championship, and Pete gives me a *twenty-thousand-dollar* raise," Harrick says in an embarrassed tone today.

Asked about the 1995-96 season, on the eve of it, Harrick told me, "Heavy lies the head ... [that wears a crown]." He had said that to others. He first heard the Shakespeare line—which actually starts *Uneasy* lies the head, in *Henry IV*—from an English instructor ages ago. He would tell confidants, curious why he didn't appear as elated as they believed he should after winning a title, "I'm still nine down." He felt the extraordinary burden, unique to only him of all of John Wooden's successors, of defending a UCLA crown. "You created a monster, now you have to feed the monster," he says. "It took a lot to feed it."

That fateful Friday evening—October 11, 1996—Harrick took high schoolers Jason and Jarron Collins, and Earl Watson to feed at Monty's Steakhouse high above Westwood. UCLA hoopsters Kris Johnson, Jelani McCoy, and Bob Myers attended, in accordance with the NCAA's dining rule of one host, or current player, per one recruit. Cameron Dollar and Charles O'Bannon tagged along, at the last moment. A witness says Dollar and O'Bannon included oysters Rockefeller and shrimp scampi in their orders and barely touched either dish. Many years later, both Dollar and O'Bannon say they were just hungry college kids looking for free grub, and Harrick did not bicker about including them. They knew anyone who dined with Harrick was never allowed to pick up a check, or even pay a portion of it. Harrick flashed his university credit card and turned in the $1,085 receipt on an expense-account form four days later.

The report traveled through channels. Athletic department snoops were keen to keep an eye on Harrick due to his son Glenn's sale of a five-year-old Chevy Blazer, registered to Jim Harrick, to recruit Baron Davis's sister—Lisa Hodoh, who worked on the UCLA campus—a month earlier. An investigation determined that no NCAA rule had been violated, that Hodoh had paid fair-market value for the rig. But Pete Dalis did not appreciate Harrick not informing him about that vehicle sale (for a couple of weeks), which led to Dalis being completely blind-sided by reporters who, on the surface, believed they had something salacious.

Dalis questioned the veracity of Harrick's expense account and launched an investigation. To Dalis and faculty athletic representative Donald Morrison, Harrick said his wife, Sally, and assistant coach Michael Holton's wife, LaShell, had arrived late to the function and shared peach cobbler with the group. Nothing was mentioned about O'Bannon and Dollar, so the ratio of current players to recruits was acceptable, according to Jim Harrick's accounting. The two extra bodies on the form were the two wives. Dalis and Morrison queried Harrick two more times, and Harrick insisted his version was fact.

Steve Lavin had attended the fateful supper, but he left early with Treena Camacho, his girlfriend at the time who worked in Pete Dalis's office. After being coached by Harrick, Michael Holton confirmed to Dalis that LaShell had, in fact, attended the dinner. That all played out over three weeks.

Late the morning of Saturday, November 2, Harrick met with Holton before a basketball group went to the Rose Bowl to watch UCLA play football against Stanford. Harrick told Holton he had decided to tell Dalis the truth, *that they're a little upset with you; they don't know why you said ...* that LaShell had attended the dinner when, in fact, she did not. [In fact, Harrick had not approached Dalis with "the truth."] Holton was royally flummoxed and told Harrick that he had to see Dalis, that he owed Dalis an apology. Harrick told Holton that he'd take care of it, believing the drama would just disappear.

Perhaps Harrick was relying on the top part of page sixty-three in his Guidelines, which states that an assistant *is undeniably loyal to all staff members, especially head coach [sic].* "Lies left and right," says a source familiar with the chronology of events. "Buffoonery. [Harrick] pulled a dirty one on Holton." Holton finally reached Dalis to profusely apologize about his deceit. Holton, at Dalis's request, kept the details of that conversation to himself.

Armed with the devastating leverage, Dalis placed a call to the Pauley court to summon Harrick to Dalis's office after practice on Tuesday, November 5. At 5:45 P.M. Harrick left the egg yolk for the final time as coach of the UCLA basketball team. He climbed those metal stairs that switched back halfway up. Dalis and Young were waiting, and Dalis again queried Harrick about those present at the now-infamous Monty's dinner. Harrick again insisted that the two wives were there. Finally, Dalis said, *Then why did Michael Holton tell me* ... caught in his own canard, Harrick bowed his head.

Dalis told Harrick he could resign by ten the following morning, and be paid for the full season, or be sacked with no compensation for violating an ethical-conduct clause in his contract. He would not resign. He tried to get them to allow him to coach the '96-97 season, a promising one considering Cameron Dollar and Charles O'Bannon would be seniors, powerful and mobile center Jelani McCoy had a year of collegiate seasoning, and Toby Bailey, J.R. Henderson, and Kris Johnson were juniors. Harrick would resign after the season, under his plan, with no mention of this Monty's disaster. That was not acceptable to Dalis and Young, who fired Harrick. Young likened the cover-up to Watergate.

"They call you in *off the floor*," an angry Harrick says today. That was particularly offensive to Harrick, who considered himself a teacher, the floor being *his* classroom, *his* domain. "I always wondered about Charles Young, what kind of leader he was. He never said a word to [me]. What kind of leader calls you in *off the floor* and fires you, never brings you in to talk to you, 'We're concerned of this ... we got issues with this.' I'm wondering ... I still don't know why I got fired." (He would admit to lying, to erring in judgment. "But to be fired over it? That outweighs the crime by mountains and miles.")

Odd and disturbing moments of disarray ... conclusions of his mental discipline ... Kamakawi, er, Tim Kawakami had been scrupulous in his assessment after that debacle of an ending in Eugene, Oregon.

Rumors circulated of the meeting that had taken place on the second floor of the Morgan Center. Wednesday morning it became official. Before a phalanx of media in his Beverly Hills office, Harrick attorney Robert Tanenbaum lambasted the dismissal as "draconian." Harrick was not going to receive a cash settlement from UCLA. It took several months, but Harrick's lawyers did recoup $140,000, the base of his $440,000 annual salary. When asked what John Wooden said to him the next time they chatted, Harrick says, "He says, 'You know Pete.' He knew Pete Dalis very, very well."

That evening, players and coaches—including, not insignificantly, Steve Lavin—made an impromptu visit to see Harrick in the Park Wilshire. Jim and Sally seemed happy to see them, but there were tears. The visit lasted two and a half hours. Players dedicated the upcoming season to Harrick. It seemed to boost him, but a somber mood prevailed. Harrick slipped a DVD into a television console. The championship victory over Arkansas played. "My final game," Harrick said. Discomfort filled the living room; in fact, Harrick's final game had been the epic 43-41 defeat to Princeton eight months earlier in the first round of the 1996 NCAAs in Indianapolis.

Gabe Lewullis beat Beagle-Beagle on a second backdoor cut on the right baseline—Charles had covered the first but wasn't prepared to bolt back—to cap a victory that will be forever celebrated at Princeton. The *Daily Princetonian* ran the sensational headline "David 43, Goliath 41" on March 15, 1996. Some smart-ass kid—likely a Duke student manager, according to a consensus of sources—asked Harrick in the ensuing press conference about being *out-coached* by longtime Tigers guru Pete Carril. "Son, you're not qualified to ask that," Harrick said with some venom. A bomb squad was called to the Morgan Center, but it was just a hoax played by a disgruntled fan.

(After that loss to Princeton, John Wooden informed Tony Luftman, "When success turns your head you face failure." Years later, Luftman texts me, "[Wooden's] teams handled prosperity VERRRRY well ... it's hard for young people to do, hard for anyone to do." Wooden favored an Abraham Lincoln line about prosperity, not adversity, being the ideal test of a man's character. When Luftman returned from meeting with Wooden, Cameron Dollar often said, "What Woody talkin' 'bout?")

Pete Carril had taken his team to Los Angeles in 1969 to play UCLA, whose five starters would play in the NBA and was averaging triple figures, and lost, 76-75. Carril called Wooden "Johnny." Lewullis studied medicine and is now an orthopedic surgeon—an *orthopod*—in Dover, Delaware. UCLA's first game after having won it all in Seattle was a loss to Santa Clara and guard Steve Nash—"Look at us yahoos," Nash told his teammates at the half, of having the lead on the defending champs, and then they finished it off—in the Maui Invitational.

Dalis installed Steve Lavin, barely two years from earning sixteen thousands dollars annually as UCLA's part-time coach and two weeks from the Bruins' season opener against Tulsa, as the interim head coach. (Tulsa won in overtime, 77-76, at Pauley.) By then Mark Gottfried had accepted his first top post at Murray State and Lorenzo Romar had gone to Pepperdine, where he would incur Dalis's wrath when omm'A Givens transferred from the Bruins to the Waves. Some believe the Monty's episode would have been mitigated, if not entirely averted, had Gottfried and/or Romar still been around. That's some heavy conjecture, a lot to pin on Gottfried and Romar. Suffice it to say their loyalty to Harrick has never diminished.

In the immediate aftermath of Harrick's firing, an ornery fax arrived in the UCLA athletic office that blamed Lavin for concocting the mess and accusing him of scheming for Harrick's job. The return area code traced the fax to Valparaiso University, where Jim Harrick Jr. had just been hired as an assistant basketball coach.

Had Lavin truly pulled such orchestral maneuvers, his presence at the lugubrious gathering inside the Harrick residence would have qualified as the epitome of effrontery. Harrick did seek assistants with head-coaching ambitions; *Really, what [your assistant] wants is the head job where he is working now*, Harrick wrote in his Guidelines. Lavin would earn the permanent UCLA post—based on Jim Milhorn's weighty recommendation to Pete Dalis—by nearly guiding the Bruins to the Final Four. They folded at the end of an Elite Eight game against Minnesota, which would later have its tournament appearance vacated due to NCAA penalties involving an academic scandal. But as Kris Johnson was fond of saying, "They still beat us on the court."

Harrick regrouped and obtained the Rhode Island job. Robert Carothers, the president of the university, said he had investigated Harrick's background and determined that Harrick was a man of character, conviction, faith, and resiliency. Harrick told me, at that time, he had found special significance in securing a home in a place called Providence. He guided the Rams to consecutive NCAAs, which included the Elite Eight in 1998.

That was parlayed into a premium position at the University of Georgia that lasted less then four seasons. Associate athletic director Damon Evans, striking a Rhode Island-like tone about Harrick's departure from UCLA when Georgia hired Harrick, said, *We all make mistakes.* The connection was Michael F. Adams, the Georgia president who had been an administrator at Pepperdine when Harrick coached the Waves. Senior brought Jim Jr. to Rhode Island and Georgia. Thirty victories, a 2002 Southeastern Conference divisional title, and the Bulldogs' NCAA appearance in 2002 would all be vacated due to an academic fraud scandal— among other issues—that involved Jim Harrick Jr., whom Senior had finagled onto his staff despite the state's anti-nepotism policy. Questions on a test in one of Junior's classes included;

How high is the rim on a basketball court? How many goals are on a basketball court? That exam lives in Internet infamy.

Harrick had also tried to hire his namesake son at UCLA, but Pete Dalis, citing university policy and his own misgivings, refused. Allegations of sexual harassment—again, among other issues—surfaced at Rhode Island, after Harrick left, and the university paid forty-five thousand dollars in an out-of-court settlement to a former female employee. Senior skirted anti-nepotism laws at Rhode Island by having Junior report to the athletic director instead of him. In 2006, a federal judge threw out most of a defamation lawsuit the two Jim Harricks had filed against the University of Georgia and the UGA Athletic Association.

Jim Sr. lavishes praise on Jim Jr., calling him "as good a recruiter as I've ever had" and "a great assistant coach." Senior claims Georgia officials *begged* Junior to teach that class, *didn't pay him a dime*, then threw *him* under the bus. Asked if he regrets having Junior on his staffs, Senior, obdurate as ever, says he regrets *what happened to him [Junior]*.

In 1998, the NCAA Committee on Infractions slapped UCLA with three years' probation. David Swank, the chairman of the committee, called rules violations regarding recruiting, ethical conduct, and extra benefits—Harrick bought about fifty pieces of championship jewelry for certain friends and parents, pendants for mothers and rings for fathers of players—under Jim Harrick "major violations." The penalties were ultimately deemed minor because of UCLA's corrective measures, which included firing Harrick. Said Dalis, "We did some things we shouldn't have been doing."

In the wake of all that detritus, Harrick kept busy. He scouted for the Denver Nuggets, did some consulting work in China, coached a summertime prep club team and a Bakersfield squad in the NBA Development League. He also helped Tevester Anderson try to organize a Virgin Islands national team in the FIBA Americas Olympic qualifying tournament at the Thomas & Mack Center in Las Vegas in August 2007. We made eye contact as I walked through a tunnel. "Minch!" Harrick said with a grin. The Virgin Islands lost all four of its preliminary games by an average of twenty-two points; the US—with Kobe Bryant, Carmelo Anthony, and LeBron James—strafed the Virgin Isles, 123-59.

Tragedy struck the Harrick family when Sally Lee Harrick died, at seventy, from scleroderma complications in November 2009, about six months shy of the couple's fiftieth wedding anniversary. Jim slipped into despair in his home in Rancho Santa Margarita, several miles inland from Mission Viejo, California. "I was a dead man, coach," he says of the next couple of years. A friend of mine found him sitting on a park bench and tried to make small talk, but Harrick was inconsolable. His heart had left him.

Harrick somehow attended the Wooden Classic at the Honda Center, the arena in which J.R. Henderson's free throws beat Kentucky. Harrick sat in a suite with a feeble John Wooden, who grabbed Harrick's shoulder and whispered into an ear, "I've been there. I know what you're going through." Harrick cried. Monte Harrick eventually introduced his father to a widowed parishioner named Allyson from his church. Jim took her to the Pantages Theatre to see *West Side Story*. They met once a week for a year. They had married within the previous year of my meeting him a day after Christmas 2012.

Jim moved into her grand two-story house on a corner lot in La Crescenta, in the foothills of the San Gabriel Mountains. Between them they have twenty-two grandchildren. Harrick relaxes in a plush tan micro-fiber couch in the large second-floor great room. Although his office is around the corner, on this floor,

Allyson wanted him to have this room, too, to make him feel comfortable. The walls are decorated with memorabilia from his UCLA days. Wooden's framed Pyramid of Success hangs near the entryway. A poster celebrates UCLA's rich basketball history. A framed photograph—inscribed with COACH, IF NOT FOR YOU I WOULDN'T BE IN THE NBA—of Lamar Odom adorns the far wall.

Harrick dines frequently with good friends Jerry West, Oscar Robertson, and Dave Winfield, and visits Staples Center to see his beloved Los Angeles Clippers, for whom he has season tickets. In September 2012, the Clippers hired Gerald Madkins, Harrick's former guard at UCLA, as their director of basketball operations. Harrick golfs often and provides color commentary for regional TV broadcasts of lower-level college programs. He visits Mark Gottfried at North Carolina State—Harrick even gave a pep talk to the Wolfpack baseball team—and Lorenzo Romar at Washington, and Harrick and Steve Lavin rekindled their friendship in New York in the fall of 2013.

Mark Gottfried, after he had left Alabama, joined Harrick at the site of his greatest achievement when Lorenzo Romar coached his Huskies against UCLA at Pauley Pavilion. "He was apprehensive," Gottfried says of Harrick. "He and I walked down the steps, as spectators, and we sat across from the bench. Many people came up to Jim and were positive, thanking him and me. That kind of broke the ice." Ben Howland got Harrick to run a station in UCLA's annual summer camps for kids. "I have a lot of pride in the program," Harrick says. "It was a great, great part of my life. I had a great run there. I had a great run in college basketball. No complaints. I never sniveled about anything, and I don't begrudge anybody."

Well, not exactly. As the hours pass, Harrick's voice rises. He says a UCLA executive once advised him and a football coach to *put down more people* on an expense account if it appeared exorbitant, *so it covers* or looks legitimate. So what led to his demise at UCLA was "exactly what they told me to do," Harrick says. Conversation drifts to Pete Dalis. Harrick swirls ice from a glass of tea around his mouth. "I don't mind addressing it," Harrick says.

> He's the most ... I've never worked for a human being like that in all the years of my life. John Niednagel [who studied brain tendencies and types, correlating them to athletes' performance patterns] came out to UCLA and evaluated [Dalis], too. Said he's like a Secret Service guy who sneaks around the corner always looking for things ... probably the worst thing to happen to me, with Pete Dalis, was winning it all. I don't think he could handle that, me winnin' it all. I think that was the one thing that drove him crazy. I got notoriety. He wanted all of his coaches to be submissive to him, that he was the king. But coaches are Type A personalities; they aren't going to do that.
>
> Monty's was not a violation. Charles and Cameron came, and I paid for their dinner. Now that is a violation ... [but we] made them pay the money back; such a minute little thing. Hundreds of schools do that. It's a secondary violation; they played it up like you robbed a bank or something.

Harrick and Dalis had encountered each other on occasion, at golf outings and arenas. Harrick refused to acknowledge Dalis. They passed each other once at UCLA, but Harrick declined to respond to Dalis's greeting. Dalis confirms his former coach's icy behavior toward him. It escalated outside a Staples Center restroom during the 2008 Pac-10 Conference tournament. Harrick was walking in. Dalis had just exited and said, "Hi, Jim."

Harrick became inflamed and yelled, "Fuck you!" Dalis said, "Well fuck you, too!"

Harrick was just getting warmed up. "Yeah? You're the fucking guy that ruined the UCLA basketball program. You tore down everything that John Wooden built!" Dalis tried to parry the attack. Harrick walked away. "Several people heard," Harrick says. "I didn't care what he thought. I didn't want to see him." Dalis confirms the confrontation, saying, "He lit up. Said, 'Don't ever talk to me again!' He turned around [and walked away]. I thought, *This guy is a very damaged person.* He never acknowledged what he did, and that led to him no longer being the coach. That's okay."

Harrick swishes more ice around his tongue and teeth. Regarding Michael Holton, he says he's "really good" friends with his former assistant and that he helped Holton get into the insurance business, in Portland, Oregon, after advising him to get off the merry-go-round of coaching. Holton also does some broadcasting work for the Trail Blazers.

At the 2014 Final Four in Texas, Nolan Richardson was revealed as a new member of the Naismith Basketball Hall of Fame. His ugly departure from Arkansas included him suing the university, and many Razorbacks fans believed he disgraced them and the program with his acidic comments. Acrimony was thick. A statue had not been built in his honor. A painting, of Richardson holding the 1994 championship trophy, had been commissioned, but it would not be permanently displayed inside Bud Walton Arena or in the Arkansas basketball offices; it went for six thousand dollars in an online sale. A year earlier, Jerry Tarkanian had been inducted into the hall.

Harrick believes the Bruins could have won more national championships, with the elite players they were after, and says Pete Newell once told him that Dalis and the UCLA hierarchy took a Hall of Fame career away from him. Jim Sr. and Jr. also believed Dalis sabotaged subsequent job opportunities for Senior, too, which Dalis denied. Eventually, Harrick settles and addresses his own fallibility. "I probably could have been better, too. I'm not the all-mighty guy on a white horse. I'm not perfect. I made a lot of mistakes. I certainly didn't handle the [UCLA] situation ... I coulda handled it better."

Of the three coaches who have led UCLA's top two revenue athletic programs—football and basketball—to national championships, two have been inducted into the school's athletic hall of fame; John Wooden for his ten hoops titles, Red Sanders for his (albeit mythical) football crown in 1954. Jim Harrick had failed to make that grade through 2014. An insider says his name rarely gets far in the process. On August 21, 2014, Tony Luftman forwards to me a UCLA press release about the next inductees; a water polo coach, and six athletes. "Appalling," writes Luftman.

Pete Dalis was part of the eight-person induction Class of 2008. "It's a slap in the face, and it's unnecessary," says Luftman, the former student manager. "That championship is locked away. Why not give him what he deserves? O.J. [Simpson] is in the USC hall, and he killed two people!" (Simpson was an inaugural inductee into the USC athletic hall of fame in 1996.)

It grates on Luftman that Pete Dalis occupies such a vaunted position in UCLA sports lore and Harrick does not. After the title season, J.R. Henderson spent a summer living with Luftman and his family in the San Fernando Valley. Henderson missed summer classes, which Dalis blamed on Luftman for not proctoring the player more diligently. Luftman says Dalis yelled at him in a manner that was highly inappropriate and unbecoming from someone not only with such stature at UCLA but whom Luftman had once so admired. "I would never talk to an adult the way he talked to me that day," Luftman says. "He was a bad, bad guy, a really bad guy. A bully."

Pete Dalis retired as UCLA athletic director, at the age of sixty-four, in the summer of 2002. In January 2001 Dalis had publicly disclosed that he had twice spoken with Rick Pitino to gauge his interest in the UCLA job after he had denied speaking with Pitino to Steve Lavin, his coach.

It was a public-relations fiasco of the highest order. Lavin assembled a team of lawyers to protect his livelihood. Pitino told Lavin he was never interested in the UCLA post. Dalis says if he had it to do over again he would not have informed media that he had talked with Pitino. Dalis tells me he only called Pitino upon the advice of a mutual contact, a fellow member at Bel-Air Country Club. "When you hear that stuff, okay, you at least make contact, to see if it's real," Dalis says. "He was coaching Boston ... we talked [the second time] as he was heading into Madison Square Garden, on his cell phone." It was a brief chat—Pitino's cell reception was sketchy—and the coach's interest was not *real*, but some believed the Pitino gaffe directly related to Dalis's "retirement," that Albert Carnesale, the UCLA chancellor at the time, had not appreciated the deception.

Dalis was eager to spend more time with his wife, Margaret, whom he had married late in life. His golf game suffered from 2007 knee surgery. Then he tore meniscus. But of far greater concern is a rare cancer found in his bone marrow, he informs me in the summer of 2013. It hadn't reached a stage where treatment is required, but it affects his blood structure and immune system. "The golden years," he says glumly. At Bel-Air Country Club, the old guard had recently welcomed a new member—Jim Harrick. Says Dalis, "He avoids making eye contact with me in the grill room."

Jim Milhorn is retired and living in the Phoenix area. He has a standing racquetball offer to Jim Harrick.

After a thirty-year run atop the Westwood Center on Glendon Avenue, Monty's Steakhouse closed in 1999.

Through 2014, Jim Harrick's three lieutenants from the UCLA championship run had a combined forty-six seasons of experience as head coaches, an overall record of 911-563, and had appeared in twenty-four NCAA Tournaments—in which they had a combined ten Sweet Sixteen appearances and were 27-24.

Gottfried went to Alabama, his alma mater, after Murray State. He resigned from the Crimson Tide in January 2009. He provided analysis for ESPN. He took over at North Carolina State in 2011 and guided the Wolfpack to consecutive NCAAs.

He now swears by the Guidelines—on making two-foot jump stops and executing proper V-cuts, basic shooting mechanics, an array of drills and practice habits, high-post sets and its manifold options—that Harrick provides to any coach, at any level, eager for insights and input. "We call it The System," Gottfried says. "Those last couple of years at Alabama I got away from running The System. Jim would call me mad, 'What are you doing playing that *motion* game?' I listened to my assistants; they were all talking. John Wooden told me once, 'Teach what you know and know what you teach.' Jim says, 'It's not the *oooooonly* way to play, it's just the best.' "

Gottfried says UCLA's eleventh national championship is not as valued as it should be, "which is tremendously unfair." As he sits in a plastic chair at a summer tournament in the Bishop Gorman High School auxiliary gym in Las Vegas, he staunchly believes UCLA was wrong to fire Harrick. "I'll go to my grave knowing that them firing [Harrick] was unnecessary. Things happen. People make mistakes. You can look around this gym ... " Gottfried glances to his right, at John Calipari, Larry Brown, and Roy Williams. " ... it's just a part of what we do. You can't reprimand somebody or self-impose some penalties? I truly believe that Jim Harrick would have [wound up] in the [Naismith] Hall of Fame."

Lorenzo Romar has been at Washington, his alma mater, since 2002. In 2006, Athletes In Action honored Romar with the John Wooden Keys to Life Award. A highlight of his career, he says. When his mother Dorothy died in February 2013, after a long illness, Lorenzo told nobody but his wife and daughters, and confidant Marques Johnson. That night he directed the Huskies to a victory over Arizona State. He did not want her death to become an immediate story line, as his father's stroke had been at the Final Four in 1995. Romar allowed Johnson to reveal his mother's passing during a basketball telecast the following week.

Romar bristles about Harrick not being in UCLA's hall of fame. "Doesn't seem fair to me," Romar says. "It takes a while, sometimes, for people to forgive or forget or reconsider. Years from now, maybe ... I don't know ... emotionally, people won't be tied to what happened, but they'll see there was a national championship, that there was one other coach who won a national championship. Maybe that's when he gets recognized."

When Steve Lavin became UCLA's head coach, at thirty-two, females fairly swooned before the new dark-haired debonair hoops boss. One fawned a bit when she asked me, *Who's that?* Only been on the bench since 1991, I said. After the Bruins won the championship, Lavin interviewed with Mike Krzyzewski for the spot on his staff that had been occupied by ultra loyalist Pete Gaudet; Coach K hired Quin Snyder. Remaining at UCLA did not prove to be a poor option for Lavin. By then he had had a mole removed from the bottom of his chin and, after reading a book by slick-haired hoops guru Pat Riley, had started gelling his hair and slicking it back. Down the middle and feathered was so 1980s.

Lav was ready for his close-up. The tonsorial transformation, he professed, allowed him to tend to his mane in the morning and then not deal with it the rest of the day. He joked about endorsing hair product, preferring Pennzoil to STP, and deodorant; Lavin would always dispense with his suit jacket early in games and sweat like a bricklayer.

Gottfried had publicly said it was ludicrous to throw such a pup to the wolves, or something to that effect, when Lavin—with zero experience as a head coach at any level—was given the keys to the powder blue Ferrari. Lavin didn't take to the comment kindly. After a few years, Gottfried and Lavin found themselves in the rear of an empty puddle jumper in Augusta, Georgia, and made amends.

Harrick criticized the move, too—saying with a good deal of certainty that Lavin would not be the UCLA coach the following season—on *Up Close*. That distanced the two until 2007, when Jim and Sally Harrick attended a National Association of Basketball Coaches luncheon, during the Final Four in Atlanta, emceed by Lavin. Coaches who reach the Final Four get a blue NABC blazer with silver buttons for the event; those who win it all get a blazer with gold buttons. Lavin arrived at the gold-buttoned Harrick, in his speech, and raved about his former mentor, "went on and on and on and on and on, like I was John Wooden three times over," Harrick says. Sally gave Jim an elbow in his ribs right then and said, *You're gonna forgive him right now!* "I did," Harrick says. "We talked ... good friends since." New York in the fall of 2013 provided further healing.

In his first six seasons Lavin guided UCLA to five Sweet Sixteens, a run matched only by Mike Krzyzewski over that span. (A player from the Bruins' glory years noted, When did a Sweet Sixteen equate to success *around here*?) Lavin had made some questionable moves, including all-black uniforms, with yellow sneakers, that were one and dones. John Wooden might have winced at the All Golds that the Bruins wore under Jim Harrick and the *bloomers* designed by Ed O'Bannon, but the All Blacks nearly sparked a riot. They're probably moldy and tattered, in a heap with the grubby 1985 NIT championship banner in a cobwebby corner of a toolshed out by Spaulding Field. Ben Howland completed an ignominious hat trick by unveiling all-camouflage unis during his tenure.

Lavin's twenty-three rules (which he had dubbed *Bruin Attitude*) and quips, about *Mount Rushmore* and bruising basketball games that resembled *black-and-blue division* (NFC North) football games, refreshed fans and media. Excessive repetition made them, and him, stale. Brandon Loyd, a guard from Oklahoma, would forever call Lavin *Willie Wonka* due to his enthusiastic verbiage. The natives turned on Lavin.

I once confronted Lavin about a trivial incident involving assistants Jim Saia, his boyhood pal, and Jim Spencer, another longtime friend. Lavin exploded. I had only sought his input to a potential rules violation of an extremely minor sort. He told me Lorenzo Romar had told him that I would *bury* the program the moment I got the chance. (He later apologized, I think, and owed it to inexperience.) I had not intended to write about the incident; it was so petty a "story" would have drawn laughs from all angles. But I was not *not* going to run it by Lavin. However, when I experienced my first layoff a few years later Lavin was the first to call. At a P.F. Chang's we discussed my future. And he included me in one of two limos he hired to chariot a large group to Anaheim Stadium to see his Giants play the Angels in Game 6 of the 2002 World Series—all I had to provide were a few Cuban cigars and some Heinekens.

When he retired, Pete Dalis says he was shocked by how much Lavin had changed—*gone Hollywood*—by hanging around A-listers like actor Andy Garcia. (Sigourney Weaver did drop by Pauley, too, soon after Lavin took over, for shooting lessons.

Filming started soon for *Aliens: Resurrection*, in which she would be required to make a backward half-court shot; with Lavin's coaching, she soon nailed one, and she did so on her first attempt at the studio with the cameras rolling.)

One writer had spoken in a Cold War hush when relaying to a coach from another Pac-10 program how the UCLA hierarchy had been building a dossier on Lavin. A *dossier*. What, for a pending trial in The Hague? Another scribe chided Lavin's switch of wedding venues, from an exclusive resort in Laguna Beach to Capri in the Mediterranean, due to a tsunami of RSVPs that overwhelmed the luxury beach spot. Lavin found comical, as he should have, the citation of the anecdote as character-flaw evidence.

For years Lavin refused to hang framed photos and other mementos on his office walls; they stood on the carpet, leaning against those walls. A Rick Pitino book lay on the coffee table. The basketball offices had been moved upstairs in a stylishly refurbished Morgan Center, but that didn't alter the pathology of the place. Dalis's dalliance with Pitino made Lavin huddle with his lawyers. Albert Carnesale, the chancellor, thanked Lavin for the way in which he represented UCLA—with style and grace—in a letter after the season.

In January 2002, Pete Newell told me that episode could have played out far differently had Lavin possessed thinner skin. "[Wooden] told me there were times when he felt like quitting, even with all the great things he did," said Newell, who died in 2008. "A lot of strange things can go through your mind; it's a kind of private hell that a coach lives with. Why would you allow yourself to be humiliated like that?" Wooden, in a letter to Lavin, praised him for enduring the episode with class; *Although it would be great if we never had to face adversity, the fact is that it only makes us stronger—be it physical, mental, moral, or spiritual. It is a test that we will encounter in many areas of our lives.*

Other incidents were just as disturbing. Nineteen-year-old Eric Lin was summoned to a judge and ordered to refrain from contacting Steve and Cap Lavin after threatening both with insidious e-mails. One Lin note went, *Resign or commit suicide. Gosh I hate you!* Technology had allowed some UCLA fans to further indict themselves. " ... overzealous people who are emotionally charged," Lavin told me, "and have a sense of entitlement with whom you should recruit, whom you should play, and whom you should give scholarships to; and whose scholarships you should take away." He became a regular at Matteo's, an Italian restaurant on Westwood Boulevard once favored by the Chairman of the Board; Lavin even stabbed at cheese tortellini and nipped at Valpolicella in Sinatra's burgundy-leather booth in the back, to best view who was coming and going.

Lavin was booted, without cause, in 2003, after the Bruins went 10-19—UCLA's first losing campaign since 1947-48. Dan Guerrero, a former UCLA second baseman that was hired from UC-Irvine to replace Pete Dalis, and Lavin parted on amicable terms. Lavin worked at ESPN as a studio analyst and Brent Musburger's sidekick on Big Ten telecasts. UCLA wasn't finished with Lavin, however. Because he was sacked without cause, the university owed him about $1.2 million; but for several months in 2006 the university tried to recoup $527,420 from Lavin via "recapture" contract provisions. According to legal documents, e-mails, and memos, that maneuver failed so badly it was determined that UCLA actually owed Lavin $580.

He accepted a six-year deal to run the St. John's program in 2010. He would hire Darrick Martin, who had informed Ed O'Bannon of UNLV's probation and told him he should come to UCLA, as an assistant. Early on in New York, Lavin was diagnosed with prostate cancer. He kept it at bay for more than a year when doctors said immediate surgery wasn't necessary; he ultimately underwent a successful operation.

Think there were soap operas at UCLA? At St. John's, a former dean and vice president had become one of the school's top fund-raisers, but when Cecilia Chang's vast corruption history was uncovered she hanged herself—a day into a trial for allegedly embezzling a million dollars—in November 2012. The university president and his top aide stepped down in the middle of 2013 when their connections to Chang were probed.

In May 2013, Lavin met me in Greenwich Village outside his apartment building. His penthouse, occupying the entire sixth floor, features floor-to-ceiling bookshelves on every interior wall that house thousands of tomes. We pass a street vendor, around the corner, hawking black T-shirts that read NEW YORK FUCKIN CITY and FUCK YOU YOU FUCKIN FUCK. Ahh, New York. A homeless man in a dirty, holey raincoat cheers for *Coach Lav*. He sneaks a folded ten-dollar bill inside the man's shabby topcoat. Lavin shows me the immense wooden round table at The Crosby Bar & Terrace, inside the Crosby Street Hotel, that he uses to close recruits; on their official visits, this is where Lavin tries to get blue chippers to commit to St. John's.

In the terrace courtyard out back Lavin nurses a cold with a bowl of tomato soup. Checkups have shown he is cancer-free. Three times he cries recalling his father, Cap, who had passed away three months earlier. Cap provided Steve with regular notes, on avoiding clichés and redundancy, to keep his deliveries fresh, when Steve was at ESPN. Lavin was on a bus with his team to Syracuse when his father rang his cell phone. Cap, home from hospice, wanted to hear his youngest child's voice. Before dawn Steve received word that his father had died. Lavin caught the next flight from Syracuse to San Francisco.

Lavin eventually glows about the ability of that UCLA championship team to pass, to be unselfish. "I've never seen a better open-court passing team," he says.

We got the ball off the boards, or off a turnover, quickly and converted at high speeds for baskets ... and when we took it out of the net, our ability to take other teams' scores away with one of our own [was tremendous]. There was a willingness to share the ball that was exceptional for any generation of basketball. People didn't talk about that part. To me, when I go back and watch the films or highlight tapes, what stands out is the unselfishness and the enjoyment of the pass. It was a group that enjoyed making that one extra pass.

Since 1975, and through 2014, only one UCLA team has given out more than the 653 assists that the Bruins accumulated in their 1994-95 season. The UCLA vultures wanted much more than a pound of flesh from Lavin, though. In 2011 an Internet story was labeled "Why We Hate Steve Lavin." The author stated that *our model* for a coach is John Wooden, and that Lavin took advantage of *a National Treasure.* Of course, the author was a ghost, who went by DCBruins. Eight years had passed since Lavin had coached UCLA.

Gottfried, Romar, and Lavin restrict media from attending most of their practices. Every fall, returning players at North Carolina State, Washington, and St. John's kind of cringe during the first practice of the season. Soon, they know, they'll be running the first of so many seventeens.

Marquis Burns admits that, for years, he has debated leaving UCLA for New Mexico State in January 1995. The Fifth Beatle had played only thirty-six total minutes, and scored nine points, in five games for the Bruins. "It's twofold," he says. "Sometimes, yeah, I wish I had stuck it out. But I wouldn't have been happy. I wouldn't have known what it's like to play, to start a college game, to play significant minutes. If I never made that move, would I have really been happy? You just don't know. That's life in general, right?" He works in Information Technology for Coca-Cola and lives in Pasadena, California. He never married. He sounds happy.

In Las Cruces, New Mexico, he scored a career-best sixteen points for New Mexico State in a victory over UNLV soon after becoming eligible. But an academic scandal had been brewing, which cost Neil McCarthy his coaching job and landed the Aggies on probation. Burns transferred again, to UC-Riverside, which didn't work out either. He finished his degree requirements back at UCLA. He enjoyed being a regular student, with no extra-curricular responsibilities. He did not miss basketball.

Burns stays in touch with Toby Bailey, Tyus Edney, and Ike Nwankwo, and he's a regular whenever those championship Bruins gather for a reunion. He is philosophical about living with decisions and building character. "I hold those guys in my heart. I missed not sharing that with them, but I think I had to [transfer], to get that experience."

Kristaan Johnson played in Russia, Turkey, China, Qatar, and Lebanon. He shot video with a camera during some turbulent times in Beirut. He walked down a street, with the threat of mortars or grenades or gunfire at every step, without fear. In 2002, he earned MVP honors for scoring thirty-two points to lead Al Rayyan, of Qatar, to an Asia Champions Cup victory in Kuala Lumpur over Al-Ittihad and former UCLA teammate J.R. Henderson. He rode in an Al Rayyan soccer player's red Lamborghini Diablo. He boasts of a six-month whirlwind romance with "the Madonna of Turkey," he says. He is working for an Internet scouting venture, doing some analysis for West Coast Conference games, and he assists the hoops team at Pacific Palisades High School. Multiple former UCLA teammates, when this went to print, were concerned that Johnson had been putting on weight.

In his native Washington, omm'A Givens is an officer for a charitable agency. Kevin Dempsey is the executive chef of a five-star restaurant in San Jose. On the other side of the San Francisco Bay, Bob Myers has an executive office inside the Oracle Arena, where he is the general manager for the Golden State Warriors.

After UCLA he provided analysis on Bruins radio broadcasts for two seasons and earned a degree at Loyola Law School. Sports agent Arn Tellem took Myers under his wing, and Myers excelled as an agent. Warriors co-owner Joe Lacob hired Myers for the front office and, a year later, handed the reins of the team to him in April 2012. At thirty-seven, he was the second-youngest GM in the NBA. He is married with two young daughters. He keeps John Wooden quotes in his cell phone. A favorite is, "Don't measure yourself by what you've accomplished but by what you should've accomplished with your ability."

Ike Nwankwo cannot take thirty steps in the sprawl of Bangkok without someone hollering a hello or greeting him with an animated wave. His six-ten stature and dark complexion make Nwankwo easy to spot, and he constantly returns big grins and salutations.

The emergence of Jelani McCoy after the title season forced Nwankwo to bolt for Long Beach State. But he took only enough credits to be eligible for the 49ers; he would earn his degree at UCLA. His father, Nkem, was always perplexed why Ike didn't accept a Stanford scholarship out of high school and study law. "A Stanford degree, that's instant respect," Nkem told Ike. "People sit up in their chair. You can't pass that up to do basketball." But Ike couldn't pass up doing basketball at the most renowned college hoops program in the world.

In June 2001, Nwankwo had just finished a season in Moscow and returned to Houston to celebrate his father's sixty-fifth birthday with his mother and three sisters. But Nkem, an author and professor who taught English literature at Tennessee State, never made it home; he suffered a fatal heart attack. He was buried in the Nigerian village of Nawai, where he was born. On the funeral program, *barrister* was written next to Ike's name. "He was telling people back in the village that I was already an attorney," says Nwankwo over a Singha beer in his buddy's loud sports bar near Soi Nana, Bangkok's infamous red-light district. "I don't necessarily know how proud he was that I was a basketball player."

Nwankwo played pro ball in Turkey, Poland, Portugal, Russia, Puerto Rico, and Venezuela. Told that Kris Johnson received cash bonuses of up to five hundred dollars in Qatar for important victories, Nwankwo laughs; when he played for Dynamo Moscow he received bonuses double that amount. In Istanbul in 2003, he grabbed a crude map from a female hotel concierge to tend to his visa at the US embassy, but a bellboy gave him a simpler route as he hustled to the street. He returned to find the woman bawling, until she saw him. The quicker route enabled Ike to avoid being near an HSBC building precisely when a truck bomb killed twenty-seven and injured more than 450 people. The woman hugged the air out of Ike's lungs. He framed her ink-scrawled map.

He represented Nigeria in the 2003 FIBA Africa championship in Egypt and the 2006 FIBA World championship in Japan, and he spent time on the preseason rosters of the Los Angeles Lakers, Miami Heat, and Houston Rockets. He never made the regular-season roster of an NBA team, but his short stint with the Rockets did include a warm welcome from Nigerian center and idol Akeem Olajuwon. Nwankwo, however, has never been in the presence of a figure like Ed O'Bannon.

"I've met a lot of people who have been more successful than Ed O'Bannon, some of the greatest players in the game," he says.

Rob Miech

"But none of them ... I don't know if I can put this into the proper words. The way [O'Bannon] carried himself, the leader he was, helped me kind of grow up in many ways. I don't know if he knows that. He carried himself with such class and dignity, he reminded me of Arthur Ashe." Nwankwo has always wondered how O'Bannon handled what appeared to be a disappointing and frustrating career after UCLA.

Nwankwo visited a friend in Bangkok in 2008. He returned a year later, to play for the Thailand Tigers of the Asean Basketball League, and hasn't left. He started the Top Flight Basketball Academy with a dozen kids, and he now counts more than two hundred children from the city's several international schools as pupils. He employs three coaches. He takes a select group to the States every summer, with a prime stop always being a camp at Pauley Pavilion. He hopes to expand the academy into Vietnam and Singapore. Nwankwo doesn't plan to ever leave Bangkok. "The people have embraced me and my program. It's a beautiful thing. Humbling. I love the lifestyle. I can make a difference here in a lot of ways."

A prominent part of his portfolio, which has helped Nwankwo obtain sponsorship deals, is a photograph of him and his fellow Bruins surrounding President Bill Clinton. "I didn't really have that much to do with what happened on the floor, but all of the great opportunities made available to me in my adult life, the way people look at me and how they view me, have been because I was part of that team. I refer to that time almost daily."

Cameron Dollar, who delivered handsomely in the game of his life in which perfection—or something close to it—had been required, is anchored in the city where he produced that singular golden athletic effort.

372

He had been coaching at Seattle University for four seasons when he landed in Las Vegas to scout schoolboys at a club tournament in July 2013. He had shepherded Seattle from independent to Division-I status, and he counts alum Elgin Baylor as a fan and friend. Baylor led the nation in rebounding in the 1956-57 season. The Chieftans (now Redhawks) played Kentucky in the 1958 NCAA finale, in which Baylor made nine of thirty-two shots for twenty-five points, and yanked down nineteen rebounds, in the 84-72 loss. Seattle was a regular NCAA participant in the 1950s and 1960s, but the program drifted into obscurity. Baylor calls Dollar frequently and visits a few times every season from his Los Angeles home. Dollar and Seattle U are so tight he has a lifetime contract—a five-year deal with an automatic annual rollover stipulation.

Dollar had been brave when he donned that suit and scaled those steps at the Morgan Center to meet Pete Dalis during his recruiting visit. As someone who earned such immediate praise from Dalis, Dollar is especially embarrassed to have played such a part in Harrick's downfall—by attending that fateful recruiting dinner with Charles O'Bannon. "That was all on me and Charles," he says.

> We weren't the "hosts," but we wanted to go. We told them we would pay for it ourselves ... me and Charlie are college kids; well, all right, we'll take off [from the restaurant, without paying]. Later on we realized that the thing Harrick was getting in trouble for was that. We were like, "Son of a bitch ... we could have paid for it." It wasn't like it was groundbreaking. Know what I'm saying? Yeah, it sucks, cuz he was looking out for us. It was a bad deal, a bad deal all around.

Charles and Cameron made restitution for their Monty's meals, improper extra benefits in the NCAA lawbook, and both served twenty hours of community service. It's no small irony that Dollar, who had muttered that *plantation* line just loud enough for Jim Harrick to hear in practice, also frequently runs his Redhawks through seventeens. He texts me, *Generation to generation. LOL.*

Toby Bailey sits in a couch in the The Westin lobby in Las Vegas and raves into his cell phone about Tony Snell, a six-foot-seven shooting guard from the University of New Mexico. Since his playing days ended two years earlier, Bailey has a brawny upper body from hitting the gym diligently. He is getting into the agent business, with Rival Sports Group based in Beverly Hills. Bailey and a colleague have pinpointed the smart and savvy Snell as their major target. They would sign Snell, who would be selected by the Chicago Bulls with the twentieth pick in the first round of the 2013 NBA draft.

The beginning of Bailey's career was a bit different than Snell's. The euphoria of being drafted, in the second round, by the hometown Lakers was fleeting. Bailey was soon dealt to the Phoenix Suns, for whom he played seventy-three games, starting twelve. Bailey went to Italy, Belgium, Germany, and Spain. In Catalonia, where he balled for Basquet Manresa, his wife was more popular than him; the former Tracey Milburn, who played soccer at UCLA, was a member of a local *futbol* team and received regular ink in the papers. His teammates posted articles about his wife on a corkboard and called him Soccer Mom.

In Greece, Bailey had produced two solid seasons—and had a lucrative, multi-year deal in the works with Real Madrid—when an operation for a bulging disk turned into a staph infection that kept him in a hospital for a month. Two more weeks, he says, and he would have been paralyzed. "It was eating away at my spine." He underwent another procedure, after brother Moose flew to Greece to assist him on the long flight home, at a hospital in Torrance, California. "People don't know all the things that went on behind the scenes. When you have as much success as we had in college, it's rough in the NBA ... embarrassing. I didn't catch the best breaks, but I made the best of it."

Bailey is blessed, he says, to have had all those chats with John Wooden. He's the one Bruin who capitalized on tapping the legendary figure for such invaluable lessons, which he depended upon during his foreign adventures. "I was humbled to see how people live overseas. It's not about materialistic stuff. It's about family. Unless you travel and see what the world has to offer, I don't think anyone can be completely wise or compassionate."

He wonders if it was just by chance that Ed and Charles O'Bannon, and J.R. Henderson all have homes in the Las Vegas area. Even Tyus Edney spent a while living in Southern Nevada; I bumped into him at a UNLV football practice, where a relative was playing. "Out here you don't have to deal with the questions as much," Bailey says in between scouting college players in Las Vegas tournaments. " 'Why didn't you have a ten- or twelve-year NBA career?' I get it all the time. I can only imagine what Ed gets. But I'm over it. I live in L.A. I'm from L.A. I'll die in L.A. I was forced to confront it early, and I'm okay with it. I'm fortunate I had the career I had. No regrets.

"As far as UCLA, we might not get the credit we deserve. Of all the championship teams at UCLA, they mostly talk of the Wooden era. But our team stacks up against a lot of [those] teams, and we won the last one ... and we were really exciting to watch."

The Outback restaurant serenades Charles O'Bannon, J.R. Henderson, and me with the "Rock Lobster" by the B-52s, "Let the Good Times Roll" by The Cars, and "Nights in White Satin" by the Moody Blues. We order steak and chicken, mashed potatoes and onion rings. But we are a long way from Westwood, and the States. We are in Nagoya, Japan, where Charles's Panasonic team is staying for its two weekend games against Henderson's Aishin Sea Horses in Kariya (pronounced *Korea*), about a thirty-minute drive to the southeast. It's the end of January 2013, one of the final times the two former Bruins will play pro ball against each other.

After today's shootaround in Kariya, longtime Sea Horses coach Kimikazu Suzuki tapped an odd page in his Guidebook when he handed each player a three-page critique of Aishin's last game, an embarrassing title-game defeat to Panasonic in a Tokyo holiday tournament. Aishin executives did not digest the outcome well. Suzuki no doubt feels that heat, thus the bizarre memo. An assistant typed English versions, and the following is exactly how they were worded, for Henderson and Big Boy; *on the rebound, we should have at least tipped a ball toward outside or boxed out the mark man ... you can go stop the outlet pass just a little bit ... we need to have stronger desire to win ... losing a game even one point means that the opponent had a stronger desire ... Kitagawa can shoot well we all know that but he does not work hard enough on defense ... J.R. got blocked the shot that he normally makes, and also started making defensive and rebound mistakes.*

And Henderson and O'Bannon thought the pressures were extraordinary at UCLA. Call this Eastwood Village. Charles reviews the three pages before the appetizers arrive and says, "Uh oh, god damn!" He glances at Henderson.

"He broke down the whole game?"

"Yup."

"Damn." Charles examines each sentence. "Damn. Calling you out! Are you serious? Of course, it's in Japanese, too. They got this?"

"Yup. He went after the locals more."

"You get a review after all games, or losses?"

"This is the first time this happened. History."

"Oh my gosh."

"He didn't put in there why I wasn't makin' stuff I usually make; I was tired, boss, forty minutes guarding their best player!"

"What is this guy thinking about?" Charles looks at me and hands the letter back to J.R. "You picked a helluva weekend to visit!"

Henderson shakes his head and gives the three pages to me as keepsakes. Aishin, with its dark-suited, dour executives sitting at a baseline table, beats Panasonic on Saturday, but those board members do not attend Sunday's loss. As I depart the City Gym, I thank Suzuki for his hospitality and inquire about the Friday memo, asking him if that represented inordinate pressure he was feeling heading into the weekend? He loosened his collar like Rodney Dangerfield, smiled widely, nodded, shook my hand, and said, "Pressure relieved!"

By then Henderson had switched places with O'Bannon in the second and third spots, respectively, on the Japan Basketball League's career scoring chart. Of course, that isn't Henderson's name anymore. Since July 2007, when he became a naturalized Japanese citizen, Henderson has been known as J.R. Sakuragi—announcers howl *Sahh-kurr-a-geeee*; the last consonant is hard, like "geese." In Japanese, it translates to cherry blossom tree. It's also the surname of a main character in the Japanese anime series *Slam Dunk* who plays basketball, a tall redheaded *jerk with a heart of gold* who is adaptive, agile, and has superior stamina for Team Shohoku.

The Vancouver Grizzlies drafted Sakuragi, but his NBA career consisted of thirty games, with no starts, and only two three-point baskets. Toby Bailey, Tyus Edney, and Sakuragi participated on Washington's entry in an NBA summer league in Boston. J.R. had been performing well when Wizards coach Lionel Hollins helped him stretch his legs on the court at halftime. "He was dominating," Bailey says. "Tyus and I said, 'If the *head coach* is stretching him ... are you kidding me? He's making the team.' That doesn't happen." Hollins leaned J.R.'s right leg waaaaay back, and even Bailey and Edney heard the hamstring pop. The Wizards sent Henderson home the next day. Says Bailey, "Then he went to Japan and never stopped."

By then Aishin had filled both of its foreign roster spots. However, Kimikazu Suzuki still enticed Henderson to come to Japan. Suzuki was quite familiar with the player, having watched him play so frequently as a Bruin. He knew Henderson's teammates called him Nerf, and he projected JBL stardom for the lithe and versatile six-nine powerhouse. The Sea Horses initially paid Henderson a full season's salary, nearly two hundred thousand dollars, just to observe the team, to determine if he might like Japan—which also enabled his hamstring to heal properly. Then Junior Burrough returned late after the holiday break and got cut. In Japan, punctuality—saving face—is everything. Henderson was healthy, he played and dominated, and he became the foundation of the franchise.

Sakuragi and O'Bannon are certain they've seen *yakuza*, or leaders of Japan's underworld, speeding down city streets and running stop lights in their old, dark Mercedes-Benz 500s. "Our guys are terrified of them," Sakuragi says. He once instructed the driver of the team bus to swing open its door, in transit, to yell at a biker gang that had encircled the coach. The hoodlums, notorious *yankees* who yearn to keep alive the former *bosozoku* ("reckless tribe," in English) motorcycle gang lifestyle, wore dark jumpsuits and rode choppers. The driver kept the door closed. Says Sakuragi, "Teammates were scared. They said, 'No, no, no, don't say anything.' " During a tour of a Kariya electronics facility, Sakuragi was shocked to see an entire floor manned by robots; he backed up so one didn't run over his toes.

Aishin recorded the best record in the league in eight of Henderson's first eleven seasons, in which the Sea Horses won four Emperor's Cup championships. "If he gets into foul trouble, they become not even a normal team, a below-average team," says Charles. "They don't know what to do without him." Officials have difficulty with Sakuragi. Much of the petulance he still carries seems produced by, and directed at, the refs. "I've heard, 'You're too good, so not fair,' and 'You have an advantage, so no foul' ... 'I saw it, but sorry,' " Sakuragi says of blatant fouls by others, on him, that are not called, and phantom fouls that are whistled on him. "They say, 'J.R., maybe it's a foul, but sorry.' I say, 'He hit me on the arm!' They say, 'Yeah, I agree,' but no whistle. Aishin has a huge advantage, and I'm it."

Against Panasonic that Sunday, sixteen-year-old Tatsuki Nagasaki sat three rows from the City Gym court and wore a surgical mask over his face and a blue UCLA sweatshirt. A blue UCLA backpack lay at his feet. He acquired the gear online. Through an interpreter, Nagasaki could barely contain his excitement talking about Sakuragi, his favorite player.

At the end of the 2012-13 season, which the Sea Horses capped with a JBL title, Sakuragi had two seasons remaining on his handshake agreement with Suzuki. In Japan, that's like a written contact signed in blood. Aishin finished 2013-14 at 40-14, a game behind Wakayama in the Western Division of the new twelve-team, two-division National Basketball League. The Sea Horses lost a decisive Game 3 in the semifinals to Wakayama by fourteen points. Sakuragi averaged 12.1 points, 7.7 rebounds, and 3.4 assists; Kevin "Big Boy" Young tallied averages of 8.8 points and 6.8 boards.

Suzuki counts many governmental figures as friends, which aided Henderson in a naturalization process that entailed written and oral exams, and a rudimentary knowledge of Hiragana characters. His new classification benefitted the Sea Horses, since Sakuragi doesn't count as one of their two foreign-player roster spots and only one foreigner can occupy the floor. Aishin has a decided edge with Sakuragi and Big Boy on the court at the same time. In addition, Sakuragi plays for Suzuki on the Japanese national team.

But that doesn't do Sakuragi's relationship with Japan justice. He is low key and unassuming, and actions have always meant more than words to him, all of which mirrors the Japanese way of life. The Land of the Rising Sun is Sakuragi's adopted homeland to the degree that he doesn't believe he will ever leave. Kariya is a rich agricultural area, which suits the country boy from Bakersfield very well. Sakuragi and his wife, Christina, jog outside their apartment complex past fields of rice paddies. He was raised in a religious household, but he considers himself more spiritual after the events of January 4, 2009.

That night he walked into Club Midas, a popular hip-hop spot in the Roppongi section of Tokyo, with his usual intentions of infidelity. Before he even began prowling, Sakuragi was overcome with hypocrisy and shame. He walked out. He divorced wife Jennifer, who lives in Florida with their daughter Hailee. J.R. had only briefly met Christina, through friends, but when he rang her after the divorce she told him she had prayed that he would call. They were married within a year.

Their apartment building is gray and Eastern Bloc-ish. While modest and cubicle-like, their unit is warm and welcoming. On a narrow wall in the back, above a computer and desk, hangs a painting—*Broad Road and Narrow Gate*—by contemporary Christian artist Ain Vares, a native of Estonia. A main street filled with light, like a mini-Las Vegas, draws people to its bars and nightlife like moths. Off to the left, a few individuals meander through an alley and up a mountain to a cross. Most visitors, J.R. says, don't notice those people who decline to be lured to the glitz and glamour.

He returns to his moment of truth in that Tokyo club and how that affected him. "Rebirth is the exact word," Sakuragi says. "It was life changing in every respect. [Lifestyle] had everything to do with it. I didn't respect marriage. I was disrespecting it all the time. Just immature. No wisdom." A jerk that needed to prove to himself, and maybe someone else, that he still had a heart of gold.

As he drives me to the Nagoya airport, Sakuragi's knees rest upon the black dashboard of his boxy gray Toyota BB. But he steers from the front right seat in complete comfort, yielding legroom for enough headroom to accommodate Kareem Abdul-Jabbar. He uses his home in Henderson, Nevada, for a base when he reunites with family in the States during the summer, but he considers his crimson Japanese passport invaluable. "This is my home. I feel comfortable here. I go to the States, I feel uncomfortable. I don't feel like any part of the US is home for me."

Charles O'Bannon is introduced as *O-bannnn-ooooo* in the City Gym. He had loose knee particles flushed out in November 2012, which hindered him for a few months. Former Georgetown center Jameel Watkins is a low-post force for Panasonic, so he's the guy who monopolizes the foreign spot on the floor. O'Bannon not only does not play much, he understands that his professional career is coming to a close as we share an exquisite shabu-shabu dinner in Kariya. Shoes outside the flimsy-walled room, we sit cross-legged on the floor at a low table. Drunken laughter from neighbors amplifies into the evening.

Like Cameron Dollar, Charles regrets that he was involved in what led to the ouster of Jim Harrick at UCLA. "That was just bad," O'Bannon says.

> It got blown out of proportion, and it was very unfortunate that I was a part of that … they were looking for any reason to get Coach Harrick, who is a friend and a father figure. For him to lose his job over something like that; so petty. It was really disheartening. We went because we were family. Me and Cam, we don't have much money and we wanted to go to dinner, too. Coach is like, "Okay, come on. Let's go." We're college students. Okay, let's go. We didn't think twice about it. We sat at a separate table. We included our bill with "that table over there." Had we known the repercussions, we wouldn't have gone. There were lies being told, people weren't forthcoming. We didn't expect it to be such a big deal.

Detroit, which specialized in a black-and-blue, deliberate style of hoops, drafted Charles near the top of the second round in 1997. Over two seasons he played in forty-eight games for the Pistons, starting once. He went to Poland, where he experienced a disheartening season for Slask Wroclaw. Fans spit on him. He closes his eyes and shrugs. "Just talking about it pisses me off. They actually hated our team. Being a black person over there, I felt a little racism as well. It's not for everybody; everybody can't do this. You have to adapt wherever you go or you'll get swallowed up."

He landed with Tokyo-based Toyota, one of the more stable and successful Japanese teams. He preceded Sakuragi in Japan by a year. Other than the two months he played with Tyus Edney at Benetton in Italy—where he earned more than forty thousand dollars, in the spring of 2003—Charles spent the vast majority of his pro career in Japan after a successful tryout for Toyota in San Diego. An eleven-year-old boy knew all about his UCLA days and was grateful for Charles's autograph after a Toyota game. That kid was Atsunobu Hirao, and he grew to play beside Charles on Panasonic for the 2012-13 season. Hirao often regaled teammates with stories about the O'Bannons and the Bruins and 1995. O'Bannon had reconstruction surgery on his left ACL during his Japanese career; unlike Ed, Charles opted for an autograft procedure that used material from his own hamstring.

Japan had always been an itinerant spot for Charles. Unlike Sakuragi, who is so entrenched here, Charles kept few possessions in his apartments. He commuted to and from practice in Osaka on a scooter. Twice he failed the naturalization process. He chats with his older brother for counsel as soon as he returns to Las Vegas, for good, in the summer of 2013. He might attend culinary school; Charles Jr. raves about the salmon, steaks, pasta, broccoli, and omelettes his father prepares.

O'Bannon owns a thirty-five hundred square-foot, two-story frame stucco home in Las Vegas, complete with pool and spa, that he and his wife, Valencia, bought in 2003. He first met her when he was eleven, at Victoria Park. She had a rewarding career as a Southwest Airlines flight attendant. He coaches Charles Jr. on the highly rated club squad Team Vegas Elite. Junior played on the Bishop Gorman High varsity as a freshman in 2013-14, when Senior helped coach the Gaels' freshmen to an undefeated season. In late April 2014, Junior received a scholarship offer from UNLV.

Charles Sr. says nobody knows him from his Detroit days, or Japan. "They know me for UCLA. That makes me proud to have been a part of that. UCLA dominated college basketball, and to have been a part of its only title in ... [almost] forty years? That's special. My boy gets recognized for that name. He's so proud to be Chuck. There's a lot of pressure with that name."

George Zidek was in a hotel room in Washington, D.C., where he partook in an academic All-America awards presentation and dinner a couple of months after the title season. UCLA media liaison Bill Bennett accompanied Zidek, and he gaped at the room-service tray that arrived at Zidek's door. Bennett felt like one of the guys in *Diner* who peeked over Big Earl's shoulder, from the adjoining booth, and tallied that Big Earl had ordered, and was wolfing down, the entire left side of the menu. Bennett, though, thought Zidek had ordered both sides. They *had* told Zidek he could order what he wanted.

Today Zidek zips around Prague, and Europe, at breakneck speed. He consults for a Russian league, helps manage the Czech Republic national team, and provides television analysis for the Euroleague, which requires him, at least once a week, to fly to Barcelona for studio work.

When home he pops into his grand renovation project, a multi-story apartment building in a historical section of Prague, at least once a day to keep various workers on their toes. In April 2013 he proudly shows me the shell of an edifice. Wearing yellow hard hats, we descend to the basement. During the previous brutal winter, Ukrainian workers rid the muck and grime between every brick, of the walls and archways, with toothbrushes. Once he visited and a few of those workers were passed out—drunk—on the dirt floor down here. "*Fuckeeen* Ukrainians," Zidek says with disdain. He figures to spend close to the equivalent of three million US dollars on the project. Peter Schultz, Zidek's benefactor at UCLA and still a close friend, says Zidek, his wife, and their three children will be wealthy because of his wise real estate investments.

Zidek still sleeps two hours a night, maybe. He thinks nothing of it because that intense drive turned him into a productive Bruin and an NBA player. When he was with the Nuggets in Denver, a stint in an overnight sleep clinic determined nothing. He battled back and knee issues as a pro. Medication helped him cope with a herniated disk in 2000 and earn a lucrative single-season salary at Real Madrid. Lithuania (with Tyus Edney), Turkey, Germany, and Poland were other club stops. At the end of his career, he was hailed as somewhat of a hero when he helped Nymburk—twenty-five miles east of Prague, for whom he also works as a press attaché—win a Czech Republic basketball league title.

Everywhere he goes in Prague, locals point and whisper *bass-ket*. But it's stunning to see him carrying only about 220 pounds—fifty or so fewer than he carried as a senior at UCLA. There is bone-on-bone action in his left knee, so surgery will be required someday. In a beer hall he ignores my picky-eater pleas and coaxes me to try the steak tartar; a cloth napkin is quickly employed, and a big soft pretzel and stein of Pilsner Urquell never tastes so good. I mention his anxiety. "I get very nervous if I have nothing to do," he says. I'm soon trying to match his loping gait down Slezska and Vinohradska, and into Wenceslas Square. "If I have nothing to do, like on vacations, it becomes very difficult for me."

Zidek doesn't believe the Czech Republic should join the euro monetary community, a hot topic in the news and on the streets. A cabby told me that would happen within five years; Zidek despises the idea of needing to bail out fiscally irresponsible states, like Spain and Greece. Even more distressing to Zidek is the apparent rise of Communist loyalties, emanating from the hinterlands. He rails against socialism, too, and taxes that are about to spike. "We never outlawed [Communism]," he says. "We didn't outlaw it as an extreme political movement after 1989. I think they tried later, but it was too late ... I don't trust Communists; I hate them. Their influence in Parliament and in the Senate is going up. That's the saddest thing. I feel like my grandfather has to be turning over in his grave. It tells you that, as a nation, we have a very short memory."

We cross the Charles Bridge over the Vltava River. We hike up the 208 Old Castle Stairs, next to Prague Castle. The view of his city, to the south and east, is stunning, out of a fable. His voice, often cold and sharp, nearly cracks when he speaks about his good fortune, of appearing on that VHS tape when Jim Harrick was so focused on Julius Michalik. "UCLA and Los Angeles, " Zidek says, "those were the best times of my life, period."

As the Aeroflot jet descended into Kaunas International Airport, Tyus Edney peeked out a window and saw a building and runways that appeared to be run down, even abandoned. Edney thought, *What did I get myself into?* There were remnants of ancient-looking structures, while others were just big cement-block projects. Weeds grew in streets. *Gonna be a tough year.* He would learn about existing with minimal amenities, somewhat similar to how George Zidek spent the first sixteen years of his life.

Edney was nestled between Latvia, Belarus, and Poland. The fifty-mile western edge of Lithuania hugs the Baltic Sea. Zidek had convinced Edney to join him at Zalgiris Kaunas, to test himself in Europe.

By then the NBA had drained Edney. Sacramento had picked him in the second round of the 1995 draft, and he signed a two-season deal worth about $450,000. He participated in four playoff games, but the Kings won only one. He landed in Boston, as a free agent, just as Rick Pitino became the Celtics' coach, general manager, president, and CEO. The lone title he didn't nab was sanitation chief; the only hat diehard fans of the storied franchise would swear fit Pitino best. New draftee Chauncey Billups and Edney would struggle but boost each other's spirits. "Pitino's a tough coach," Edney says. "He was kind of [frequently] on Chauncey. We'd talk each other off the ledge a lot. Chauncey was on that ledge a lot. There were times when he was going to [quit] ... just go back to Colorado and do something else. He didn't even feel like he knew how to play basketball."

In the middle of February 1998, Edney and a few teammates were shooting free throws after a practice when they heard screeching on a lower level of the Celtics' training facility in Waltham, Massachusetts. They found Billups and Dee Brown as excited as if they had just escaped from prison; they had been traded, with Roy Rogers and John Thomas, to Toronto. "They were yelling at the top of their lungs in joy," Edney says. "Everyone thought, 'Why isn't that me?' I had never heard a ballplayer say, 'Why isn't that me?' If that gives you any indication of that atmosphere ... " Sixteen years and $105 million later, Billups was still playing in the NBA during the 2013-14 season.

Edney went the other way. Hello, Lithuania. He disembarked from that Aeroflot plane into the warm hugs of George and Martina Zidek, whom Tyus had shown comfort and support at UCLA in 1991. "Kind of a role reversal," Edney says. Heat, cable television, and twenty-four-hour restaurants that he had so taken for granted were now dearly missed. That global awakening would serve him well in Italy, Greece, Ukraine, Spain, and Poland.

Getting paid is often the most challenging aspect for an American hoopster in Europe, but Zalgiris Kaunas owner Shabtai

Kalmanovich treated Zidek and Edney like nobility. The short man with the long hair was an extravagant extrovert, which belied a ruthless streak he had needed as either a double or triple agent, between Shin Bet of Israel and the KGB. He had always loved basketball, so when he bought Zalgiris he hired coach Jonas Kazlauskas, who almost guided Lithuania to a massive upset of the US in a semifinal of the 2000 Summer Olympics in Sydney.

Zalgiris won its domestic league and upended Europe when a massive roll in the Euroleague, the most important continental tournament, ended with its victory over Kinder Bologna in the finale. Edney won Euroleague Final Four MVP honors. Zidek lifted Edney on the court—Seattle in 1995, Munich in 1999. Kalmanovic flew Hank and Barbara Edney, and Tyus's older brother Russell in First Class to Munich, where five-star accommodations awaited them. Similar arrangements were made for Peter Schultz and Jiri Zidek Sr. to see George. They were all shuttled to a fine restaurant in a convoy of black Mercedes-Benz G63 AMGs. "G wagons," says Tyus Edney.

The Zalgiris arena held barely five thousand fans, but it was always packed. Kalmanovich, from his courtside seat, always sang the Lithuanian anthem loudest before every game. At a celebration Edney stood on a stage, held onto the straight silver-based trophy that flared out like an Art Deco champagne bucket, and gazed out at deliriously happy fans shedding tears. "Unbelievable," he says. The team attended victory celebrations all over Lithuania. "It was as if we had won for the whole country, not just for our own little city. It was such a big deal. Everywhere we went crowds would follow us." Edney's parents accompanied Tyus back to Lithuania, and they were stunned by the attention from the moment the plane landed. Says Hank Edney; "It was the biggest thing in Lithuania since they were set free from Russia."

Kalmanovich's wild and crazy life ended in November 2009, not far from Vladimir Putin's office in Moscow, when assassins sprayed bullets into the passenger side—where he sat—of his black Mercedes S500. He was hit ten times and died instantly. The murder occurred in rush-hour traffic at a stoplight. Police found $1.5 million in cash in the Mercedes, and it believed the shooting was related to a debt—instead of paying off Kalmanovich, a debtor chose to wipe him out—or gangster turf disputes.

After a season at Benetton Treviso, in Italy, Edney gave the NBA one last go-round with the Indiana Pacers in 2000. A sprained ankle contributed to him playing only once over four months. He played as a reserve twenty-four times. "Like a paid vacation," he says. "I almost felt guilty about being in Indiana. I wanted to go back to Italy and play for stuff, be part of a team, win. And I was fortunate that Mike [D'Antoni] was the coach [at Benetton], too."

Edney began a nine-year European adventure in which he spent five seasons in Italy. When he returned with any of those teams to Lithuania, the crowds stood en masse to applaud him. Edney became UCLA's director of basketball operations for Ben Howland in 2010. At the Wooden Classic in Anaheim in 2012, Edney might have displayed the most emotion I had ever witnessed. Clipboard in hand as he sat on the bench, a game against San Diego State was slipsliding away. Edney fumed. He stomped on the court in front of the UCLA bench. I had never seen him frown, but this qualified as true anger. Edney does not hesitate to explain his attitude toward Howland. It was a pivotal juncture. Aztecs coach Steve Fischer had an advantage and was slowing down the pace to bleed the clock. Howland did not react to the ploy by pressing the issue, maybe having his guys get into the Aztecs' grilles and denying outlets, with any sense of urgency.

"I got mad," Edney says. "I got up and … didn't yell at Howland, but it was at a point where they were doing something … coach Fischer is a veteran. He was delaying or pausing or stalling. I was already mad with how the game had been going. Then he's pulling this. I don't know what [Howland] was doing. I got up, 'Coach, don't you see what he's doing? He's trying to stall.' [Howland says], 'Oh, all right, yeah. Yeah.' He starts ... dude, come on. Yeah, a lot of frustration."

Howland received his dismissal, and replacement Steve Alford retained Edney in the same capacity. Edney was grateful, but Baron Davis and Ed O'Bannon were among a few former Bruins irritated that such a famous UCLA figure had not been made a full-fledged assistant—by either regime—with the power to recruit, visit prospects in their homes, and woo them and their parents with his contagious powder blue passion.

In his office he is low key and unassuming, but his eyes dance when the subject is UCLA basketball. Edney says that moving up from DBO, to assistant coach, is just about timing. "Obviously, with all the change ... you know, I'm getting to know them. They don't know me. I understand. They say it's the nature of the business. Just got to be patient." Are you itching to get out there, to recruit? "Yeah, yeah. I want to get out there."

In 2009, Sonny Vaccaro invited Edney to become the face of a lawsuit—to protect players' likenesses and images, which would grow in scope and size—against various companies and the NCAA. Knowing he was about to embark on a coaching career and believing, rightfully so, that a connection to such legal action could hamper such prospects, Edney declined. At least eight others did, too. Ed O'Bannon would accept Vaccaro's offer. "I just decided not to do it," Edney says. "But I believed in it. You just never know what's going to happen. I definitely support [O'Bannon]. I knew it was a good thing he was doing."

Edney knows about image infringement. When he was in Europe, a friend congratulated him about a new Coke Zero commercial in the States. Edney said, "Uh, excuse me?"

Unbeknownst to him, he was featured in a television advertisement for the soft drink. An announcer describes how UCLA *stared fate straight in the eye* and the smallest man on the court made the game's *most gargantuan shot.* Footage featured Edney's remarkable drive against Missouri. Nobody had contacted Edney, or his legal representatives, about using his image in the commercial. Edney's attorney sought, and received, compensation. Edney is incredulous. "I was not even contacted about that? 'Do you mind if we do this?' Nothing. It just didn't seem right."

As the calendar turned to 2014, Edney formed the company WHERE WERE YOU WHEN? It peddles T-shirts and caps bearing Edney's outline—both hands up, body a bit leaning back—and "4.8," the time left on the clock that he beat to crush the Tigers. It would also be an outlet for fans to record where they were and what they were doing as dramatic sporting moments unfolded before them on television screens at home, in bars, in airports, or even while at other athletic venues.

In the spring of 2014, UCLA beat Tulsa and Stephen F. Austin to reach the Sweet Sixteen in the NCAAs, only to lose once again to Bruins-crusher Florida and coach Billy Donovan. In 2006 and 2007, Donovan joined Mike Krzyzewski in the unique fraternity of back-to-back NCAA champs since John Wooden. Fittingly, the Gators had to get by UCLA, in the national final in 2006 and a national semifinal the following year, for Donovan to achieve such status. Henry Iba (Oklahoma State, 1945 and '46), Adolph Rupp (Kentucky, 1948 and '49), Phil Woolpert (San Francisco, 1955 and '56), and Ed Jucker (Cincinnati, 1961 and '62) also nailed the double. Only Wooden has won at least three consecutive NCAA titles, and it might be safe to presume nobody will ever match his seven in a row.

Connecticut and first-year coach Kevin Ollie—the guard that Jim Harrick had so coveted out of high school in 1991—would cap the 2014 NCAAs by defeating Kentucky, denying the Wildcats a ninth national championship; the Bruins would retain their three-title edge over Kentucky. Tony Luftman probably speaks for many, many UCLA fans when he makes a corollary to LBJ's space-race quote about never wanting to go to bed by the light of a Communist moon; Luftman fears the night he lays himself down to sleep by the light of a bluegrass moon if Kentucky ever passes UCLA in NCAA men's basketball titles in his lifetime.

I ask Edney about a dream job. He will coach, probably for a very long time, and pass along the vast amount of knowledge he has culled. He pauses. "Coming back here would be a dream job," he says, as if he knows getting the top gig at UCLA from within, a la Steve Lavin, would require the oddest, damnedest series of circumstances. "That's later, maybe. You never know. But, you know, it's not easy to coach here. I have a lot of respect for everyone who coaches here."

Ed O'Bannon felt like a Crash Test Dummy. His left knee had been poked and prodded and twisted in so many workouts by so many medical personnel for so many NBA teams. The elation of the NBA draft had long worn off. Again, serendipity and Ed O'Bannon were not bedfellows. A salary cap was first established for the 1995 draft, his draft, at SkyDome (now Rogers Centre) in Toronto. The previous year, Glenn Robinson went first and inked a ten-year pact for sixty-eight million dollars. In '95, Joe Smith was tabbed first and signed a three-year deal worth nearly nine million bucks.

The real capper arrived moments before the ninth pick would be announced. New Jersey was up. O'Bannon had quickly learned how the cameras homed in on a prospect just seconds before his name would be called. The cameras tipped it all off. They focused on O'Bannon. The Nets. On the other side of the country, in a system that had nothing to do with up-tempo strategy or finesse schemes, on a roster of mediocrity and selfishness, coached by Butch Beard. O'Bannon is the picture of unhappiness as he climbs that stage. In 1994, ninth pick Eric Montross signed an eleven-year contract for seventeen million dollars; O'Bannon's three-year deal guaranteed him less than four million dollars.

In a preseason game in Phoenix, O'Bannon was confused why the crowd booed New Jersey teammate Jayson Williams every time he touched the ball. Phoenix had drafted Williams in 1990, he explained to O'Bannon, but he did not want to play there; he was a New York native and desired to ball for an Eastern team. The Suns were forced to trade Williams, to Philadelphia, that October; the Sixers dealt him to New Jersey in 1992.

O'Bannon was a West Coast guy playing on the East Coast. He sat in the visitors' locker room in Phoenix and glared at Williams. "You kiddin' me? That's all it took? You just refused to come?" Williams nodded. "If I could go back a month I woulda just refused," O'Bannon says today. "I woulda been like, 'I ain't goin'. Find somewhere else for me. Trade me. I'll be a bad guy, but keep me on the West Coast. I'm not goin' back [to New Jersey].'"

He liked Nets general manager Willis Reed, the famous former New York Knick. But O'Bannon never worked up the nerve to inquire why Reed had drafted him. "I never got the balls," O'Bannon says. "The person I am today? I'd ask him. Better yet, if I had the emotional aptitude then as I do now I would tell him, 'Don't even do it. I ain't doin' it, bro. When my name comes up, I'd rather fall a few places than get drafted early and go to you.'"

O'Bannon got homesick. He felt sorry for myself. He played sparingly. The Nets went 30-52. Beard got sacked. John Calipari was hired. Because Calipari had spent so much time in the collegiate ranks, O'Bannon thought he'd get opportunities in his sophomore pro season. He didn't. "I didn't really care for [Calipari], to be honest with you," O'Bannon says. "He and I didn't have a whole lot of conversations." Their final chat took place when Calipari called O'Bannon in his Secaucus condo to inform him he'd been traded to Dallas in February 1997.

"He was better than Grant Hill in college," says Jim Harrick, comparing O'Bannon to the former Duke star that logged 997 NBA games over seventeen seasons. "If you don't have confidence, as a professional athlete, you'll never go anywhere. He lost his confidence, got motherfucked by Butch Beard the whole time he was at New Jersey, and he never developed, never formed. Everybody asks, 'What happened to Ed O'Bannon?' He was a long way from home, lost his confidence ... such a grind. I saw him play in New Jersey and he wasn't nearly the player I had envisioned. He never got the time to show what he could do. People didn't know how good he was. My god was he good. Shit. Good lord."

O'Bannon couldn't shake Beard, who was tight with Dallas coach Jim Cleamons and had been added to the Mavericks' staff. In September 1997 O'Bannon was traded to Orlando, which broke him. The Magic preseason roster overflowed, forcing O'Bannon to sit on the floor past the end of the bench. At the end of a blowout loss Chuck Daly, who had turned the Detroit Pistons into winners, peered at Ed and nodded toward the court.

Ed shook his head. Daly did a double take. Huh? Get in there! Ed again shook his head. Thanks coach, but no thanks. It was the only time in his life that Ed O'Bannon refused to enter a basketball game. That kick-started a sojourn that landed him in the hinterlands of Wisconsin and the CBA, and included overseas posts in Italy, Spain, Greece, and a pleasurable three-month respite—in which he made ten grand a month—for Boca Juniors in Argentina. Upon landing at LAX after each season, his first stop would be In-N-Out for double doubles. While O'Bannon was in

Buenos Aires, in March 2000, the twenty-four-year-old Seattle Kingdome—on whose lease taxpayers still owed $125 million—was imploded.

He once returned to the States with nearly ten thousand dollars, in hundred-dollar bills, in each shoe. On a trip home from Athens, he hid a Rolex in a sock and a shoe in the depths of his gym bag. (Take that, revenuers.) A Polish team still owes O'Bannon forty thousand dollars. On another Polish squad, O'Bannon travelled twenty-four hours—a bus to another bus, to an airport to catch a plane, and then another bus—to reach a European Cup game in the Russian outpost of Ostrov, south of St. Petersburg near the Latvian border. O'Bannon's famished teammates tore into what looked like mushy broccoli oatmeal. In America, O'Bannon wouldn't have fed such a dish to a dog. His boys dipped bread in it, wolfed it down. O'Bannon followed suit, putting mind over matter. "I chewed it and swallowed it. I made the best of it. At that point I told myself I could do it; went into survival mode."

I ask him which gave first, his knee or his heart, in relation to basketball. He pauses. Great question, he says. His heart wasn't in it, for sure. "I've never really figured that out," O'Bannon says.

> I've always kind of asked myself that question. You sit there and wonder, What happened? A million things can and do cross my mind. Why didn't I play as well as I should have, or wanted to? Was it because my knee wasn't one hundred percent well? Why wasn't it one hundred percent? Was it because I just didn't want to be on [New Jersey]? Psychologically, I was done when they called my name and got drafted [by the Nets].
>
> I also piss myself off when I think about that, because I should have forgotten about the team. I'm in the league. I should be happy that I'm playing in the NBA, damn

what team I'm playing on. Grab your nuts and pull up
your bootstraps, and play. Who cares what team you're
on? That's what I shoulda been thinking. I'm upset with
myself, that I didn't think that, and because I didn't
think that, well, mentally ... I was physically hurt before
the season even started, but I was also psychologically
hurt before the season even started. I don't know.

Today, he can neither straighten his left leg, nor bend it, as
much as his right. The left wheel gives out on him on occasion. He
can feel the swelling; sometimes, the left knee is considerably
warmer than the right one. In the NBA, he had blood and other
liquid drained from the knee five times. "Probably, in hindsight, I
think my [left] knee didn't quite take to the graft like it was
anticipated. The swelling never really went down." The thigh and
calf muscle on his left leg are not as pronounced, due to atrophy,
as those on his right leg. Arthritis has kicked in, too. "I spent so
much time not playing on it, [the calf and thigh] got smaller. Yet, I
came back too soon; it sounds like I probably should have waited
two years before I could play [for UCLA], but I just couldn't do
that."

When O'Bannon tried out for a Chinese league in Oregon, in
the fall of 2004, he knew it was over. None of those officials knew
what he had accomplished in 1995. He left his black Nike high-
tops—a basketball player's dearest possessions—atop a dorm-
room bed.

The ledger shows that the UCLA stars of the 1995 national
championship season—Ed and Charles O'Bannon, Tyus Edney,
George Zidek, J.R. Henderson, and Toby Bailey—combined to
play 640 games (starting 157) in the NBA, where they earned a
total of $9.1 million. Arkansas star Corliss Williamson alone
played twelve NBA seasons, starting 293 of 822 games, and made
$42.7 million. "What I never wanted was to have to explain

myself or make excuses, on why or how my career ended up," O'Bannon says. "My NBA career came and went. I'm good. If I'm good and my family's good, and my parents are good, what's the problem?"

Ed reviews a game-by-game log of his 128 NBA games, in which he started thirty-four times, tallied 634 points, grabbed 316 rebounds, made $3.91 million, and recorded a single double-double. "Man, there are a lot of zeroes on this thing," he says. He lays the sheets on a restaurant table.

> I wasn't meant to play in the NBA. I went through the knee [surgery] for a reason. I went through these hard times in the NBA ... because I'm strong enough. I was strong enough to be the number one player in the country in high school, get to college, and have it ripped away, and I'm strong enough to have that tossed aside, and regain it ... to be the number one player in college ... then that's ripped away once I get to the NBA. Now I build from that. There's something bigger for me in this lifetime. A lot of times, that's the problem with a lot of guys who are in the NBA; they need that to define them. I don't need the NBA to define me. I'm a human being.

Waves of players dropped into UCLA for a spell, after the title season, and prospered in the NBA. From Trevor Arriza to Baron Davis to Jason Kapono, et al, there were fifteen Bruins who, through 2013, had combined to log 109 NBA seasons, with eight All-Star appearances, four championships, and $437.6 million in salaries; six of those players had contracts that guaranteed them another $193.3 million.

None of them, however, own an NCAA championship ring. O'Bannon takes immeasurable pride in the role he played in the latest, lone chapter of UCLA basketball glory, the only crown over a span of nearly forty years. "I love the fact that I was part of Coach Wooden's legacy and I added to his tradition," he says.

> There are just a few of us who were part of that team. No matter who went to that school and no matter how many guys went through that program, I'm one of a few that was on a team that won a national championship and got my number retired [seven Bruins have had their numbers retired]. Hell, and I'm one of two Bruins to win the John R. Wooden Award. That's way more prestigious than any [NBA] MVP or [collegiate] MOP trophy.

Mark Whicker, the veteran *Orange County Register* columnist, believed the 1994-95 edition of the Bruins was the finest of the program's eleven championship squads. Of the Final Four teams in Seattle in 1995, only UCLA had won its conference championship. Plus, this was the first UCLA team that required six victories to earn a trophy. Integration, television, freshman eligibility, rule alterations, foreign recruiting, and many other factors stoke a comparison debate, but Whicker didn't dabble in gray area. *Around UCLA*, he wrote, *this sensational 1995 basketball team should always be remembered as champion of champions.*

Having been led by three seniors gave it additional distinction. Ed O'Bannon, Tyus Edney, and George Zidek were three of the Bruins' top four scorers, a combined level of experience and expectation that has disappeared in a collegiate game that is now dominated by entitled youngsters looking to play one season before cashing in. Moreover, through 2014, only three championship teams since UCLA's singular season of resurgence have been led, in scoring, by fifth-year seniors. Of those, only Maryland of 2002 had two other seniors among its next three scorers. But scoring leader Juan Dixon had used a redshirt season at the start of his career when he qualified late and entered school in January. Dixon hadn't been forced into a rehabilitation regimen of more than a year, like O'Bannon, to return to some semblance of his old self.

O'Bannon had grossed about $7 million in his professional career. He and Rosa, pregnant with their third child, married on June 20, 1998. The ceremony was in their Torrance home, and she does not let him forget that he showed late ... to his own wedding, under his own roof. His bachelor party at a friend's glorious hilltop San Fernando Valley home had been a riot. Ed slept in, let the fog lift, went to a Coco's in Cerritos for a big breakfast with his parents and other relatives, and returned to his parents' house to shower and shave. (He's still sorry, Rosa.) He says that was the finest day of his life.

He begrudgingly heeded Rosa's advice and purchased a comfortable two-story home in Anthem, in the foothills of Henderson, Nevada. Rosa knew escaping the congestion of Los Angeles and Golden State tax burdens would be wise moves for the family. Ed would not miss certain people, though. There was a limit, too, to ignoring a widespread label as one of the NBA's all-time draft busts.

When he was selling a brawny Chevrolet Suburban outside his Torrance home, a prospective buyer rang the number in the windshield and knew whom he was calling. The guy left a message. "Hey, O'Bannon! It's only fitting that you're selling your truck! You probably ran through all your money. You're so bad you can't even make the Clippers! You suck!" O'Bannon thought, *You gotta be pretty miserable in your life to actually decide you want to pick up the phone and be pissed off at someone else, for something that has nothing to do with you.* "I didn't do anything to this guy," O'Bannon says. "I forced myself to remember that, that there's always bad people that will do anything they can to bring you down."

O'Bannon, his wife, and three kids made the one-way drive up Interstate 15 to start a new chapter in Las Vegas. After he left his favorite sneakers in that Oregon dormitory, I found him at Green Valley High School. He had befriended Gators coach Adam Patai, at church, and Patai invited O'Bannon to tutor promising forward Billy White. O'Bannon, though, soon left the campus for good. He had been found to have a record of felony domestic violence and grand theft auto. Administrators knew it was a case of stolen identity because the person on the rap sheet was a five-foot-seven Hispanic man, but rules were rules. O'Bannon spent two years clearing the mess with the Social Security office.

He soaked up the sun the rest of 2004 and into '05. He would take a kid or two to school, maybe hit the gym for a workout, but afternoons were devoted to the backyard, grillin' something for lunch, watchin' one of his college or prep games on tape on the flatscreen in the patio corner, and relaxin' in the pool with a tumbler of Jack Daniel's and Coke. He'd consume a 1.75-liter bottle of Jack a week. "The next chapter. Everyone handles it in his own way. Some guys take to drinking; I know I drank heavily. Drink in one hand, remote in the other. Didn't have a care in the world."

Rosa grew tired of Ed's inertia, dirty dishes in the sink, and nothing on the table or in the oven, for dinner, when she got home at eight-thirty. She had embarked on a career in high school administration. She forced him to begin the next stage of his life, whatever that may be. Ed had obtained the business card of a Findlay Toyota manager from former UNLV coach Bill Bayno, and Rosa pressured Ed to make that call.

Cliff Findlay, an automobile magnate and former UNLV center who once got schooled by Elvin Hayes of Houston, favored giving opportunities to former athletes. He liked their competitive natures and team-player dispositions. Bo Belinsky, who threw the first no-hitter in Dodger Stadium in his fourth career start for the Los Angeles Angels in 1962, spent the final ten years of his life working for Findlay. He and general manager Rich Abajian had also once hired former National League batting champion Bill Madlock and Jason Thomas, who played quarterback at USC and UNLV.

Ed, though, had never envisioned himself as a *used-car salesman* ... "that guy," he says. "Bad hair. Bad breath." But he finally rang Abajian and accepted an entry-level position. Coaching from fellow salesman Eric Ludwick—a former UNLV pitcher who threw in the majors in the late 1990s and was part of the trade that sent slugger Mark McGwire from Oakland to St. Louis—helped O'Bannon adjust his attitude and take pride in helping people.

It worked. Canvassing the lot on a 115-degree day in the middle of the summer became second nature. His mantra became, *I'm not here to sell you a car, but I'll be more than happy to help you buy one.* When he sold two vans to Las Vegas native Andre Agassi, the former tennis star heaped accolades on O'Bannon for his amazing championship season and bemoaned that O'Bannon never played for UNLV. O'Bannon figures he has sold two thousand vehicles.

It would have been a highlight to have been on the lot the day the staff became perplexed at a boxed-in Smart car that needed to be relocated; Ed hopped in and, with his neck and noggin popping through the sun roof, negotiated a twenty-eight-point turn to free the thing.

One blazing summer day, I did observe him in action. We had planned to have one of what became many lunches, but he was busy with an older woman and her adult son. He led them to vehicles to the right, then to the left. He did not smile. She was a friend of a friend, a referral, but O'Bannon innately felt as if he were being used. He apologized as he leaned into the window of my car. I told him, not necessary; this is your livelihood. I remained in the parking lot for three hours. I visited the interior of the dealership, to use the facilities, and saw him with them at a table, sifting over paperwork, crunching numbers. *He's closing*, I thought. *Yes.* Still, he did not smile.

The charade finally ended with no sale. He visited my car and frowned. Ed O'Bannon greatly dislikes being used. The woman would buy a vehicle in Southern California. Frustrating, he says. For the most part, the six-eight introvert has enjoyed the art of introducing himself to strangers. "Since I started working here I've gotten comfortable with conversation, with meeting people," he says. "What I don't like is the negotiation, of having to 'convince' someone to buy a vehicle. Never been good at it. Don't want to be good at it. I find a way to make a living by doing what I do my way, as opposed to being 'that car salesman,' that guy I don't want to be. I'm not here to squeeze someone."

At Bishop Gorman High, he manned a big tote board that displayed scores and statistics of an expansive tournament when Corliss Williamson squeezed through a door. He had been coaching at a small Southern college and was scouting prospects. Ed recognized Corliss, who just ... couldn't ... place ... Ed re-introduced himself, shook Corliss's hand. "What's up? Howya been?" said Corliss. They exchanged small talk and O'Bannon's former title-game adversary went his way. "I felt like he was happy to see me; I was happy to see him," O'Bannon says. Williamson eventually became an NBA assistant coach for the Sacramento Kings.

O'Bannon relied on Harrick's Guidelines when he coached the private Henderson International School for one season, but the team played poorly and got axed in a wide swath of budget cuts. Harrick has tried to convince Ed not to explore further coaching possibilities, that his position at the dealership is a secure and stable career.

In 2009, O'Bannon drove to Summerlin to pick up buddy Michael Curtis, the former UNLV walk-on guard, to attend a Rebels game at the Thomas & Mack Center. Curtis had first met O'Bannon at Pauley Pavilion in December 1993, when the Rebels got pummeled. The two reunited, via the automotive business, when O'Bannon moved to Las Vegas. Curtis was delayed so O'Bannon settled into a couch to watch Curtis's two sons, Parker and Spencer, play *NCAA Basketball 09*, an Electronic Arts Sports video game. O'Bannon was stunned when he saw a figure of Milk Duds-like complexion—like his—bald and left-handed, wearing a white UCLA jersey bearing the number thirty-one. It was Ed O'Bannon. He was watching himself.

Curtis laughed as he entered the room and said, "The worst part is, you're not getting anything for that, are you?" O'Bannon did not laugh. He would accept Sonny Vaccaro's offer to be the face of what at first looked like a potentially debilitating lawsuit against the NCAA, and EA Sports and Collegiate Licensing Company, for using athletes' images and likenesses in perpetuity. *O'Bannon* v. *NCAA* was filed, in Northern California, on July 21, 2009. Curtis jokes that he and O'Bannon combined for thirty-one points that December day in 1993 at Pauley, that he tallied a single point and Ed poured in thirty. Actually, O'Bannon had sixteen points and seven boards, while Curtis played three minutes and sank one of two free-throw attempts. It stuns Curtis, whose own image appeared on another video game, that what began in his living room would end up in a court of law and will escalate to even higher legal arenas. "It all started in my house. The crazy thing is we were just hanging out. He's this big name in basketball, but he's just a great friend of mine. I only have great things to say about him."

Until it went to trial in June 2014, the case had morphed and expanded and shifted like a blob. Some observers speculated that the NCAA could be hit with penalties of several billion dollars. Due to the antitrust nature of the case, that severe figure would be tripled, possibly dealing a crippling financial blow to the governing body of collegiate sports. But that was an extreme potential *denouement*. On the eve of the trial, Michael Hausfeld, the lead attorney for the O'Bannon team, chose not to pursue monetary damages as part of the suit. That streamlined the case, taking a verdict away from a jury to leave it solely up to US District Judge Claudia Wilken, a Stanford graduate.

Late the afternoon of Friday, August 8, 2014, Wilken ruled in favor of O'Bannon, citing that the NCAA's limits on what top-tier college basketball and football players can receive for playing sports "unreasonably restrain trade" in violation of antitrust laws. The ninety-nine-page ruling slammed the NCAA and contained an injunction that prevents it from keeping those players from getting a limited share of revenues—via a trust after they leave college, of at least five thousand dollars per collegiate season—in an appeals process.

As expected, the NCAA announced it would appeal. A legal expert told me that move—at the state level, in the Ninth Circuit Court of Appeals—could take two years. (Chief Judge Alex Kozinski, who earned his undergrad and law degrees at UCLA, would ultimately assign three judges to that panel.) Both sides had already threatened to appeal to the highest level; a decision by the Supreme Court, should it decide to hear the case, would likely tack on another ten years. Two weeks later Hausfeld sought more than fifty-two million dollars, in fees and expenses for his firm and the forty-two that aided the plaintiffs, from the

NCAA through Wilken's court. The new rules would be instituted in the next basketball and football recruiting cycles, in July 2015.

Sonny Vaccaro called the verdict the proudest moment of his life. He said he and O'Bannon were on a "quest, not a job." Vaccaro didn't want to act like a "giddy teenager," but he didn't know what else he could have done in his life that held more importance.

Pretty cool stuff, Ed O'Bannon texted me three hours after the decision was made public. That qualified as an emotional outburst for such a cool, reserved soul, who does not partake in Facebook or Twitter; too distracting from real-world responsibilities. At the dinner table, Ed and Rosa kept their children informed about the progress of the case, that much of what they heard from others or saw on the Internet was baseless, conjecture, or fluff. By nightfall of August 8 he was being hailed as the Curt Flood of college sports. Toby Bailey re-Tweeted a photograph of the license plate—THANX ED—that Charles O'Bannon had placed on the Ford Explorer his older brother had bought him after Ed was drafted. *A lot of kids are going to need one of these license plates*, Bailey wrote. A prominent author told me the court victory was a fitting coda to Ed O'Bannon's association with basketball.

That roller-coaster ordeal might have been deflating, in time alone, but O'Bannon never wavered once he became a part of it. He spent years discussing tactics, in person, with teams of lawyers on both coasts. He was called into depositions. During the summer of 2013, O'Bannon had been seeking a broadcasting gig for a couple of weeks, until that company discovered his involvement with the legal action. He had wanted to explore coaching opportunities, too. "But no coach will touch me right now," he said at that time. (Don't be surprised if he ends up on the coaching staff at either North Carolina State or Washington.) O'Bannon told a PBS *Frontline* reporter, " ... selfishly speaking, I want the way the NCAA does business, I want that to change." During the five-year ordeal, O'Bannon received occasional text messages—*hang in there ... be strong ... keep the faith ...*—from Marques Johnson.

At the start of the 2013 NCAAs, Ed hosted a ballroom gathering for about a thousand fans at the South Point in Las Vegas. O'Bannon settled a score by winning a free-throw shooting contest against former UNLV guard Freddie Banks, who had beaten O'Bannon in the same challenge in 2012. A short, fat guy with turkey-drumstick calves, wearing a UCLA T-shirt under a garish Hawaiian garment, walked by O'Bannon, who said, "Go, UCLA!" The guy hardly nodded at the man who willed that school to its lone season of glory since John Wooden. O'Bannon slightly shook his head and grinned.

I brought him that week's *Sports Illustrated*. He smiled. He was forty-third on the magazine's ranking of the fifty most powerful people in sports, a spot ahead of Barack Obama. UFC president Dana White, Dallas Mavericks owner Mark Cuban, and Michael Jordan brought up the rear of the poll. That week, someone had sent to Ed a picture of him guarding Jordan in an NBA game. The scene flashed on a sports show, and the friend snapped his smart phone in time. O'Bannon made that the main image on the face of his phone. The magazine poll wowed him, but only a tad. "I didn't really think it was that big of a deal, [but] it was pretty cool that I'm in front of Mr. President. Wow. I don't know what it means, if anything. But somebody thinks so. I think it's pretty cool." For the only occasion in our many talks, totalling maybe one hundred hours over nine months, we shared a drink; Jack and Coke toasts, to his ranking, in red plastic cups.

The magazine's nutshell explanation of O'Bannon's stature highlighted his role as the lead plaintiff in the NCAA lawsuit and his "threshold for settlement [that] may reshape college sports." Madeline O'Bannon told Ed that he had a higher calling. "I'm excited that I have the opportunity to represent my fellow basketball players," he says.

> The feedback I'm getting, personally, has been one hundred percent positive. Everyone I talk to seems to be in our corner. As a man, that's what you want; the respect of your peers. I seem to have it and I will do all that I can to keep it. I want to represent my family, my parents, my wife, and my kids ... I want to represent *black* men ... um, you know, I want to represent UCLA the right way. I have an opportunity to be a positive influence on a lot of people's lives, and, hopefully, it will turn out that way.

In 1963, the TV rights to air the basketball tournament through 1968 were sold for $140,000; in 1991 CBS Sports agreed to its first billion-dollar (multi-year) TV deal. The contract surpassed ten billion dollars about the time Vaccaro filed the lawsuit. Mark Gottfried says the scholarship model, getting a free education to play sports, was a fair deal for decades. View those above figures again to know when it went askew for players. "I'm not sure I've ever coached a more genuine and real human being than that guy," Gottfried says. "He's not one of those vindictive guys who would hold a grudge against anybody. His motive, I think, is pure. It's just the right thing. It could change college athletics more than anything in our lifetime if they win, which I think they will." Gottfried's prediction was validated.

O'Bannon was touched when Harry Flournoy, a member of the Texas Western squad that upended Kentucky for the 1966 title, and Oscar Robertson and Bill Russell joined his legal team. O'Bannon was having a particularly edgy day when Russell called about a vehicle purchase. With that settled, he asked how Ed was doing. Ed told him. Russell soothed O'Bannon with some insights about challenges and difficulties he had endured in his life. Afterward, O'Bannon found a picture of Russell on the Internet. With a few clicks he made it the screen saver on his computer monitor.

He had always had a clean-shaven dome and mug, but O'Bannon grew a beard. It looked like steel wool. Charles called his older brother Osama bin Laden. At a tournament at Bishop Gorman, O'Bannon's former high school coach Wayne Merino said it was uncanny how he resembled James Harden. *Copying Harden, eh?* I like his game, Ed said, and consider him a friend, "but this is *all* Bill Russell." He proudly stroked the beard. That's the image on the cover of this book. O'Bannon had met Russell because Russell has been friends with Cliff Findlay for decades and a regular customer. O'Bannon enjoyed Russell's rollicking laughter and that scraggly, gray-flecked beard. "I don't know what he's gone through, probably a whole lotta stuff. But his laugh is so infectious," O'Bannon says.

> That's the beauty of Mr. Russell. The fact that he's gone through all he's gone through, and he can still not only laugh but make everyone around him laugh. He sat in Rich's office for two days, telling stories and jokes. His beard is all knotty; he's a funny lookin' dude. Later on he becomes part of this lawsuit. I can't thank him and Mr. Robertson enough. I can't express to them what it means to me, that they agreed with what I'm doing and want to be a part of this. It's unbelievable.

The night before the lawsuit started, O'Bannon fielded a call from Harry Flournoy that gave him a considerable boost heading into the uncharted territory of a much different court. O'Bannon had been ambivalent, unsure of what would transpire. But

Flournoy settled him, to where O'Bannon put Flournoy's wisdom and insight on grand par with his maternal grandfather, Alton Hamilton.

Word had trickled around on some blow-hard grapevine that O'Bannon had regretted, to whatever degree, getting involved in the lawsuit. I relayed that to him on Wednesday, August 6, in the dealership. It stunned him. Nothing could be further from the truth, he says. Would he do it again? "In a New York minute." The entire process had been affecting the college landscape in positive ways for athletes, he acknowledged. He talked about USC instituting four-year scholarships, as opposed to the previous industry norm of one-year pacts that were re-drawn annually at the behest of the school, as one example of recent changes. Rosa O'Bannon became a fan of Judge Wilken—the questions she asked and the methodical manner in which she operated—during the trial. That had to have been heightened on August 8.

Tony Luftman—to whom Kris Johnson has never apologized for repeatedly smacking in the back of his head on the bus after UCLA beat Oklahoma State in Seattle—and O'Bannon stay in regular contact. Luftman asked O'Bannon who he might like to play him, if a movie were ever made about his life. O'Bannon quickly named Idris Elba, a versatile British entertainer maybe best known for his role in the HBO hit series *The Wire*.

A broadcast veteran, Luftman worked for CBS Sports Net's *Lead Off* show for a stretch. He presented evidence for a topic and backed it up with opinions and insight, much like his lawyer brother and father would do in a court of law. A UCLA administrator sent Luftman a terse email, calling him disloyal, after Luftman—on air—disagreed with Dan Guerrero's hiring of Steve Alford to replace Ben Howland. Luftman had reasoned, *They're asking [Alford] to do something he's never done; win a championship.* Hitting forty years, in the spring of 2015, with only one championship seemed highly probable to Luftman. In

February 2014, Luftman arranged a *Lead Off* interview with O'Bannon and asked him mostly questions about the lawsuit for three and a half minutes. "Why not me?" O'Bannon said.

(Steve Alford, by the way, made it four consecutive UCLA hoops coaches to make debatable uniform decisions when the Bruins lost that Sweet Sixteen game to Florida, in March 2014, wearing short-sleeved dark blue jerseys. *New York Post* writer Phil Mushnick, an observer of college basketball for nearly fifty years, fumed. He wrote, "there is no more identifiable, famous, glory-synonymous uniform ... than the home-and-aways worn by UCLA ... as tethered to a tradition as are Yankee uniforms." The most famous uniforms in the 123-year history of college basketball, Mushnick deduced, and UCLA eschewed them.)

Luftman and O'Bannon share a tight friendship. When some prominent boosters, instead of UCLA's five student managers, visited the White House with coaches and players after the title season, Luftman was hurt beyond words. He kept his sorrow to himself for decades. On Saturday, July 19, 2014, Luftman was in Las Vegas on business and, as usual, he visited with Ed. At one point Ed paused and seemed embarrassed. He told Luftman that if he had known what had transpired with the managers' exclusion on that trip, something he had only recently discovered, he would have met with Jim Harrick, maybe even Pete Dalis, and said, *If he doesn't go, I don't go.* For the first time since that omission, Luftman found peace. He admits he might be too sensitive and emotional, but the heavy weight of that wrong had been lifted forever with O'Bannon's declaration.

Ten days later a hundred-year-old, three-foot-wide pipe burst on Sunset Boulevard, flooding the Morgan and Wooden centers, and Pauley Pavilion with an estimated twenty million gallons of water. The court was underwater, buckling in spots. Andrew Pruter and Tony Luftman exchanged text messages in which they jokingly confirmed that they'd meet at Pauley in ten minutes with towels on their shoulders to "sop up the wet spots." The status of the egg yolk out in the entryway was unclear, but Dan Guerrero said experts had assured him that the building would be able to play host to the upcoming hoops season.

O'Bannon stayed busy between the filing of the lawsuit and the trial, as he became baptized into Catholicism at the Los Angeles parish that Rosa and her family had long attended and finished his degree requirements at UCLA. Rosa sewed and stitched an elegant garment, of white cotton and linen and silk, to transform Ed into a kind of apostle for his immersion. "I don't want to say Jesus, but he looked like some religious figure," says a jubilant Madeline O'Bannon. Heads turned inside a Denny's at the lead figure of the O'Bannon party of about a dozen. Edward III had teary eyes when he told his grandmother, "I'm so proud of dad."

Ed Jr. had attended church in his youth with his parents and brother, and he did say, not long after that final buzzer blared in Seattle to cap his intense five-year Bruins baptism by fire, that his guys *walk by faith, not by sight.* In Nevada, church had been a somewhat regular Sunday family event, along with movies or bowling, and a backyard barbecue. He had hoped completing the rite of passage would exemplify to his children the unshakable courage of his convictions. "*He* doesn't give you more than you can handle, doesn't put you in a position you can't handle," Ed says. "In my opinion, you have to have faith, to have understanding, to have purpose. [But] I strongly believe you have to have your own relationship with God. I think it absolutely helps me … physchologically, mentally, emotionally, spiritually."

A year of study at the University of Nevada, in Reno, didn't satisfy Aaron O'Bannon—LIL O'B, according to the tiny jersey he wore on his father's Senior Night—so he matriculated to a trade school in Rancho Cucamonga, California. He enjoys tinkering on engines and other mechanical gadgets. Jazmin accepted a scholarship to play basketball at Utah Valley University in the fall of 2014.

Edward III will be a six-foot-seven junior forward for Liberty High School in 2014-15. His famous father helps coach him. Edward III has been a bit dismayed that many teammates are receiving recruiting calls and letters from college basketball coaches; he hasn't received much attention. That could change with a strong junior season, his dad tells him. In the meantime, the right-handed youngster eagerly anticipated a UNLV baseball camp in mid-August. His father, wearing red shorts and a satiny white UNLV BASEBALL polo, had taken him to batting cages—nearly throwing out his left arm pitching to him—to prep Edward III for the camp. The son is glad that his father didn't let him quit baseball.

Should Edward III blossom on the basketball court and Charles Jr. continues to excel, and both were to attract the coach of a certain Western powerhouse—that has more championship banners in its rafters than any other program but has been experiencing a drought of nearly twenty years—it would be quite fascinating to watch a pair of O'Bannons again represent UCLA inside Pauley Pavilion. But Charles Jr. did receive that offer from UNLV, and if Edward III were to be extended such a proposal ... could Rebels fans contain themselves if *two* O'Bannons finally don UNLV uniforms?

Showing his kids the value of an education, Ed O'Bannon Jr. trekked back and forth, between Las Vegas and Los Angeles—a baseball in the hand that wasn't occupied by the steering wheel of his Ford F-150—for most of 2011 to earn his UCLA degree. He had pondered finishing those studies down the road at UNLV, to complete a most unique full circle. Instead, as if pulled by some ineffable lodestone, O'Bannon deemed that anything less than a piece of UCLA sheepskin would tarnish his legacy as a Bruin. Indeed, he had left that place much better than he found it. In one class, a couple of students whispered and glanced his way. One finally asked, *Pardon me, are you Lamar Odom?* Another kid told him he chose to attend UCLA because of that 1995 championship. "He had wanted to go to a school with a basketball tradition," O'Bannon says. "To me, that's a positive influence on someone's life, a pretty cool deal."

He stayed at his parents' home, in Cerritos, when he made all those weekly trips—down on Sunday and back on Wednesday, or down on Monday and back on Thursday. He never got a speeding ticket. Not proud of that, he says. He corrects himself. "Yes I am." He'd return from campus late. A fervent runner, he'd trek six miles only after reading papers or completing other homework. Running has always relaxed O'Bannon. He worried his parents, however; a tall black man dashing around the streets of Cerritos at three in the morning would surely draw some undesired attention.

There weren't many passersby. Still, once in a while there would be stares. Faint recognition. What's that? Branches in the wind? A few insomniacs or bakers or graveyard shifters did doubletakes. Could it be ... Ed O'Bannon, the guy who once played ball at UCLA, who won that NCAA championship, loping in and out of the moonlight and the haziness of the streetlamps, and standing on the street corner ... shadowboxing?

Acknowledgements

I had left my usual spot at the Pauley Pavilion courtside media table, even with the free-throw line opposite the visitors' bench, to ask Ed O'Bannon about this climax to his incredible journey. Hundreds of balloons and thousands of students, professors, administrators, family, friends, and fans—and an ecstatic Larry Pierce—filled Pauley Pavilion for the post-championship celebration. I was gone for three minutes; enough time for someone with larceny on his mind to snatch my black computer bag that contained fifteen notebooks with play-by-play details from every game, post-game quotes, practice observations and insights, cassette tapes with comprehensive interviews, a little black book with phone numbers of players, their parents and publishing contacts, a series of exacting book outlines, and a computer with stories and features and pages upon pages of notes from the entire 1994-95 season.

The colorful Seattle Final Four logo on the side of the bag—an NCAA media gift (doled out annually by the organization at its marquee event) that allowed me, for the first time, to keep everything related to the book in one "safe" place—must have proved too attractive to someone with a nefarious streak; he could not have imagined what he had nicked. I never heard about that bag or any of its contents. The book project was squelched.

So this completes the most unfinished business of my life. To the person who swiped that bag, I owe you a couple of twenties and a hug; with the passage of time, it's a far, far, far better story today. And having written my first book, published in 2012, gave me the experience to do this one justice.

I owe much to one person. Without his extensive involvement this does not exist. He was the backbone of that team and season, so his role would be no less in the chronicling of that championship campaign, all the twists and turns that led to it, how and why it happened, and what became of the key figures that affected the only hoops crown in UCLA's cabinet that does not bear John Wooden's signature.

I ran my vague idea, to document that time and those people, by Ed O'Bannon in an impromptu meeting in his office at Findlay Toyota, in Henderson, Nevada, on December 1, 2012. I had just finished the biggest project of my life. This one beckoned. It picked me. But if Ed declined to participate, it could not be attempted. Without his involvement, an accounting of that period would be sorely incomplete. With his involvement, I knew everyone else would accommodate, and I'd be off to Thailand, Japan, the Czech Republic, and elsewhere to hear their stories, to dredge up the details of their lives and that season, to scrape away the film of time, with a toothbrush, to reveal certain truths. Phone conversations, or e-mail queries, wouldn't suffice; I had to see every one of them in person.

That informal meeting with O'Bannon lasted two hours. He told me he would never forget my ashen face in the minutes after the discovery of my computer-bag heist. He stood, and shook my hand. He was in. My next twenty-one months were suddenly spoken for, save for the mourning of my father. Ed O'Bannon generally doesn't do introspection, but he did with me. Twice, in our hours upon hours of lunches and interviews, he halted. I felt I had pushed or pressed too much. I tapped the digital recorder off. No, he said. It had just stunned him to actually hear himself speak what, until then, had only been thoughts, personal ruminations that were sometimes decades old. This is, or was, cathartic for him. He was enjoying the process. He tapped the digital recorder on. "Let's go," he said. He asked for nothing; in fact, half the time he picked up the bill.

I have known few mortals with such courage, willpower, and strength, of mind and body. One isn't with me anymore; hopefully I learned from him over almost exactly fifty years.

To the other—Thanx, Ed.

NOTES

I tapped scores of people, for their opinions and insights and recollections, for this book, and their comments in that gathering and research process—as directly told to me—is represented by "says," or the present tense. Quotes, thoughts, or ideas from newspaper articles, magazine features, or other publications are expressed in the past tense, or "said." Bill Bennett, in the UCLA sports information department, was—as usual—invaluable in providing access to a vast vault of history. Statistics, records, facts, and figures were culled from media guides, official NCAA box scores and Final Four tournament guides, databases, papers of record, sports-reference.com, and the *Blue Ribbon* annual that is a bible of the game. A detailed accounting of exclusive material follows.

Chapter 1

My main sources were interviews and correspondence with Ed O'Bannon Jr., Tony Luftman, Jim Harrick, Lorenzo Romar, Mark Gottfried, Toby Bailey, George Zidek, J.R. Henderson, Charles O'Bannon, Marquis Burns, Steve Lavin, Tyus Edney, Ed O'Bannon Sr., Madeline O'Bannon, Dr. Michael R. Shapiro.

Chapter 2

My main sources were interviews and correspondence with Jim Harrick, Jerry Tarkanian, Ed O'Bannon Jr., Helen Gillette, Mark Gottfried, Lorenzo Romar, Steve Lavin, Pete Dalis, George Zidek, Peter Schultz, Tyus Edney; *They Call Me Coach*, by John

Wooden; *Tark*, by Jerry Tarkanian; *Runnin' Rebel*, by Jerry Tarkanian; *Blue Ribbon 1990-1991 College Basketball Yearbook*, by Chris Wallace; *The Wizard of Westwood*, by Dwight Chapin and Jeff Prugh; *Embracing the Legend*, by Jim Harrick; "Edwin Wendell Pauley Sr.," by Wolfgang Saxon; "L.A.'s invisible builder," by Christopher Reynolds; "Something special about the first: How '64 Bruins made John Wooden," by Alexander Wolff; "Call Him Irreplaceable," by Alexander Wolff; "Wise In The Ways Of The Wizard," by Curry Kirkpatrick; "Empty Chancellor's House Raises Questions," by Larry Gordon; "Heartache and Headache," by Robyn Norwood.

Chapter 3

My main sources were interviews and correspondence with Marques Johnson, Ed O'Bannon Jr., Pete Dalis, Lorenzo Romar, Peter Schultz, Madeline O'Bannon, Ed O'Bannon Sr., Kris Johnson, Jim Harrick, Tony Luftman; "Urban Legend," by Bill Plaschke; "At The Top Of His Profession," by John Papanek; *They Call Me Coach*, by John Wooden; "John Wooden: Untouchable record, incomparable man," by John Feinstein; "Paul Called All-Time Dirtiest Player," by Mal Florence; *The Wizard of Westwood*, by Dwight Chapin and Jeff Prugh; "UCLA: Simple, Awesomely Simple," by Curry Kirkpatrick; "Hello, Drip, Drip! Goodby, UCLA," by Joe Jares; "The Race Will Get Hotter in the Desert," by George Dohrmann; "Chasen's Chili Is History as Once Star-Studded Eatery Closes," by *Los Angeles Times* staff report; "Quiet reflection," by Mike Terry; "Tape-Delayd UCLA Games in Pauley Helped Launch a Legend's Career," by Larry Stewart; "Wise In The Ways Of The Wizard," by Curry Kirkpatrick; "Gilbert UCLA Godfather," by Alan Greenberg and Mike Littwin; "The dark side of the UCLA basketball dynasty," by Chris Dufresne; "Sports of The Times: The Ghosts and Goblins of Westwood," by William C. Rhoden; *Embracing The Legend*, by Jim Harrick; *Wooden: A*

Coach's Life, by Seth Davis; *Tark*, by Jerry Tarkanian; "At Home With 'Papa G' – Baasketball Stars, Estranged Sons," by Glenn F. Bunting; *They Shoot Coaches, Don't They?* by Mark Heisler; "Sport: A Patron Called Papa Sam," by *Time* magazine; "John Wooden's legend eclipses his competitive fire," by Sally Jenkins; "Sports Figure Is Indicted – 4 Days After Death," by William Overend and William Nottingham; "Wooden Remembers Booster," by Neil Amdur; "Clippers' Johnson Arrested," by Associated Press; "Basketball Notes," by Russ White; "Saga Of Papa Sam And The One That Got Away," by Jim Murray; "Marques Johnson: L.A. streetball 101," by Ronnie Flores; "After 63 years, Palisades High English teacher closes the book," by Louis Sahagun; "One Last Hurrah in Hyannis," by Frank Deford; *A Sense Of Where You Are*, by John McPhee; "Flashback: 1961: The Bel-Air/Brentwood Fire," by Cecilia Rasmussen.

Chapter 4

My main sources were interviews and correspondence with Ed O'Bannon Jr., Ed O'Bannon Sr., Madeline O'Bannon, LeRoy Pedigo, Jim Harrick, Jerry Tarkanian, Mark Gottfried, Marques Johnson, Pete Dalis, Jim Milhorn, Peter Schultz, Lorenzo Romar, Charles O'Bannon, Dr. Michael R. Shapiro; "Brother!" by Tom Krasovic; "O'Bannon Brothers Team Up at U.C.L.A." by Tom Friend; *TARK: College Basketball's Winningest Coach*, by Jerry Tarkanian and Terry Pluto; *The Last Great Game*, by Gene Wojciechowski; "In a Switch, UNLV Can Defend Title," by Danny Robbins; "It Just Might Be Time For Another Banner In The U.C.L.A. Gym." by Michael Martinez; "O'Bannon in floodgate of UCLA's Rebel talent," by Rob Miech; "Youth Basketball: O'Bannons Wary of Sale Pitch," by Elliott Almond; "It's A Family Affair," by Richard Hoffer; "Bred To Be A Superstar," by Douglas S. Looney; "Todd Marinovich: The Man Who Never Was," by Mike Sager; "O'Bannon decides he'll play at UCLA," by Frank Burlison;

"O'Bannon falls, Bruins regroup," by Rob Miech; "One False Move," by Richard Demak; "Minnesota Vikings' Adrian Peterson says no to cadaver tendon," by Michael Baldwin; "O'Bannon battles his dreams," by Karen Crouse; "O'Bannon Is Making Move Back to Old Form," by Steve Berkowitz; "Harrick-Bashing Is Affecting Team," by Elliott Almond; "Finally a Home," by Paul McLeod; "From Sweet to Elite," Jerry Crowe; "There's More Than One Reason Why UCLA's Rated No. 1," by Mark Alesia; "Tarkanian, NCAA Settle for $2.5 million," by Larry Stewart; "Parenthood becomes O'Bannon's reality," by Rob Miech; "O'Bannon watches out for 'kids,' " by Mark Whicker.

Chapter 5

My main sources were interviews and correspondence with Bill Bennett, Doug Erickson, Jim Harrick, Mark Gottfried, Lorenzo Romar, Steve Lavin, Ed O'Bannon Jr., J.R. Henderson, Charles O'Bannon, George Zidek, Andrew Pruter, Tony Luftman; *Onward Christian Athletes*, by Tom Krattenmaker; "Brother!" by Tom Krasovic; "Johnson Finally Gets to Throw Weight Around," by Tim Kawakami; "Restricted-earnings Coaches Agreed To Work For Peanuts," by Travis Miller; "Parenthood becomes O'Bannon's reality," by Rob Miech.

Chapter 6

My main sources were interviews and correspondence with Marques Johnson, Kristaan Johnson, Tyus Edney, Cameron Dollar, George Zidek, Ed O'Bannon Jr., Ed O'Bannon Sr., Madeline O'Bannon, Charles O'Bannon, Pete Dalis, Lorenzo Romar, Mark Gottfried, Jim Harrick, Steve Lavin; "Kris Johnson Sent to Class for Violence Intervention," by Greg Sandoval; "Round Mound of

Sound," by Tim Kawakami; "Past the Pain," by Jon Wilner; "Bruins show who isn't No. 1 team." by Mark Alesia.

Chapter 7

My main sources were interviews and correspondence with Jim Milhorn, Jim Harrick, J.R. Henderson, Toby Bailey, Ed O'Bannon Jr., Tony Luftman, Lorenzo Romar, and Mark Gottfried; *Embracing The Legend*, by Jim Harrick; "UCLA breezes by Northridge," by Rob Miech; "Deep roster poses problem for Harrick," Art Thompson III; "O'Bannon gets dream game," by Rob Miech; "Anaheim Arena to Be Site of Wooden Classic Dec. 3," by Lon Eubanks.

Chapter 8

My main sources were interviews and correspondence with Tony Luftman, Jim Harrick, J.R. Henderson, Steve Lavin, Ed O'Bannon Jr., Charles O'Bannon, Tyus Edney, Tim Kawakami, and Toby Bailey; "Henderson free throws lift UCLA," by Rob Miech; *The Wizard of Westwood* by Dwight Chapin and Jeff Prugh; "UCLA: Simple, Awesomely Simple," by Curry Kirkpatrick; "UCLA Was A Mistake," by Lew Alcindor and Jack Olsen; "Something special about the first: How '64 Bruins made John Wooden," by Alexander Wolff; "Hank Gathers' legacy endures 20 years after tragic on-court death," by Wendell Maxey; *Embracing the Legend*, by Jim Harrick; *Pistol: The Life of Pete Maravich*, by Mark Kriegel; "Jimmer dominance at BYU reminiscent of Maravich," by Peter Finney Jr.; "Wooden on Pete Maravich: 'His style would not cut it with me.'" by Beth Harris.

Chapter 9

My main sources were interviews and correspondence with George Zidek, Peter Schultz, Jim Harrick; Tyus Edney, Ed O'Bannon Jr., Charles O'Bannon, Ike Nwankwo; Mark Gottfried, and Lorenzo Romar; *The Atlantic And Its Enemies,* by Norman Stone; *Savage Continent,* by Keith Lowe; *Voices From Chernobyl,* by Svetlana Alexievich; "Upheaval in the East; From All Czechoslovakia, a Joyful Noise," by John Tagliabue; "The Oral History of 2013," by Jessie Kissinger; Jan Culik's lecture at the University of Siena, Italy, on June 2, 2006; *Iron Curtain: the crushing of Eastern Europe, 1944-1956*, by Anne Applebaum; "Zidek's Had His Gut Czech; UCLA Center Feels at Home," by Dick Weiss.

Chapter 10

My main sources were interviews and correspondence with Jim Harrick, Ed O'Bannon Jr., Tyus Edney, Charles O'Bannon, Tim Kawakami, Lorenzo Romar, Mark Gottfried; "Bruins kiss No. 1 goodbye," by Mark Alesia; "Harrick: Always a Question," by Tim Kawakami; *Embracing the Legend,* by Jim Harrick.

Chapter 11

My main sources were interviews and correspondence with Jim Harrick, Mark Gottfried, Ike Nwankwo, Ed O'Bannon Jr., Tyus Edney, Lorenzo Romar, Steve Lavin, J.R. Henderson, Charles O'Bannon; "Henderson gets defense," by Rob Miech; "Pauley fans awaken Bruins," by Rob Miech; "Edney dunks, UCLA romps," by Mark Alesia; "Latest in Bruin Highlight Club is 'Air' Edney," by Tim Kawakami.

Chapter 12

My main sources were interviews and correspondence with
Jim Harrick, Ed O'Bannon Jr., Toby Bailey, George Zidek, J.R.
Henderson, Charles O'Bannon, Mark Gottfried, Lorenzo Romar;
Runnin' Rebel, by Jerry Tarkanian; "UCLA gets a big KO at
McKale," by Mark Alesia; "Dempsey's hoops dreams delayed," by
Scott Yamaguchi; "For Michigan Coach Bill Frieder, Getting Good
Players Is In the Cards," by United Press International; "On The
Prowl," by Robyn Norwood; "Frieder Was Near, but So Far, Far
Away," by Mike Downey; "Edney Leaves Them Tongue-Tied," by
Mike Downey; "Coaches root for horses, don't they?" by Hank
Wesch; "Trip to Arizona Gives Bruins a Sweeping View," by Tim
Kawakami; "O'Bannon is setting a good example for UCLA," by
Rob Miech.

Chapter 13

My main sources were interviews and correspondence with
Jim Harrick, Ed O'Bannon Jr., Charles O'Bannon, Marques
Johnson, Toby Bailey, Tony Luftman, Andrew Pruter, Tyus Edney,
J.R. Henderson, George Zidek, Mark Gottfried, Steve Lavin; "After
Getting Close Calls, Bruins Survive Close Call," by Tim Kawakami;
"Steady He Goes," by Robyn Norwood; "Harbour Rebounds With
New Thumb," by Lowell Cohn; "Cal looking for respect in
victory," by Art Thompson III; "Haste Made Waste," by Alexander
Wolff and Don Yeager; "Bozeman Gives Credit To Time Served,"
by Mike Wise; "Morgan State Coach Todd Bozeman is making the
most of his second chance," by Michael Wilbon.

Chapter 14

My main sources were interviews and correspondence with Jim Harrick, Mark Gottfried, Ed O'Bannon Jr., Tyus Edney, George Zidek, Toby Bailey, Tony Luftman, Charles O'Bannon, Lorenzo Romar, Steve Lavin; "UCLA guts out the win," by Mark Alesia; "Zidek slams door on USC's defense," by Art Thompson III; *They Call Me Coach*, by John Wooden; *The Wizard of Westwood*, by Dwight Chapin and Jeff Prugh; "Mack Calvin waited it out with USC to beat UCLA in 1969," by Jerry Crowe; "Bob Boyd Taking a Year Off From His Retirement," by Mal Florence; "Stall Wars," by Mike Terry; "Boyd feels connected again," by Ben Bolch; "College Coaches Are Starting To Worry About Sales Pitch to Youngest Murray," by Jeff Fellenzer; "UCLA guts out the win," by Mark Alesia; "Zidek slams door on USC's defense," by Art Thompson III; "Raveling Says Move Was His Idea," by Lonnie White; "Raveling Cites Love for L.A. in Staying as USC's Coach," by Lonnie White; "Press does wonders for Bruins," by Rob Miech; "A Timely Push Propels Bruins Past Notre Dame," by Tim Kawakami.

Chapter 15

My main sources were interviews and correspondence with Ed O'Bannon Jr., Charles O'Bannon, Jim Harrick, Toby Bailey, J.R. Henderson, Andrew Pruter, Lorenzo Romar, Mark Gottfried, Steve Lavin, George Zidek, Tony Luftman; "A year later, O'Bannon wants to make amends," by Rob Miech; *Embracing The Legend*, by Jim Harrick; "Harrick's Motivational Tool Gets UCLA in Gear, 74-66," by Tim Kawakami; "Seattle preparing to Blow Huge Stadium to Kingdome Come," by Kim Murphy; "UCLA is sky-high after 98-83 win," by Rob Miech; "Henderson Has His Day in the Sun," by Tim Kawakami.

Chapter 16

My main sources were interviews and correspondence with Ed O'Bannon Jr., Jim Harrick, Mark Gottfried, Cameron Dollar, Charles O'Bannon, Toby Bailey, Lorenzo Romar, Steve Lavin, Ike Nwankwo; "UCLA Fends Off Arizona, 72-70," by Tim Kawakami; *Embracing The Legend*, by Jim Harrick; "When Going Gets Tough, Bruins Get a Bit Tougher," by Tim Kawakami; "UCLA takes step toward No. 1 rating," by Jim Thomas; "UCLA Gives Duke Lesson in Higher Ed," by Tim Kawakami.

Chapter 17

My main sources were interviews and correspondence with Ed O'Bannon Jr., Jim Harrick, Toby Bailey, Tony Luftman, J.R. Henderson, Charles O'Bannon, Mark Gottfried, Lorenzo Romar; "Givens' Athletic Skills Are Only Half His Story," by Percy Allen; "At 18, a Veteran of Hard Road," by Thomas Bonk; "Pac-10 title isn't nearly enough," by Mark Alesia; "UCLA secures berth," by Rob Miech; *Embracing The Legend*, by Jim Harrick; The Wizard of Westwood, by Dwight Chapin and Jeff Prugh; "Freedom rings for UCLA," by Rob Miech.

Chapter 18

My main sources were interviews and correspondence with Ed O'Bannon Jr., Charles O'Bannon, Jim Harrick, Steve Lavin, Mark Gottfried, Lorenzo Romar, Toby Bailey, George Zidek, Peter Schultz; "UCLA wraps up Pac-10," by Rob Miech; "UCLA seals it with a kiss," by Jim Thomas; "Seniors O'Bannon, Edney Rule the Night for Bruins," by Tim Kawakami.

Chapter 19

My main sources were interviews and correspondence with Ed O'Bannon Jr., Ed O'Bannon Sr., Jim Harrick, Toby Bailey, Tyus Edney, Charles O'Bannon, Cameron Dollar, Jim Milhorn, Hank Edney, Lorenzo Romar, Mark Gottfried, Tony Luftman, Andrew Pruter, George Zidek, Steve Lavin, J.R. Henderson, Kevin Young, Brendan Jacobson; *Embracing the Legend*, by Jim Harrick; "Golden Panthers or Paper Tigers?" by Bob Nightengale; "UCLA flexes its muscles," by Mark Alesia; "Bruins Fret Over Injury to Edney," by Tim Kawakami; "Ex-coach Weltlich gets last word on referees with novel approach," by Jerry Potter; "A Happy Edneying for UCLA," by Tim Kawakami; "Edney's shot gives Bruins a Sweet victory," by Rob Miech. "Edney's Injury Called a Sprain, Bruins Rest Easy," by Tim Kawakami; "There's More Than One Reason Why UCLA's Rated No. 1," by Mark Alesia.

Chapter 20

My main sources were interviews and correspondence with Ed O'Bannon Jr., Jim Harrick, Toby Bailey, Tyus Edney, Charles O'Bannon, Cameron Dollar, George Zidek, Andrew Pruter, orenzo Romar, Mark Gottfried, Tony Luftman, Jim Milhorn, Pete Dalis, Steve Lavin, J.R. Henderson, Marquis Burns, Bill Bayno; *Embracing the Legend*, by Jim Harrick; *They Call Me Coach*, by John Wooden; "Bruins' rapid start routs Mississippi St.," by Rob Miech; "Kingdome Comes," by Tim Kawakami.

Chapter 21

My main sources were interviews and correspondence with Ed O'Bannon Jr., Jim Harrick, Toby Bailey, Tyus Edney, Charles O'Bannon, Cameron Dollar, George Zidek, Andrew Pruter,

Lorenzo Romar, Mark Gottfried, Tony Luftman, Steve Lavin, J.R. Henderson, omm'A Givens, Jim Milhorn, Bill Bayno; *Embracing the Legend*, by Jim Harrick; "Bruins' rapid start routs Mississippi St.," by Rob Miech; "Kingdome Comes," by Tim Kawakami; " 'Take Him, Tyus' – He Takes Bruins Along," by Mike Downey; "Edney Finally Finds a Way," by Tim Kawakami; "Huskies' Lorenzo Romar is coaching with a heavy heart," by Todd Dybas.

Chapter 22

My main sources were interviews and correspondence with Ed O'Bannon Jr., Cameron Dollar, George Zidek, Charles O'Bannon, Jim Harrick, Toby Bailey, Tyus Edney, Hank Edney, Andrew Pruter, Lorenzo Romar, Mark Gottfried, Tony Luftman, Pete Dalis, J.R. Henderson, Steve Lavin, Dr. Michael R. Shapiro; " 'Big Nasty' And 'The Terminator' Are On A Collision Course," by Gwen Knapp; "Zidek's Had His Gut Czech," by Dick Weiss; "Applause needed for trailblazer Richardson," by Dan Wetzel; "Nolan Richardson goes rogue," by Eamonn Brennan; "Razor Sharp," by Alexander Wolff; "Dollar Goes a Lot Further," by Tim Kawakami; "Past Champs Look Wooden By Comparison," by Mark Whicker; "Scotty Thurman Remembers," by senior analyst; "Campus mourns death of disabled persons advocate," by Jennifer Morita; "No timeouts," by Mark Heisler. *Embracing the Legend*, by Jim Harrick.

Aftermath

My main sources were interviews and correspondence with Jim Harrick, Mark Gottfried, Lorenzo Romar, Steve Lavin, Pete Dalis, Ed O'Bannon Jr., Tyus Edney, George Zidek, J.R. Henderson, Toby Bailey, Cameron Dollar, Charles O'Bannon, Ed O'Bannon Sr., Madeline O'Bannon, Tony Luftman, Jim Milhorn, Michael Curtis,

Marquis Burns; Financial analysis, by the official *NCAA Final Four Tournament Records Book*; "Bad Blood," by Tim Kawakami; "Out To Dinner, Out Of A Job," by Alexander Wolff; "Princeton 43, UCLA 41," by Zachary Kwartler; "Heartache and Headache," by Robyn Norwood; "NCAA Gives UCLA Mild Rebuke," by Tim Kawakami; "Beyond Just Desserts?" by Mark Kram; "Harrick Travels Coast to Coast," by Tim Kawakami; *The Smart Take from the Strong*, by Pete Carril; "The Coach Fouls Out," by Jeffrey Kluger; "Past Champs Look Wooden By Comparison," by Mark Whicker; "This Is No Lie: Harrick Deserves an Opportunity," by Chris Dufresne; "Former UCLA coach Harrick to lead Bakersfield Jam," by Mason Kelley; "The Dean of Corruption," by Steve Fishman; "Red Storm rises at St. John's," by Frank Rosario and Dan Mangan; "Former Bruin is now Japan's J.R. Sakuragi," by Jerry Crowe; "Spy with 'Twisted Biography' Laid to Rest in Tel Aviv, by Alexander Bratersky; "Lithuanian businessman killed in Moscow," by Julija Jisko; "To Russia With Love," by Alexander Wolff; "Former KGB spy shot dead in Moscow," by Luke Harding; "The Power 50," by *Sports Illustrated*; "Survivor," by Rob Miech; "Bob Myers has had quite a hoop journey," by Ben Bolch; "GM Bob Myers ready to mold Warriors into winners," by Antonio Gonzalez; "Sonny Vaccaro calls O'Bannon win his proudest," by Rachel Axon; "Judge releases ruling on O'Bannon case: NCAA loses," by Steve Berkowitz; "Next steps in O'Bannon case," by Michael McCann; "O'Bannon attorneys seek $52.4M in costs, fees, paid for by NCAA," by Steve Berkowitz.

BIBLIOGRAPHY

Abel, Greg. "Still Going End to End." *Los Angeles Times*, March 14, 2005.

Alexievich, Svetlana. *Voices From Chernobyl*. New York: Picador, 2006.

Alcindor, Lew, and Jack Olsen. "UCLA Was A Mistake." *Sports Illustrated*, November 3, 1969.

Alesia, Mark. "There's More Than One Reason Why UCLA's Rated No. 1." Los Angeles *Daily News*, January 30, 1994.

----------. "Bruins show who isn't No. 1 team." Los Angeles *Daily News*, November 23, 1994.

----------. "Bruins kiss No. 1 goodbye." Los Angeles *Daily News*, January 6, 1995.

----------. "Edney dunks, UCLA romps." Los Angeles *Daily News*, January 15, 1995.

----------. "UCLA gets a big KO at McKale." Los Angeles *Daily News*, January 20, 1995.

----------. "UCLA guts out the win." Los Angeles *Daily News*, February 3, 1995.

----------. "Pac-10 title isn't nearly enough." Los Angeles *Daily News*. March 1, 1995.

----------. "UCLA flexes its muscles." Los Angeles *Daily News*, March 18, 1995.

Allen, Percy. "Givens' Athletic Skills Are Only Half His Story." *Seattle Times*, March 15, 1994.

Almond, Elliott. "Youth Basketball: O'Bannons Wary of Sales Pitch." *Los Angeles Times*, April 29, 1990.

----------. "Harrick-Bashing Is Affecting Team." *Los Angeles Times*, January 27, 1993.

Amdur, Neil. "Wooden Remembers Booster," *The New York Times*, February 4, 1982.

Applebaum, Anne. *Iron Curtain: the crushing of Eastern Europe, 1944-1956*. New York: Doubleday, 2012.

Araton, Harvey. "Hall Election Completes One of Game's Great Comebacks." *The New York Times*, April 8, 2013.

Associated Press. "Clippers' Johnson Arrested." *Deseret News*, July 26, 1988.

Axon, Rachel. "Sonny Vaccaro calls O'Bannon win his proudest." *USA Today*, August 8, 2014.

Backman, Melvin. "Moody's Revises NCAA's Credit Outlook to Negative." *The Wall Street Journal*, June 24, 2013.

Baldwin, Michael. "Minnesota Vikings' Adrian Peterson says no to cadaver tendon." *The Daily Oklahoman*, September 15, 2012.

Barron, David. "UH-UCLA classic played 43 years ago elevated the game." Houston Chronicle, January 20, 2011.

Berkowitz, Steve. "O'Bannon Is Making Move Back to Old Form." *The Washington Post*, December 16, 1992.

----------. "Judge releases ruling on O'Bannon case: NCAA loses." *USA Today*, August 8, 2014.

----------. "O'Bannon attorneys seek $52.4M in costs, fees, paid for by NCAA." *USA Today*, August 23, 2014.

Bolch, Ben. "Boyd feels connected again." *Los Angeles Times*, March 1, 2008.

----------. "Bob Myers has had quite a hoop journey," *Los Angeles Times*, December 22, 2012.

Bonk, Thomas. "At 18, a Veteran of Hard Road." *Los Angeles Times*, September 20, 1994.

Boyer, Zac. "Robert Griffin III Surprised To Learn He Had ACL Surgery." *Fredericksburg Free Lance-Star*, May 23, 2013.

Brady, Erick, and Steve Berkowitz. "Six active players join O'Bannon lawsuit against NCAA." *USA Today*, July 18, 2013.

Bratersky, Alexander. "Spy With 'Twisted Biography' Laid to Rest in Tel Aviv." *The St. Petersburg Times*, November 10, 2009.

Brennan, Eamonn. "Nolan Richardson goes rogue." ESPN.com, February 16, 2010.

Bunting, Glenn F. "At Home With 'Papa G' – Baasketball Stars, Estranged Sons." *Los Angeles Times*, April 23, 1990.

Burlison, Frank. "O'Bannon decides he'll play at UCLA." *Long Beach Press-Telegram*, August 7, 1990.

Carril, Pete. *The Smart Take from the Strong.* New York: Simon & Schuster, 1997.

Chapin, Dwight, and Jeff Prugh. *The Wizard of Westwood.* New York: Warner, 1973.

Cohn, Lowell. "Harbour Rebounds With New Thumb." *San Francisco Chronicle*, January 4, 1995.

Colombet, P., Allard, M., Bousquet, V., De Lavigne, C., and Flurin, P.H. "The History of ACL Surgery." www.maitrise-orthop.com.

Crouse, Karen. "O'Bannon battles his dreams." *The Orange County Register*, December 26, 1992.

Crowe, Jerry. "From Sweet to Elite." *Los Angeles Times*, March 27, 1992.

----------. "Former Bruin is now Japan's J.R. Sakuragi." *Los Angeles Times*, January 21, 2008.

----------. "Mack Calvin waited it out with USC to beat UCLA in 1969." *Los Angeles Times*, February 2, 2009.

Davis, Seth. *Wooden: A Coach's Life*. New York: Times Books, 2014.

Deford, Frank. "One Last Hurrah in Hyannis." *Sports Illustrated*, June 28, 1976.

----------. "The Ring Leader." *Sports Illustrated*, May 10, 1999.

Demak, Richard. "One False Move." *Sports Illustrated*, April 29, 1991.

Dillman, Lisa, and Steve Springer. "Fraternity of Coaches is Stunned." *Los Angeles Times*, November 7, 1996.

Dohrmann, George. "The Race Will Get Hotter in the Desert." *Los Angeles Times*, February 13, 1997.

Downey, Mike. "Frieder Was Near, but So Far, Far Away." *Los Angeles Times*, April 4, 1989.

----------. "Edney Leaves Them Tongue-Tied." *Los Angeles Times*, January 29, 1995.

----------. " 'Take Him, Tyus' – He Takes Bruins Along." *Los Angeles Times*, April 2, 1995.

Dufresne, Chris. "This Is No Lie: Harrick Deserves an Opportunity." *Los Angeles Times*, March 27, 1997.

----------. "The dark side of the UCLA basketball dynasty." *Los Angeles Times*, June 8, 2010.

Dybas, Todd. "Huskies' Lorenzo Romar is coaching with a heavy heart." *Tacoma News-Tribune*, March 8, 2013.

Eubanks, Lon. "Anaheim Arena to Be Site of Wooden Classic Dec. 3." *Los Angeles Times*, March 23, 1994.

Feinstein, John. "John Wooden: Untouchable record, incomparable man." *The Washington Post*, June 5, 2010.

Fellenzer, Jeff. "College Coaches Are Starting To Worry About Sales Pitch to Youngest Murray." *Los Angeles Times*, August 26, 1993.

Fernas, Rob. "Scandals in the Wind." *Los Angeles Times*, March 30, 2003.

Finney, Peter Jr. "Jimmer dominance at BYU reminiscent of Maravich." *New York Post*, March 24, 1022.

Fishman, Steve. "The Dean of Corruption." *New York* magazine, February 24, 2013.

Florence, Mal. "Paul Called All-Time Dirtiest Player." *Los Angeles Times*, June 25, 1978.

----------. "Bob Boyd Taking a Year Off From His Retirement." *Los Angeles Times*, June 28, 1988.

Flores, Ronnie. "Marques Johnson: L.A. streetball 101.' ESPN.com, August 19, 2011.

Friend, Tom. "O'Bannon Brothers Team Up at U.C.L.A." *The New York Times*, December 5, 1993.

Gonzalez, Antonio. "GM Bob Myers ready to mold Warriors into winners." Associated Press, May 17, 2012.

Gordon, Larry. "Empty Chancellor's House Raises Questions." *Los Angeles Times*, December 8, 1992.

Greenberg, Alan, and Mike Littwin. "Gilbert UCLA Godfather." *Los Angeles Times*, February 1, 1982.

Harding, Luke. "Former KGB spy shot dead in Moscow." *The Guardian*, November 3, 2009.

Harrick, Jim, with John McGill and Tom Wallace. *Embracing The Legend*. Chicago: Bonus, 1995.

Harris, Beth. "Wooden on Pete Maravich: 'His style would not cut it with me.' " Associated Press, March 29, 2006.

Heisler, Mark. *They Shoot Coaches, Don't They?* New York: Macmillan, 1996.

----------. "No Timeouts." *Los Angeles Times*, July 16, 1995.

Hoffer, Richard. "It's A Family Affair." *Sports Illustrated*, January 31, 1994.

Jares, Joe. "Hello, Drip, Drip! Goodby, UCLA." *Sports Illustrated*, December 15, 1969.

Jenkins, Sally. "John Wooden's legend eclipses his competitive fire." *The Washington Post*, June 12, 2010.

Kanigher, Steve. "O'Bannon: Fairness the basis of beef with the NCAA." *Las Vegas Sun*, March 19, 2010.

Kaplan, David E., and Alec Dubro. *Yakuza: Japan's Criminal Underworld*. Berkeley: University of California Press, 2003.

Kawakami, Tim. "Harrick: Always a Question." *Los Angeles Times*, January 7, 1995.

----------. "Latest in Bruin Highlight Club Is 'Air' Edney." *Los Angeles Times*, January 15, 1995.

----------. "Trip to Arizona Gives Bruins a Sweeping View." *Los Angeles Times*, January 22, 1995.

----------. "After Getting Close Calls, Bruins Survive Close Call." *Los Angeles Times*, January 27, 1995.

----------. "A Timely Push Propels Bruins Past Notre Dame." *Los Angeles Times*, February 6, 1995.

----------. "Harrick's Motivational Tool Gets UCLA in Gear, 74-66." *Los Angeles Times*, February 10, 1995.

----------. "Henderson Has His Day in the Sun." *Los Angeles Times*, February 12, 1995.

----------. "UCLA Fends Off Arizona, 72-70." *Los Angeles Times*, February 20, 1995.

----------. "When Going Gets Tough, Bruins Get a Bit Tougher." *Los Angeles Times*, February 22, 1995.

----------. "UCLA Gives Duke Lesson in Higher Ed." *Los Angeles Times*, February 27, 1995.

----------. "Round Mound of Sound." *Los Angeles Times*, March 1, 1995.

----------. "Seniors O'Bannon, Edney Rule the Night for Bruins." *Los Angeles Times*, March 12, 1995.

----------. "Bruins Fret Over Injury to Edney." *Los Angeles Times*, March 19, 1995.

----------. "A Happy Edneying for UCLA." *Los Angeles Times*, March 20, 1995.

----------. "Kingdome Comes." *Los Angeles Times*, March 26, 1995.

----------. "Dollar Goes a Lot Further." *Los Angeles Times*, March 29, 1995.

----------. "Edney Finally Finds a Way." *Los Angeles Times*, April 2, 1995.

----------. "Edney's Injury Called a Sprain, Bruins Rest Easy." *Los Angeles Times*, April 3, 1995.

----------. "Johnson Finally Gets to Throw Weight Around." *Los Angeles Times*, January 14, 1996.

----------. "Bad Blood." *Los Angeles Times*, November 10, 1996.

----------. "Harrick Travels Coast to Coast." *Los Angeles Times*, May 6, 1997.

----------. "NCAA Gives UCLA Mild Rebuke." *Los Angeles Times*, May 1, 1998.

Kindred, Dave. "I'm a Good Guy Now." sportsonearth.com, September 4, 2012.

Kirkpatrick, Curry. "UCLA: Simple, Awesomely Simple." *Sports Illustrated*, November 30, 1970.

----------. "Who Are These Guys?" *Sports Illustrated*, February 5, 1973.

----------. "Wise In The Ways Of The Wizard." *Sports Illustrated*, November 31, 1981.

Kelley, Mason. "Former UCLA coach Harrick to lead Bakersfield Jam." *Bakersfield Californian*, June 13, 2006.

Kisko, Julija. "Lithuanian businessman killed in Moscow." *Baltic Reports*, November 4, 2009.

Kissinger, Jessie. "The Oral History of 2013." *Esquire*, December 2013.

Kluger, Jeffrey, and Paige Bowers, and Greg Fulton. "The Coach Fouls Out." *Time*, May 19, 2003.

Knapp, Gwen. " 'Big Nasty' And 'The Terminator' Are On A Collision Course." *Philadelphia Inquirer*, April 3, 1995.

Kram, Mark. "Beyond Just Desserts?" *Philadelphia Daily News*, March 12, 1997.

Krasovic, Tom. "Brother!" *San Diego Union-Tribune*, January 10, 1994.

Krattenmaker, Tom. *Onward Christian Athletes*. Lanham: Rowman & Littlefield, 2010.

Kriegel, Mark. *Pistol: The Life of Pete Maravich*. New York: Free Press, 2008.

Kwartler, Zachary. "Princeton 43, UCLA 41." *Princeton Alumni Weekly*, March 14, 2011.

Lawlor, Frank. "Lithuanians Ambush Kinder Bologna in Final." *The New York Times*, April 24, 1999.

Looney, Douglas S. "Bred To Be A Superstar." *Sports Illustrated*, February 22, 1988.

Lowe, Keith. *Savage Continent.* New York: St. Martin's, 2012.

Martinez, Michael. "It Just Might Be Time For Another Banner In The U.C.L.A. Gym." *The New York Times*, November 15, 1991.

Maxey, Wendell. "Hank Gathers' legacy endures 20 years after tragic on-court death." *USA Today*, March 4, 2010.

McCann, Michael. "Sports Law." *Sports Illustrated*, September 1, 2012.

----------. "Next steps in O'Bannon case." SI.com, August 11, 2014.

McCollough, J. Brady. "One-man rebellion: Sonny Vaccaro takes on the NCAA." *Pittsburgh Post-Gazette*, June 16, 2013.

McLeod, Paul. "Finally, a Home." *Los Angeles Times*, January 31, 1992.

McPhee, John. *A Sense Of Where You Are.* New York: Farrar, Straus and Giroux, 1978.

Miech, Rob. "O'Bannon in floodgate of UCLA's Rebel talent." *Pasadena Star-News*, August 7, 1990.

----------. "O'Bannon falls, Bruins regroup." *Pasadena Star-News*, October 15, 1990.

----------. "A year later, O'Bannon wants to make amends." *Pasadena Star-News*, January 13, 1994.

----------. "Parenthood becomes O'Bannon's reality." *Pasadena Star-News*, October 16, 1994.

----------. "UCLA breeze by Northridge." *Pasadena Star-News*, November 27, 1994.

----------. "O'Bannon gets dream game." *Pasadena Star-News*, December 2, 1994.

----------. "Henderson free throws lift UCLA." *Pasadena Star-News*, December 3, 1994.

----------. "Henderson gets defensive." *Pasadena Star-News*, January 8, 1995.

----------. "Pauley fans awaken Bruins." *Pasadena Star-News*, January 13, 1995.

----------. "O'Bannon is setting a good example for UCLA." *Pasadena Star-News*, January 23, 1995.

----------. "Press does wonders for Bruins." *Pasadena Star-News*, February 6, 1995.

----------. "UCLA is sky-high after 98-83 win." *Pasadena Star-News*, February 12, 1995.

----------. "UCLA secures berth." *Pasadena Star-News*, March 2, 1995.

----------. "Freedom rings for UCLA." *Pasadena Star-News*, March 6, 1995.

----------. "UCLA wraps up Pac-10." *Pasadena Star-News*, March 10, 1995.

----------. "Edney's shot gives Bruins a Sweet victory." *Pasadena Star-News*, March 20, 1995.

----------. "Bruins' rapid start routs Mississippi St." *Pasadena Star-News*, March 24, 1995.

----------. "Survivor." *Basketball Times*, February 2002.

----------. "Findlay a man of few words with a large footprint." *Las Vegas Sun*, February 12, 2009.

----------. "Westwood to the Far East." *Basketball Times*, June 2013.

Miller, Travis. "Restricted-earnings Coaches Agreed To Work For Peanuts." *Chicago Tribune*, April 6, 2000.

Morita, Jennifer. "Campus mourns death of disabled persons advocate." *Daily Bruin*, April 27, 1995.

Murphy, Kim. "Seattle Preparing to Blow Huge Stadium to Kingdome Come." *Los Angeles Times*, March 26, 2000.

Murray, Jim. "Saga Of Papa Sam And The One That Got Away." *Los Angeles Times*, January 22, 1975.

Myslenski, Skip. "Kid From Gans Now The Man." *Chicago Tribune*, March 29, 1995.

NCAA Staff. "Financial Analysis." *The Official 2001 NCAA Final Four Tournament Records Book*. Indianapolis: NCAA, 2000.

Nightengale, Bob. "Golden Panthers or Paper Tigers?" *Los Angeles Times*, March 14, 1995.

Nikolaou, P.K., Seaber, Anthony V., Glisson Richard R., Ribbeck, B.M., and Bassett, F.H. III. "Anterior cruciate ligament allograft transplantation." *American Journal of Sports Medicine*, September-October 1986.

Norwood, Robyn. "On The Prowl." *Los Angeles Times*, March 15, 1988.

----------. "Heartache and Headache." *Los Angeles Times*, March 6, 2003.

----------. "Steady He Goes." *Los Angeles Times*, March 10, 2004.

Overend, William, and William Nottingham. "Sports Figure Is Indicted – 4 Days After Death." *Los Angeles Times*, November 26, 1987.

Papanek, John. "At The Top Of His Profession." Sports Illustrated, November 10, 1980.

Plaschke, Bill. "Urban Legend." *Los Angeles Times*, February 14, 2001.

Potter, Jerry. "Ex-coach Weltlich gets last word on referees with novel approach." *USA Today*, January 25, 2005.

Rasmussen, Cecilia. "Flashback: 1961: The Bel-Air/Brentwood Fire." *Los Angeles Times*, January 18, 1991.

Reynolds, Christopher. "L.A.'s invisible builder." *Los Angeles Times*, March 6, 2003.

Rhoden, William C. "Sports of The Times: The Ghosts and Goblins of Westwood." *The New York Times*, March 14, 2003.

Robbins, Danny. "In a Switch, UNLV Can Defend Title." *Los Angeles Times*, November 30, 1990.

Rosario, Frank, and Dan Mangan. "Red Storm rise at St. John's." *New York Post*, May 4, 2013.

Rushin, Steve. "The King Reigns Supreme." *Sports Illustrated*, January 21, 1991.

Sager, Mike. "Todd Marinovich: The Man Who Never Was." *Esquire*, May 2009.

Sahagun, Louis. "After 63 years, Palisades High English teacher closes the book." *Los Angeles Times*, March 9, 2013.

Sandomir, Richard. "Russell Redux: A Private Man Bursts Back Into the Public Eye." *The New York Times*, June 16, 2000.

Sandoval, Greg. "Kris Johnson Sent to Class for Violence Intervention." *Los Angeles Times*, February 14, 1998.

Saran, Rajat. "Evaluation of Anterior Cruciate Ligament repair with Illiotibial Band." *People's Journal of Scientific Research*, Vol. 3(2), July 2010.

Savage, Jim. *The Encyclopedia of the NCAA basketball tournament*. New York: Dell, 1990.

Saxon, William. "Edwin Wendell Pauley Sr." *The New York Times*, July 29, 1981.

Senior analyst. "Scotty Thurman Remembers." Bleacherreport.com, December 18, 2008.

Slezak, Carol. "From Death, Athletic Life." *Inside Sports*, April 1996.

Solomon, Jon. "NCAA targets Sonny Vaccaro again, only this time in Ed O'Bannon lawsuit." *The Birmingham News*, August 23, 2012.

Staff report. "For Michigan Coach Bill Frieder, Getting Good Players Is In The Cards." United Press International, October 28, 1987.

Staff report. "The Top 50." *Sports Illustrated*, March 11, 2013.

Staff report. "Chasen's Chili Is History as Once Star-Studded Eatery Closes." *Los Angeles Times*, April 2, 1995.

Staples, Andy. "Ed O'Bannon v. the NCAA: A complete case primer." SI.com, April 2, 2013.

Stone, Norman. *The Atlantic And Its Enemies*. Great Britain: Basic, 2010.

Stewart, Larry. "Tarkanian, NCAA Settle for $2.5 million." *Los Angeles Times*, April 2, 1998.

----------. "Tape-Delayd UCLA Games in Pauley Helped Launch a Legend's Career." Uclabruins.com, December 14, 2012.

Tagliabue, John. "Upheaval in the East; From All Czechoslovakia, a Joyful Noise." *The New York Times*, December 12, 1989.

Tarkanian, Jerry, and Terry Pluto. *Tark*. New York: McGraw-Hill, 1988.

----------, with Dan Wetzel. *Runnin' Rebel*. Champaign, Ill.: Sports Publishing LLC, 2005.

Taylor, John. *The Rivalry: Bill Russell, Wilt Chamberlain, and the Golden Age of Basketball*. New York: Random House, 2005.

Terry, Mike. "Stall Wars." *Los Angeles Times*, February 8, 2000.

----------. "Quiet reflection." *Los Angeles Times*, February 15, 2007.

Thomas, Jim. "UCLA takes step toward No. 1 rating." *South Bay Daily Breeze*, February 22, 1995.

----------. "UCLA seals it with a kiss." *South Bay Daily Breeze*, March 12, 1995.

Thomas, Katie. "Ex-Players Join Suit vs. NCAA." *The New York Times*, March 10, 2010.

----------. "Image Rights vs. Free Speech in Video Game Suit." *The New York Times*, November 15, 2010.

Thompson, Art III. "Deep roster poses problem for Harrick." *The Orange County Register*, November 27, 1994.

----------. "Cal looking for respect in victory." *The Orange County Register*, January 29, 1995.

----------. "Zidek slams door on USC's defense." *The Orange County Register*, February 3, 1995.

Time magazine editorial. "Sports: A Patron Saint Called Papa Sam." February 25, 1974.

Tracevskis, Rokas M. "Kaunas' most colorful son buried." *The Baltic Times*, November 11, 2009.

Transcript. "Talk Today." *USA Today*, January 21, 2005.

US District Court for the Northern District of California. Case 4:09-cv-01967-CW, December 17, 2010.

Wachter, Paul. "The ESQ&A: Sonny Vaccaro." *Esquire*, March 18, 2013.

Wagner, Dick. "Long Beach Poly's Tyus Edney Plays Above Expectations." *Los Angeles Times*, January 10, 1991.

Wallace, Chris. *Blue Ribbon 1990-1991 College Basketball Yearbook*. New York: Bantam, 1990.

Weiss, Dick. "Zidek's Had His Gut Czech." *New York Daily News*, April 4, 1995.

Wesch, Hank. "Coaches root for horses, don't they?" *San Diego Union-Tribune*, October 31, 2006.

Wetzel, Dan. "Applause needed for trailblazer Richardson." Yahoo! Sports, May 18, 2010.

----------. "Making NCAA pay?" Yahoo! Sports, July 21, 2009.

----------. "Robertson joins suit vs. NCAA." Yahoo! Sports, January 26, 2011.

Whicker, Mark. "O'Bannon watches out for 'kids.' " *Orange County Register*, February 21, 1995.

----------. "Past Champs Look Wooden by Comparison." *Orange County Register*, April 7, 1995.

White, Lonnie. "Raveling Cites Love for L.A. in Staying as USC's Coach." *Los Angeles Times*, July 12, 1994.

----------. "Raveling Says Move Was His Idea." *Los Angeles Times*, November 22, 1994.

White, Russ. "Basketball Notes." *Orlando Sentinel*, June 16, 1985.

Wilner, Jon. "Past the Pain: Brother's Loss Reconciled, Johnson Gains Control." Los Angeles *Daily News*, March 12, 1998.

Wilbon, Michael. "Morgan State Coach Todd Bozeman is making the most of his second chance." *The Washington Post*, March 18, 2010.

Wise, Mike. "Bozeman Gives Credit To Time Served." *The Washington Post*, December 22, 2006.

Wojciechowski, Gene. *The Last Great Game*. New York: Plume, 2012.

Wolff, Alexander. "Call Him Irreplaceable." *Sports Illustrated*, April 11, 1988.

----------. "Razor Sharp." *Sports Illustrated*, April 11, 1994.

----------, and Don Yeager. "Haste Made Waste." *Sports Illustrated*, September 9, 1996.

----------. "Out To Dinner, Out Of A Job." *Sports Illustrated*, November 18, 1996.

----------. "To Russia With Love." *Sports Illustrated*, December 15, 2008.

----------. "Something special about the first: How '64 Bruins made John Wooden." *Sports Illustrated*, June 4, 2010.

----------. "When Worlds Collide." *Sports Illustrated*, February 11, 2013.

Wooden, John. *They Call Me Coach*. New York: Bantam. 1973.

Yamaguchi, Scott. "Dempsey's hoop dreams delayed." *Daily Bruin*, January 31, 1996.

9 781632 634467